To my kind of man,
who has been described thusly,
"He would rather read a book
than watch sports!"
Happy 1987.
Kathy

THE
STORY OF
ENGLISH

THE
STORY OF
ENGLISH

ROBERT McCRUM
WILLIAM CRAN
ROBERT MacNEIL

faber and faber

LONDON · BOSTON

BBC PUBLICATIONS

First published in 1986 by
Faber and Faber Limited
3 Queen Square
London WC1N 3AU
and
BBC Publications
A division of BBC Enterprises Ltd
35 Marylebone High Street
London W1M 4AA

Designed by Julia Alldridge
Typeset by Keyspools, Golborne, Warrington
Colour reproduction by Wensum Graphics, Norwich, Norfolk
Printed in Great Britain by W S Cowell, Ipswich, Suffolk
Bound by Butler & Tanner, Frome, Somerset
All rights reserved

British Library Cataloguing in Publication Data
McCrum, Robert
The story of English
1. English language – History
I. Title   II. Cran, William   III. MacNeil, Robert
420′.9   PE1075

ISBN 0 571 13828 4 (Faber and Faber)
ISBN 0 563 20247 5 (BBC)

When we see men grow old and die at a certain time one after another, from century to century, we laugh at the elixir that promises to prolong life to a thousand years; and with equal justice may the lexicographer be derided, who, being able to produce no example of a nation that has preserved their words and phrases from mutability, shall imagine that his dictionary can embalm his language, and secure it from corruption and decay . . .

Dr Samuel Johnson, from his Preface to *A Dictionary of the English Language*, 1755

A living language is like a man suffering incessantly from small haemorrhages, and what it needs above all else is constant transactions of new blood from other tongues. The day the gates go up, that day it begins to die.

H. L. Mencken, from *The American Language*, 1919

CONTENTS

TABLE OF ILLUSTRATIONS

Introduction

SPEAKING OF ENGLISH

———◆———

"The English language", observed Ralph Waldo Emerson, "is the sea which receives tributaries from every region under heaven." On a much smaller scale, the same might be said of this book, which is published to coincide with a television series. Its authors have drawn on a wealth of original material collected during the making of the films, together with a wide range of published and unpublished sources, to tell the story of our language. To adapt Shakespeare slightly, we have been "at a great feast of language and stolen some of the scraps". Our work has been inspired by first-hand sound recordings of a great variety of contemporary English – in the United Kingdom and Ireland, in North America, in Australia, in the Caribbean, in India and South-East Asia, and in post-colonial Africa. We have been fortunate enough to have an experience of the living language across the world that is denied to many scholars and we have incorporated the highlights of our research, recorded on film and sound tape in the years 1983–5, into the text.

We have tried to tell the whole story. Some academic studies tend to dwell on the catalogued literary past rather than on the messier, teeming present, on Chaucer and Noah Webster at the expense of Caribbean creole or space-speak. Until recently, the focus of scholarship has been on the Anglo-American story, and while giving proper weight to this main narrative, we have also explored some of the newer sub-plots of the language, in places like China, Singapore, Holland and West Africa. A more accurate title for this book might have been *The English Languages*, an idea to which we shall return in the final chapter.

We have also paid attention to the everyday spoken English of fishermen, wheelwrights, cowboys, folk singers, priests, doctors, sugar planters, computer hackers, etc., talking about their work in their own variety of the language. This approach emphasizes an important truth about language which the fixity of print can sometimes obscure: that it is always in flux, and that its form and expression are beyond the control of schoolteachers or governments. What is more, when you look at language under a microscope, you can see it changing almost as you watch it: words and phrases, pronunciations and rhythms become widely imitated at astonishing speed. Watching the rough-cut of the programme about Black English, one of our production assistants was amazed to discover that her ten-year-old son was imitating the latest slang from the Philadelphia ghettos – in London.

We know that for many people English has become synonymous with English Literature. While focusing on the spoken word, we have also looked to the literary innovators of our language and quoted their opinions. In some cases their views on English emerge as asides in well-known novels or essays. It has been one of the pleasures of the research to consider the canon of English and American writing from a new perspective. (The "bel canto" English and American writers have tended to be the most perceptive in their comments on the language. Charles Dickens says more than Jane Austen, Mark Twain more than Henry James.) The balance between the spoken and the written is partly shaped by the story itself. The first Anglo-Saxons were illiterate. The present generation of English users have more ways to write and record it than ever before.

The English language surrounds us like a sea, and like the waters of the deep it is full of mysteries. Until the invention of the gramophone and the tape-recorder there was no reliable way of examining everyday speech. Anyone who has spent time with the quasi-scientific writings of the phoneticians could be forgiven for thinking that their laborious notations hardly explain the mysteriously fluid substance they are trying to analyse. The music of our language eludes transcription. Similarly, written English has always been the preserve of the educated minority, and gives us tantalizingly few clues about the English of earlier centuries. English is – and always has been – in a state of ungovernable change, and the limits of scholarship are demonstrated by phrases like the famous "Great Vowel Shift", hardly more informative than the "unknown land" of early cartography.

There is another part of language that is almost impossible to analyse: its genius. When William Morris – idealizing the German and Scandinavian roots of English – proposed the replacement of lieutenant by *steadholder*, grotesque by *whimwork*, and omnibus by *folkwain*, his suggestions were seen for what they were, a new romanticism. The absurdity of such usages comes partly from their artificiality and partly from an intangible sense of language appropriateness. The essayist and Anglophile Logan Pearsall Smith, who wrote one of the best books on the language, courageously faced up to the inexpressible side of this subject in some memorable paragraphs about "the genius of the language", which he defined as, "the power that guides and controls its progress", a passage that should perhaps be pinned up in Departments of Linguistics throughout the world.

> We each of us possess, in a greater or less degree, what the Germans call "speech-feeling", a sense of what is worthy of adoption and what should be avoided and condemned. This in almost all of us is an instinctive process; we feel the advantages or disadvantages of new forms and new distinctions, although we should be hard put to it to give a reason for our feeling. We know, for instance, that it is now wrong to say "much" rather than "many thanks", though Shakespeare used the phrase; that "much happier" is right, though the old "much happy" is wrong, and that *very* must in many cases take the place once occupied by *much*. We say a picture was *hung*, but a murderer was *hanged*, often, perhaps, without being conscious that we make the distinction. . . .

Grammarians can help this corporate will by registering its decrees and extending its analogies; but they fight against it in vain. They were not able to banish the imperfect passive, "the house is being built", which some of them declared was an outrage on the language; the phrase "different to" has been used by most good authors in spite of their protests; and if the Genius of the Language finds the split infinitive useful to express certain shades of thought, we can safely guess that all opposition to it will be futile.

Second only to the mystery of the subject, and related to it, is the sheer difficulty of writing about the English language. Treating it as a science is deadening for most people. Treating it, as we have done, as a mixture of social history, literature and linguistics still does not overcome the problem that language is also gesture, tone and context. We hope that constructing each chapter in the shape of a journey moving through time and space gives our subject a touch of the colour and drama that it sometimes seems to lack.

True to the popularizing credo of the television series, we decided that the world was our oyster (or *erster*, as they are alleged to say in Brooklyn), a phrase whose origins have become buried, like so much of our language, in the whispers of the past. We have relished the challenge, and our aim has been to make this book a straightforward narrative that ranges widely over the numerous varieties of English. In the same spirit, we have tried to give the chapters a sense of *place* – our experience of language and the laws governing its evolution suggests that geography is one of the fundamental factors: the English–Gaelic division of the Scottish Lowlands and Highlands is a case in point. For those who want to go further into the by-ways and backwoods of language, there are extensive notes and source materials at the end. In the same spirit of accessibility and readability, we have avoided using technical jargon and phonetic symbols, and we have also tried to steer clear of what the late American journalist Peter Lisagor of the *Chicago Daily News* used to call "out of town words", for example *polymorphic*, *isogloss* and *homophone*. (We should, in passing, add that this book does not address itself in any serious sense to the *theory* of language, though some linguistics is implicit in most chapters.)

The logic of this global approach has led us to make a basic descriptive decision: rather than talk about *accents* and *dialects* of English, we talk of *varieties*. Again and again we found that the line between *accent*, *dialect* and *language* is not a sure or a steady one and is often disputed, even by specialists. Is Scottish English, for instance, a language or a dialect? The experts find it hard to be certain. It has been said that "a language is a dialect with an army and a navy", but *my* accent often turns out to be *your* dialect. There are other problems. If we say that an accent is a set of sounds peculiar to a region, and that a dialect includes peculiarities not only of sound, but also of grammar and vocabulary, the definition excludes what is often the *class* basis of an accent, irrespective of locality. The English language is a continuum of speech. Using *variety*, we avoid the pejorative overtones of *dialect*. As countless scholars have pointed out, Standard English is itself only a dialect, albeit a prestigious one. On the other hand, there is no point in pretending that certain kinds of English are not *perceived* to be superior. Many Americans, for instance, will tell a speaker of British English that his or her speech is "better" than theirs. The news readers of the Singapore Broadcasting Corporation seem to parody BBC English in an attempt to emulate the British model. Inverted snobbery makes a middle-class British rock star like Mick Jagger adopt what he thinks is a "Cockney" accent. In the South and West of the United States, it is currently fashionable to adopt "country" usages and rhythms.

If our approach seems more journalistic than scholastic, we felt this was appropriate for a subject that, unlike many academic studies, is both popular and newsworthy. Hardly a week goes by without a news story, often on the front page, devoted to some aspect of English: the "decline" of standards; the perils and hilarities of Franglais or Japlish; the adoption of English as a "national" language by another Third World country. For all the dry connotations of the word, "language" is good box-office. Inside the newspapers – of Britain and the United States especially – columns on language generate, as in the case of William Safire on the *New York Times*, the paper's biggest mailbag.

English has also become big business, perhaps the United Kingdom's richest natural resource, marketed with considerable skill and professionalism throughout the world, from Australia to Zanzibar. Denis Forman, Chairman of Granada Television, expressed an aspect of this idea in his McTaggart Lecture at the 1984 Edinburgh Festival:

> Of [English] assets, Shakespeare is the greatest. His value on the national balance sheet can be computed by assessing the total profit of the Shakespeare industry in the current year in terms of domestic and foreign trade and grossing this up over, say, twenty years, thereby reaching a current market valuation ... If then the government were to pass a bill privatizing the full range of Shakespearian copyright, it could even be that the capital value of Associated Stratford Industry plc would considerably exceed the £297 million set as the price for British Leyland's Jaguar.

In the last ten years, the global selling of the language has reached astonishing proportions, from China's revolutionary English language policy, to the publication of the *MacQuarie Dictionary of Australian English*, to the near-total anglicization of international trade and politics, from OPEC to summitry.

We have tried to reflect the fact that language belongs to each one of us, to the flower-seller as much as to the professor, which is of course the explanation for such popular interest: everyone uses words, even if, at first, they don't stop to think about them. But when they do, language can generate an astounding amount of heat. What is it about language that makes people so passionate, and so curious? The answer is that there is almost no aspect of our lives that is not touched by language. We live in and by language. We all speak and we all listen: so we are all interested in the origins of words, and their rise and fall. How did *nice* once mean "foolish or wanton"? Why did we never adopt *neverness* as a synonym for "eternity"? We travel more and more: so visitors to London are intrigued to discover that Rotten Row is a corruption of *la route du roi* (the King's way). We are all in some senses political, and so is language. People have been killed in Northern Ireland for their pronunciation of the ABC. In Canada, STOP signs get repainted ARRÊT by the Quebecois. Sexual identity has become a political issue, and so have titles like *Mr*, *Mrs* and *Ms*. In Britain, some women have become *wimmin*, to avoid the "sexist" use of the word "men". National pride will stimulate arguments about Franglais, or AmerEnglish. As citizens of a constantly changing world, which is revealed in language, we can become irrationally aggressive or defensive about usages like "hopefully" and "gay", or rival pronunciations like "con'troversy" versus "contro'versy", to name a famous one. People tend to fasten their anxieties about the changing world on to words. In the right context, a split infinitive can look like the end of civilization as we know it.

The heat of language is matched by its myths. From the hoary old chestnut that Shakespearean English is alive and well and living in the Ozark mountains, to the belief that the speech of Merseyside is attributable to bad colds and blocked noses, to the racist slur that Blacks speak the way they do because they have thick lips, there are several popular superstitions which we have, where possible, tried to demolish. In the process, we may have fallen victim to a few myths ourselves, probably the inventions of a local informant with a taste for mischief. In our efforts to be truthful and accurate, we have at times sympathized with Algernon in *The Importance of Being Earnest*: "It is perfectly phrased, and quite as true as any observation in civilized life should be." In the end, truth and untruth, legends and apocryphal tales, all go to make up what W. H. Auden once called "our marvellous native tongue".

None of this would have come to anything, either on television or in print, without the practical help and guidance of a number of people, whom we would like to thank. Above all, this project is the brainchild of Brian Wenham, then Controller of BBC2, who first responded to the idea, commissioned a pilot programme and arranged for co-production finance. If Brian Wenham was the godfather, Roger Laughton in the Department of Network Features was the midwife, seeing the series through some difficult times at the BBC, and bringing some characteristically distinctive ideas to the project during its long gestation. The television series is also indebted to the co-producers, MacNeil-Lehrer-Gannett Productions in the United States. Both the book and the series owe a special thank you to Matthew Evans, Chairman of Faber and Faber, for his generous support and encouragement from first to last.

On the editorial side, we are very grateful to our three main consultants, Dr Robert Burchfield, Chief Editor of the *Oxford English Dictionary*, Stuart Flexner, Editor-in-Chief of the *Random House Dictionary*, and Professor Sir Randolph Quirk, all of whom have made many invaluable contributions, and saved us from countless errors of fact and interpretation. For those that remain, we take full responsibility.

In addition to the overall guidance of our consultants, each programme and chapter benefited hugely from the involvement of many scholars throughout the world who gave us of their time and expertise far beyond the call of duty. For chapter one: Dr J. C. Wells, Professor John Honey, and Professor Peter Strevens. For chapter two: Professor Tom Shippey, Dr

Michael Clanchy, Professor Bruce Mitchell, and Dr Christopher Page. For chapter three: Professor F. G. Cassidy, and Professor Stanley Ellis. For chapter four: Professor John Braidwood, Professor A. J. Aitken, and Professor Cratis Williams. For chapter five: Professor Alan Bliss, Professor J. L. Henry, Dr Séamas Ó'Catháin, Professor Harold Paddock, and Dr Loreto Todd. For chapter six: Professor J. L. Dillard, Dr John Holm, Dr Loreto Todd, Dr Arthur Spears, and Dr Michael Cooke. For chapter seven: Professor Jack Chambers, and Professor John Fought. For chapter eight: Professor Robert Eagleson, Professor John Bernard, Professor Arthur Delbridge, and Dr W. S. Ramsun. For chapter nine: Professor Mervyn Morris, Professor Edwin Thumboo, Professor Peter Trudgill, Professor E. K. Brathwaite, and Professor Eldred Jones.

We owe an important thank you to the production team who brought the series to the screen: to our producers, Peter Dale and John Pett; to our assistant producers Vivian Ducat and Dr Howard Reid; to our tireless series cameraman, David South, who also provided many of the finest illustrations in this book; to his assistant, Frank Bigg, to our sound-recordist, Anthony Wornum, to our production assistants, Anthea Cridlan and Hilary Harrison, and last but not least, our series film editor, Richard Spurway, and his assistant Philippa Spurway. We should also like to thank Julia Alldridge, Bob Cummins, Maureen Dewick, Alan FitzJohn, Nicky Fox, Andrew Godfrey, John Goodyer, Sarah Hardie, Graham Hare, Lorelle Harker, Kenneth Hasler, Kate Jennings, Anne Leleu, John McGlashan, Doug Mawson, Sid Morris, Sue New, Stephen Oliver, Denise Perrin, Liz Ross, Clive Siddall, Janet Sinclair, Pat Southam, Sarah Stacey, Edwin Tingey, Al Vecchione, and Marcus Wilford.

Finally, for those who wonder about a book with three authors, it was written by Robert McCrum, in collaboration with William Cran, and with invaluable editorial suggestions from Robert MacNeil, who also contributed the passages on English in Nova Scotia and Canada, and many insights into other aspects of the English language in North America.

1 The Voyager space probe with a tape-recorded English greeting "on behalf of the people of our planet".

I

AN ENGLISH-SPEAKING WORLD

On 5 September 1977, the American spacecraft Voyager One blasted-off on its historic mission to Jupiter and beyond. On board, the scientists, who knew that Voyager would one day spin through distant star systems, had installed a recorded greeting from the people of the planet Earth. Preceding a brief message in fifty-five different languages for the people of outer space, the gold-plated disc plays a statement, from the Secretary-General of the United Nations, an Austrian named Kurt Waldheim, speaking on behalf of 147 member states – in English.

The rise of English is a remarkable success story. When Julius Caesar landed in Britain nearly two thousand years ago, English did not exist. Five hundred years later, *Englisc*, incomprehensible to modern ears, was probably spoken by about as few people as currently speak Cherokee – and with about as little influence. Nearly a thousand years later, at the end of the sixteenth century, when William Shakespeare was in his prime, English was the native speech of between five and seven million Englishmen and it was, in the words of a contemporary, "of small reatch, it stretcheth no further than this iland of ours, naie not there over all".

Four hundred years later, the contrast is extraordinary. Between 1600 and the present, in armies, navies, companies and expeditions, the speakers of English – including Scots, Irish, Welsh, American and many more – travelled into every corner of the globe, carrying their language and culture with them. Today, English is used by at least 750 million people, and barely half of those speak it as a mother tongue. Some estimates have put that figure closer to one billion. Whatever the total, English at the end of the twentieth century is more widely scattered, more widely spoken and written, than any other language has ever been. It has become *the* language of the planet, the first truly global language.

The statistics of English are astonishing. Of all the world's languages (which now number some 2700), it is arguably the richest in vocabulary. The compendious *Oxford English Dictionary* lists about 500,000 words; and a further half million technical and scientific terms remain uncatalogued. According to traditional estimates, neighbouring German has a vocabulary of about 185,000 words and French fewer than 100,000, including such Franglais as *le snacque-barre* and *le hit-parade*. About 350 million people use the English vocabulary as a mother tongue: about one-tenth of the world's population, scattered across every continent and surpassed, in numbers, though not in distribution, only by the speakers of the many varieties of Chinese. Three-quarters of the world's mail, and its telexes and cables, are in English. So are more than half the world's technical and scientific periodicals: it is the language of technology from Silicon Valley to Shanghai. English is the medium for 80 per cent of the information stored in the world's computers. Nearly half of all business deals in Europe are conducted in English. It is the language of sports and glamour: the official language of the Olympics and the Miss Universe competition. English is the official voice of the air, of the sea, and of Christianity: it is the ecumenical language of the World Council of Churches. Five of the largest broadcasting companies in the world (CBS, NBC, ABC, BBC, CBC) transmit in English to audiences that regularly exceed one hundred million.

English has a few rivals, but no equals. Neither Spanish nor Arabic, both international languages, have this global sway. Another rival, Russian, has the political and economic under-pinning of a world language, but far from spreading its influence outside the Soviet empire, it, too, is becoming mildly colonized by new words known as *Russlish*, for example *seksapil* (sex appeal) and *noh-khau* (know-how). Germany and Japan have, in matching the commercial and industrial vigour of the United States, achieved the commercial precondition of language-power, but their languages have also been invaded by English, in the shape of *Deutchlish* and *Japlish*.

The remarkable story of how English spread within predominantly English-speaking societies like the United States, Canada, Australia and New Zealand is not, with the benefit of hindsight, unique. It is a process in language that is as old as Greek, or Chinese. The truly significant development, which has occurred only in the last one hundred years or so, is the use of English, taking the most conservative estimates, by three or four hundred million people for whom it is not a native language. English has become a *second* language in countries like India, Nigeria or Singapore where it is used for administration, broadcasting and education. In these countries, English is a vital alternative language, often unifying huge territories and diverse populations. When Rajiv Gandhi appealed for an end to the violence that broke out after the assassination of his mother, Mrs Indira Gandhi, he went on television and spoke to his people in English. In anglophone Africa, seizures of power are announced in English. Then there is English as a *foreign* language, used in countries (like Holland or Yugoslavia) where it is backed up by a tradition of English teaching, or where it has been more recently adopted, Senegal for instance. Here it is used to have contact with people in other countries, usually to promote trade and scientific progress, but to the benefit of international communication generally. A Dutch poet is read by a few thousands. Translated into English, he can be read by hundreds of thousands.

The emergence of English as a global phenomenon – as either a first, second or foreign language – has recently inspired the idea (undermining the claims we have just made) that we should talk not of English, but of many Englishes, especially in Third World countries where the use of English is no longer part of the colonial legacy, but the result of decisions made since independence. But what kind of English is it? This is a new and hotly contested debate which we shall explore fully in chapter nine. The future, of course, is unpredictable, but one thing is certain: the present flux of English – multi-national standard or international Babel? – is part of a process that goes back to Shakespeare and beyond.

"THE QUEEN'S ENGLISH"

Throughout the history of English there has been a contest between the forces of standardization and the forces of localization, at both the written and the spoken levels. The appearance of the first substantial English dictionaries in the eighteenth century was a move towards written standardization. It was Victorian England that realized the idea of "the Queen's English", a spoken standard to which the "lesser breeds" could aspire.

There is an old Hindi proverb that "language changes every eighteen or twenty miles". Despite the influence of television and radio, you can still find a surprising number of regional varieties of spoken English within the United States, Canada and Australia, and especially within the British Isles. Here, depending on which county you are driving through, a donkey can still be called a *moke*, or a *cuddy*, or a *nirrup*, or a *pronkus*. In the English Lake District *deg*, *frap*, *heft*, *joggle*, *nope*, *scaitch* and *whang* all mean "to beat". While it is true that local idioms are not as strong as they were, we probably underrate their resilience and attribute more power to the levelling forces of television and radio than they deserve. A conversation between a Dorset shepherd and an Aberdonian farmworker can still be a dialogue of the deaf.

In the early nineteenth century, these regional differences were even more distinctive, but as the industrial towns of Lancashire and the Black Country mushroomed, and the countryside was stripped of its rural workforce, a steady improvement in literacy helped to disseminate more widely a standard of written English. The industrial revolution meant roads, canals and, above all, trains: people travelled more, both geographically and socially. We have only to read the novels of Charles Dickens to see the truth of George Bernard Shaw's famous dictum that "it is impossible for an Englishman to open his mouth without making some other Englishman despise him". The pressures of class ambition speeded up the emergence of a standard form of English speech. Writing less than a generation after the beginning of universal elementary education in England, Thomas Hardy, in *Tess of the d'Urbervilles*, drew an interesting contrast between Tess and her mother:

> Mrs Durbeyfield habitually spoke the dialect; her daughter, who had passed the Sixth Standard in the National School under a London-trained mistress, spoke two languages; the dialect at home, more or less; ordinary English abroad and to persons of quality.

The emergence of Received Pronunciation (RP) – the outward and visible sign of belonging to the professional middle class – went hand in hand with the rise of an imperial Civil Service and its educational infrastructure. The Education Act of 1870 not only established the English public school as the melting-pot of upper- and middle-class speech and society, but

2 Thomas Hardy, born and educated in Dorset, reproduced "the dialect" and "ordinary English" in his novels.

3 William Wordsworth is remembered by neighbours in Grasmere rehearsing his poetry in a Cumberland murmur.

4 William Ewart Gladstone never lost traces of his Lancashire accent.

5 Public Schools like Winchester eradicated regional speech.

6 Kipling's Indians spoke "a clipped, uncertain sing-song".

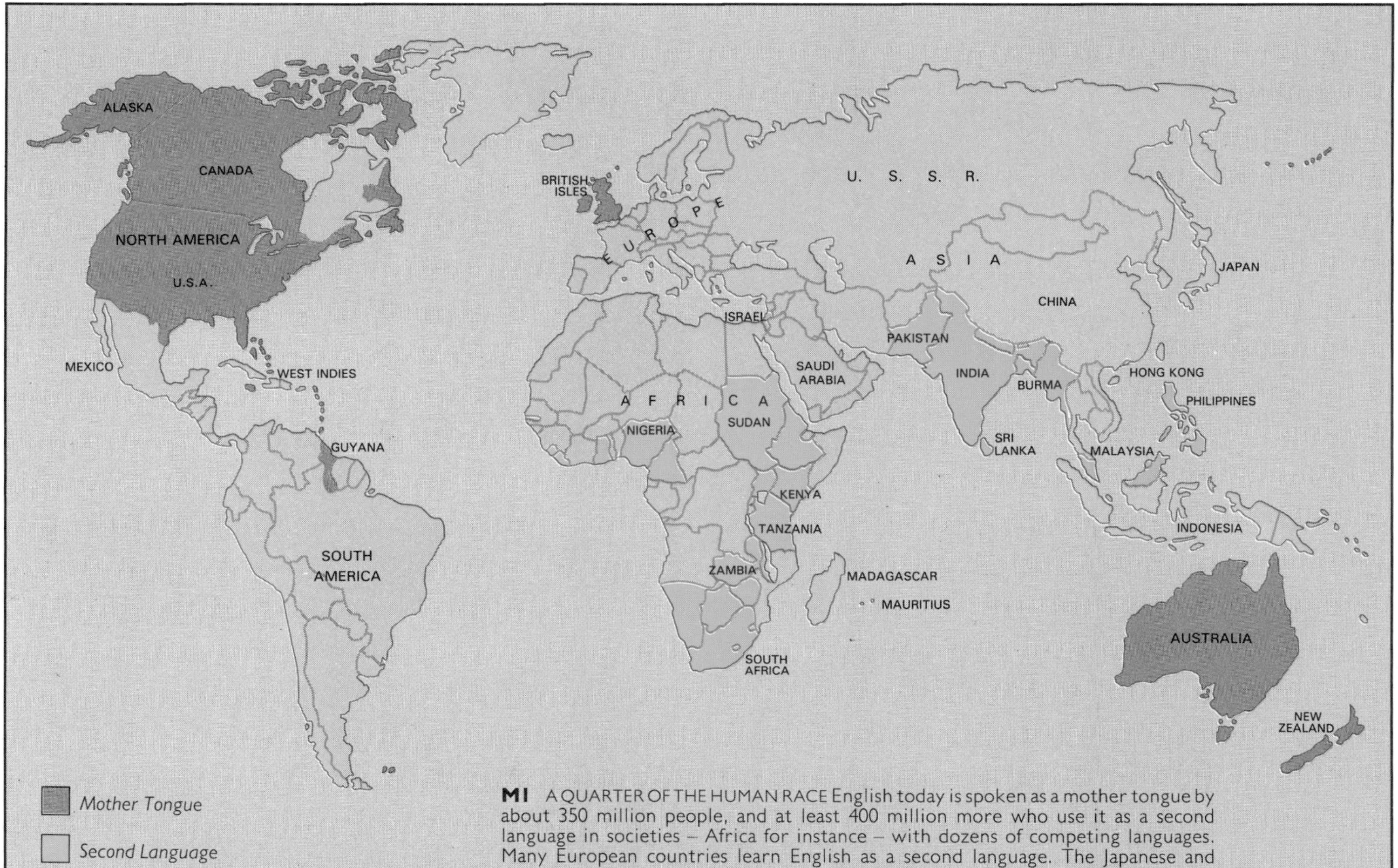

M1 A QUARTER OF THE HUMAN RACE English today is spoken as a mother tongue by about 350 million people, and at least 400 million more who use it as a second language in societies – Africa for instance – with dozens of competing languages. Many European countries learn English as a second language. The Japanese and Chinese appear to be fascinated by English. It is also the language of international business and politics, transcending ideological and religious divisions. In total, there are probably more than a billion speakers of English, at least a quarter of the world's population.

Mother Tongue

Second Language

Map labels: NEW ZEALAND, AUSTRALIA, JAPAN, PHILIPPINES, INDONESIA, HONG KONG, MALAYSIA, CHINA, BURMA, SRI LANKA, INDIA, PAKISTAN, U. S. S. R., A S I A, MADAGASCAR, MAURITIUS, SAUDI ARABIA, ISRAEL, KENYA, TANZANIA, SUDAN, A F R I C A, NIGERIA, ZAMBIA, SOUTH AFRICA, E U R O P E, BRITISH ISLES, ALASKA, CANADA, NORTH AMERICA, U.S.A., MEXICO, WEST INDIES, GUYANA, SOUTH AMERICA also started a boom in English preparatory schools. Now the children (mostly boys) of country squires, city nobility, army officers, imperial civil servants, small-town lawyers, doctors, clergymen and suburban dentists could be brought together from the ages of eight to eighteen, drawn from many parts of the country, and educated in one confined space, often isolated market towns like Wellington, Sherborne, Tonbridge and Worksop.

The contrast in the English speech of the educated elite before and after the Education Act is startling. Before 1870, many of the most eminent Victorians retained their regional accents throughout their lives. Sir Robert Peel (Harrow and Oxford), one of England's most famous Conservative prime ministers, never disguised his Midlands speech. Lord Stanley, later fifteenth earl of Derby (Rugby and Cambridge), spoke "a sort of Lancashire patois". His Liberal opponent, William Gladstone, spent his childhood in Liverpool and his "Lancashire burr" survived both Eton and Oxford, which suggests he was under virtually no social pressure to lose it. Frederick Temple, a headmaster of Rugby School, had a "marked provincial accent" which his unruly boys loved to mimic as "Bies, yer getting ruude: this must cease". But he was not scorned for his speech. Even at Eton, the shrine of English private education, the Reverend J. L. Joynes, one of the poet Swinburne's tutors, is known to have pronounced "died" as "doyed", and to have attacked the "oidle" in his sermons. All these idiosyncrasies were noticed, but they were not stigmatized.

By the 1890s, all this had changed. A new generation of post-Education Act schoolmasters would rebuke the boy who said "loike" for "like". Accent levelling was not only applied from above: peer pressure among the schoolboys themselves was a powerful incentive for a new boy to acquire the approved tone. From the 1880s, at Bedford Modern School, local boys with a North Bedfordshire accent "were so mercilessly imitated and laughed at that, if they had any intelligence, they were soon able to speak standard English". By the end of the nineteenth century some ambitious parents began to fear the local schools where their children might "pick up an accent". Non-standard English was now seriously stigmatized as the mark of the under-educated. At Oxford it had become virtually a condition of social acceptance among undergraduates that one should "speak the Queen's English with a specific accent and intonation".

This "specific accent" was RP – a term that entered common currency at the end of the nineteenth century, the educated accent of London and south-east England. There was nothing wholly new in this. Three centuries before, an Elizabethan writer had described the most desirable form of English, "the usuall speach of the Court, and that of London and the shires lying about London within lx myles, and not much above". But now, for the first time, the public and preparatory schools were spreading this preferred English nationwide, so much so that in 1917 the phonetician Daniel Jones christened standard spoken English "Public School Pronunciation (PSP)", a label that did not stick.

RP was not confined to the public schools which had a special and wider administrative role to play within Victorian society: to provide the British Army and the imperial Civil Service with a steady flow of well-spoken recruits. At the height of the empire, RP was widely recognized throughout the colonies as the voice of authority. Indeed, it was jealously preserved as such. In George Orwell's *Burmese Days*, when the Burmese butler at the club shows an unacceptable proficiency ("I find it very difficult to keep ice cool now"), he is rebuked by the white *sahib*:

> "Don't talk like that, damn you – 'I find it very difficult!' Have you swallowed a dictionary? 'Please, master, can't keeping ice cool' – that's how you ought to talk. We shall have to sack this fellow if he gets to talk English too well."

Within privileged parts of the empire – the officer corps of the Indian Army, for instance – the aspiration towards RP became total. As one retired officer in the Indian armed services remarked, "Our teachers drilled into our minds that the thing to aspire to was what is known as the King's English."

If the identification of RP with power, education and material success encouraged imitation, it also stimulated a distinct antipathy, and many people resented its implicit snobbery. The speech of army officers, for instance, became the subject of parody: *chahnce* for "chance", *pahchase* for "purchase", *bahd* for "bird" and *evenchalleh* for "eventually". This style of speech has continued to be teased in books like *Fraffly Well Spoken*, and *The Sloane Ranger's Handbook*. The evolution of an identifiable upper middle-class standard was matched by the emergence of rural and working-class stereotypes flourishing alongside educated speech both in Britain and throughout the empire. It is clear from the works of a writer like Rudyard Kipling that the phenomenon of the officers speaking RP and the troops speaking English vernacular was widely recognized. In a ballad like "Danny Deever", the voice of the rank-and-file is unmistakable:

> *"What are the bugles blowin' for?" said Files-on-Parade.*
> *"To turn you out, to turn you out," the Colour-Sergeant said.*
> *"What makes you look so white, so white?" said Files-on-Parade.*
> *"I'm dreadin' what I've got to watch," the Colour-Sergeant said.*

Like many of Kipling's *Barrack Room Ballads*, "Danny Deever" is full of Cockney: *'ollow* for "hollow", *'and* for "hand", *an'* for "and", *o'* for "of", and *hangin'* for "hanging". It is a stylized version of English Cockney, but it conforms to the popular idea of the English working man's speech, in or out of the army. (It is an irony of English speech distinctions that the "assured" upper and "indifferent" lower classes should share the casual *in'* pronunciation, in sharp contrast to the correct *ing* articulation of the ever-anxious middle classes.)

During the First World War, RP and Cockney collided not merely face to face, but down telephone wires. We have entered the age of the recorded voice and electrically transmitted sound. For the first time in the history of language it was possible to listen to another voice without being in the presence of the speaker – and to hear that voice again and again. Today, we take these inventions for granted, but the first recordings of the speech of the Poet

Laureate, Alfred Tennyson (with a noticeable Lincolnshire burr), and even Queen Victoria herself (the old lady pronounced a high-pitched "Good evening" for posterity) must have seemed miraculous.

7 Winston Churchill exploited the power of radio to rally "the English-speaking peoples" in the Second World War.

8 John Reith took great pains with the English of the new BBC.

"NATION SHALL SPEAK PEACE UNTO NATION"

The years from the end of the First World War in 1918 to the end of the Second World War in 1945 were the heyday of radio in Britain and the United States, the years of Roosevelt's fireside chats to the American people and of Winston Churchill's wartime broadcasts. The establishment in Britain in 1922 of the first radio broadcasting service, the BBC, was a milestone for the English language. As one of its first executives wrote: "The broadcasting of aural language is an event no less important than the broadcasting of visual language [printing], not only in its influence on human relations, but in its influence upon the destinies of the English language." From the first, the BBC had a global – and in those days imperial – attitude towards the English language. Its motto ran "Nation shall speak peace unto nation", and no one doubted what the tongue should be. The question was: what kind of English?

In an era of rapid change, there was, first of all, the question of acceptable vocabulary. New inventions could provoke furious public debate: should *airman* be recognized in favour of *aviator*? A British broadcasting authority would have to make such rulings. Then there were foreign borrowings to cope with. Would a mass radio audience understand *Zeitgeist*, *Weltanschauung* and *Übermensch*, or should the BBC voice say *time-spirit*, *world-outlook* and *superman*? And what about that old British bugbear, Americanisms? What attitude should the new BBC take towards such coinings as *cocktail*, *joy-ride*, *pussyfoot*, *road-hog* and *sneak-thief*? And, perhaps most sensitive of all, what English accent should the BBC adopt?

The approach to a solution, reached in 1926, was to set up the so-called *Advisory Committee on Spoken English* (ACSE). This high-powered group of experts included the poet

Robert Bridges, a northerner who argued unsuccessfully for the adoption of a Northern Standard, the American scholar Logan Pearsall Smith, and the Irishman George Bernard Shaw, but was composed chiefly of RP speakers, men such as the lexicographer C. T. Onions; the scientist Julian Huxley; the art historian Kenneth Clark; and Alistair Cooke, then a young journalist. The Committee's declared task was to arbitrate on the usage and pronunciation of words, English and foreign. Decisions were reached by a simple vote, an arbitrary procedure that, in 1936, for example, sensibly favoured *roundabouts* against *gyratory circuses*, but, less sensibly, proposed *stop-and-goes* instead of *traffic lights*. Arbitrations on usage were probably much less influential for the evolution of a spoken Standard English than judgements about pronunciation. Alistair Cooke remembers how the ACSE settled the pronunciation of "canine":

> Shaw brought up the word "canine", and he wanted the recommendation to be "cay-nine" . . . And somebody said, "Mr Shaw, Mr Chairman, I don't know why you bring this up, of course it's "ca-nine". Shaw said, "I always pronounce things the way they are pronounced by people who use the word professionally every day." And he said, "My dentist always says 'cay-nine." And somebody said, "Well, in that case, Mr Chairman, you must have an American dentist." And he said, "Of course, why do you think at 76 I have all my teeth!"

The first Director General of the BBC, Lord Reith, a Scot, himself believed in a broadcast English that would give no offence, as he recalled in a television interview towards the end of his life:

> What I tried to get was a style or quality of English which would not be laughed at in any part of the country. I was as vehemently opposed to what variously has been called the Oxford accent or the south-eastern accent – such as the *theatah*, the *fahside*.

According to Reith, "the language, the speech and pronunciation . . . that the announcers were taught to speak . . . was the very best thing we could do". He was, of course, describing RP. Bridges alone seriously challenged the implicit assumption that RP was the only socially acceptable accent for radio. The establishment of a uniform BBC English was partly designed to promote a sense of impersonality and impartiality. A sober recital, it was felt, would seem more accurate. In the early days, the newsreaders wore dinner jackets and, when nothing newsworthy was deemed to have occurred, they said so – and played classical music instead.

Like many pioneers, Reith was an idealist. His broadcasting corporation reflected his aspirations. First, there was the hope that the BBC would promote English on a global scale. "We cherish the decision", as one pamphlet put it, "that our language will remain as we know it now, the optimistic even seeing in it a future world language." Much more potent, and much more pervasive, was this belief: "It would appear . . . that the higher a community climbs on the social scale, the greater is the degree of uniformity in speech. Whenever language is spoken, there is present in the minds of the speakers the notion that there is a 'right way' of speaking it . . ." Lord Reith's BBC was determined to promote this "right way". Accent was one of the factors that perpetuated social inequality, sustained class barriers, and put the lower classes at a disadvantage. "You cannot raise social standards without raising speech standards," observed one member of the Committee. Overseas, BBC English – transmitted by eight so-called Empire announcers, and later by the World Service – was intended to unite the colonies, later the Commonwealth. Gradually, the English of the airwaves took over from the English of the imperial Civil Service, a vital means of communication among people without a common language.

Within the British Isles, the spread of RP by the BBC, first on radio, then on television, helped to reinforce what was an already strong connection in many people's minds between education and "Standard English" – usually perceived as the pronunciation found in the public schools, the universities, the professions, the government and the church. The influence of this association was, in its day, enormous, even though RP was spoken by only about 3 per cent of the British population, a tiny fraction of the world's English-speaking community. Henry Cecil Wyld, Merton Professor of English Language and Literature at Oxford from 1920 to 1945, and credited with the dictum that "No gentleman goes on a bus", expressed a common view when he wrote of RP that it was: "The best kind of English, not only because it is spoken by those often very properly called the best people, but also because it has two great advantages that make it intrinsically superior to every other type of English speech – the extent to which it is current throughout the country and the marked distinctiveness and clarity of its sounds." Even in the United States a refined pronunciation of the King's English became desirable: in the Hollywood films of the 1930s stars playing upper-class Americans affected "posh" accents. (The fascination was not entirely one way. Raymond Chandler, now wholly identified with Los Angeles, liked to stress his English public-school education. In 1958, the year before his death, he wrote to John Houseman, a friend from Hollywood days, "I have had a lot of fun with the American language; it has fascinating idioms, is constantly creative, very much like the English of Shakespeare's time, its slang and argot are wonderful . . .") Later, in the 1950s, Wall Street and Madison Avenue executives hired English secretaries to add a touch of class to their dealings with the public.

As RP became widespread – thanks to imitation by the upwardly mobile – it became necessary to distinguish between two types: the mainstream version, "unmarked RP", and the elite version, "posh English", known as "marked RP" (*bleck het* for "black hat", *hice* for "house"). The characteristic of this accent is that it is chiefly recognized by those who don't speak it. To non-RP speakers, it is known as talking "with a plum in the mouth" or "lah-di-dah" or "fraffly-fraffly". It was to identify this latter kind of English that Professor Alan Ross coined his famous and controversial distinction between U and non-U, observing that "among European languages, English is, surely, the most suited to the study of linguistic class-distinctions". Ross (whose work was popularized by Nancy Mitford) was concerned with what he called "the linguistic demarcation of the upper class" (for instance, people who said *table napkin* instead of serviette, or *wireless* rather than *radio*). In Britain it is a well-known preoccupation, but the notion that one kind of pronunciation (and usage) is superior to another runs very deep in many languages.

9/10/11 The accents of class. Harold Wilson and Arthur Scargill, both of the Labour Party, have not "standardized" their speech. Edward Heath took elocution lessons to enhance his acceptability to the Conservative Party.

"THE BEST KIND OF ENGLISH"

An accent has two vital functions: first, it gives us a clue about the speaker's life and career; second, an accent will give a good indication of the speaker's community values, and what he or she identifies with. A New York taxi-driver who says "Toid and Toity toid" is not only giving away his Brooklyn origins, but expressing pride in his roots. Jimmy Carter's unabashed southern accent proclaimed his determination to be an outsider in Washington. When a British miners' leader like Arthur Scargill stands on a platform in front of several thousand Yorkshire miners and shouts, "Courage, comrades!" exploiting the Northern English u-sound in "courage", he is making a very obvious gesture of solidarity.

Research into popular attitudes towards accents in Britain produces a surprisingly uniform reaction. Speakers of RP – identifiable only by voice – tend to be credited with qualities such as honesty, intelligence, ambition, even good looks. After RP, there is a league table of acceptable accents. Dublin Irish and Edinburgh Scottish are high on the list, which then descends through Geordie (the accent of Newcastle and the North-East), Yorkshire and West Country, until we reach the four least valued accents in Britain: Cockney, Liverpool Scouse, Birmingham and Glaswegian. Some local accents rate a higher score for sincerity and friendliness than RP, but not many. The RP speaker, compared with the speaker of non-standard English, has a better chance of asserting his rights, whether in a court of law, or when negotiating credit with a shopkeeper or bank manager – in any situation, in fact, where credibility is at a premium. This power extends to advertising on local radio. Most businesses, locally advertising their goods to the citizens of Glasgow, Liverpool or Birmingham, do not make their appeal in the local accents but in the RP of national broadcasting. British broadcasters who have non-standard accents have been known to receive hate-mail. Other findings suggest that women are more likely than men to modify their accent towards RP. Men will tend to cultivate a local accent, often as a badge of male solidarity and "mateship".

It is one of the iron laws of this story that language is always on the move, and this is as true of the words we use as of the way we say them. Significant language changes will occur even in the course of one lifetime. During the Second World War, the BBC tried to use well-known personalities with local accents, such as the Yorkshireman Wilfred Pickles, as newsreaders. The experiment was abandoned after listeners complained. During the 1960s and 1970s, however, rapid social change was reflected by a widening of the accent spectrum heard on BBC broadcasts. Actors like Albert Finney, Tom Courtenay and Frank Finlay, who had been taught to lose their flat Northern accents at the Royal Academy of Dramatic Art, now found that they were suddenly in vogue. Today, Brian Redhead, who proudly declares his Newcastle origins, is one of the BBC's most popular broadcasters, though he too gets his share of abusive mail attacking his accent. Running parallel to this process, the use of modified RP became much more widely acceptable. Three recent British Labour Party leaders – Harold Wilson, James Callaghan and Neil Kinnock – have non-RP backgrounds, and all speak a kind of English that, while advertising a certain pride in their regional origins, essential for their political credibility, at the same time makes a number of significant concessions to a widespread national respect for BBC English. Similarly, within the Conservative Party, the leadership of Britain's landed and monied interests has been conducted by two politicians – Edward Heath and Margaret Thatcher – whose acquired RP vowels are notoriously unstable. The weakening (though certainly not the abolition) of the English class system has led to a lessening of the power of English class accents.

Even RP itself has changed. The phonetician Dr J. C. Wells has demonstrated what he regards as "the clear differences between the RP of fifty years ago and the RP of today". One of the most obvious changes, in his opinion, is in the voice, which used to have a much tenser quality. This has much to do with fashion:

> Working-class culture has come to be admired in many ways . . . People are now a bit embarrassed to be seen imitating upper-class behaviour. It has become smart to go down-market, and this is reflected of course in their pronunciation.

A brief look at a public school like Winchester – for most people a bastion of RP speech – illustrates this trend perfectly. According to the boys themselves, "When you walk down the street, people say, 'Posh, oh'." "People tend to think that people at public school have a very posh accent – very lah-di-dah." However, they consider this view to be a long way from the reality: "There are very few people who still have posh accents. People don't want to be seen to be different. The posh accents are ironed out when you get here." As another boy put it, "Anyone who did have an upper-class accent would have to change it very quickly . . . so the plummy accent's gone. They get levelled out to a general middle-class accent." There are many theories about the way this "levelling out" occurs. Professor Wells has an interesting theory about changes in RP. He believes that they come from below, that is, from Cockney or London English:

> I think that many features of Cockney do move up-market. One notices today the spreading out of what I call "l vocalization". Now this is the use of a kind of "w" sound instead of an "l" in the middle of words like "milk" or "middle". In this case, we have clear evidence that these pronunciations are spreading out geographically and socially from the south-east of England.

"Posh" or "Cockney", between 1870 and 1945, British English was scattered throughout the world by war, empire and broadcasting, fostering the beginnings of English as a global *lingua franca*. The decline of the British Empire after the Second World War should have spelt the slow decline of English as a world language, in the way that French has declined. Yet, as our story will show, the English language now entered a new phase not merely as an international tongue, as Spanish or French are, but as a world language. It was saved by the United States, the first superpower in history.

THE VOICE OF AMERICA

On 8 May 1945, a few hours after announcing to the world the surrender of Hitler's Third Reich to the combined allied armies, Winston Churchill appeared on the balcony of Buckingham Palace with the King and Queen to acknowledge the cheers of the British people. Among the millions who witnessed the scene was the distinguished American radio commentator Edward R. Murrow, reporting on the event for his audience back home. This was a symbolic moment of transition. After 1945 the dominant voice in the English-speaking world was no longer British but American. For the next generation and more, the enormous strategic, economic and cultural interests of the United States – expressed through international English-speaking institutions like UNESCO and NATO, and corporations like Exxon, Ford and IBM – ensured that the English language would survive and flourish long after its parent culture could no longer sustain it.

The war in Europe had brought Americans first to bases in England and Italy and then, after D-Day, to France, and later Germany. By the fall of Berlin, the administration of formerly Nazi-occupied territories was at least partly in American hands. The language of the GI was vivid, profane, prone to military-style abbreviations like *R and R*, and, like the British, heavily influenced by the German of the enemy, in words like *blitz* (from *Blitzkrieg*) and *flak* (from the German acronym for Fliegerabwehrkanone, an anti-aircraft gun). The American military's propensity for acronyms created a famous one, *snafu* ("situation normal, all fucked up"), a word which has now entered the American lexicon.

Once peace was declared, Americans became deeply involved (through the Marshall Plan) with the European economy. The *black market* was already a popular phrase. Off-duty, the

American troops would use their privileged position to make the most of the local girls, offering cigarettes and *nylons* (invented in 1938) in exchange for the euphemistic "good time". Some new Americanisms – *pin-up*, for example – had precise etymologies. When the United States came into the war, it was decided that the GIs should have their own newspaper. In the spring of 1942, the magazine writer Hartzell Spence listed what he thought the new magazine, *Yank*, should contain. "Every issue", he said, "should have a pin-up picture for soldiers to pin up on the barracks wall to remind them of the girls back home." Recalling the early days of *Yank*, Spence remembers that, "We took to calling it 'the pin-up' and sent photographers out to shoot 'pin-up' pictures. I had never heard the expression before. It was a spontaneous coinage to meet the need and it sort of passed into the language." Or had it not already done so? It is typical of language (and our experience of it) to be "in the air". The issue of *Life* for July 1941 had already declared that "Dorothy Lamour is No. 1 pin-up girl of the US Army." Soldiers, sailors, pilots and marines popularized the term in bars and barracks throughout the world. For British troops, Vera Lynn, "the forces' sweetheart", was a favourite pin-up; for Americans, Betty Grable. The most artistic was probably Rita Hayworth, a photo of whom is said to have been taped to Fat Boy, the atomic bomb dropped on Hiroshima in August 1945.

This terrible event introduced a new and grim vocabulary into the English language: *fireball, mushroom cloud, test site, countdown, fallout, fusion, fission, chain reaction* and *atomic holocaust*. The bomb influenced Japan – and the American-dominated Far East – in another fundamental way. In the aftermath of defeat, among scenes of unparalleled devastation and demoralization, the full might of the American economy was imported to get the Japanese (and to a lesser extent, the whole Pacific) economy on its feet again. *It pays to advertize* had been an American business slogan since 1914. Now American civilian and military administration took charge on a colossal scale. In due course, Japanese families would find their way of life infiltrated by a whole series of potent brandnames: Lucky Strike, Marlboro, Budweiser, Schlitz, Gillette, Kodak, Maxwell House. Japanese children learnt to eat American breakfast cereals – Kellogg's cornflakes, for instance – and to drink Coca-Cola. In the post-war Pacific, especially Japan, this process of commercial infiltration was christened *Coca-colonialism*. This dependence on American technology and finance has introduced some 20,000 English words into regular use in Japan. The language trade has gone both ways. The fashionable American term *honcho* is of Japanese origin, and dates from the American occupation of Japan. *Honcho* (from a Japanese word meaning "squad-leader") was used to mean leader or boss ("Who's the honcho on this project?") and, travelling from California in the late 1960s, became a verb meaning to take effective action, to force something into effect, a word first widely popularized by John Ehrlichman during the Senate Watergate hearings.

After the Bomb, the *Cold War*, a phrase that entered the dictionaries in 1947, marked the emergence of the United States and the Soviet Union as the two superpowers. For the first time in the history of the language, English – American English – was unequivocally "the language of democracy". It was Winston Churchill who championed this identification: "We must never cease to proclaim in fearless tones the great principles of freedom and the rights of man, which are the joint inheritance of the English-speaking world and which, through Magna Carta, the Bill of Rights, the habeas corpus, trial by jury, and the English common law find their expression in the Declaration of Independence." Now, with English-speaking America ranged against the Soviet Union, both its democratic ideals and the language of those ideals – "life, liberty and the pursuit of happiness" – became closely identified with a fundamental geo-political struggle. The radio station Voice of America conducted many of its broadcasts in American English. For underground movements in Soviet Russia and the satellite countries of the Eastern bloc, it was the publication of their manifestos in English that drew world attention to their struggles. Many "liberation movements" and "freedom fighters" in the Third World came to adopt local versions of the Declaration of Independence to inspire their followers – often against the retreating British Empire.

The first superpower crisis, the Korean war, which gave us words like *brainwashing* and *chopper* (for "helicopter"), ended in July 1953. It was the last war to be reported extensively on newsreel by companies like Pathé, Movietone and Rank. A few weeks before the ceasefire, the Coronation of Queen Elizabeth II in Westminster Abbey was the first event to capture a mass television audience around the world. The age of television communications had arrived. Throughout the 1950s, American television and movies combined to bring American English and the American way of life – as interpreted by Hollywood – to a world audience. Many immigrants to the United States have said they first learned English by repeating much-loved lines in the cinemas of Europe. There had been many American films before the 1950s, but their influence was largely confined to Britain and America, and the richer European countries. After the Second World War, the technology of film-screening was more widely available and, except in France, Italy, Sweden and Britain, there was virtually no local film production (or television broadcasting) to balance the available diet of American-made (and American-spoken) material. Never had propaganda for the English language been presented in such an entertaining form.

The influence of the movies on the spread of English was – and still is – incalculable, an influence now intensified by the worldwide distribution of American television programmes and advertising. The images and phrases from Madison Avenue – "Try it, you'll like it", "Does she, or doesn't she?", "Where's the beef?" – have become the small change of our everyday conversation and are, perhaps, one of the United States' most successful and pervasive exports. Products like vacuum cleaners, tissues and photo-copiers are known worldwide as Hoovers, Kleenex and Xeroxes. The advertiser, John O'Toole, describes the advertisers' export of American English:

> The depiction of American life, or at least the popular myth of American life, the good life, a lot of free and easy laughter, and people hanging around in bars and cocktail parties, all looked very attractive and it was associated with American products. In so doing it made the American way of life attractive – and with it the American language.

12 Betty Grable, one of the first "pin-up girls". (Rita Hayworth's picture was attached to the Hiroshima A-bomb.)

13 American advertising has spread the English language by a process the French call "Coca-colonialism".

If there was one event that brought together all these post-war influences affecting the spread of American English – East/West tension, Coca-colonialism, and mass culture – it was the Vietnam war. The war, and the opposition to it, created a sizeable new vocabulary and, because it was a television war, many new words moved rapidly into the language: *defoliate, napalm, firefight, friendly fire, search-and-destroy mission*, and, of course, the famous *domino theory*, the belief that if Vietnam went Communist, the rest of South-East Asia would fall to Communism too, like a row of dominoes. Vietnam also threw up a kind of language that reflected official doubts about America's involvement, and, once involved, official anxiety to present a "dirty war" in the best possible light. In 1965 the conflict was pronounced not to have "worsened" but to have *escalated*. The elimination of armed resistance in the thousands of small South Vietnamese villages infiltrated by the Vietcong was called *pacification*. Even the dead were renamed and became *inoperative combat personnel*. Vietnam was a verbal as well as a military minefield. "You always write it's bombing, bombing, bombing," Colonel David H. E. Ofgor, air attaché at the US Embassy in Phnom Penh, complained to reporters. "It's not bombing. It's air support."

The Vietnam war traumatized American society at every level. Even the language of protest was affected. *Hawks* and *doves* acquired a new meaning. So did *moratorium*: formerly an authorization to postpone payment of debt, the word now came to mean an anti-war demonstration (for a delay/moratorium in the bombing of North Vietnam). Those who did not join the forces of dissent became known as *the silent majority*, a phrase first made popular by President Nixon in a television address on 3 November 1969, shortly after the biggest anti-war moratorium. He said, "If a vocal minority ... prevails over reason and the will of the majority, this nation has no future as a free society ... And so tonight – to you, the great silent majority of my fellow Americans – I ask for your support."

THE "NETWORK STANDARD"

American broadcasting, of course, had long been the most potent medium of the English language. And, like the English at the BBC, it evolved its own all-American accent, known as "Network Standard", the accent of television newscasters, in which the regional characteristics of Southern or Texan or Brooklyn speech would be modified in the interests of clarity, intelligibility, and neutrality. This was discovered to be generally admired by most Americans. Among prominent American newscasters, the case of Dan Rather, the most watched television news broadcaster in the United States, is typical. He grew up a Texan with a Texan accent, but on the air he works hard to avoid peculiarities of pronunciation, and even went to a speech teacher to improve his elocution:

> I worked on my own for a while trying to say *e* as in "ten" correctly. Texans, including me, tend to say *tin*. I also tried to stop dropping *g*s. It never seemed to be a problem except sometimes when I was tired (still the case I fear), I tended to say *nothin'* instead of "nothing".

Similarly, on the "MacNeil-Lehrer Newshour", Robert MacNeil consciously modifies his use of the Canadian *ou* vowel in such words as "house".

Just as BBC English has its broader-based demotic partner in "Cockney", so we find that American English flourishes at a second, broader level. Partly expressed in songs and films, the classic mid-American voice known throughout the world of tourism is more nasal, deliberate and harsh than the softer, more polished tones of the television network standard. Just as Cockney is seen as "inferior" to "BBC English", so this broader, blue-collar American voice is associated with the less-privileged sectors of American society. Stuart Flexner, Editor-in-Chief of the *Random House Dictionary*, and author of *I Hear America Talking*, makes an interesting prediction about American English:

> We Americans are still moving and communicating from one part of the country to another. As easterners and midwesterners continue to move to the sun belt, the local Florida and Texas speech patterns will be diluted; as people continue to leave large cities for small ones and for rural areas, pockets of local dialects will tend to weaken or disappear. Perhaps someday in the future regional dialects will be no more. Then we may have only two dialects, that of educated, urban Americans and that of rural and poor Americans.

If the distinctive local varieties of American English do not fade in quite the way Flexner suggests, it is possible that people will express at least two speech loyalties, a local one (Texas, Florida, Brooklyn, Chicago, Wyoming) and a socio-national one, either Network Standard (or something close to it) or mid-American English.

Rich or poor, the experience of the network newscasters is in contrast to that of the nation's presidents. Unlike Britain, the Network Standard has virtually no class connotation. A strong regional accent has never been a hindrance in reaching the White House. Far from apologizing for, or correcting, the speech of their origins, grand or humble, some American presidents have worn their accents like a badge. Abraham Lincoln spoke, it is said, "with a wilderness air and a log-cabin smack". He pronounced the word "idea" more like *idee* ("eye-dee"), and the word "really" like a drawled Kentucky *ra-a-ly* ("rah-ly"). Theodore Roosevelt, educated at Harvard, spoke the English of the first families of New York. In the New York state legislature, he would call out, "Mister Speakah! Mister Speakah!" and a newspaper imitated his drawl by quoting him as saying he was "r–a–w–t–h–e–r r–e–l–i–e–v–e–d". Woodrow Wilson, the professor from Princeton, spoke with an academic dryness. According to Teddy Roosevelt, "his elocution is that of a Byzantine logothete". Franklin D. Roosevelt had the patrician vowels of old Eastern money, with intonations that would sound mid-Atlantic to us. Harry Truman, who succeeded him, had the flat, uncompromising, twangy sounds of Missouri, and Dwight Eisenhower had what most Americans consider the typical speech of the American Mid-West (as did Richard Nixon and Gerald Ford). But John F. Kennedy had the Boston Irish accent that his privileged upbringing did little to soften. It was much caricatured because Kennedy both dropped some *r*s, as in *vig-uh* (vigour), and put extra *r*s in, as in *Cub-er* (Cuba). His vice president and successor, Lyndon Johnson, had a strong South Texas accent, and Jimmy Carter the speech of rural Georgia.

Each of these strong regional identities was greeted with scorn by a few, became a joke for a while, and then seemed unremarkable. The idea of the "President's English" is unthinkable. What has offended Americans is not the presidential accent, but lapses of taste in presidential speech. Some Americans were shocked less by Richard Nixon's "crimes" than by the fact that the famous White House tapes revealed him to have the profane vocabulary of a gangster. Only Ronald Reagan has a spoken English that is the epitome of Network Standard, appropriately for the president known as "the great communicator", who started his career as a radio announcer and movie actor.

ENGLISH WHERE IT'S AT

Ronald Reagan exemplifies another trend which is having its impact on American English – the growing power and influence of California, the state in which he made his political career. In the words of an American broadcaster, California is "the state where the future happens first". Its influence on the English language correlates with its social and economic muscle. The most populous state, with twenty-five million inhabitants, about a tenth of the American population, it contributes about $450 billion per annum, 12 per cent of GNP, and its per capita income is significantly higher than the national average. California contains representatives of virtually every ethnic group in the United States, including very substantial numbers of Hispanics, Chinese, Koreans and Vietnamese. Ever since the late 1960s, it has been famous for its experiments in lifestyle, from the surfers to the Valley-girls to the EST freaks to the gay community of San Francisco. Its main industries are all state-of-the-art: nuclear power, oil prospecting, cinematography, space research at Edwards Air Base, and the computer business of Silicon Valley. A highly mobile population and the presence of the world's number one media city, Los Angeles, ensure that the speakers of Californian English are among the most influential users of English in the world.

The computer industry in Silicon Valley is a textbook illustration of the way in which the language coined in California is quickly adopted throughout the English-speaking world. The heartland of America's electronics industry is a super-rich suburb immediately north of San José, half an hour's drive south of San Francisco. It is the home of more than 3000 companies, including famous information-technology names like Apple and Hewlett-Packard. Alongside the giants there are dozens of smaller companies spawned from the frustrated talent of other companies and from the computer science graduate programmes of nearby Stanford University at Palo Alto. The streets have names like Semiconductor Drive. The valley is the home of the video game, the VDU, the word processor, the silicon chip and, for the English language, it is a rich jargon factory. Words like *interface*, *software*, *input*, *on-line* and *data-processing* are already in the dictionary. *High-tech*, *computer hacker*, *to access*, *diskette* and *modem* will be added to subsequent editions.

To be able to use such words easily is to be *computer-literate*. But it is the jargon phrases of Silicon Valley, reapplied to non-computing circumstances to make a kind of high-tech slang, that may eventually prove as influential on the language in the long run. John Barry, a columnist on one of Silicon Valley's myriad journals, *Infoworld*, has a list of such usages, plus their slang translations:

> He's an *integrated* kind of guy. (He's got his act together.)
> He doesn't have *both drives on line*. (He isn't very coordinated.)
> He's a *read-only memory*. (He never learns anything. He keeps saying the same thing over and over again – from *ROM*, a computer part that cannot be altered by the user.)
> I'm *interrupt-driven*. (My life is frantic, disorganized.)
> She's *high res*. (She's on the ball.)
> She's *low res*. (She's none too sharp – from *high* and *low resolution*.)
> They're in *emulation mode*. (They're copy cats; they're rip-off artists.)
> He had a *head-crash*. (He snorted too much cocaine.)
> He's in *beta-test stage*. (He's "wet behind the ears".)

American computerese has also invaded other languages. French has *les applications batch*, *digitalizer*, *semi-conductor*, and the ubiquitous *interface*. German has *repeat funktion*, *der Highbyte*, *Resetknopf* (reset button), *das HP-Top-Management* and *der High-Speed-*

Prozessor-Bus. Italian has *bufferizare* (to buffer), *shiftare* (to shift-key), *hardwarista* (hardware designer), *debuggare* (to debug), and *randomizzazione* (random access).

The Silicon Valley story highlights the way in which American English permeates the world in which we live through its effortless infiltration of technology and society. In fact, there is evidence that within the last decade or so, this process has evolved to the point where English is no longer wholly dependent on its British and American parents, and is now a global language with a supra-national momentum. English is now everyone's second language, and has a life of its own in totally non-English situations. A Japanese businessman might learn English to do deals in Brazil. A Russian might learn English to do research in Berlin. An Arab doctor might learn English to practise in Amsterdam. And when an Italian pilot learns English, it's to talk to ground control in Spain or Kuwait. The age of global English is symbolized by the launching of Voyager One, and the words of Kurt Waldheim:

> As the Secretary-General of the United Nations, an organization of a hundred and forty-seven member states who represent almost all of the human inhabitants of the planet Earth, I send greetings on behalf of the people of our planet . . .

A UNIVERSAL LANGUAGE

The emergence of a language that could unite the world is the realization of a dream that goes back to the late seventeenth century and the beginnings of global consciousness itself. Such ambitions had a special flowering a century ago when, in 1887, Dr Zamenhof launched Esperanto, still the most popular of the many artificial languages, currently used by between seven and twelve million people. But neither Esperanto nor Interlingua, Novial and Interglossa, all man-made hybrids, have real roots in any community. They remain a slightly stilted monument to late-Victorian scientific rationalism.

The global English of our times has all the benefits of the standardizing process we have been describing. There is a recognized standard in Britain and America. There is also an agreed, standardized vocabulary and spelling system. Or nearly. Global English speaks with two voices: British and American. A student in, say, Japan or Saudi Arabia is confronted with not one version, but two, a distinction recognized by the main language schools, like Berlitz, who offer either British English or American English to their pupils. The differences are essentially differences of accent, inflection, spelling and, above all, vocabulary: *apartment* versus *flat*, *buddy* versus *mate*, *candy* versus *sweets*, *diaper* versus *nappy*. There are so many different expressions that America's Associated Press and Britain's Reuters news agencies have to translate English into English. The Reuters office in New York has a twelve-page list of common terms requiring translation and many are the books that compile jokes about *box*, *knock up* and *fag*.

British or American, the language is basically the same, and its global stature is backed up by massive English-language training programmes, an international business that – in textbooks, language courses, tape cassettes, video programmes and computerized instruction – is worth hundreds of millions of pounds or dollars to the economies of the US and the UK. The English language is now one of Britain's most reliable exports. In the ironic words of the novelist Malcolm Bradbury, it is an ideal British product, "needing no workers and no work, no assembly lines and no assembly, no spare parts and very little servicing, it is used for the most intimate and the most public services everywhere. We call it the English language . . ." Dr Robert Burchfield, Chief Editor of the *Oxford English Dictionary*, has remarked that "any literate, educated person on the face of the globe is deprived if he does not know English".

The first level of the global sway of English is to be found in those countries, formerly British colonies, in which English as a second language has become accepted as a fact of cultural life that cannot be wished away. In Nigeria, it is an official language; in Zambia, it is recognized as one of the state languages; in Singapore, it is the major language of government, the legal system and education; and in India, the Constitution of 1947 recognizes English as an "associate" official language. In the heady early days of independence, the first prime minister, Nehru, declared that "within one generation" English would no longer be used in India. By the 1980s, most Indians would admit that, like it or not, English was as much a national language of India as Hindi.

The cross-cultural spread of English is unprecedented in other ways. It is more widely used than any of the other colonial languages like French, Portuguese or Spanish. It even has a wider use than some of the languages associated with international non-Western religious traditions, like Arabic or Sanskrit. In countries like India and Nigeria, English is used at all levels of society: in local English-language newspapers and broadcasting, in public administration, in university education, in the major industries, the courts and the civil service. Indeed, with nearly 200 languages, India needs English to unify the country. Professor Lal, a champion of Indian English, who runs a well-known writers' workshop, claims that in simple numerical terms, in a country of 750 million, "more Indians speak English and write English than in England itself . . . You know what Malcolm Muggeridge said: 'The last Englishman left will be an Indian.'"

English in India is vital for science and industry. Professor Yash Pal from India's Department of Science and Technology explains:

> English is probably the most important link language in science. That's because science developed in the UK, and then, of course, in the US, particularly after the last war, at such tremendous growth that most scientists find it easier to get along with each other if they know English.

English is not simply a vital means of intercommunication for the scientific community, it also, almost unconsciously, provides the everyday basic vocabulary. Professor Yash Pal continues: "There are all kinds of standard terms in computer programmes and then of course the management jargon like 'the critical path'. One doesn't even notice that they are English words."

The power of English in Indian life also extends to fundamentals like choosing a wife. In the Institute of Home Economics, in Delhi, one of the girls remarked that 95 per cent of Indian men "do definitely consider English as a prerequisite for brides ... We are still very much influenced by what the British left us ... English represents class." Another girl explained why English was so much more attractive than Hindi:

> Every guy wants his wife to know English so that she can move about with him in the society. If you go to parties and clubs you'll be more attracted towards a person who's talking in English rather than Hindi ... You're so much more attracted towards Western culture these days.

The students even distinguish between British and American English. In class, for formal writing, and to impress their parents, they will use British English. Colloquially, they use American English:

> We're getting to use American English more these days. That's because of the influence of movies ... The books you read are mostly published in America and written by American authors ... One has a tendency to pick up that kind of speech, any slang that they use.

Professor Lal summarizes the situation: "There are more Indians speaking better English than ever before, and there are more Indians speaking worse than ever before." The flowering of local English traditions in an un-English context can be seen in the development of national literatures in India and Nigeria. R. K. Narayan and Salman Rushdie exploit the richness of Indian English; Amos Tutuola and Chinua Achebe write in Nigerian English; and all of them do so as writers exploring national cultures in a language that is, for them, at once national and international. In Rushdie's words: "English, no longer an *English* language, now grows from many roots; and those whom it once colonized are carving out large territories within the language for themselves. The Empire is striking back." The result of this fusion is that the English language is being enriched from within. An Indian writer might use the phrase *Himalayan blunder* for "a grave or serious mistake", or a homely proverb like *as honest as an elephant*. An African writer might refer to a *knocking-fee* for a "bribe", or *snatch boys* for "pickpockets". Some vivid African English idioms include: *where there is dew there is water*; *wisdom is like a goat skin – everyone carries his own*; and *to eat each other's ears* (to talk privately). A similar process is at work in former white colonies, Australia, for example. A once predominantly Anglo-Saxon society now has a significant proportion of non-English immigrants (Italians, Yugoslavs, Sri Lankans, Greeks). For these new Australians, English is a foreign language: who can predict what new uses they will put it to?

At a second, equally important, level global English has become the one foreign language that much of the world wants to learn. While this appears to be a nearly universal aspiration, some countries (Singapore, Japan, China, Indonesia and the Philippines) exhibit it more than others. One basic force is an international need and desire to communicate. The more

English-speaking the world becomes the more desirable the language becomes to all societies. English is the language of the "media" industries – news-journalism, radio, film and television. Almost any international press conference held to disseminate information about an internationally significant event will be conducted in English. The roll-call of contemporary world figures who speak to the press in English includes the Chancellor of West Germany, Helmut Kohl; the Libyan leader and Islamic fundamentalist, Colonel Qadhafi; the President of Pakistan, General Zia; and former President Marcos of the Philippines; in the recent past, moreover, it was well known that the leaders of France and Germany, Valéry Giscard d'Estaing and Helmut Schmidt, used to speak to each other in English.

The demands of modernization, technological change and international bank funding, still largely controlled by Anglo-American corporations, provide the main reason for global English, the language of the multinational corporations. Of the leading countries in world trade, eight are countries in which English either is an official language or was an official language in colonial times: Australia, Canada, India, Malaya, New Zealand, South Africa, the United Kingdom, and the United States. These countries accounted for more than 25 per cent of the world's imports in 1974. By contrast, the leading French-speaking countries (Belgium, Canada, France and Switzerland) accounted for only 15 per cent, the second highest figure for a language bloc.

Many multinational Japanese companies (like Nissan or Datsun) write international memoranda in English. The Chase Manhattan Bank gives English instructions to staff members on three continents. Aramco – a big oil multinational – teaches English to more than 10,000 workers in Saudi Arabia. In Kuwait, the university's language centre teaches predominantly English, much of it highly specialized. "The engineering faculty has its own English language, geared to its own profession," the director, Dr Rasha Al-Sabah, reports, "so we provide a course in engineering English." The pressure to learn English in this environment is strictly commercial. A businessman who doesn't know English and who has to run to his bilingual secretary is at a serious competitive disadvantage. The "necessity of English" has created some interesting business enterprises, perhaps the most famous being the IVECO heavy truck company. Based in Turin, financed by French, German and Italian money, staffed by Europeans for whom English is only an alternative language, it none the less conducts *all* its business in English. Giorgio Bertoldi describes a monthly board meeting in which "the vast majority of the people attending are Italian, or French, or German. But the common language is English. Everybody talks English and the minutes of these meetings are written in English." Peter Raahauge, a Dane, commented that "you wouldn't get a job at a certain level in IVECO if you didn't speak good English". Company executives take courses to improve their proficiency. Jean Pierre Neveu, an IVECO product planner, points out that, for successful trading in the international truck market, the advantage of communicating with the outside world in English is that the company gets its answers in English. "This gives two advantages. One is first to have a language which is easier for everyone to understand, and second, it does without any translation."

14 President Seaka Stevens: "The use of English both at home here and internationally will be very good."

15 When Rajiv Gandhi came to power he addressed the Indian people in English.

What is true of individuals and companies applies, writ large, to countries. If the people do not know English they cannot benefit from multinational development programmes. The classic case is China's. For centuries, China preserved a lofty isolation from the outside world. After the Revolution of 1949 it sustained a Marxist contempt for Anglo-American culture. Briefly, in the 1960s, there was a Russian-learning phase. Then, in the late 1970s and 1980s, the decision to develop China's industrial and technological base by encouraging Western investment and Western expertise has led to a crash-programme of English teaching. Chinese television began to transmit several English-language classes each week, with titles like *Yingying Learns English* and *Mary Goes to Peking*. The most popular was a BBC-produced series, *Follow Me,* which achieved an audience of more than fifty million and transformed the presenter of the programme, Kathy Flower, into a media celebrity. Kathy Flower describes the contemporary craze for English in China: "You go into a shop and find two 60-year-olds practising the dialogue from *Follow Me* the night before." The passion for English drives people to make extraordinary sacrifices. A young man whose monthly wages are 36 yuan spends one third of his total income on English classes, dictionaries, cassettes, novels.

For a developing country like China, Singapore or Indonesia, English is vital. As well as being the language of international trade and finance, it is the language of technology, especially computers, of medicine, of the international aid bodies like Oxfam and Save The

Children, and of virtually all international, quasi-diplomatic exchanges from UNESCO, to the WHO, to the UN, to Miss World, to the Olympic Committee, to world summits. The textbook case in the new Pacific prosperity sphere is Singapore. Now the most prosperous Far East Asian society after Japan, Singapore is a multi-ethnic society which has been rigorously educated in English by its long-time prime minister, Lee Kuan Yew, who was not above lecturing his ministers and civil servants on the necessity of good grammar. Until the mid-1980s, the English First policy was seen as integral to the island's success. Now, with a falling growth rate, and the first stirrings of real opposition to the ruling People's Action Party, the future of Singapore English (see chapter nine) is perhaps less certain.

FROM JAPLISH TO FRANGLAIS

The power of English is not confined to the invention and manufacture of new technology. All major corporations advertise and market their products in English. Nowhere is this more dramatically apparent than in present-day Japan. Of all the things that Japan has imported from the West (to which Tokyo advertising bears witness), few have had as great an impact as English words. The Japanese have always borrowed words, first from the Portuguese and Dutch who landed in trading ships in the sixteenth and eighteenth centuries, but since the end of the Second World War so many new words have been added to the Japanese vocabulary – more than 20,000 by some estimates – that some fear the language will lose its identity. Special dictionaries have been produced to explain the meaning of, for example, *inflight*, *infield*, *input* and *influenza*. Better than these straight imports there is Japlish (or Janglish): fascinating new formations like *man-shon* (mansion), Japanese for an apartment/condominium, or *aisu-kurimu* (ice-cream). Ownership is important. If you don't live in a *man-shon* you live in a *mai-homu* (my home). The Japanese now have *mai-kaa*, *mai-town*, and *mai-com* (my computer). Television has embraced Japlish with enthusiasm. One nightly baseball programme is called *Ekusaito Naita* (Excite Niter). Another popular programme of songs is called *Reffsu Go Yangu* (Let's Go Young). It was inevitable that when a new weekly glossy magazine was launched in Tokyo in 1985, it bore the name *Friday*. Even the hit songs in the Tokyo top twenty have English titles.

English as the language of international pop music and mass entertainment is a worldwide phenomenon. In 1982, a Spanish punk rock group, called Asfalto (Asphalt), released a disc about learning English, which became a hit. The Swedish group Abba records all its numbers in English. Michael Luszynski is a Polish singer who performs almost entirely in English. There is no Polish translation for words like "Baby-baby" and "Yeah-yeah-yeah". Luszynski notes wryly that a phrase like "Słysze warkot pociągu nadjedzie na torze" does not roll as smoothly in a lyric as "I hear the train a-coming, it's rolling down the line ..." This will sound better to a Pole, or, on the other side of the world, to a Japanese simply because they grew up listening to English and American lyrics. With a few exceptions, the culture of popular entertainment and mass consumerism is an Anglo-American one, expressing itself in a variety of English.

Perhaps the most scientific study of the invasion of a language by English comes from Sweden. Professor Magnus Ljung of Stockholm University, investigating "Swinglish", the English hybrids in the Swedish language, questioned some two thousand Swedes. Sixty per cent claimed that their Swedish was being "corrupted" by watching English television programmes. Twenty-six per cent blamed English books, newspapers and magazines for the same process. Fourteen per cent admitted that their Swedish was changing but could not attribute the change to any particular cause. More than half confessed to using the English plural *s* instead of the Swedish *or, ar, er*. A characteristic piece of Swinglish is *baj baj* (bye bye), or *tajt jeans* (tight jeans). The difficulty about such language surveys is that people tend to blame changes in language for changes in society. The Swede who deplores English television is probably venting his anxieties about the development of Swedish society. Complaints about language are as old as complaints about the weather.

Inventions like *baj baj* are natural in English-invaded countries throughout the world. In Hong Kong, a discotheque becomes a *dixie-go*. To be a "swinger" in Ecuador is *travoltarse* (from John Travolta). In Germany, teenagers wear *die Jeans* and listen to *die Soundtrack*. The French have probably now abandoned the fight against *le weekend, le drugstore, le playboy* and *le bifteck* (though not against some other imports). In Russia, a Muscovite can drink a *viskey* or a *dzhin-in-tonik* and go to a *dzhazz-saission*. Even Spain's prestigious dictionary of Castilian, *The Dictionary of the Royal Academy*, the virtually "official" voice of Castilian Spanish, now admits *whisky*, together with several English technical terms (*escaner* for *scanner*) in the latest edition.

The global influence of English can be measured by the opposition of its old rival, French, "the most meagre and inharmonious of all languages" according to Horace Walpole. For centuries, French was the international language *par excellence,* as the phrase goes. The French have cherished their language through the Académie Française, but it was not until the mid-1970s that successive Presidents became sufficiently concerned to come officially to the defence of the French language. "We must not let the idea take hold that English is the only possible instrument for industrial, economic and scientific communication," said President Pompidou. He, and his successor Giscard d'Estaing and, later, President Mitterrand's Socialists, took a series of government-sponsored initiatives to check the spread of *la langue du Coca-Cola*, abolishing borrowed words where possible and inventing suitable French alternatives. *Hot money* became *capitaux fébriles, jumbo jet* became *gros porteur* and *fast food* turned into *prêt-à-manger*. Despite these efforts, it is estimated that, in a newspaper like *Le Monde*, one word in 166 will be English. Another calculation claims that about one-twentieth of day-to-day French vocabulary is composed of *anglicismes*.

The darker, aggressive side of the spread of global English is the elimination of regional language variety, the attack on deep cultural roots. Perhaps the most dramatic example of the power of English can be found in Canada, which shares a 3000-mile border with the USA. Canadian English has been colonized by American English, especially in the mass media, and the French-speaking third of the community, living mainly in Quebec, has felt threatened to breaking point. Formerly the "two solitudes", living an uneasy co-existence, Canada since 1945 has had a powerful Quebec separatist movement, sustained as much by opposition to that northward glacier, the American language and culture, as by historic resentment of English-speaking Canada. It developed enough political steam to elect a provincial government in 1976 which, the next year, enacted the notorious "charter of the French language" – better known as Loi 101. English billboards, posters and storefronts were banned. Students were not allowed to attend English-language Quebec schools unless one of the parents had been educated in English at a Quebec elementary school. Many other minorities, Greek, Italian, and Chinese, protested. One result is that there are now more than a thousand unregistered students in Montreal Catholic schools illegally studying English. "We decided to have a fairly high-profile campaign offering instruction in English to all comers," the Secretary General of the provincial association of Catholic schoolteachers is reported as saying. "It was a flagrant defiance of the law. We had to have special classes. We 'borrowed' school board property." Teachers for these special classes – in some cases accounting for one sixth of all pupils – were hired unofficially and paid under the table. The explanation is simple. Parents want their children's education to be useful to them. As one businessman commented: "I don't mind having to Francicize my business. Here we do everything in French. [Only about 15 per cent of Quebec province's six million inhabitants consider English to be their first language.] But when it comes to my family, I'm going to fight like a tiger."

Legislation like Loi 101 shows the desperate measures necessary to stem the tide of English. The campaign has changed the English Canadian perception of their French neighbours, and the official policy of bilingualism means that French is safe for a few more generations. But all the legislation in the world cannot disguise the fact that even in the French-speaking parts of Canada the reality of the English-speaking world is inescapable. French-speaking air-traffic controllers have to use English in Canadian airspace. The banks of Quebec have to deal in English outside the province. Even Canadian English is under attack. American textbooks, especially American dictionaries, predominate in schools.

The marriage of English and various First World languages has made the headlines. Much less publicized and studied is the English spoken (and increasingly written) in the Third World. English itself, as we shall see, is such a hybrid (of Old Norse, German, Latin and Norman French) that it is peculiarly susceptible to pidginization. It is pidgin English not standard British or American English that is the language in Black Africa. The singer Fellala Fakooti expresses his need for what he calls "broken English" to reach a bigger audience:

> If I want all the Africans to hear me well, I cannot sing in this language [*his mother tongue*] because they wouldn't understand me well. So I have to speak in the language that they all understand, and that is broken English.

There are many countries with huge populations whose command of English falls into this category: Uganda with about 13 million, Cameroon with about 8 million, Zambia and

Zimbabwe with 6 and $7\frac{1}{2}$ million, Bangladesh with at least $3\frac{1}{2}$ million (more than New Zealand or Ireland). The same is true of English-dominated countries like the Philippines and Pakistan. The President of Sierra Leone, Seaka Stevens, explains the pragmatic reason for English-language education in his country. "If you want to earn your daily bread, the best thing to do is to learn English. That is the source from which most of the jobs come."

It is the non-linguistic forces – cultural, social, economic and political – that have made English the first world language in human history and instilled its driving force. Language is neutral, passive: only the uses to which it is put make it active. Why is it that English can inspire astonishing affection not only among those who speak and write it as their mother tongue, but also among those for whom it is a foreign language? The richness and power of English was summarized in the nineteenth century by the great German philologist Jakob Grimm when he wrote, "In wealth, wisdom and strict economy, none of the other living languages can vie with it." But is it, in fact, "better", "superior", "more expressive", "richer" than other languages?

"WEALTH, WISDOM AND STRICT ECONOMY"
First, we must dispose of some myths. English is not intrinsically easier to learn than French or Russian, nor is it more lyrical, more beautiful, mellifluous or more eloquent than any other language. Such judgements are almost meaningless. Lyrical for whom? English is, moreover, highly idiomatic. How does one begin to explain phrases like "put up with" and "get on with it". English has some impossible characteristics. The *th* is famously difficult for foreigners who find a sentence like "What's this?" hard to pronounce. There are some very rare and difficult vowels: the vowel sound in *bird* and *nurse* occurs in virtually no other language. There are no fewer than thirteen spellings for *sh*: *shoe*, *sugar*, *issue*, *mansion*, *mission*, *nation*, *suspicion*, *ocean*, *conscious*, *chaperon*, *schist*, *fuchsia*, and *pshaw*. An old bit of doggerel for foreign students advises:

> *Beware of* heard, *a dreadful word*
> *That looks like* beard *and sounds like* bird,
> *And* dead: *It's said like* bed, *not* bead –
> *For goodness' sake, don't call it* deed!

Various distinguished minds have grappled with this problem. The more spoken English seemed standardized on the air, the greater seemed the need for a simplified spelling system. Such proposals were often heard during the inter-war years. In 1930, a Swedish philologist, R. E. Zachrisson, proposed an international language, essentially English, to be called *Anglic*. For all its logic, its drawbacks can be easily demonstrated in the Anglic version of a famous sentence: *Forskor and sevn yeerz agoe our faadherz braut forth on this kontinent a nuw naeshon, konseevd in liberti* . . . In 1940, the British Simplified Spelling Society mounted a campaign for New Spelling which lobbied hard for government approval. Perhaps the most famous champion of simplified spelling was George Bernard Shaw who bequeathed part of his large fortune to the cause of a more regular English spelling. But at the time of writing, new generations of school children are still grappling with a spelling system that dates back to William Caxton.

On the other hand, the English language has three characteristics that can be counted as assets in its world state. First of all, unlike all other European languages, the gender of every noun in modern English is determined by meaning, and does not require a masculine, feminine or neuter article. In French, by contrast, the moon is *la lune* (feminine) while the sun, for no obvious reason, is *le soleil* (masculine). Worse, in the Germanic languages, is the addition of the neuter gender. In German the moon is *der Mond* (masculine), the sun is *die Sonne* (feminine), while child, girl and woman, are *das Kind*, *das Mädchen* and *das Weib*, all neuter. As Mark Twain put it, "In German, a young lady has no sex, but a turnip has."

The second practical quality of English is that it has a grammar of great simplicity and flexibility. Nouns and adjectives have highly simplified word-endings. This flexibility extends to the parts of speech themselves. Nouns can become verbs and verbs nouns in a way that is impossible in other languages. We can *dog* someone's footsteps. We can *foot* it to the bus. We can *bus* children to school and then *school* them in English.

A few years ago, General Alexander Haig, a White House chief of staff under Richard Nixon and later Secretary of State, was widely criticized (and parodied) for using nouns as verbs in a highly idiosyncratic way, known as *Haigspeak*: phrases like "I'll have to caveat any response, Senator, and I'll caveat that", "Not the way you contexted it, Senator", and "There are nuance-al differences between Henry Kissinger and me on that." From one point of view, however, Haig was merely displaying the virtuosity of English, if not its grace.

Above all, the great quality of English is its teeming vocabulary, 80 per cent of which is foreign-born. Precisely because its roots are so varied – Celtic, Germanic (German, Scandinavian and Dutch) and Romance (Latin, French and Spanish) – it has words in common with virtually every language in Europe: German, Yiddish, Dutch, Flemish, Danish, Swedish, French, Italian, Portuguese, and Spanish. In addition, almost any page of the *Oxford English Dictionary* or *Webster's Third* will turn up borrowings from Hebrew and Arabic, Hindi-Urdu, Bengali, Malay, Chinese, the languages of Java, Australia, Tahiti, Polynesia, West Africa and even from one of the aboriginal languages of Brazil. It is the enormous range and varied source of this vocabulary, as much as the sheer numbers and geographical spread of its speakers, that makes English a language of such unique vitality. In the words of H. L. Mencken, one of the greatest writers on English, "A living language is like a man suffering incessantly from small haemorrhages, and what it needs above all else is constant transfusions of new blood from other tongues. The day the gates go up, that day it begins to die."

Supple in grammar, maddeningly inconsistent in spelling and pronunciation, English has its strengths and weaknesses. English as a world language is sustained by another elusive quality – its own peculiar genius. The arts of speech and literature have been perhaps the special contribution of the English people to European culture, or at least the one for which they are most respected! This, one could speculate, may have something to do with the history of the language. After the Norman invasion, English was neglected and ill-considered by the Latin-writing and French-speaking authorities; so it was unregulated and unimposed upon; from the earliest times it was naturally the language of protest and dissent, the language of the many rather than the few. Its genius was, and still is, essentially democratic. It has given expression to the voice of freedom from Wat Tyler, to Tom Paine, to Thomas Jefferson, to Edmund Burke, to the Chartists, to Abraham Lincoln, to the Suffragettes, to Winston Churchill, to Martin Luther King. It is well equipped to be a world language, to give voice to the aspirations of the Third World as much as the inter-communication of the First World.

Today, in this new global state, English is probably finding more variety of expression and more local colour than at any time since the Elizabethan "golden age". When the language was confined to English and North American shores, it became progressively schooled by generations of grammars and dictionaries. Although that tradition lives on, its influence is counterbalanced by the sheer teeming diversity of the language in the age of mass communications, from the "Spanglish" of Miami and Los Angeles, to the "Slanguage" of the Antipodes, even the jargon of astronauts and computer hackers. Beyond the Anglo-American hegemony, there are newer English-using cultures for whom the precepts of Dr Johnson and Noah Webster are not binding. The Indianization and Africanization of English is introducing a multi-cultural dimension to the language that is without precedent in the history of any language. It is from the Krio of West Africa, the "nation language" of Jamaica, the "Singlish" of Singapore, and the pidgins of Hawaii and Melanesia that English is getting constantly recharged with the voltage of innovation. From this international perspective, the kaleidoscope of English today is perhaps closer in spirit and self-expression to the Shakespearian extravaganza than at any time since the seventeenth century. Spoken and written, it offers a medium of almost limitless potential and surprise, though it would be rash indeed to predict its future evolution.

The story of all languages is full of surprises. The year the Anglo-Saxons first crossed the sea to the former Roman province of Britannia, in AD 450, the odds against English becoming a world language were about a million to one. It was then an obscure sub-branch of the Germanic family of languages and not even native to the British Isles. In the course of this book we shall see how a language that was born of invasion itself became an invader on a global scale, and how it was thus possible, at the end of 1983, for a nomadic, drought-plagued African tribe, the Tuareg, to delay their annual migration to fresh pastures by ten days, in order to catch the last episode of *Dallas*.

16 The father of English literature, Geoffrey Chaucer, reading to the court at Windsor.

2
THE MOTHER TONGUE

The making of English is the story of three invasions and a cultural revolution. In the simplest terms, the language was brought to Britain by Germanic tribes, the Angles, Saxons and Jutes, influenced by Latin and Greek when St Augustine and his followers converted England to Christianity, subtly enriched by the Danes, and finally transformed by the French-speaking Normans.

From the beginning, English was a crafty hybrid, made in war and peace. It was, in the words of Daniel Defoe, "your Roman-Saxon-Danish-Norman English". In the course of one thousand years, a series of violent and dramatic events created a new language which, by the time of Geoffrey Chaucer, is intelligible to modern eyes and ears without the aid of subtitles.

The English have always accepted the mixed blood of their language. There was a vague understanding that they were part of a European language family, but it was not until the eighteenth century that a careful investigation by a gifted amateur linguist began to decipher the true extent of this common heritage.

"THE COMMON SOURCE"

In the early days of the Raj, Sir William Jones, a British judge stationed in India, presented a remarkable address to the Asiatick Society in Calcutta, the fruits of his investigations into ancient Sanskrit. A keen lawyer, Jones had originally intended to familiarize himself with India's native law codes. To his surprise, he discovered that Sanskrit bore a striking resemblance to two other ancient languages of his acquaintance, Latin and Greek. The Sanskrit word for father, transliterated from its exotic alphabet, emerged as *pitar*, astonishingly similar, he observed, to the Greek and Latin *pater*. The Sanskrit for mother was *matar*; in the Latin of his school days it was *mater*. Investigating further, he discovered dozens of similar correspondences. Though he was not the first to notice these similarities, no one before Sir William Jones had studied them systematically. The Sanskrit language, he announced to the Asiatick Society on that evening of 2 February 1786, shared with Greek and Latin "a stronger affinity . . . than could possibly have been produced by accident; so strong, indeed, that no philologer could examine them all three, without believing them to have sprung from some common source, which, perhaps, no longer exists."

17 William Jones, an amateur linguist who stumbled on the roots of English while stationed in India.

18 Jakob Grimm established the important connection between a *p* in Latin (*piscis*) and an *f* in English (*fish*).

Two centuries of linguistic research have only strengthened Jones's basic proposition. We now know that the languages of about one-third of the human race come from this Indo-European "common source". These include the European descendants of Latin, French and Spanish, a great Slavic language, Russian, the Celtic languages, Irish and Scots Gaelic, and the offshoots of German – Dutch and English. A second important breakthrough in the search for the truth about "the common source" came from the folklorist Jakob Grimm, better known, with his brother Wilhelm, as a collector of fairy tales. "Grimm's Law" established beyond question that the German *vater* (and English *father*) has the same root as the Sanskrit/Latin *pitar/pater*. Words such as *me, new, seven* and *mother* were also found to share this common ancestry. Now the Indo-European basis for the common source was clear.

It is sometimes said that you can deduce the history of a people from the words they use. Clever detective work among some fifty prehistoric vocabularies has now led to a reconstruction of the lifestyle of a vanished people, the first Indo-European tribes, the distant forebears of contemporary Europe. From the words they used – words for winter and horse – it seems likely that the Indo-Europeans lived a half-settled, half-nomadic existence. They had domestic animals, oxen, pigs and sheep, they worked leather and wove wool, ploughed the land, and planted grain. They had an established social and family structure, and they worshipped gods who are the clear ancestors of Indian, Mediterranean and Celtic deities.

Who these people were, and when exactly they lived, is a hotly disputed mystery.

According to the Garden of Eden myth, they lived in the fertile crescent of Mesopotamia, but this theory was exploded by nineteenth-century archaeology. Today, there are some who argue for the Kurgan culture of the Russian steppes, others for the farming culture of the Danube valley. The dates vary from 6000 BC to 4500 BC. The most widely accepted theory locates the environment of the Indo-Europeans in a cold, northern climate in which common words for *snow*, *beech*, *bee* and *wolf* played an important role. Furthermore, none of these prehistoric languages had a word for the sea. From this, and from our knowledge of nature, it is clear that the Indo-Europeans must have lived somewhere in northern central Europe.

Two innovations contributed to the break-up of this Central European society: the horse and the wheel. Some of the Indo-Europeans began to travel east and, in the course of time, established the Indo-Iranian languages of the Caucasus, India, Pakistan and Assam. Others began to drift west towards the gentler climates of Europe. Their descendants are found in Greece, Italy, Germany, and the Baltic. Both the Rhine and the Rhône are thought to take their names from the Indo-European word meaning *flow*. English has much in common with all these languages. A word like *brother* has an obvious family resemblance to its Indo-European cousins: *broeder* (Dutch), *Bruder* (German), *phrater* (Greek), *brat* (Russian), *bráthair* (Irish), and *bhratar* (Sanskrit).

THE CELTS

One of the earliest westward migrations was made by a people whose descendants now live in Cornwall, the highlands of Scotland, Ireland, Wales and Brittany: the Celts. These Gaelic-speaking tribes were natives of the British Isles long before the English. Today, the people of Wales prefer to call themselves *cymry*, or "fellow-countrymen", a reminder that they – together with the Irish, Scots and Cornish – are the true Britons.

The language of Wales – *Cymraeg* – is part of a Celtic family stretching north to the islands of the Hebrides and south to the remoter parts of Brittany. Welsh and Breton, in fact, are very closely related, and the traditional Breton-French onion sellers who used to bicycle through the valleys of Wales every summer were able to communicate with their Welsh-speaking customers.

The Welsh have remained as fiercely independent in words as in deed. The Cambrian mountains, the mountain range that gave the fleeing Britons a refuge from the conquering Anglo-Saxons, isolated the Welsh language from outside influence for centuries. Even at the beginning of the industrial revolution, in which the coal mines of Wales were to play such a vital part, the vast majority of the people still spoke Welsh. In the great social and economic upheavals of Victorian Britain there were some who believed that Welsh culture was being irreparably threatened and they fled to Patagonia. In retrospect, they were unduly alarmist. Despite the anglicizing inroads of intermarriage, education and industrialization, the persistence of Welsh language and culture is remarkable. At the turn of the century, two-thirds of the Welsh were bilingual, and according to a recent census, some 527,600 (or some 20 per cent) still claim to be Welsh speakers.

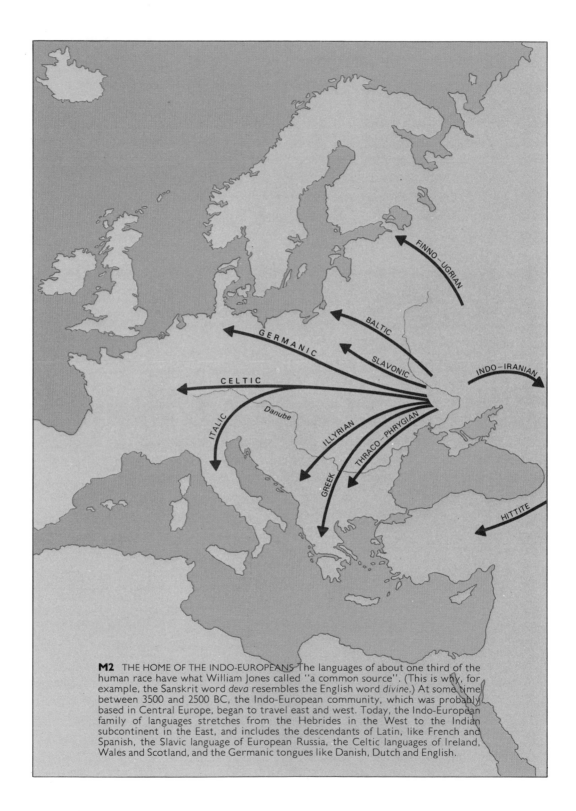

M2 THE HOME OF THE INDO-EUROPEANS The languages of about one third of the human race have what William Jones called "a common source". (This is why, for example, the Sanskrit word *deva* resembles the English word *divine*.) At some time between 3500 and 2500 BC, the Indo-European community, which was probably based in Central Europe, began to travel east and west. Today, the Indo-European family of languages stretches from the Hebrides in the West to the Indian subcontinent in the East, and includes the descendants of Latin, like French and Spanish, the Slavic language of European Russia, the Celtic languages of Ireland, Wales and Scotland, and the Germanic tongues like Danish, Dutch and English.

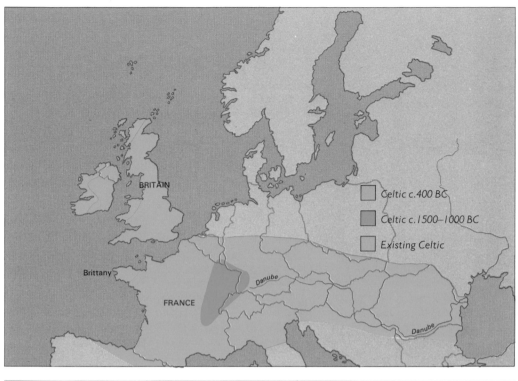

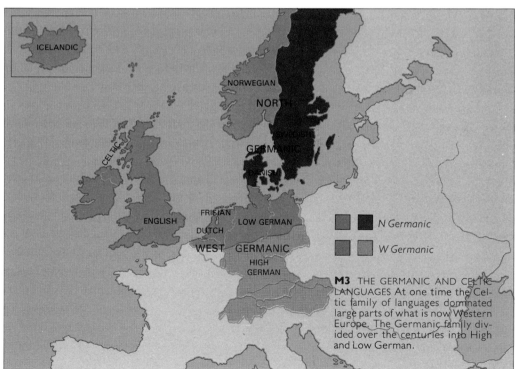

Celtic c.400 BC

Celtic c.1500–1000 BC

Existing Celtic

BRITAIN

Brittany

Danube

FRANCE

Danube

ICELANDIC

NORWEGIAN

NORTH

CELTIC

GERMANIC

DANISH

ENGLISH

FRISIAN

DUTCH

LOW GERMAN

WEST GERMANIC

HIGH GERMAN

N Germanic

W Germanic

M3 THE GERMANIC AND CELTIC LANGUAGES At one time the Celtic family of languages dominated large parts of what is now Western Europe. The Germanic family divided over the centuries into High and Low German.

Today, Welsh language and culture flourish. It is used in education, and it has theoretical equality with English in law and administration. Welsh nationalists have successfully campaigned – like the Quebec separatists – for bilingual road signs. The Welsh language television station, S4C, is popular and successful. The annual Eisteddfod keeps alive an idea of Welsh culture that goes back to the days when their ancestors enjoyed the sovereignty of the island called Britannia. The strength of this Welsh culture has permeated the English spoken in Wales. Eluned Phillips, winner of the Eisteddfod Crown, believes that Welsh–English speakers can always be identified by the lilt of their speech. She remarks that even with Richard Burton, who spoke almost perfect Standard English, his Welsh roots were recognizable in "the melodious lilt of his voice and the sing-song way he used to talk English, the resonance, the rounded vowels – in the music of the language".

The Welshness of the English spoken in Wales also appears in sentence construction. According to Eluned Phillips:

> In Welsh we tend to invert our sentences, perhaps putting the adjective after the noun . . . I was talking to a neighbour the other day. She is from the valleys and we were talking about a young Welshman who had died. What she said to me was, "Pity it was that he died so early", which is really a literal translation of the Welsh . . . We also have a habit of using throwaway words – *like*, *indeed*, *look you* – and I think this originally started because we couldn't finish the translation from Welsh in time. So a word like "indeed" became an important stop-gap.

The Welsh contribution to English literature is also distinctive, and Eluned Phillips believes that this, too, has deep Celtic roots. "You can always tell when a Welshman is writing in English because of the flamboyance of their descriptions. I think that comes down from the old Celtic warriors who used to go into battle [against the Anglo-Saxons] not only with terror in their veins, but with red hot waves of ecstasy."

The Celtic Britons had the misfortune to inhabit an island that was highly desirable both for its agriculture and for its minerals. The early history of Britain is the story of successive invasions. One of the most famous was the landing of Julius Caesar and his legions in 55 BC. After a difficult start, the Roman Empire kept the British tribes in check – or at any rate at bay – beyond Hadrian's Wall. The evidence of the splendid palace at Fishbourne, near Chichester, suggests that many Celtic Britons became quite Romanized. The poet Martial claimed, with the boastfulness of poets, that his work was read even in the remote island of Britannia. A few Roman words crept, corrupted, into British usage: place-names like Chester, Manchester and Winchester, are derived from the Roman word *castra* meaning a camp. Once the legions withdrew (traditionally in AD 410) and the Empire collapsed, this achievement was threatened. Along the shores of Europe, a new generation of raiders was turning its attention to the misty, fertile island across the water.

The tribes which now threatened the Celtic chiefs of Britain were essentially Germanic, another branch of the Indo-European migration. After the Celts, the movement of the

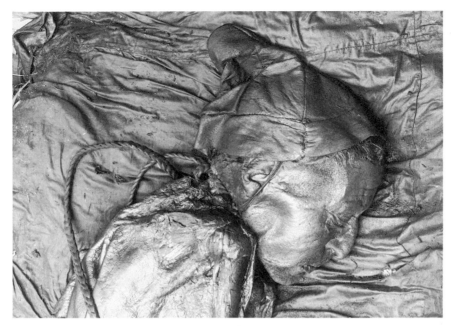

19 The ancestors of the English-speaking peoples sacrificed to Mother Earth. Some of their victims, astonishingly preserved, are now on show in Denmark.

Germanic people into the Baltic region, Northern Germany, Denmark and the Netherlands produced two more massive branches in the great language tree of Europe. To the north, there were the Norse tongues of Scandinavia; to the south, the family of West Germanic languages. This second branch divided into the High German and the Low German. The first serious historian of these Germans was the Roman writer Tacitus, who gives us the earliest picture of the tribes that became the first Englishmen.

Tacitus was writing near the zenith of the Roman Empire. The armies of Rome were garrisoned across Europe from Britannia to Bucharest, throughout the known world. There was an obvious fascination with the unruly peoples of the North, especially the troublesome ones like the Germans. In his *Germania*, "On the Origin and Geography of Germany", Tacitus makes a colourful evaluation of the character and customs of the tribes that absorbed so much of Rome's political and military power. The Germans, he says, have the virtues Rome has lost. They love freedom; their women are chaste; there is no public extravagance. He characterizes the various tribes. The Tencteri excel in horsemanship, the Chatti have "hardy bodies, well-knit limbs and fierce countenances", the Suebi tie their hair in a knot, and so on. But no picture is perfect. There are, Tacitus writes, seven tribes about whom there is "nothing particularly noteworthy" to say, except that they worship the goddess, Mother Earth, "a ceremony performed by slaves who are immediately afterwards drowned in the lake". One of these seven barbarous tribes was "the Anglii", known to history as the Angles, who probably inhabited the area that is now known as Schleswig-Holstein.

By a curious irony, the savage and primitive rituals of the Anglii have not been entirely forgotten. Peat-water has a curious property. In the nineteenth century, Danish farmers, digging for peat, uncovered the bodies of some sacrificial victims, presumably of the Angles, perfectly preserved in a bog. Known as the *Moorleichen* (swamp corpses), or bog people, they are now on view in a number of Danish museums. One man had been strangled. Another's throat had been cut. They are astonishingly well preserved: you can see the stubble on one man's chin. These leathery corpses are the distant ancestors of the English-speaking peoples.

The speech of the Anglii belonged to the Germanic family of languages. Further south, probably living among the marshy islands of coastal Holland, were the Frisii (Frisians), a raiding people whose descendants still live and farm in the area known as Frisia or Friesland, and speak a language that gives us the best clue to the sound of Anglo-Saxon English. Most people would probably associate Frisia with cows. It is an identification the native Frisians seem proud of. In the central square of the main town, Leeuwarden, where you might expect to find an equestrian memorial to a local hero, there is a larger-than-life statue of a milk-laden cow. Today there are about 300,000 Frisian speakers who travel up and down the dykes and canals, working the flat, marshy land much as their ancestors have done for centuries. The Frisian for cow, lamb, goose, boat, dung and rain is *ko*, *lam*, *goes*, *boat*, *dong* and *rein*. And the Frisian for "a cup of coffee" is *in kopke kofje*.

The similarity between Frisian and English, both with strong Germanic roots, emphasizes how close English is to German, Dutch and Danish. The Germanic echoes in all these languages betray their oldest and deepest roots. And it is no accident that the Dutch, for instance, often seem to speak English with as much ease as the English themselves. The evidence of a place like Friesland suggests that if that linguistic cataclysm, the Norman Conquest of 1066, had not occurred, the English today might speak a language not unlike modern Dutch.

20 Jean Leroux, a Breton, can converse in Gaelic with his Welsh cousins.

21 Place-names like Avon, Thames, Exe and Wye are a reminder of Britain's Celtic past.

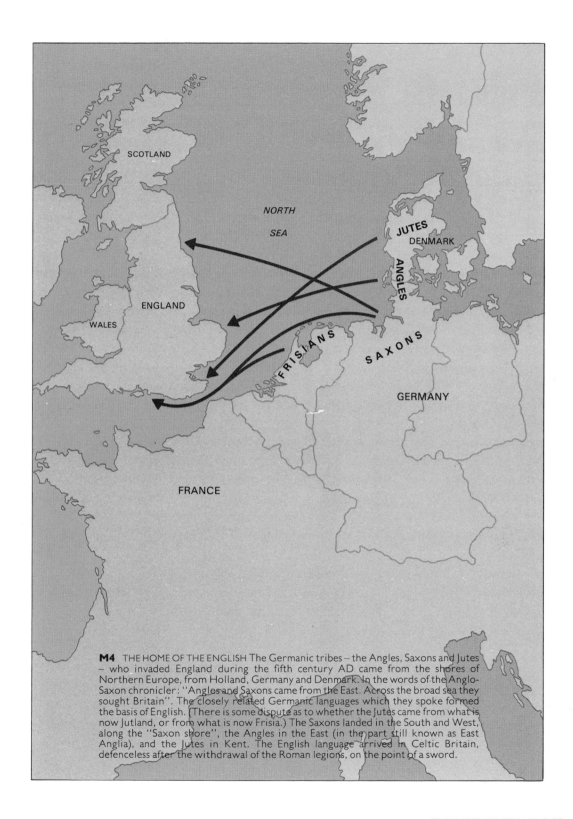

M4 THE HOME OF THE ENGLISH The Germanic tribes – the Angles, Saxons and Jutes – who invaded England during the fifth century AD came from the shores of Northern Europe, from Holland, Germany and Denmark. In the words of the Anglo-Saxon chronicler: "Angles and Saxons came from the East. Across the broad sea they sought Britain". The closely related Germanic languages which they spoke formed the basis of English. (There is some dispute as to whether the Jutes came from what is now Jutland, or from what is now Frisia.) The Saxons landed in the South and West, along the "Saxon shore", the Angles in the East (in the part still known as East Anglia), and the Jutes in Kent. The English language arrived in Celtic Britain, defenceless after the withdrawal of the Roman legions, on the point of a sword.

THE MAKING OF ENGLISH

According to their own record of events, *The Anglo-Saxon Chronicle*, the first invaders of the British Isles – the Angles, Saxons and Jutes – sailed across the North Sea from Denmark and the coastal part of Germany, still known as Lower Saxony, in the year AD 449. By all accounts, they had lost none of their taste for terror and violence. "Never", wrote the chronicler, "was there such slaughter in this Island." The native Britons were driven westward, fleeing from the English "as from fire". The English language arrived in Britain on the point of a sword.

The process of driving the British into what is now called the "Celtic Fringe" did not happen overnight. The most successful resistance was organized by a *dux bellorum* (as Nennius called him) named Artorius – probably the legendary King Arthur – who managed to establish an uneasy peace for perhaps a generation. In the long run, though, the Anglo-Saxons – "proud warmakers, victorious warriors" – were unbeatable. They put the Britons to flight at places like Searoburgh (Old Sarum) and elsewhere, occupied old Romano-British settlements like Camulodunum (Colchester) and Verulamium (St Albans), and strengthened their control over some of the most fertile parts of the islands. In the course of the next 150 years they set up seven kingdoms (Northumbria, Mercia, East Anglia, Kent, Essex, Sussex and Wessex) in an area which roughly corresponds to present-day England. They called the dispossessed Britons *wealas*, meaning "foreigners", from which we get the word *Welsh*.

The extent to which the Anglo-Saxons overwhelmed the native Britons is illustrated in their vocabulary. We might expect that two languages – and especially a borrowing language like English – living alongside each other for several centuries would borrow freely from each other. In fact, Old English (the name scholars give to the English of the Anglo-Saxons) contains barely a dozen Celtic words. Three of these, significantly, refer to features of the British landscape that the English could not have known in their flat, marshy continental homelands: *crag*, *tor* (a high rock) and *combe* (a deep valley, as in High Wycombe). Another likely borrowing is *puca*, an evil spirit, who eventually turns up as Puck, Shakespeare's mischief-maker.

Place-names tell a similar story. Some modern river names are Celtic, not English (*Avon* means "river"), and some towns have Roman-British names: *Londinium* became London – the Old Irish *lond* means "wild". *Lindum Colonia* became Lincoln, partly derived from the Welsh *llyn* meaning "lake". *Dubris* – also *dwfr* for "water" in Welsh – became Dover. But most English place-names are English or Danish. When, for instance, the English settled amongst the ruins of *Isurium* they called their town *Aldeburgh*, which means simply Old Town. One or two place-names give a vivid indication of the mutual antipathy, the yawning communication gap that existed between the two sides. Cheetwood in Lancashire is a tautology. *Cheet* is an old Celtic word for "wood". It is as though the English could not be bothered to learn the language of the island they had conquered. Again, in Oxfordshire, there's a place called Brill, which comes from Bre-Hill. Yet *bre* is the Celtic for "hill". Whoever named the place in Old English obviously did not understand even the most common words of the native language. This is a pattern we shall find repeated again when the English language travelled to North America and Australia.

The hostility went both ways. A fragment of an early Welsh folk song tells of a young man going "with a heart like lead" to live in "the land of the Saxons". To this day the gap between the English on the one hand and the Welsh, the Scots and the Irish on the other, is often huge. The Welsh campaign for bilingualism; the Scots proudly retain separate legal and education systems and frequently despise the *Sassenachs*, a Scots Gaelic version of "Saxons"; and the Irish have been at war with the people they now, ironically, call "the Brits" on and off for nearly eight centuries. On the face of it, the English language has been indifferent to the Celts and their influence. Yet the lyrical spirit of the Celts imbues English literature and speech from the earliest ballads to the present day. In the way that some of the greatest Roman poets came from the provinces, many of the finest writers in English – for example, Swift, Burns, Burke, Scott, Stevenson, Wilde, Shaw, and Dylan Thomas – are of Celtic origin. English speakers have a huge debt to the poetic mind of the Celts, and it was the scattered people of Scotland, Ireland and Wales who took the English language on many of the world journeys we shall be describing.

To the Celts, their German conquerors were all Saxons, but gradually the terms *Anglii* and *Anglia* crept into the language, also referring to the invaders generally. About 150 years after the first raids, King Aethelbert of Kent was styled *rex Anglorum* by Pope Gregory. A century later the Venerable Bede, writing in Latin, composed a history of what he called "The *English* church and people". In the vernacular, the people were *Angelcynn* (Angle-kin) and their language was *Englisc*. By AD 1000, the country was generally known as *Englaland*, the land of the *Angles*.

Gradually, the Anglo-Saxons settled down and began farming their new property. They were an agricultural people. Their art is full of farming, and so is their vocabulary. Everyday words like *sheep*, *shepherd*, *ox*, *earth*, *plough*, *swine*, *dog*, *wood*, *field*, and *work* all come from Old English. After the hard struggle of daily life in the fields, they loved to celebrate, from which come words like *glee*, *laughter* and *mirth*. Not all the words have the same meaning now. *Mirth* used to mean "enjoyment", or "happiness" and even "religious joy". *Merry*, as in Merry Christmas or Merry England, could mean no more than "agreeable" or "pleasing".

It is impossible – unless you go in for tortuous circumlocution – to write a modern English sentence without using a feast of Anglo-Saxon words. Computer analysis of the language has shown that the one hundred most common words in English are all of Anglo-Saxon origin. The basic building-blocks of an English sentence – *the*, *is*, *you* and so on – are Anglo-Saxon. Some Old English words like *mann*, *hus* and *drincan* hardly need translation. Equally, a large part of the Anglo-Saxon lexicon – for example, a word like *tungdwitega* meaning "an astrologer" – is, to us, totally incomprehensible. These roots are important. Anyone who speaks or writes English in the late twentieth century is using accents, words and grammar which, with several dramatic modifications, go all the way back to the Old English of the Anglo-Saxons. There is an unbroken continuity from *here* to *there* (both Old English words).

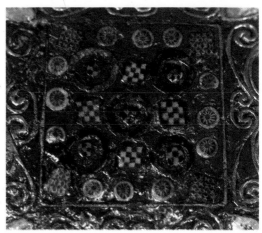

22/23 The ornaments found at the ship-burial in Sutton Hoo illustrate the sophistication of Anglo-Saxon culture. The complexity of Anglo-Saxon art is matched by their love of word-play and riddles.

When, in 1940, Winston Churchill wished to appeal to the hearts and minds of the English-speaking people it is probably no accident that he did so with the plain bareness for which Old English is noted: "We shall fight on the beaches; we shall fight on the landing grounds, we shall fight in the fields and in the streets, we shall fight in the hills; we shall never surrender." In this celebrated passage, only *surrender* is foreign – Norman-French.

Old English was not a uniform language. From the beginning it had its own local varieties, just as today, on a much larger scale, the English of California differs from the English of Auckland or of London. The regions of Old English correspond with surprising accuracy to the main varieties of contemporary spoken English in the British Isles. When a Geordie from Newcastle pronounces a word like *path* with a short *a*, or a farmer in Hardy country, in Dorchester for example, burrs his *r*s, the pronunciation is a heavily modified throwback to the local English speech of Anglo-Saxon times. Even the ancient kingdom of Kent, conquered by the Jutes from Jutland, still has a distinct speech-pattern whose origins can be traced back to that first invasion.

The Anglo-Saxons, by all accounts, were very sophisticated in the arts of speech. Theirs was, after all, an oral culture. In the late twentieth century, we work on paper, relying on typewriters, word processors and Xerox machines. If we make an agreement, we insist on seeing it in "black and white". But most Anglo-Saxons would have been unable to read or write – they had to rely on speech and memory. Their oral tradition was highly developed; they enjoyed expressing their ideas in an original, often rather subtle way. They valued understatement, and liked riddles, and poems which went in circles. These preferences suggest a certain deviousness about them, although they also liked to cultivate an air of plain bareness, which is not an unknown art even today.

The Anglo-Saxon love of ambiguity, innuendo and word-play, which remains a distinguishing characteristic of the English language to this day, can be seen very clearly in

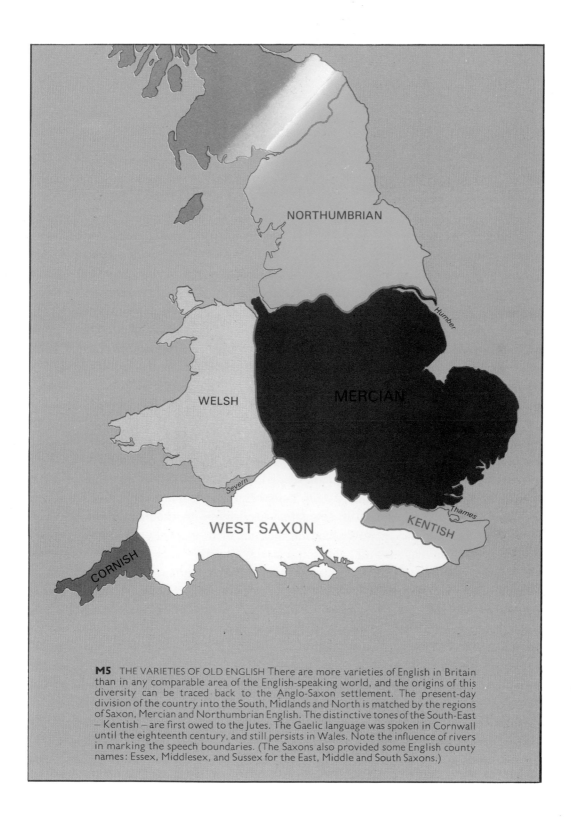

NORTHUMBRIAN

Humber

WELSH

MERCIAN

Severn

WEST SAXON

Thames

KENTISH

CORNISH

M5 THE VARIETIES OF OLD ENGLISH There are more varieties of English in Britain than in any comparable area of the English-speaking world, and the origins of this diversity can be traced back to the Anglo-Saxon settlement. The present-day division of the country into the South, Midlands and North is matched by the regions of Saxon, Mercian and Northumbrian English. The distinctive tones of the South-East – Kentish – are first owed to the Jutes. The Gaelic language was spoken in Cornwall until the eighteenth century, and still persists in Wales. Note the influence of rivers in marking the speech boundaries. (The Saxons also provided some English county names: Essex, Middlesex, and Sussex for the East, Middle and South Saxons.)

the collection of Old English verse known as *The Exeter Book of Riddles*. Riddle 69 is simply one line: "On the way a miracle: water become bone." This is ice. Riddle 45 is ostensibly about dough:

I'm told a certain object grows
in the corner, rises and expands, throws up
a crust. A proud wife carried off
that boneless wonder, the daughter of a King
covered that swollen thing with a cloth.

The same love of intricacy and interlacing is obvious in the visual art of the Anglo-Saxons, in their jewellery and their manuscripts. The jewellery discovered by archaeologists excavating the ship-burial of an Anglo-Saxon king at Sutton Hoo shows a mastery of geometric pattern, and provides the visual counterpart to the complicated minds of the first English poets. It is easy to overlook the cultural difficulties facing the Anglo-Saxons. By Roman standards, they did not have a very developed society. But they had lived more or less outside the pale of the Roman Empire and had no experience of "civilization". Everything had to be done for the first time – it was a process of trial and error. Historically, the Anglo-Saxons have had a rather mixed press; but they deserve great credit for the energy and determination with which they developed their own sense of culture.

THE WORDS OF GOD

The civilizing energies of the Anglo-Saxons received an enormous boost when Christianity brought its huge Latin vocabulary to England in the year AD 597. The remarkable impact of Christianity is reported by the Venerable Bede in a story which says as much about the collision of Old English and Latin as it does about the spread of God's word. According to the famous tradition, the mission of St Augustine was inspired by the man who was later to become Pope Gregory the Great. Walking one morning in the market place of Rome, he came upon some fair-haired boys about to be sold as slaves. He was told they came from the island of Britain and were pagans. "What a pity", he said, "that the author of darkness is possessed of men of such fair countenances." What was the name of their country? he asked. He was told that they were called Angles (*Anglii*). "Right," he replied, "for they have an angelic face, and it is fitting that such should be co-heirs with the angels in heaven. What is the name", he continued, "of the province from which they are brought?" He was told that they were natives of a province called Deira. "Truly are they *de ira*," is the way Bede expresses the future pope's reply, "plucked from wrath and called to the memory of Christ. How is the king of that province called?" They told him his name was Aella. Gregory, who appears to have had an incorrigible taste for puns, said, "Alleluia, the praise of God the Creator must be sung in those parts." Bede says that Gregory intended to undertake the mission to Britain himself but, in the end, he sent Augustine and a party of about fifty monks to what must have seemed like the end of the earth.

Augustine and his followers would have been aware that the tribes they were setting out to convert were notoriously savage. The risk must have seemed almost suicidal. But fortune smiled. Augustine and his monks landed in Kent, a small kingdom which, happily for them, already had a small Christian community. The story of the great missionary's arrival at the court of King Aethelbert is memorably reported by Bede:

> When, at the king's command, they had sat down and preached the word of life to the king and his court, the king said: "Your words and promises are fair indeed; they are new and uncertain, and I cannot accept them and abandon the age-old beliefs that I have held together with the whole English nation. But since you have travelled far, and I can see that you are sincere in your desire to impart to us what you believe to be true and excellent, we will not harm you. We will receive you hospitably and take care to supply you with all that you need; nor will we forbid you to preach and win any people you can to your religion."

After this, perhaps the earliest recorded example of English tolerance, the liberal-minded king arranged for Augustine to have a house in Canterbury, the capital of his tiny kingdom. He kept his word: Augustine's mission went ahead unhindered.

The conversion of England to Christianity was a gradual process, but a peaceful one. No one was martyred. The mission received a boost in AD 635 when Aidan, a charismatic preacher from the Celtic church in Ireland, independently began the conversion of the north. The twin sources of English Christianity are reflected in the two Old English words for its central symbol, the cross. In the north, there was the Irish version, *cros*. Down south, an earlier, German borrowing, also derived from the Latin *crux*, produced *cruc*. *Cruc* has vanished from the language, though there is a Crutched Friars Street (friars with crosses) in London to this day.

With the establishment of Christianity came the building of churches and monasteries, the corner-stones of Anglo-Saxon culture, providing education in a wide range of subjects. Bede, himself a pupil at the monastery in Jarrow, writes that not only were the great monk-teachers learned "in sacred and profane literature", they also taught poetry, astronomy and arithmetic. The new monasteries also encouraged writing in the vernacular, and all the plastic arts. Astonishing work in stone and glass, rich embroidery, magnificent illuminated manuscripts, were all fostered by the monks, as was church music and architecture.

The importance of this cultural revolution in the story of the English language is not merely that it strengthened and enriched Old English with new words, more than 400 of which survive to this day, but also that it gave English the capacity to express abstract thought. Before the coming of St Augustine, it was easy to express the common experience of life – sun and moon, hand and heart, sea and land, heat and cold – in Old English, but much harder to express more subtle ideas without resort to rather elaborate, German-style portmanteaux like *frumweorc* (*fruma*, beginning and *weorc*, work = creation). Now, there were Greek and Latin words like *angel, disciple, litany, martyr, mass, relic, shrift, shrine* and

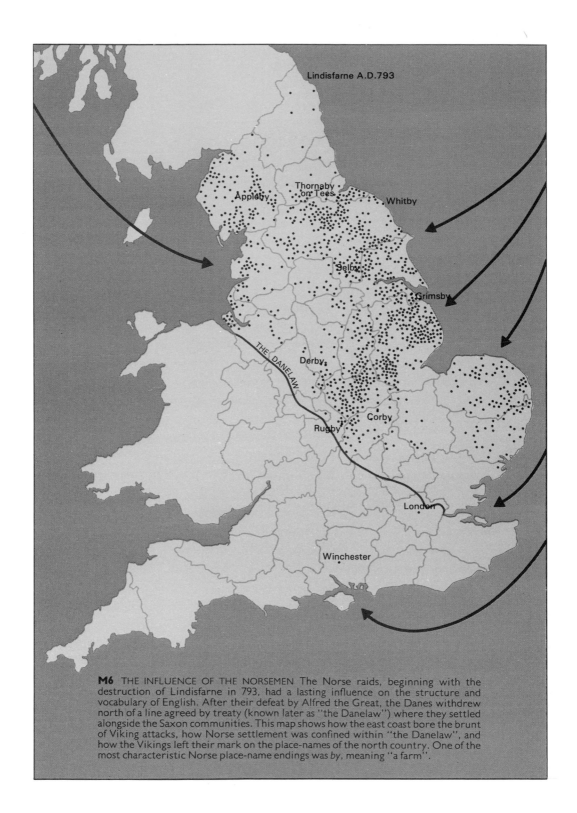

Lindisfarne A.D.793

Appleby

Thornaby on Tees

Whitby

Selby

Grimsby

THE DANELAW

Derby

Corby

Rugby

London

Winchester

M6 THE INFLUENCE OF THE NORSEMEN The Norse raids, beginning with the destruction of Lindisfarne in 793, had a lasting influence on the structure and vocabulary of English. After their defeat by Alfred the Great, the Danes withdrew north of a line agreed by treaty (known later as "the Danelaw") where they settled alongside the Saxon communities. This map shows how the east coast bore the brunt of Viking attacks, how Norse settlement was confined within "the Danelaw", and how the Vikings left their mark on the place-names of the north country. One of the most characteristic Norse place-name endings was *by*, meaning "a farm".

psalm ready to perform quite sophisticated functions. The conversion of England changed the language in three obvious ways: it gave us a large church vocabulary; it introduced words and ideas ultimately from as far away as India and China; and it stimulated the Anglo-Saxons to apply existing words to new concepts.

Church words came from Latin, Greek and Hebrew. *Disciple, shrine, preost, biscop, nonne* and *munuc* (monk) all have Latin origins. *Apostle, pope* and *psalter* are borrowed, via the Scriptures, from Greek. *Sabbath* comes from Hebrew. *Angelos* (messenger) and *diabolos* (slanderer) were transformed into *angel* and *devil*, central figures in the Madame Tussaud's of early Christianity. *Easter* is a curiosity: the word preserves the name of *Eostre*, the pagan goddess of dawn. To understand the speed and completeness with which the language of the Bible was absorbed into Old English, we have only to think of the way in which our own contemporary vocabulary has become permeated by the language of psychology and psychoanalysis with words like *ego, id, angst* and *subconscious.*

The oriental origins of the Christian faith introduced words from the Bible – *camel, lion, cedar, myrrh* – which must have seemed as exotic and strange to a seventh-century Englishman as, say, recent borrowings from Japanese culture like *kamikaze* and *ju-jitsu* did at first. Also from the East came exotic words like *orange* and *pepper*, the names *India* and *Saracen*, and *phoenix*, the legendary bird. *Oyster* and *mussel* are both Mediterranean borrowings, while *ginger* comes ultimately from Sanskrit.

Perhaps most interesting of all is the way Old English reinvented and rejuvenated itself in the face of this Latin cornucopia by giving old words new meanings. *God, heaven* and *hell* are all Old English words which, with the arrival of Christianity, became charged with a deeper significance. The Latin *spiritus sanctus*, or Holy Spirit, became translated as *Halig Gast* (Holy Ghost); *feond* (fiend) was used as a synonym for Devil, and Judgement Day became, in Old English, *Doomsday*. The Latin *evangelium* (good news) became the English *god-spell* which gives us *gospel*. To this day, the power of the English language to express the same thought or

24 The Lindisfarne Gospels. The monastery was sacked in 793.

25 The Alfred Jewel, inscribed with the words "Alfred had me made", symbolizes Alfred's appreciation of the written word.

object in either an early vernacular or a more elaborate Latinate style is one of its most remarkable characteristics, and one which enables it to have a unique subtlety and flexibility of meaning.

By the end of the eighth century, the impact of Christianity on Anglo-Saxon England had produced a culture unrivalled in Europe. The illuminated manuscripts of the famous monastery at Lindisfarne, on Holy Island off the Northumbrian coast, show how words and pictures had both achieved a kind of perfection. But in the eighth and ninth centuries this culture faced another threat from what was to become the second great influence on the making of English – the sea-warriors from the North.

THE VIKING INVASIONS

The mass movement of the Scandinavian peoples between the years AD 750 and 1050, one of the great migrations of European history, began as plunder-raids and ended as conquest and settlement. People from what is now known as Sweden established a kingdom in part of European Russia. Adventurers from Norway colonized parts of the British Isles, the Faroes and Iceland, pushed on to Greenland and eventually the coast of Labrador. And the Danes – also called Norsemen – conquered northern France (which became Normandy) and finally England. Collectively, these peoples are referred to as the Vikings, a name which is thought to come either from the Norse *vik* (a bay, indicating "one who frequents inlets of the sea") or from the Old English *wic*, a camp, the formation of temporary encampments being a prominent feature of Viking raids. In the past, the Vikings have been described as daring pirates but, while there is obviously much truth to the stereotype, recent scholarship likes to emphasize the long-term peaceful benefits of the Norse landings. It has been suggested, too, that the native Anglo-Saxons took advantage of the Viking raids to settle old scores with each other. Unlike the Anglo-Saxon race war against the Celts which preserved virtually no trace of the Celtic languages in English, the Danish settlers had a profound influence on the development of Old English.

The Viking raids against England began in earnest in the year AD 793 when the monasteries of Jarrow and Lindisfarne were sacked in successive seasons and plundered of gold and silver. By the middle of the ninth century almost half the country was in Viking hands. The Norsemen, referred to by the Anglo-Saxons as "Danes", turned their forces against the jewel in the crown: the kingdom of Wessex.

The king of Wessex was a young man named Alfred who had inherited the throne in 871 after his brother was killed beating off the first of the Danish attacks from the North. It is perhaps a measure both of Alfred's qualities and of the desperate situation in Wessex that Alfred was chosen in preference to his brother's sons. For a time, the Vikings seemed unstoppable. By 878 Alfred was reduced to taking refuge with a small band of followers in the marshes of Somerset on the island of Athelney. The story of Alfred burning the cakes while brooding on the plight of his kingdom symbolizes the gravity of his situation. This was the moment at which it became suddenly possible that English might be wiped out altogether.

With no English-speaking kingdoms left, the country would gradually speak Norse. The turning point came that same year. Alfred raised a fresh army of men from Somerset, Wiltshire and Hampshire, and, surprising the Danes, overwhelmed them at the battle of Ethandune, a victory commemorated by a white horse carved on the hillside.

The subsequent Treaty of Wedmore saved Wessex. The Danes withdrew to the North. Alfred and the English-speaking Saxons ruled in the South and the country was partitioned roughly along the line of Watling Street, the old Roman road that ran from London to Chester. Having won the war, Alfred set out to make sure he won the peace. His problem was that his power-base was too small to guarantee that the peace with the Danes would hold, or that Englishmen living outside Wessex in, for example, Mercia (Worcestershire and Warwickshire) would not be gradually drawn into the Danish empire.

As king of Wessex Alfred had sovereignty only over people who lived in the counties of the south-west centred on Dorset, Wiltshire, Somerset and Hampshire, based around the capital city, Winchester. He had no power over, for example, people who lived in Oxfordshire or Shropshire. Yet his continued survival against the Vikings depended on men and money from the counties outside Wessex. Somehow he had to retain political control of territory that was not his. He did this by appealing to a shared sense of Englishness, conveyed by the language. Alfred quite consciously used the English language as a means of creating a sense of national identity.

Without Alfred the Great the history of the English language might have been quite different. He set about restoring his kingdom to its former greatness. He began rebuilding the monasteries and the schools. It was his inspiration to use English, not Latin, as the basis for the education of his people. At the age of nearly forty, amidst what he called the "various and manifold cares of this kingdom", he learnt Latin so that he could translate (or arrange for the translation of) various key texts, notably Bede's *Historia Ecclesiastica Gentis Anglorum (History of the English Church and People)*. Alfred describes his English-language campaign in a famous preface:

> Therefore it seems better to me ... that we should also translate certain books which are most necessary for all men to know, into the language that we can all understand, and also arrange it ... so that all the youth of free men now among the English people ... are able to read English writing as well.

There is one story (recorded by his biographer, Bishop Asser) that perhaps demonstrates more than any other Alfred's understanding of books and language. When he was young, Asser writes, Alfred was sitting, with some other children, at his mother's feet. She had on her lap a book written in English, and the boy was struck by the beauty of the decorated initial on the first page. As the story goes, his mother said that she would give the book to whoever could learn the book and repeat it to her. So Alfred went away, learnt the book, returned to his mother, repeated the text, and won the prize. Not only does the story convey – as it was designed to do – the future king's drive and tenacity, it also reveals his belief in the importance of culture. Alfred understood that his people needed history to remind them of their loyalties. So he instituted a chronicle, a record of current events, unique in Europe. The saviour of the English language, he was also the founder of English prose. No other English monarch is remembered as "Great".

After Alfred, the Danes and the Saxons lived alongside each other for generations, more or less at peace. Because both their languages had the same Germanic roots, the language frontier broke down and a kind of natural pidginization took place that gradually simplified the structure of Old English. Professor Tom Shippey, who has made a close study of the mingling of Saxon and Viking culture, vividly explains the process:

> Consider what happens when somebody who speaks, shall we say, good Old English from the south of the country runs into somebody from the north-east who speaks good Old Norse. They can no doubt communicate with each other, but the complications in both languages are going to get lost. So if the Anglo-Saxon from the South wants to say (in good Old English) "I'll sell you the horse that pulls my cart," he says: "Ic selle the that hors the draegeth minne waegn."
>
> Now the old Norseman – if he had to say this – would say: "Ek mun selja ther hrossit er dregr vagn mine."
>
> So, roughly speaking, they understand each other. One says "waegn" and the other says "vagn". One says "hors" and "draegeth"; the other says "hros" and "dregr", but broadly they are communicating. They understand the main words. What they don't understand are the grammatical parts of the sentence. For instance, the man speaking good Old English says for one horse "that hors" but for *two* horses he says "tha hors". Now the Old Norse speaker understands the word *horse* all right, but he's not sure if it means one or two because in Old English you say "one horse", "two horse". There is no difference between the two words for horse. The difference is conveyed in the word for "the" and the old Norseman might not understand this because his word for "the" doesn't behave like that. So: are you trying to sell me one horse or are you trying to sell me two horses? If you get enough situations like that there is a strong drive towards simplifying the language.

Before the arrival of the Danes, Old English, like most European languages at that time, was a strongly inflected language. Common words like "king" or "stone" relied on word-endings to convey a meaning for which we now use prepositions like "to", "with" and "from". In Old English, "the king" is *se cyning*, "to the king" is *thaem cyninge*. In Old English, they said one *stan* (stone), two *stanas* (stones). The simplification of English by the Danes gradually helped to eliminate these word-endings, as Tom Shippey explains:

> Nowadays we say the same thing for all the plurals. We say, *stone, stones* and *king, kings*. The language became simplified because these complications become very difficult to keep going when you have to speak to someone who does not have a total grasp of it, and perhaps especially difficult if you're

talking to someone who has a 90 per cent grasp of it. The vital 10 per cent is just enough difficulty to give the wrong impression. It's very much the situation you have now between the Danes and the Swedes. They think they can understand each other; they say they can understand each other. But they go away from the same conversation with different opinions about what's actually been agreed.

A little church in Kirkdale, North Yorkshire, tells the story of the way the Vikings almost won the war and how they lost the peace. In the porch is a sundial. Lovingly chiselled into the stone is the resoundingly Viking name of the man who made it: Orm Gamalsson. But on closer inspection the inscription turns out to be worked in Old English, not Old Norse. Barely one hundred years after his people had invaded Britain, Orm Gamalsson is writing (and presumably thinking) in English. Evidence of the way Saxon and Dane lived alongside each other is in the place-names that survive to this day. Saxon place-names are easy to spot. Places, like Clapham, ending in *ham* (meaning a settlement), *ing* (as in Worthing), *stowe* (as in Hawkstowe), *sted* (as in Oxted) and *ton* (as in Brighton) are all likely to be of Saxon origin. Viking place-names have similarly characteristic endings. Anywhere ending in *by* (meaning originally a farm, then a village) is almost certainly of Danish origin, as in *Grimsby* or *Derby*. Another Viking place-name ending is *wick* as in Swainswick, Keswick and Chiswick. *Thorpe* (Danish) and *thwaite* (Norwegian) are also common Viking names, as is *toft* (meaning a plot of land), and *scale* (a temporary hut or shelter).

The place-names along a stretch of the Lincolnshire coast give an indication of the way in which Saxon and Dane co-existed, and how the Danes had to work hard to find land for themselves. Lincolnshire is flat and marshy and liable to flooding from the sea. The Anglo-Saxons lived inland in places like *Covenham* and *Alvingham*. But less than five miles away, Danes lived in *North Thoresby*. Towards the coast itself, having established a sea-dyke to drain the marshland and make the land workable, Danish settlements were established in *Grainthorpe* and *Skidbrooke*. (Evidence from a study of the type of land settled indicates that the incoming Danes often left the English undisturbed and settled on the less good, still empty land.) The best hint of the mixing of Saxon and Dane comes from a place-name like *Melton*. Melton was almost certainly *Middletoun* in Old English. When the Vikings came they would have recognized the meaning of the name, but replaced the Old English *middle* with the Scandinavian *meddle*, giving *Meddleton*, and finally *Melton*.

The impact of Old Norse on the English language is hard to evaluate with much accuracy, precisely because the two languages were so similar. Nine hundred words – for example, *get*, *hit*, *leg*, *low*, *root*, *skin*, *same*, *want* and *wrong* – are certainly of Scandinavian origin and typically plain-syllabled. Words beginning with *sk* like *sky* and *skein* are Norse. There are probably hundreds more we cannot account for definitely, and in the old territory of the Danelaw in Northern England literally thousands of Old Norse borrowings, words like *beck* (stream), *laithe* (barn) and *garth* (yard) survive in regional use. *Riding*, derived from an Old Norse word meaning 'a third part', was used to indicate the division of an English county,

Yorkshire, until recently. *Riding* is also used in Canada to describe a parliamentary constituency. There is another influence derived from these northern invaders we shall look at later: the beginnings of Scots English.

In many cases the Old Norse borrowings stood alongside their English equivalents. The Norse *skirt* originally meant the same as the English *shirt*. The Norse *deyja* (to die) joined its Anglo-Saxon synonym, the English *steorfa* (which ends up in the dictionaries as *starve*). You can *rear* (English) or *raise* (Norse) a child. Other synonyms or near-synonyms include: *wish* and *want*, *craft* and *skill*, *hide* and *skin*. Thanks to the Danes, the language was given another dimension, more light and shade, and more variety.

The fusion of Saxon and Viking is epitomized in *Beowulf*, a poem of some 3000 lines, the greatest single work of Old English literature, as intricate and subtle as the illuminated manuscripts painted at the same time. It reveals a reflective and ruminative temper of mind, obsessed with the transience of life, with heroism, and with the keeping of dignity in the face of defeat. These lines are typical of the mood of the poem:

> *There's no joy from harp-play,*
> *gleewood's gladness, no good hawk,*
> *swings through the hall now, no swift horse*
> *tramps at threshold: the threat came:*
> *falling has felled a flowering kingdom.*

Other surviving poems from this time emphasize the character of the Anglo-Saxon experience. The poets write of the cruel sea, ruined cities, the life of the minstrel, and of war and exile. The pinnacle of the Vikings' achievement – and of Danish integration into English society – was marked around the year AD 1000 when Cnut, king of Denmark (known to legend as wise King Canute), inherited the English throne, conquered Norway and ruled over most of the Scandinavian world. From then on their story is one of rapid decline.

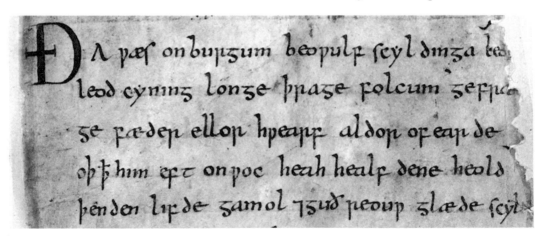

26 The manuscript of *Beowulf*. The lines begin: "Then in the strongholds was Beowulf of the Scyldings, beloved king of the nation, for a long time famed among peoples . . ."

THE NORMAN INVASION

In 1066 the English language once again showed an astonishing adaptability in surviving another major linguistic collision following the landing of the Norman French at Hastings. It was the limpid English prose of *The Anglo-Saxon Chronicle* that recorded this event, in a few doom-laden paragraphs:

> Then Count William came from Normandy to Pevensey on Michaelmas Eve [28 September], and as soon as they were able to move they built a castle at Hastings. King Harold was informed of this and he assembled a large army and came against him at the hoary apple-tree, and William came against him by surprise before his army was drawn up in battle array. But the king nevertheless fought hard against him, with the men who were willing to support him, and there were heavy casualties on both sides. Then King Harold was killed and Earl Leofwine his brother, and Earl Gyrth his brother, and many good men, and the French remained masters of the field. . . .

The Norman victory at Hastings changed the face of English forever. Harold was the last English-speaking king for nearly three hundred years. It was, in the words of one scholar, "an event which had a greater effect on the English language than any other in the course of its history". In the short run it must have seemed like a disaster for the English. The Normans seized control of their new territory with systematic rigour. Norman castles, built by English workmen, were garrisoned by Norman soldiers and used as strong points to hold down the countryside. The English royal family and Harold's court had been destroyed in battle. William established his own regime, rewarding those who had supported his expedition across the Channel. The English poet Robert of Brunne wrote:

> *To French and Normans, for their great labour,*
> *To Flemings and Picards, that were with him in battle,*
> *He gave lands betimes, of which their successors*
> *Hold yet the seizin, with full great honour.*

William also purged the English church: Norman bishops and abbots gradually took over in the cathedrals and monasteries. For several generations after the Conquest all important positions in the country were dominated by French-speaking Normans.

William's coronation in Westminster Abbey on Christmas Day 1066, an act of triumph, symbolized the condition of England for the next two hundred years. He was crowned in a ceremony that used both English and Latin. He himself spoke the French of Normandy and though he tried to learn English at the age of forty-three he was too busy to keep it up. So from 1066 there were three languages in play and the overwhelming majority of English people experienced the humiliations of a linguistic apartheid: religion, law, science, literature were all conducted in languages other than English, as words like *felony, perjury, attorney, bailiff* and *nobility* testify.

27 Harold, the last English-speaking king for three hundred years.

28 The Bayeux Tapestry, a masterpiece of Saxon artistry, tells the story of the Norman victory at the Battle of Hastings.

A twelfth-century miracle story expresses the bitter resentment the English felt. A friend of St Wulfric of Haselbury, a certain Brother William, laid hands on a dumb man who had been brought to him. At once the man could speak both English and French. The local parish priest, Brichtric, complained that this was unfair. He had served the church faithfully for many years and yet Brother William had made it possible for a total stranger to speak two languages while he, Brichtric, had to remain dumb in the presence of his bishop. Though he was a priest, Brichtric knew little or no Latin, and no French.

Going by the written record alone, the supremacy of Norman French and Latin seems total. In 1154, the English monks who wrote *The Anglo-Saxon Chronicle* abandoned their work for ever. A great silence seems to descend on English writing. In court, church and government circles, French was established as the smart and Latin as the professional language. There is, for instance, the story of Bishop William of Ely, Chancellor of England during the reign of Richard the Lionheart (Coeur de Lion). Disgraced politically, the bishop

29/30 "Castle" comes from French, which was now the language spoken in the great Norman fortresses and cathedrals.

31 Stokesay Castle, Salop.

tried to escape from England in 1191 disguised as a woman and carrying under his arm some cloth for sale. He reached Dover safely but was discovered when he was asked by an English woman what he would charge for an ell of cloth. He could not reply because he knew no English – and it was inconceivable that his low-born captors could speak French.

The Norman kings were often totally ignorant of English, although Henry I, who had an English wife, was an exception and could speak some English. No doubt in upper-class circles it was the fashionable thing to speak French. To this day the use of French words in conversation is thought to show sophistication, or *savoir-faire*. The situation is summarized by the historian known as Robert of Gloucester:

> *For but a man know French men count of him little.*
> *But low men hold to English and to their own speech yet.*
> *I think there are in all the world no countries*
> *That don't hold to their own speech but England alone.*

Though French had the social and cultural prestige, Latin remained the principal language of religion and learning. The English vernacular survived as the common speech, obviously a matter of pride for Robert of Gloucester. The mingling of these three powerful traditions can be seen in the case of a word like *kingly*. The Anglo-Saxons had only one word to express this concept, which, with typical simplicity, they made up from the word *king*. After the Normans, three synonyms enter the language: *royal*, *regal*, and *sovereign*. The capacity to express three or four different shades of meaning and to make fine distinctions is one of the hallmarks of the language after the Conquest, as word groups such as *rise-mount-ascend*, *ask-question-interrogate*, or *time-age-epoch* suggest.

Yet the use of French in England was probably natural to only an elite of churchmen and magnates. The continuity of the English language in the mouths of the mass of ordinary people was never in doubt. Why did English survive? Why was it not absorbed into the dominant Norman tongue? There are three reasons. First and most obvious: the pre-Conquest Old English vernacular, both written and spoken, was simply too well established, too vigorous, and, thanks to its fusion with the Scandinavian languages, too hardy to be obliterated. It is one thing for the written record to become Latin and French (writing was the skilled monopoly of church-educated clerks), but it would have needed many centuries of French rule to eradicate it as the popular speech of ordinary people. The English speakers had an overwhelming demographic advantage. Pragmatically, it is obvious that the English were not going to stop speaking English because they had been conquered by a foreigner.

Second, English survived because almost immediately the Normans began to intermarry with those they had conquered. Of course, in the first generation after the Conquest, there were bound to be deep divisions within society. There is a document dating from around 1100 addressed to "all his faithful people, both French and English, in Herefordshire" from Henry I. But this did not last. Barely one hundred years after the invasion, a chronicler wrote that "the two nations have become so mixed that it is scarcely possible today, speaking of free men, to tell who is English and who is of Norman race". One can imagine the situation of a minor Norman knight living in a small manor in the English countryside surrounded by English peasants, served in the house by English maids, his estates managed by an English steward, and his children playing with English children. He would have to pick up some English to survive, and to quell the natural resentment of his subjects. There is plenty of evidence of the peaccful co-existence of Norman overlords and English subjects. There were French towns alongside the English at Norwich and Nottingham. Southampton still has a French Street, one of its principal thoroughfares in the Middle Ages. Petty France in London is known to anyone who has had to visit the Passport Office.

The great historian Ordericus Vitalis provides good evidence of the decline of French in educated society, both courtly and clerical. The son of a Norman knight and an English mother, Ordericus was born less than a decade after the Conquest near Shrewsbury and was taught Latin by a local priest. At the age of ten he was sent to continue his education in a monastery in Normandy. There, he writes (in Latin, of course), "like Joseph in Egypt, I heard a language which I did not know". In other words, he knew no French.

Thirdly, and perhaps most importantly, in 1204, thanks to the military impetuosity of King John, the Anglo-Normans lost control of their French territory across the Channel. Many of the Norman nobility, who had held lands in both countries and divided their time between them, were forced to declare allegiance either to France or England. Simon de Montfort's family separated their estates in this way: "My brother Amaury", said de Montfort, "released to me our brother's whole inheritance in England, provided that I could secure it; in return I released to him what I had in France." This process of separation reached a turning point in 1244 when the king of France made a decisive move, announcing that, "As it is impossible that any man living in my kingdom, and having possessions in England, can competently serve two masters, he must either inseparably attach himself to me or to the king of England."

"COMMON MEN KNOW NO FRENCH"
In the early years of the thirteenth century, long before the outbreak of hostilities with France known as the Hundred Years War, we find English making a comeback at both the written and the spoken level. Church sermons, prayers and carols especially are expressed in English. The first known appearance of an English word in a Latin document occurs in an account of a court case brought by Henry III against some of his citizens. The clerk, trained in Latin, who recorded the proceedings found himself lost for the right Latin word to describe the king's suit. Instead, we find him writing in English that it is *nameless* (or, as we should say, "pointless"). More and more records were now kept in English; more and more upper-class Englishmen were keeping up their French only for the sake of appearances. The great silence that had apparently fallen over the written language from 1066 to 1200 began to be broken, at first with a few simple messages and then with a flood of documents.

English writings like *The Owl and the Nightingale* and the *Ancrene Riwle* are probably the tip of an iceberg of lost manuscripts: and of course church sermons and hymns would undoubtedly have been given in English. Anti-French feeling – complaints that London is full of foreigners – was greatly provoked during the reign of Henry III, which ended in 1272. Henry was wholly French and surrounded himself with French favourites. The confused situation is exemplified by the Barons' revolt of Simon de Montfort in the middle of the century – for all his ancestry, it was distinctly anti-French in spirit. At the same time, the English bishop Grosseteste (obviously of Norman blood) denounced Henry's French courtly circle as "not merely foreigners; they are the worst enemies of England. They strive to tear the fleece and do not even know the faces of the sheep; they do not understand the English tongue . . ."

At the end of the thirteenth century, Edward I, who was very conscious of his Englishness, whipped up patriotic feeling against the king of France, declaring that it was "his detestable purpose, which God forbid, to wipe out the English tongue". The growing power and spread of the vernacular is expressed by a contemporary poet who wrote:

> *Common men know no French*
> *Among a hundred scarcely one*

Even among the educated classes it seems clear that French had become an *acquired*, not a natural, language. There is a little textbook dating from the mid-thirteenth century written by a knight known as Walter of Bibbesworth. It was designed to teach English-speaking children how to learn French "which every gentleman ought to know". (Throughout Europe, French was the language of chivalry, just as in the eighteenth and nineteenth centuries it was the language of diplomacy.) Two hundred years after the Norman Conquest, the descendants of William's knights were almost certainly acquiring French in the schoolroom, not the cradle.

English had now become much more self-assertive. The new note of nationalistic pride in the language is sounded in the introduction to a long biblical poem called *Cursor Mundi*: "This book is translated into English for the love of the English people, English people of England, and for the common man to understand . . ." As English-language consciousness grew, churches and universities tried to stop the decline of French. For instance, the foundation statutes of Oriel and The Queen's College (1326 and 1340) at Oxford University required that the undergraduates should converse in French and Latin. At Merton things were obviously going to the dogs. There was a report that the Fellows spoke English at High Table and wore "dishonest shoes". The battle for French was a losing one, partly because English French was certainly not a prestige dialect, a point that Chaucer makes with his usual irony when he writes about the Prioress:

> *And Frenssh she spak ful faire and fetisly,*
> *After the scole of Stratford atte Bowe,*
> *For Frenssh of Parys was to hir unknowe.*

The Hundred Years War with France (1337–1454) provided a major impetus to speak English, not French. At the same time, the outbreak of the mysterious disease known as "The Black Death", by making labour scarce, improved and accelerated the rise in status of the English working man (a process that culminated in the Peasants' Revolt of 1381). It caused so many deaths in the monasteries and churches that a new generation of semi-educated, non-French and Latin speakers took over as abbots and prioresses. After the plague, English grammar began to be taught in schools, to the detriment of French. In 1325, the chronicler William of Nassyngton wrote:

> Latin can no one speak, I trow,
> But those who it from school do know;
> And some know French, but no Latin
> Who're used to Court and dwell therein,
> And some use Latin, though in part,
> Who if known have not the art,
> And some can understand English
> That neither Latin knew, nor French
> But simple or learned, young or old,
> All understand the English tongue.

English now appears at every level of society. In 1356, the mayor and aldermen of London ordered that court proceedings there be heard in English; in 1362, the Chancellor opened Parliament in English. During Wat Tyler's rebellion in 1381, Richard II spoke to the peasants in English. In the last year of the century the proceedings for the deposition of Richard II (together with the document by which he renounced the throne) were in English. Henry IV's speeches claiming the throne and later accepting it were also in English. The mother tongue had survived.

MIDDLE ENGLISH

But English had changed; it had become the form known to scholars as Middle English, a term devised in the nineteenth century to describe the English language from AD 1150 to 1500. The distinction – given the collapse of Old English writing – is partly artificial. Much of what is called Middle English is no more than a record in *writing* of what had already happened to *spoken* Old English. Thus, while *spoken* Old English had almost certainly lost most of its inflections by the time of the Norman Conquest, it is not until *written* Middle English that the changes show up in the documents. Perhaps the most vital simplification, now fully established, was the loss of Old English word endings, which were replaced by prepositions, words like *by*, *with* and *from*.

An example of what happened in the transition from Old English to Middle English is shown in the story of the letter *y*. In Old English, *y* represented, in some cases, the sound which French scribes wrote as *u*: a short vowel. So Old English *mycel* became Middle English *muchel*, which ends up as Modern English *much*. But when *y* stood for a long vowel the long *u* was written by the French scribes as *ui*. So the Old English *fyr*, becomes the Middle English *fuir* and the modern *fire*. To make the matter more complicated, the original vowel sound, short or long, represented by the Old English *y*, sounded different in different parts of the country. In the North and East down to the East Midlands as far as London, the short vowel sound became roughly like that represented by modern English *i*, as in *kin*. In Kent and parts of East Anglia it became the sound represented by *e*, as in *merry*. In the West Country, it became the sound now represented by *oo* as in *mood*, but in those days spelt *u*. The same word at the same period in Middle English was therefore spelt differently in different parts of the country. Old English for "kin", *cyn*, for example, could be *kyn*, *ken*, or *kun*. In the case of *byrgen* (which had Middle English variants *birien, burien, berien*) Modern English has kept the western spelling, *bury*, while using the Kentish pronunciation, *berry*, while *busy* reflects the western spelling but is pronounced as the London/East Midlands "bizzy".

So what had happened to the language map of England? The short answer is that it had not changed much from Anglo-Saxon times, though with the development of written English it had developed strong local forms, written and spoken. For instance, the author of *Cursor Mundi*, already quoted, notes that he found the story of the Assumption of Our Lady in southern English and translated it for "northern people who can read no other English". And even Chaucer launches *Troilus and Criseyde* with his famous "Go, litel book", adding

> *And for ther is so gret diversite*
> *In Englissh and in writyng of oure tonge,*
> *So prey I God that non myswrite the,*
> *Ne the mysmetre for defaute of tonge.*

Spoken English differed from county to county as it does in rural districts to this day. The five main speech areas – Northern, West and East Midlands, Southern and Kentish – are strikingly similar to contemporary English speech areas. Within the East Midlands, one small nucleus of power, trade and learning – the triangle of Oxford, Cambridge and London – shared the same kind of English, which may be said to have become the basis for Standard English in the twentieth century.

Stanley Ellis, an authority on English speech varieties, has devoted his life to studying the bizarre nuances and definitions of English speech. He takes his tape-recorder into the English countryside and by a process of gentle inquiry discovers local variations in usage, of both vocabulary and accent. In this passage, he is trying to establish the local Yorkshire for a watercourse. His informant speaks broad Yorkshire, pronouncing "no" as *nae*, "nude" as *noody* and "leap" as *lope*.

| STANLEY ELLIS: | You've been in farming all your life. Farming's altered a lot, hasn't it? |
| INFORMANT: | Oh, my God, there's no comparison to when I started. |

ELLIS:	In the old days, how did you get your drainage to the fields? The gutters would be drains, and the gutters would then run out into the . . .?
INFORMANT:	The beck.
ELLIS:	Ah yes. The beck. Now what's the difference between a beck and a gutter?
INFORMANT:	Why of course the beck's considerably wider than th' gutter . . . We used to bathe in th' beck you know. Oh aye. Went hollocking down here and it was nowt to be nude and leap into th' water.

Not only does Ellis establish the distinction between *beck* and "gutter", and *hollocking* for "galloping", he also collects a piece of authentic folk practice – bathing in the river. In another part of the country, in Kent for example, the conversation would have been different. David North is one of Ellis's pupils. His conversation with a local farmer goes as follows:

DAVID NORTH:	What do you call a stretch of water at the edge of a field that you drain the field with?
INFORMANT:	A stretch of water? A pond?
DAVID NORTH:	Well, the sort of thing along the hedge to drain –
INFORMANT:	Oh, the ditch, the dyke – well, some people call it dyke. My old people called it ditch.

And so on. The one thing missing on the page of print, of course, is the sound. In the first extract, the Yorkshireman is hard for most people to understand; in the second, the man from Kent is easier, even though he says *doik* for "dyke" and *oi* for "I". This is simply because he is geographically closer to the Standard English dialect of London. To put it another way, if Edinburgh not London were the capital of the British Isles, Standard English would sound like Scottish English. There is nothing special about Standard English except that it happens to be the speech of the capital, the *prestige* English.

"FIRST FOUNDEUR AND EMBELLISSHER OF OUR ENGLISH"

The career and achievement of one man, Geoffrey Chaucer, exemplifies the triumph of London English. By making a conscious choice to write in English, he symbolizes the rebirth of English as a national language. Born in 1340 of a provincial middle-class family in the wine trade, he was, in the custom of the time, educated as a squire in a noble household, later joining the king's retinue. He began his writing life as a translator and imitator. His later work offers some clues to the life of the poet. In *The Parlement of Fowles* he tells how he reads in bed at night because he cannot sleep. From 1370 to 1391, Chaucer was busy on the king's business at home and abroad. He is recorded negotiating a trade agreement in Genoa, and on a diplomatic mission to Milan, from which he acquired a taste for Italian poetry. Petrarch was still alive in Florence and Boccaccio was lecturing on Dante, though there is no way of knowing if Chaucer met either of them. During these years he composed much of his best work: *The House of Fame*, *The Parlement of Fowles*, *Troilus and Criseyde* and translated the *Consolation of Philosophy* by Boethius.

It is likely that it was around this time that he began to work on his masterpiece, *The Canterbury Tales*, poems which he would either read aloud in the traditional manner or, as was becoming the practice, pass around for reading. In the final years of his life, with England divided by fierce political rivalries, Chaucer's career at court faltered. The last reference to him comes in December 1399, when he took a lease on a house in the garden of Westminster Abbey. He died on 25 October 1400 and was buried in the Abbey.

Recognized as a great poet in his lifetime, in both France and England ("noble Geffrey Chaucier" as a French poet called him), he is one of those writers of genius on whom English has always depended for its important transformations. He took as his subjects all classes of men and women: the Knight, the Prioress, and the famous Wife of Bath. Chaucer was alive to the energy and potential of the language of everyday speech. He pokes fun at Yorkshire speech; he dazzles the reader with word-play, and he mocks the pretensions of people who claim to know French and Latin. He writes of the Summoner:

> *Wel loved he garleek, oynons, and eek lekes,*
> *And for to drynken strong wyn, reed as blood;*
> *Thanne wolde he speke and crie as he were wood.*
> *And when that he wel dronken hadde the wyn,*
> *Than wolde he speke no word but Latyn.*

Of the Friar, Hubert, he says:

> *Somewhat he lisped, for his wantownesse,*
> *To make his English sweete upon his tonge;*

Chaucer benefited enormously from the preceding three hundred years of language evolution. This can be shown in one line, the words of Criseyde, spoken to her knight, Troilus:

> *Welcome, my knyght, my pees, my suffisance*

Welcome, my knyght are all original English words, though *knyght*, from the Old English *cniht*, "boy", has, under French social and military influence, come to connote a vast structure of concepts and feelings. *Peace* is one of the earliest words recorded as borrowed from French after the Conquest, replacing English *grith*. *Suffisance*, a grand, rather abstract word for "satisfaction" is another French borrowing, from an obviously Latin source. The richness of Middle English, Latinized and Frenchified by Christianity and Conquest, inspires the opening lines of Chaucer's *Prologue to the Canterbury Tales* which many have quoted before and which we must quote again:

> *Whan that Aprill with his shoures soote*
> *The droghte of March hath perced to the roote,*
> *And bathed every veyne in swich licour*
> *Of which vertu engendred is the flour ;*
> *Whan Zephirus eek with his sweete breeth*
> *Inspired hath in every holt and heeth*
> *The tendre croppes, and the yonge sonne*
> *Hath in the Ram his halve cours yronne,*
> *And smale foweles maken melodye,*
> *That slepen al the nyght with open eye*
> *(So priketh hem nature in hir corages) ;*
> *Thanne longen folk to goon on pilgrimages . . .*

It was Dryden, writing in the seventeenth century, who gave most eloquent expression to the debt the English language owes to its first major poet:

> He must have been a Man of a most wonderful comprehensive Nature, because, as it has been truly observed of him, he has taken into the compass of his *Canterbury Tales* the various Manners and Humours (as we now call them) of the whole *English* Nation, in his Age . . . The Matter and Manner of their Tales, and of their Telling, are so suited to their different Educations, Humours, and Callings, that each of them would be improper in any other mouth . . . 'Tis sufficient to say, according to the Proverb, that *here is God's plenty.*

Chaucer's time also saw the emergence of English surnames, family names. In Anglo-Saxon peasant society it was enough for a man to be identified as Egbert or Heorogar. Later, a second stage would produce the "son of" prefix or suffix – Johnson, Thomson, Jobson. As English

32/33 Geoffrey Chaucer was "the worshipful fader & first foundeur & embellissher of ornate eloquence in our Englissh . . .", according to William Caxton.

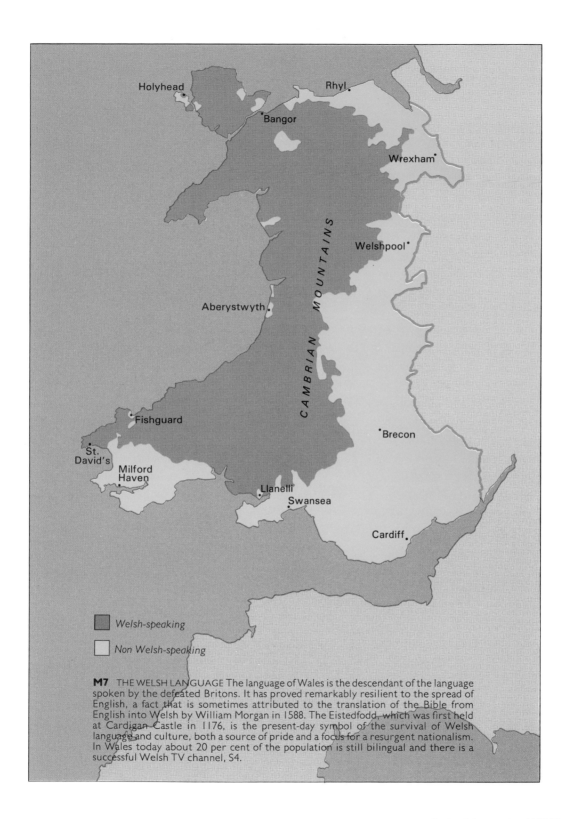

Holyhead

Rhyl

Bangor

Wrexham

Welshpool

C A M B R I A N   M O U N T A I N S

Aberystwyth

Fishguard

Brecon

St. David's

Milford Haven

Llanelli

Swansea

Cardiff

Welsh-speaking

Non Welsh-speaking

M7 THE WELSH LANGUAGE The language of Wales is the descendant of the language spoken by the defeated Britons. It has proved remarkably resilient to the spread of English, a fact that is sometimes attributed to the translation of the Bible from English into Welsh by William Morgan in 1588. The Eistedfodd, which was first held at Cardigan Castle in 1176, is the present-day symbol of the survival of Welsh language and culture, both a source of pride and a focus for a resurgent nationalism. In Wales today about 20 per cent of the population is still bilingual and there is a successful Welsh TV channel, S4.

society became more sophisticated, Christian or first names were not enough. People began to be identified by where they lived, hence *Brooks, Rivers, Hill* and *Dale*. Or more specifically: *Washington, Lincoln* or *Cleveland*. The next most common form of identification was occupation: *Driver, Butcher, Hunter, Glover, Sadler, Miller, Cooper, Weaver, Porter, Carpenter, Mason, Thatcher, Salter, Waxman, Barber, Bowman, Priest, Abbot, Piper, Harper, Constable*. Then there were continental names of people/families from abroad: *Fleming, French, Holland*. The Welsh contributed *Evans* (a version of Johns), *Owens*, and *Rhys* (Reece). The Welsh *Ll* underwent phonetic assimilation, giving us both *Floyd* and *Lloyd*. Shakespeare's Captain Fluellen was the English version of Llewellyn. In Scotland, *Mc* or *Mac* is well known as *son of*, a prefix attached to occupations as in the South: *McPherson* means "son of the parson". A few names go back into Scottish mythology. *McCormack* means "son of Chariot-Lad" and *McRory* means "son of Red-King". The arrival of the Norman French also introduced names like Fitzjohn, Gascoygne, Francis, Lorraine, Baillie, Gerard, Gerald, Raymond and Vernon. Geoffrey Chaucer himself had a French first name and a half-French surname. Chaucer (from the Old French *chaustier*, shoemaker) came from his grandfather's residence in Cordwainer (Leatherworker) Street.

Chaucer wrote in English, but the language of government was still officially French. Yet only seventeen years after the poet's death, Henry V became the first English king since Harold to use English in his official documents, including his will. In the summer of 1415, Henry crossed the Channel to fight the French. In the first letter he dictated on French soil he chose, symbolically, not to write in the language of his enemies. This national statement indicates a turning point, as decisive in its own way as Alfred's use of English in the ninth century. Henry's predecessor, Edward III, could only swear in English; now it was the official language of English kings.

Henry V's example clearly made an impression on his people. There is a resolution made by the London brewers, dating from the year of Henry's death, 1422, which adopts English by decree:

> Whereas our mother tongue, to wit, the English tongue, hath in modern days begun to be honorably enlarged and adorned; for that our most excellent lord king Henry the Fifth hath, in his letters missive, and divers affairs touching his own person, more willingly chosen to declare the secrets of his will [in it]; and for the better understanding of his people, hath, with a diligent mind, procured the common idiom (setting aside others) to be commended by the exercise of writing; and there are many of our craft of brewers who have the knowledge of writing and reading in the said English idiom, but in others, to wit, the Latin and French, before these times used, they do not in any wise understand; for which causes, with many others, it being considered how that the greater part of the lords and trusty commons have begun to make their matters to be noted down in our mother tongue, so we also in our craft, following in some manner their steps, have decreed in future to commit to memory the needful things which concern us.

IOANNES WICLEFVS ANGLVS.
Quanta fuit rabies odijque potentia vestri,
Pontifices olim, carnificesque truces!
Ossa in tumata diu vobis muisa virorum
Sanctorum, requie non potuere frui?
Cum priuillegio.

34 After the Conquest, Henry V was the first king to use English for his official correspondence.

35 John Wyclif. "The pearl of the Gospel … trodden underfoot by swine."

The importance of this statement is that the brewers have decided to adopt English *writing*. The next step was for written English to be expressed in printed form and for this crucial development we must look at the life and work of William Caxton, as important for the language, in his own way, as Geoffrey Chaucer, whose work he printed.

William Caxton "was born and learned mine English in Kent in the Weeld (Weald) where I doubt not is spoken as broad and rude English as is in any place of England". He had an eventful life as a merchant and diplomat, learned the art of printing on the Continent and then, in retirement, introduced the press into England around the year 1476, setting up his press within the precincts of Westminster Abbey. He was an attractive, original and thoroughly English character: a man of gusto and humour, of business acumen and pronounced political loyalties. He was perhaps the first editor-publisher, printing the works of Chaucer, and other poets like Gower, Lydgate and Malory; but he also translated bestsellers from France and Burgundy, and was himself a compulsive writer who obviously delighted in printing his own works. For the history of English spelling, Caxton's decision to reproduce the English of London and the South-East is crucial. Caxton and his successors gave a special currency to London English.

Caxton's decision was not as simple as it would seem in retrospect. There were several standards with rival claims. It was not easy for a writer and printer in the fifteenth century to choose a version of English that would find favour with all readers. In one of his prefaces,

Caxton himself describes some of the difficulties he encountered when he came to print English for the first time. He was sitting in his study, he says, and without any new work to hand, picked up a book that had recently been translated from Latin into French, a paraphrase of Virgil's *Aeneid*. Then, says Caxton, he "concluded to translate it into English, and forthwith took a pen and ink, and wrote a page or two". But when he came to read through what he had done, he found he had used so many "strange terms" he was afraid that he would be accused of translating in a way that "could not be understood by common people". Then he describes how he consulted "an old book" to improve his translation but found "the English so rude and broad that I could not well understand it". He compared this with some Old English, which he found "more like to Dutch than English". Next there were the problems of regional variation: "Common English that is spoken in one shire varies from another." He tells a story, expressed here with all the wonderful idiosyncrasy of Middle English spelling and syntax:

> In so moche that in my dayes happened that certayn marchauntes were in a shippe in tamyse, for to have sayled over the see into zelande, and for lacke of wynde, thei taryed atte forlond, and wente to lande for to refreshe them. And one of theym named Sheffelde, a mercer, cam in-to an hows and axed for mete; and specyally he axyd after eggys. And the goode wyf answerde, that she coude speke no frenshe. And the marchaunt was angry, for he also coude speke no frenshe, but wolde have hadde egges, and she understode hym not. And thenne at laste a nother sayd that he wolde have eyren. Then the good wyf sayd that she understod hym wel. Loo, what sholde a man in thyse dayes now wryte, egges or eyren? Certaynly it is harde to playse every man by cause of dyversite & chaunge of langage. For in these days every man that is in ony reputacyon in his countre, wyll utter his commynycacyon and maters in suche maners & termes that fewe men shall understonde theym. And som honest and grete clerkes have ben wyth me, and desired me to wryte the moste curyous terms that I coude fynde. And thus bytwene playn, rude, & curyous, I stande abasshed. But in my judgemente the comyn terms that be dayli used ben lyghter to be understonde than the olde and auncyent englysshe. And for as moche as this present booke is not for a rude uplondyssh man to laboure therin, ne rede it, but onely for a clerke & a noble gentylman that feleth and understondeth in faytes of armes, in love, & in noble chyvalrye, therfor in a meane bytwene bothe I have reduced & translated this sayd booke in to our englysshe, not ouer rude ne curyous, but in suche termes as shall be understanden, by goddys grace, accordynge to my copye.

When Caxton settled for the idiosyncrasies of the English he heard in the streets of London – "right" for instance reflects the fifteenth-century pronunciation "richt" (*ch* pronounced as in *loch*) – he (and printers like him) helped to fix the language on the page before its writers and teachers had reached a consensus. It is to this that English owes some of its chaotic and exasperating spelling conventions.

The printing press, which made the spread of learning and knowledge so much easier, was a communications revolution, the cornerstone of the European Renaissance, that introduced a torrent of Latin words into the language. Fifteenth-century English poetry is over-burdened with what one critic called "half-chewed Latin". The Scottish poet Dunbar was similarly afflicted:

> Hale sterne superne! Hale, in eterne
> In God's sight to schyne!
> Lucerne in derne, for to discerne
> Be glory and grace devyne;
> Hodiern, modern, sempitern . . .

This sort of writing provoked Bishop Reginald Pecock to make what is, perhaps, the first proposal (in a long tradition of such proposals) to "purify" the English language. Latinate borrowings, he argued, should be purged. Instead of *impenetrable*, he proposed *ungothroughsome*; instead of *inconceivable*, he suggested *not-to-be-thought-upon-able*. Pecock was not taken seriously; by the eighteenth century, however, such suggestions were given more weight.

The growing prestige and supremacy of the London standard is reflected in the fact that Mak, the sheep-stealer in one of the early miracle plays, attempts to impose upon the Yorkshire shepherds by masquerading as a person of some importance and affects a "Southern tooth". The vitality, if not the sophistication, of English culture is clear from the other plays of the fifteenth century: *Mankind*, for instance, one of the hits of its time, which was written around 1470, was designed for a company of strolling players, who would have been professionals. The script includes the taking of a collection during the performance, the first recorded instance of commercial acting. It has some crowd-pulling bawdiness:

> It is wretyn [written] with a coll [coal], it is wretyn with a coll,
> He that schitith with his hoyll [hole], he that schitith with his hoyll,
> But [unless] he wippe his ars clene, but he wippe his ars clene,
> On his breche [breeches] it shall be sen, on his breche it shall be sen . . .

The play would have been performed in a church porch or in an inn-yard and because the play requires only six actors the company could be highly mobile. Such troupes became enormously popular throughout Europe in the sixteenth century. Eventually the best of the English groups settled in London and built the original open-air theatres. The first appeared in 1576, when Shakespeare would have been twelve years old. The players in *Mankind* were the ancestors of the King's Men and the Elizabethan dramatic tradition. Hamlet's excitement at the news that the Players are coming to Elsinore gives us some idea of the enthusiasm with which such troupes were greeted.

Mankind tells the story of a hard-working peasant. Under the spell of the devil Titivillus and the Seven Deadly Sins, Mankind is made to swear an oath of loyalty to Satan. Then Titivillus, the forerunner of the Iago-character in Shakespeare, prepares to ensnare Mankind in a speech loaded with malice.

TITIVILLUS   Goo your wey, a dev[i]ll wey, go yowr wey all!
                  I blisse yow with my lifte honde – foull yow befall!
                  A[nd] bringe yowr avantage into this place.
                  [*Exeunt. Manet Titivillus.*]
                  To speke with Mankinde I will tary here this tide,
                  Ande assay his goode purpose for to sett aside.
                  The goode man Mercy shall no lenger be his g[u]ide.

In the end, having been saved from suicide, the deadliest sin of all, the peasant repents and is forgiven. The language in *Mankind* – original, funny, and high-spirited – is thoroughly and recognizably English. (One could, in fact, imagine having a conversation with "Mankind" himself in the street.) It has emerged from the shadow of Latin and French and exploits the versatility it has acquired during the last thousand years. The stage is now set for the English of William Shakespeare and the Elizabethans.

36 Strolling players. By Caxton's time, English was becoming recognizable to modern ears.

37 The only painting with any claim to represent a likeness of the poet, complete with earring.

3
A MUSE OF FIRE

About 150 years after the death of Elizabeth I, Samuel Johnson looked back with some pride on the achievements of her reign:

> From the authors which rose in the time of *Elizabeth*, a speech might be formed adequate to all purposes of use and elegance. If the language of theology were extracted from *Hooker* and the translation of the Bible; the terms of natural knowledge from *Bacon*; the phrases of policy, war, and navigation from *Ralegh*; the dialect of poetry and fiction from *Spenser* and *Sidney*; and the diction of common life from *Shakespeare*, few ideas would be lost to mankind, for want of *English* words in which they might be expressed.

The achievements of these astonishing years – an age of national crisis, seafaring adventure and artistic splendour – are inescapably glorious. Elizabeth I came to the throne in 1558 at the age of twenty-five. William Shakespeare, her most famous subject, was born six years later in 1564. Her successor, James I, who gave his name to another English masterpiece, the Authorized Version of the Bible, died in 1625. During their reigns, about seventy years, the English language achieved a richness and vitality of expression that even contemporaries marvelled at.

But there is an irony to the commonplace that this was the golden age of the English language. For contemporaries, their native tongue was barely ready, after centuries of Latin and French, for serious literary and scholarly purposes. England was a small nation, just beginning to flex its international muscles. Its spokesmen, anxious to stake out a European reputation for its writers as well as its admirals and statesmen, tended to stray into pardonable hyperbole. Richard Carew, author of *An Epistle on the Excellency of the English Tongue*, compared Shakespeare to Catullus and Marlowe to Ovid. Sir Philip Sidney himself, a true Elizabethan, at once a poet, courtier and soldier, observed: "But for the uttering sweetly and properly the conceite of the minde . . . which is the ende of thought . . . English hath it equally with any other tongue in the world."

The reasons for this great surge in the English language and its literature lie in the unprecedented rate of change experienced by European society during these years. This

38 Francis Bacon preferred Latin to English which, he wrote, will ''play the bankrupts with books''.

39 Thomas More's new words included *absurdity*, *contradictory*, *exaggerate*, *indifference*, *monopoly* and *paradox*.

40 The oldest known representation of a printing press, published in Paris in 1507.

41 According to one champion of the English language, ''this present period [is] the verie height thereof.''

short period, the lifespan of one man, saw the confluence of three immensely influential historical developments: the Renaissance, the Reformation and the emergence of England as a maritime power.

"THE NEW WORLD OF ENGLISH WORDS"

The Renaissance had different effects in every European country. In England, there had occurred, in the years since Caxton set up his printing press at Westminster, a communications revolution, probably not matched until the present age of word processors and videos. The printing press transformed society. Before 1500 the total number of books printed throughout Europe was about 35,000, most of them in Latin. Between 1500 and 1640, in England alone, some 20,000 items in English were printed, ranging from pamphlets and broadsheets to folios and Bibles. The result was to accelerate the education of the rising middle class. Some estimates suggest that by 1600 nearly half the population had some kind of minimal literacy, at least in the cities and towns. The economics of the book trade also encouraged the spread of the vernacular. Outside the universities, people preferred to read books in English rather than in Latin or Greek, and printers naturally tried to satisfy their customers' demand.

Gradually, the sheer popularity of English began to tell. In 1531 Sir Thomas Elyot, statesman and scholar, published *The Book Named the Governour*, perhaps the first book on education printed in English. He had plenty of new words to play with – *education* and *dedicate*, for example. Elyot himself was uneasy about some of his usages. He apologized for introducing the word *maturity*, which he admitted was "strange and dark" (obscure), but which, as he put it, would soon be "facile to understande as other wordes late commen out of Italy and Fraunce". Besides, such borrowings from Latin were part of "the necessary augmentation of our language".

English could not escape the influence of the classics. The revival of learning and the study of classical models produced a new breed of scholar-writers from Thomas More to Francis Bacon, who, turning their backs on the dog-Latin of the Middle Ages, devoted themselves to the cultivation of style, often disdaining what they saw as the awkwardness of the mother tongue. When Tudor men of letters wrote in English, they embellished their prose with Latinate words. Latin, after all, was still the universal medium of the written word, and Bacon, like many of his contemporaries, actually preferred to write in Latin, which he considered the proper medium of scholarship. The ransacked classical past provided new words like *agile*, *capsule* and *habitual* (from Latin), and *catastrophe*, *lexicon* and *thermometer* (from Greek).

Many of these borrowings did not simply have a literary origin. The Renaissance was also a scientific revolution and English had to accommodate these changes. New discoveries and new inventions needed new descriptions, creating words like *atmosphere*, *pneumonia* and *skeleton*. Galileo was redefining the natural world: an *encyclopaedia* would now be needed to *explain* the idea of *gravity*. Vesalius had transformed man's understanding of the human

42 Elizabeth I, who reigned for forty-five years, was an enthusiastic patron of plays and pageants.

43 Sir Walter Ralegh spelt his name many ways, including "Rauley", a clue to its pronunciation.

44/45 John White was a gifted amateur painter whose drawings suggest the profound influence of the native American Indian culture on the place-names and the vocabulary of the first English settlement in the New World.

anatomy : *excrement*, *strenuous* and *excrescence* are all new words from these years. In physics, the work of scientists like William Gilbert was introducing words such as *paradox*, *external* and *chronology*. (Recourse to Latin and Greek for such purposes continues in the late twentieth century, for example in *video*, *television*, and *synthesizer*.)

By no means all of these new words were Latin or Greek in origin. There were French borrowings like *bigot* and *detail*; Italian architectural borrowings like *cupola*, *portico* and *stucco*; bellicose Spanish words (reflecting contemporary conflicts) like *desperado* and *embargo*; nautical words from the Low Countries like *smuggle* (*smuggeler*) and *reef* (*rif*). In these times sailors were the messengers of language. Part of their vocabulary would have been "Low Dutch" words like *fokkinge*, *kunte*, *krappe* (probably derived from Latin) and *bugger* (originally a Dutch borrowing from the French), words that are sometimes inaccurately said to be "Anglo-Saxon". From the poetry of Spenser (who invented *braggadocio* in *The Faerie Queen*) to the slang of the sailors who defeated the Armada, there was, throughout English society, a new urge to use English to communicate.

The importance of the Renaissance to the English language was that it added between 10,000 and 12,000 new words to the lexicon. In 1658, looking back on the myriad coinings of the previous century, Milton's nephew, Edward Philips, summarized the experience in the title of his glossary, "The New World of English Words".

"ENGLISHE MATTER IN THE ENGLISCHE TONGUE"

In contrast to the internationalism of the worlds of scholarship and commerce, Tudor politics – the Reformation, and the growth of national feeling – emphasized the splendid isolation of Shakespeare's "sceptr'd isle". Throughout the Tudor century, England fought with her continental neighbours. Henry VIII broke with Rome. Elizabeth I was threatened by the superpowers of the age, France and Spain. The spirit of the Armada – a small island beating off a huge invasion fleet – was matched by an independent-minded queen. "I thank God", she told her Parliament, "I am endowed with such qualities that if I were turned out of the realm in my petticoat, I were able to live in any place in Christendom."

The fortunes of the English language during these years echoed the battles between England and Europe. Many were as proud of their mother tongue in all its vernacular plainness as they were of defying the pope or defeating the Spanish. There were some who wanted to stem the flood of foreign borrowings. Thomas Chaloner, for instance, is often quoted for his attack on writers who "serche . . . out of some rotten Pamphlet foure or fyve disused woords of antiquitee, therewith to darken the sence unto the reader". Critics had a phrase for these new "woords of antiquitee", calling them *inkhorn terms* – and much ink was spilt arguing their merits for the language.

The battle between "inkhorn terms" and "plainnesse", raging throughout the middle years of the century, even became a popular issue in the playhouses. Ben Jonson has a scene in which the poet Marston is purged of Latinate borrowings like *retrograde*, *reciprocal*, *defunct* and *inflate*, words that are now everyday currency. His rival, Shakespeare, summarized the debate with a typically striking phrase. When Berowne finally declares his love for Rosaline in *Love's Labour's Lost* he announces that he will shun "taffeta phrases, silken terms precise". Instead

> *. . . my wooing mind shall be express'd*
> *In russet yeas and honest kersey noes.*

The upshot of these twin traditions, native and foreign, was the emergence of a language, to quote Logan Pearsall Smith, "of unsurpassed richness and beauty, which, however, defies all the rules". Almost any word could be used in almost any part of speech. Adverbs could be used for verbs, nouns for adjectives; nouns and adjectives could take the place of verbs and adverbs. In Elizabethan English you could *happy* your friend, *malice* or *foot* your enemy, or *fall* an axe on his neck. A *he* is used for a man and a *she* for a woman, along with many usages that would now be regarded as breaking the normal rules of English. And no Elizabethan wrote with greater boldness than Shakespeare. He could *out-Herod Herod*, he could *uncle me no uncle*, he used expressions like *how she might tongue me*, and he wrote that *Lord Angelo dukes it well in his absence*.

These innovations and inventions were partly coined to meet a need: and partly they exhibited the kind of cultural courage we associate with the Elizabethans. As Ben Jonson remarked in his *Discoveries*, "A man coins not a new word without some peril and less fruit; for if it happen to be received, the praise is but moderate; if refused, the scorn is assured."

THE BRAVE NEW WORLD

One man, a quintessential Elizabethan, a jack of all trades, who was not afraid of scorn and not afraid to take risks, was Sir Walter Ralegh. He, and scholar-explorers like Richard Hakluyt, and adventurers like Francis Drake, travelled far beyond the bounds of Christendom, circumnavigating the globe, plundering the Caribbean, and exploring what they called "the New World", the Americas. It was in these years that England first moved into that pivotal position between Europe and North America that she was to occupy so prosperously for three hundred years.

Ralegh was a West Countryman, born and brought up in the county of Devon. The antiquary and gossip John Aubrey wrote that "Notwithstanding his so great Mastership in Style and his conversation with the learnedst and politest persons, yet he spake broad Devonshire to his dying day." The Queen is said to have called him "Water", teasing his accent, but he was proud of his Devon speech, which demonstrated his roots and connections. For ten years, until he married one of her ladies-in-waiting, Ralegh was the Queen's special favourite. To his rivals he was maddeningly versatile. He sacked Cadiz, he wrote poetry, flattering his Queen as "Cynthia, Lady of the Sea", and he was above all a tireless entrepreneur and seagoing explorer. There was, of course, an element of rivalry with men like Drake and Hawkins in this, but Ralegh also had dreams of something more permanent than plunder. It was his guidance and inspiration that led to the first English-speaking communities in the New World.

The story of what was to become the first American settlement starts in the late 1570s when Sir Humphrey Gilbert, under charter from Elizabeth, claimed Newfoundland for England. Heading south, he was drowned in a storm with the famous last words "We are as neer to heaven by sea as by land." Ralegh, who was Gilbert's half-brother, took up the mission on his death. He chartered two ships to sail to the New World in 1584, where they made landfall on 13 July, on the coast of North Carolina, near a place soon to be called Roanoke Island. Richard Hakluyt's account conveys the explorers' excitement. It was an age when, it seems, no one could write a dull sentence. The land, Hakluyt noted, was:

> very sandie, and lowe towards the waters side, but so full of grapes [scuppernongs], as the very beating and surge of the Sea ouerflowed them, of which we founde such plentie, as well there, as in all places else, both on the sande, and on the greene soile on the hils, as in the plaines, as well on euery little shrubbe, as also climing towardes the toppes of the high Cedars, that I thinke in all the world the like aboundance is not to be founde: and myself having seene those parts of Europe that most abound, find such difference as were incredible to be written.

They admired the scene (unchanged to this day). Others, with an almost Conradian gesture of curiosity and confidence, fired a single shot, and, as Hakluyt wrote, "a flocke of Cranes (the most part white) arose . . . with such a crye redoubled by many Ecchoes, as if an armie of men had shouted all together". They met Algonquin Indians, whom they described as "gentle, loving and faithful". Then they came home, bringing with them two Indians, Manteo and Wanchese, to give Ralegh, who had remained in England, first-hand knowledge of the new possession which, in a typically flattering gesture, he named Virginia, after his Queen.

The next spring, Ralegh commissioned a second expedition, a colonizing mission this time. Accompanied by Manteo and Wanchese, some 168 adventurers, including the artist John White (who was to become first Governor of the colony) and Thomas Hariot, a scientist, returned to Roanoke. Hariot described what he found with the excitement of a man confronted by an exotic new landscape. The flora and fauna were in many respects completely unfamiliar. There was, for instance, a fruit we now know to be the persimmon that was "as red as cheries and very sweet: but whereas the cherie is sharpe sweet, they are lushious sweet". In such a situation, many new words had to be coined. There is no record of these, but we do have John White's drawings, a wonderfully naturalistic record of a continent "sitting for its portrait".

The wonder was short-lived. Relations with the Indians deteriorated rapidly, as food became scarce and the Englishmen raided the Indian fish-traps. By the summer of 1586, the two sides were in a state of open war. The now-besieged colonists had to beg a rescue from Sir Francis Drake, returning from a voyage of plunder in the Caribbean.

Undiscouraged by the failure of this first colony, Ralegh organized another, on an even grander scale, to establish "the Cittie of Ralegh in Virginea". Each man was granted 500 acres as an inducement to go. By July 1587 Governor White had established a base on Roanoke Island. A month later, White's daughter, Eleanor, married to Ananias Dare, gave birth to a girl, christened Virginia, the first child of English parentage to be born in the New World. There were few other joys. The Indians were hostile from the beginning. When they killed one of the colonists "wading in the water alone, almost naked, without any weapon saue onely a smal forked sticke, catching Crabs", the situation became desperate. White was prevailed upon by the other colonists to return to England for help, mainly food and supplies.

What took place after White's departure is a mystery. He was, as it happened, unable to return as quickly as he would have liked – it was now the year of the Armada, 1588 – and all ships were needed for the defence of the realm. Finally, after many delays and crises, White set sail in March 1590, about two-and-a-half years after he had left the Roanoke colony. Arriving on the coast of North Carolina, he and his men first anchored off Roanoke Island. They blew a trumpet and sang familiar English songs to the silent landscape. There was no answer. The next day they landed. All the houses had disappeared. A palisade had been built but there was no sign of any defenders, alive or dead. White found three letters, CRO, carved on a tree, but to this day their meaning remains a mystery.

The "Lost Colony" story exemplifies the adventurous, maritime side of the Elizabethans. It also shows that the settlement of the New World was extremely hazardous and difficult. In retrospect, that settlement, and the extension of the sway of the English language into a potentially huge arena, seems inevitable, obvious and natural. At the time, Ralegh – now out of favour with the crown – was forced into bluster and self-justification. Yet he continued to express his undying faith in an English empire overseas, remarking of the New World, in a letter to Sir Robert Cecil in 1602, that "I shall yet live to see it an English Nation". At the time that must have seemed to many observers the kind of vainglorious boasting for which Ralegh was well known.

THE BARD OF AVON

The English writer whose imagination and vocabulary matched the discoveries of the New World was the poet and dramatist William Shakespeare. It is impossible to quantify the relationship between a writer of genius and the development of a language; it is both simple and obvious and yet difficult to define. But suppose that Shakespeare had lived before the age of printing, or suppose his fellow actors had not been able to preserve his plays in book form. It is lucky for us that Shakespeare lived during the first flourishing of the popular presses: centuries later we can still appreciate the extent of his powers, his compassion, his knowledge of the human heart, and above all his genius for words. This privilege was denied to the earlier masters of the oral tradition. Seven years after his death, the first volume of his works – the First Folio – was published, and established the legend: "His mind and hand went together . . . wee have scarse received from him a blot in his paper."

Shakespeare put the vernacular to work and showed those who came after what could be done with it. He filled a universe with words. *Accommodation, assassination, dexterously, dislocate, indistinguishable, obscene, pedant, premeditated, reliance* and *submerged* are just a handful of the words that make their first appearance in the Folio. Shakespeare's impact on the patterns and stuff of everyday English speech has been memorably expressed by the English journalist Bernard Levin:

> If you cannot understand my argument, and declare "It's Greek to me", you are quoting Shakespeare; if you claim to be more sinned against than sinning, you are quoting Shakespeare; if you recall your salad days, you are quoting Shakespeare; if you act more in sorrow than in anger, if your wish is father to the thought, if your lost property has vanished into thin air, you are quoting Shakespeare; if you have ever refused to budge an inch or suffered from green-eyed jealousy, if you have played fast and loose, if you have been tongue-tied, a tower of strength, hoodwinked or in a pickle, if you have knitted your brows, made a virtue of necessity, insisted on fair play, slept not one wink, stood on ceremony, danced attendance (on your lord and master), laughed yourself into stitches, had short shrift, cold comfort or too much of a good thing, if you have seen better days or lived in a fool's paradise – why, be that as it may, the more fool you, for it is a foregone conclusion that you are (as good luck would have it) quoting Shakespeare; if you think it is early days and clear out bag and baggage, if you think it is high time and that that is the long and short of it, if you believe that the game is up and that truth will out even if it involves your own flesh and blood, if you lie low till the crack of doom because you

46 Montacute House, built in the shape of an E, is a fitting symbol of the Elizabethan Renaissance.

suspect foul play, if you have your teeth set on edge (at one fell swoop) without rhyme or reason, then – to give the devil his due – if the truth were known (for surely you have a tongue in your head) you are quoting Shakespeare; even if you bid me good riddance and send me packing, if you wish I was dead as a door-nail, if you think I am an eyesore, a laughing stock, the devil incarnate, a stony-hearted villain, bloody-minded or a blinking idiot, then – by Jove! O Lord! Tut, tut! for goodness' sake! what the dickens! but me no buts – it is all one to me, for you are quoting Shakespeare.

The facts of Shakespeare's life are scarce, so meagre indeed that the eighteenth-century scholar George Steevens wrote, "All that is known with any degree of certainty concerning Shakespeare is that he was born in Stratford-upon-Avon, married and had children there, went to London where he commenced actor and wrote poems and plays, returned to Stratford, made his will, died, and was buried."

More is known now, but not much more. In the end, in spite of a mountain of scholarship, Shakespeare the man escapes us. Of many epitaphs, in many succeeding decades, none competes with the words of his own friend, Ben Jonson:

> I loved the man, and do honour his memory (on this side Idolatry) as much as any. He was (indeed) honest, and of an open and free nature: had an excellent *Phantsie*; brave notions, and gentle expressions: wherein he flowed with that facility, that sometime it was necessary he should be stopped: . . . His wit was in his own power; would the rule of it had been so too. . . . There was ever more in him to be praised than to be pardoned.

This has not stopped biographers, critics and historians creating a mountain of speculation. Why? The answer is that perhaps more than to any writer who has ever lived, the English-speaking world looks back to Shakespeare as its greatest writer, with the universality of the great. Ralph Waldo Emerson wrote:

> What point of morals, of manners, of economy, of philosophy, of religion, of taste, of our conduct of life, has he not settled? What mystery has he not signified his knowledge of? What office, or function, or district of man's work, has he not remembered? What maiden has not found him finer than her delicacy? What sage has he not outseen?

Shakespeare is universal in his appeal and sympathy not least because he wrote in a language that has become global. It is impossible, finally, to estimate his importance for the English language except to say that he is – as Dante is for the Italians or Goethe is for the Germans – an icon for speakers of his language throughout the world.

He was a country boy, born in Stratford, in the heart of Warwickshire, then a town of some 1500 inhabitants. His poetry is full of his delight in the English countryside, and many of his plays are set in or near a wood, like the neighbouring Forest of Arden. When Oberon, in *A*

Midsummer Night's Dream, plots his revenge on Titania, he tells Puck where he will find her in words that only a country boy could have written:

> *I know a bank whereon the wild thyme blows.*
> *Where oxlips and the nodding violet grows,*
> *Quite over-canopied with luscious woodbine,*
> *With sweet musk-roses, and with eglantine . . .*

And when Puck shortly afterwards reports on the transformation of Bottom, we sense that Shakespeare knows what he is talking about:

> *As wild geese that the creeping fowler eye,*
> *Or russet-pated choughs, many in sort,*
> *Rising and cawing at the gun's report,*
> *Sever themselves, and madly sweep the sky ;*

Even Shakespeare's vocabulary betrays his Warwickshire roots. In his work we find words like *ballow*, a North-Midlands word for cudgel; *batlet*, a local term, used until recently, for the bat to beat clothes in the wash; *gallow*, meaning to frighten; *geck*, a word for a fool, which was also used by George Eliot in *Adam Bede*; *honey-stalks*, a regional word for the stalks of clover flowers; *mobled* for muffled; *pash*, meaning to smash; *potch*, to thrust; *tarre*, to provoke or incite; and *vails*, a Midlands term for perks or tips. And when, in *Macbeth*, Banquo is described as "blood-bolter'd" (having his hair matted with blood) it is easy to imagine that Shakespeare was remembering that in Warwickshire snow is said to *balter* on horses' feet. (All these usages, in passing, suggest that Sir Francis Bacon, an East Anglian, could not possibly have written the works of Shakespeare.)

Shakespeare himself would have spoken a kind of Midlands English. Stratford lay at the crossroads of the three great regional speech areas of England. To the south and west were the *r*-pronouncing counties of Somerset, Dorset, Devon and Cornwall. To the north were the counties of the old Danelaw feeding into London English grammatical forms like *tells* and *speaks*, instead of *telleth* and *speaketh*: Shakespeare could use either. And eastwards, towards London, was the English of the East Midlands, noticeable for the weakness of the *r* in words like *park* and *yard*. Despite the steady process of standardization in English speech, these regional variants have remained surprisingly persistent. If you want to hear something close to the sound of Shakespeare's English, you have only to return to Shakespeare country – Warwickshire, the Cotswolds and neighbouring Gloucestershire. Here the local people still use forms of English that have strong echoes of sixteenth-century speech.

It is sometimes claimed that you have to go to the Appalachian hills, or the Ozark Mountains, to hear Elizabethan English. Yet the English cider drinkers who gather every day in the village pub at Elmley Castle use many of the typical pronunciations of Shakespeare's time. One of the Elmley Castle drinkers describes his prescription for good health, "I shall have five pints this morning, I hope, and three pints of beer tonight, and a pint of cider with my supper. And then to bed. And I don't catch a cold ..." A word like "cider" becomes *zoider*. There is the strong *r* in words like *turrn* and *hearrd*. "Farmer" becomes *varmer*, "right", "life" and "time" become *roight, loife* and *toime*. "House" and "down" sound something like *hoos* and *doon*.

A few miles from Elmley Castle, Stratford itself lies in the Vale of Evesham on the river Avon. The land around the famous river is gently rolling, well wooded, heavily settled and farmed, with the characteristic black-and-white timber constructions of many old Tudor houses scattered through the landscape. Some of the bigger houses are handsomely made of brick, timber and stone, and some, like Charlecote House (where an apocryphal story reports that Shakespeare stole deer from a certain Sir Thomas Lucy) are built in the shape of an E, a symbol of the Elizabethan Renaissance.

Stratford, the place of Shakespeare's youth and old age, was about four days' ride from London, and it was in London, during the last years of the sixteenth century, when the old Queen was ailing on her throne, that the young actor-playwright quickly caused a sensation with his plays. His brilliant forerunner, the dramatist Christopher Marlowe, wrote magnificent poetry and high-flown speeches, but his work, inspired by his Cambridge education, is formal, almost ponderous, heard best in set-pieces. With Shakespeare, literature and popular culture meet centre stage. He writes about all classes of men and women in every conceivable situation, social and political. He has a great facility, which must have come from his experience as an actor, for headlining even his greatest, most "poetic" speeches. What Hamlet says "To be or not to be: that is the question" he has summarized in one line everything that follows. This is Shakespeare's mastery of what Samuel Johnson called "the diction of common life".

Little is known about Shakespeare's education, though it is clear he was trained in Classical and Renaissance rhetoric, but he was alive to every nuance of language. He knew both about "inkhorn terms" and about "plainnesse". He could write out of the Anglo-Saxon tradition, or the Anglo-Norman, or the Classical. After he has committed the murder of Duncan, Macbeth laments what he has done:

> *Will all great Neptune's ocean wash this blood*
> *Clean from my hand? No; this my hand will rather*
> *The multitudinous seas incarnadine,*
> *Making the green one red.*

His bloody hands, he is saying, will pollute the sea. But to express how the sea will be suffused with Duncan's blood, he repeats himself, first in a rolling Latinate phrase ("The multitudinous seas incarnadine"), and secondly in plain Anglo-Saxon, for the groundlings in the pit ("Making the green one red").

A word like *multitudinous* is a reminder that Shakespeare had one of the largest vocabularies of any English writer, some 30,000 words. (Estimates of an educated person's vocabulary today vary, but it is probably about half this, 15,000.) He was, to use his own

47 The first Folio was published in 1623 by John Heminge and Henry Condell. It omits *Pericles*.

48 Shakespeare married Anne Hathaway in 1582. Her "Cottage" – Hewland Farm – was her father's house.

phrase, "a man of fire-new words". Shakespeare loved to experiment with new words. *Allurement, armada, antipathy, critical, demonstrate, dire, emphasis, emulate, horrid, initiate, meditate, modest, prodigious, vast* – all these are new to English in the sixteenth century and they all appear in Shakespeare. It is arguable that without such encouragement – the imprimatur of genius – many of these words would not have survived.

Shakespeare had an extraordinary ability to spin off memorable combinations of words. Scores of phrases have entered the language and have become, in some cases, clichés. Just one play, *Hamlet*, is a treasure house of "quotable quotes":

> Frailty, thy name is woman!
> More in sorrow than anger
> The primrose path of dalliance
> Something is rotten in the state of Denmark
> The time is out of joint
> Brevity is the soul of wit
> More matter with less art
> Though this be madness, yet there is method in it
> The play's the thing
> To be or not to be: that is the question
> A king of shreds and patches
> I must be cruel, only to be kind
> Alas poor Yorick
> A hit, a very palpable hit
> The rest is silence

Many of Shakespeare's characters are acutely alert to the music of the English language. Some, like Theseus in *A Midsummer Night's Dream*, simply want to celebrate the poetry of language and give "to airy nothing/A local habitation and a name". Others, like Mowbray in

Richard II, cannot imagine a life in exile from it:

> *The language I have learnt these forty years,*
> *My native English, now I must forgo;*
> *And now my tongue's use is to me no more*
> *Than an unstringed viol or harp;*
> *Or like a cunning instrument cas'd up*
> *Or, being open, put into his hands*
> *That knows no touch to tune the harmony.*

Some, like Caliban, are highly conscious of the enslaving power of language:

> *You taught me language; and my profit on't*
> *Is, I know how to curse. The red plague rid you*
> *For learning me your language!*

Other Shakespearian characters, Hamlet for example, simply cannot stop "the rhapsody of words"; while those like Bottom, who are basically groundlings, are doomed to get it all delightfully wrong:

> The eye of man hath not heard, the ear of man hath not seen, man's hand is not able to taste, his tongue to conceive, nor his heart to report, what my dream was. I will get Peter Quince to write a ballet of this dream. It shall be call'd "Bottom's Dream", because it hath no bottom; and I will sing it in the latter end of our play, before the Duke. Peradventure, to make it the more gracious, I shall sing it at her death.

Love's Labour's Lost, The Merry Wives of Windsor, Henry V and *Hamlet* – these plays especially are shot through with a hypersensitivity to the richness of English, the mother tongue. At the same time, Shakespeare is acutely – almost poignantly – conscious of the gap between words and meaning, as Grandpré says in *Henry V*, "Description cannot suit itself in words to demonstrate the life of such a battle." At the beginning of the play, he uses the Chorus to apologize for the inadequacy of the theatre, and the feebleness of the playwright's pen:

> *O for a Muse of fire, that would ascend*
> *The brightest heaven of invention . . .*

Then, later in the same play, the Chorus almost answers his own regret with a speech of visual magic that again appeals to the audience's imagination:

> *Now entertain conjecture of a time*
> *When creeping murmur and the pouring dark*
> *Fills the wide vessel of the universe.*

Henry V is well known for the scenes with the three captains. Shakespeare obviously enjoys the varieties of English in his native land. Captain Fluellen, a Welshman, Captain

Jamy, a Scot, and the Irish Captain Macmorris discuss the strategy of the Battle of Agincourt, and we sense that Shakespeare revels in the caricature:

> IRISH: ... tish ill done! The work ish give over, the trompet sound the Retreat.
>
> WELSH: Captain Macmorris, I beseech you now, will you voutsafe me, look you, a few disputations with you, as partly touching or concerning the disciplines of war ...
>
> SCOTS: It sall be vary gud, gud feith, gud captens bath; and I sall quit you with gud leve, as I may pick occasion; that sall I, marry.

Certain kinds of speech which deviated from the emerging standard English of London and its environs were, even in Shakespeare's day, seen as rustic, boorish and often comic. In *King Lear*, for instance, Edgar, the well-born son of the Earl of Gloucester, is forced into a variety of rural character-sketches as "Poor Tom". Towards the end of the play, he defends his blind father from their enemy, Oswald, who challenges him as a "base peasant". Edgar's reply is given in what we might call Mummerset, using *v* for *f*, *z* for *s*, the rustic *chill* for "I will" and *chud* for "I would":

> Good gentleman, go your gait, and let poor volk pass. And 'chud ha' bin zwagger'd out of my life, 'twould not ha' bin zo long as 'tis by a vortnight. Nay, come not near th' old man; keep out, che vor' ye, or Ise try whither your costard or my ballow be the harder. Chill be plain with you.

When Shakespeare moved to London he would have encountered the speech of the court, which was sufficiently different from the speech of a country town like Stratford for a sharp-eared contemporary to note what he called a "true kynde of pronunciation", an early reference to Standard English. In 1589 the writer George Puttenham wrote that:

> There be gentlemen and others that speake, but specially write, as good Southerne as we of Middlesex or Surrey do, but not the common people of every shire, to whom the gentlemen, and also their learned clarkes, do for the most part condescend.

English class snobbery has a long pedigree. There is some controversy about what this "usuall speach of the Court" would have sounded like, but we have some good clues. For instance, before the age of fully-fledged dictionaries there were fewer spelling regulations. People tended to write as they spoke. So occasionally we find *clark* for "clerk" (as here), *coffe* for "cough" and *varmint* for "vermin". Furthermore, Shakespeare's own love of word-play gives away another set of clues when we find him punning *raising* with *reason*, a word which was then, presumably, much closer to its French original, *raison*. Similarly, Lafeu and the Clown have an exchange of puns in *All's Well That Ends Well*, based on the similarity in pronunciation of *grace* and *grass*. Shakespeare (like Alexander Pope, one hundred years later) would rhyme *tea* with *tay*, and *sea* with *say*. There is probably some truth in the assertion that Elizabethan English would have sounded, to twentieth-century ears, a mixture of West Country and Irish. This was the English that was soon to be taken, in ship after ship, across the Atlantic to the New World.

THE FIRST AMERICANS

London was the focus of all this excitement. Court, Capital and City, it was also the island's greatest port, buzzing with yarns and fables about the New World and its riches. In 1605, inspired by such dreams, two companies, chartered by rival merchants, set out from London and Plymouth. Ralegh, out of favour with the new king, James I, was not involved, but there was a continuity with his earlier expedition. Richard Hakluyt was among the leading lights in the London company. And among the leaders of the Plymouth group were Ralegh Gilbert and his brother John, sons of Walter Ralegh's half-brother, Sir Humphrey Gilbert.

The pioneers were lucky. In 1606, the year in which Shakespeare wrote *Antony and Cleopatra*, three ships financed by the London company set sail on the southern route past the Azores and the Canary Islands. They cruised in the West Indies, and then headed north, intending to settle somewhere north of the Spanish in Florida and south of the French in Canada. In April 1607, they sailed into Chesapeake Bay, then – as now – a vast, shallow tidal estuary dotted with flat, scrubby islands, and teeming with fish, crab and oysters. After about a month they reached the James River and moored in six fathoms off a wooded island which they named after their new king – Jamestown.

This time the English language took root in the New World. Unlike the unfortunate settlers in Roanoke, the men of Jamestown survived, partly thanks to the leadership and determination of Captain John Smith, who pronounced the stark but simple truth that "He that will not work neither shall he eat." In due course – but not until only 38 of the original 105 who had landed were left – they were joined by more colonists.

The processes of language change are often mysterious, but strangely enough, there is still – here and there – some tantalizing, fragmentary evidence of the lost voices of the early Americans. In the Eastern United States today there is nowhere stranger, or more isolated, than the islands of the Chesapeake Bay, "the most valuable and vulnerable estuary in the world", according to one marine biologist. Tangier Island, one of the largest, is a short ride by ferry or light plane from mainland Crisfield, one of the centres for a local industry that supplies one quarter of America's oysters. It is tiny and very flat: barely three miles long, one mile wide and five feet above sea level at its highest elevation. Graves have heavy lids to prevent the corpses from floating away when the island floods. It has two churches, a guest house for summer tourists, a school, a store-café called Nice's where the local teenagers play electronic games and eat soft-shell crab sandwiches. It is very quiet. The main street is a gritty gravel path, down which the Tangierines (as they are called) walk or bicycle. The island has no cars. Arrive during the morning and it can seem almost deserted. All the men are out in the Bay catching crabs.

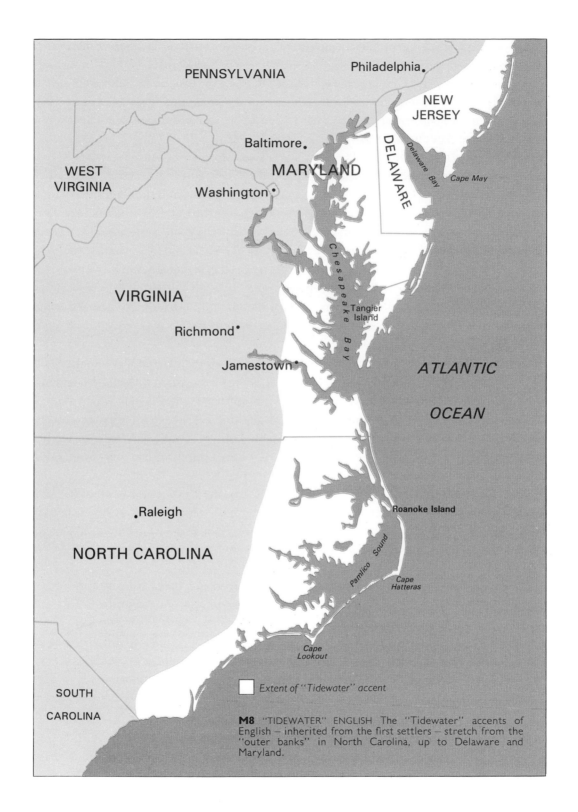

PENNSYLVANIA

Philadelphia

NEW
JERSEY

Baltimore

MARYLAND

DELAWARE

Delaware Bay

Cape May

WEST
VIRGINIA

Washington

VIRGINIA

Chesapeake Bay

Tangier
Island

ATLANTIC

Richmond

OCEAN

Jamestown

Raleigh

Roanoke Island

NORTH CAROLINA

Pamlico Sound

Cape
Hatteras

Cape
Lookout

SOUTH

CAROLINA

Extent of "Tidewater" accent

M8 "TIDEWATER" ENGLISH The "Tidewater" accents of English — inherited from the first settlers — stretch from the "outer banks" in North Carolina, up to Delaware and Maryland.

The fishermen call themselves "watermen". The word has a chequered history. In Elizabethan times, the word mainly denoted river-borne taxi-drivers "who [ply] for hire on a river". It took root in the Chesapeake Bay, mainly because the geography demanded a lot of water-transport. The comment of a local crab captain shows a typical use of the word: "My father raised me a waterman and it's all what I know how to do . . . Follow the water one year same as the next. Ain't no sense in it, but I do it just the same."

The watermen have a hard life. Their day starts about three in the morning when the men start to gather in Ray's café. There they gossip, drink Coca-Cola, eat Ray's toast, and wait for each crew to assemble. It is usually still dark when they set out into the Bay, the port and starboard lights of their long white crab boats winking over the water. By the time the dawn has broken the wharves are empty, and will remain so until the boats come back, in the early afternoon or evening, as soon as they have their quota of *jimmies* and *sooks*, mature male and female crabs. Listening to the Tangier Island watermen chatting together in Ray's café or on the boats, many English listeners could imagine they were in Devon or Cornwall. Their pattern of speech has many characteristic West Country intonations. As one fisherman remarked, "Our voice, our language, hasn't changed since people first moved to Tangier Island, or so some people have told us . . ."

The Tangierines – approximately 800 residents – say that their island was first settled in 1686 by a certain John Crockett, a Cornishman. There are no records of this, but the evidence of the Tangier Island speech is overwhelming. To English ears, they sound West Country. Most striking of all "sink" is pronounced *zink*. *Mary* and *merry* have a similar pronunciation, though this is common to much of the tidewater district. "Paul" and "ball" sound like *pull* and *bull*. For "creek" they will say *crik*. And they have a special local vocabulary: *spider* for "frying-pan", *bateau* for "skiff" and *curtains* for "blinds".

Apart from their geographical isolation, one of the reasons for the persistence of the local speech pattern is that the islanders are tightly knit. The tombs in the graveyards have recurring names: Crockett, Pruitt, Parkes, Dize, Shores. One former inhabitant of Tangier Island is David Shores, who has made a thorough study of his people's speech. He writes:

> Tangiermen are painfully aware that the way they talk is different – even bad, as they say – from the speech of the surrounding areas and seem to be ashamed of their speech in front of strangers. In speaking with them, they consciously distort a feature or two, those that they feel are the most conspicuous to others, toward that of the standard, an act for which they teasingly accuse each other, either at the time or later, of "putting on airs" or "talking proper". They are, of course, essentially single-style speakers. They do waver, however, when they are on guard. Visitors, that is, the summer tourists who stay only two or three hours, often go away amused by the strange speech they hear.

Tangier is part of the state of Virginia, but its English shares many characteristics with the most isolated communities of the Atlantic seaboard. Together with the other Piedmont/

Tidewater districts, and the "hoi toiders" or "bankers" of Okrakoke/Roanoke, North Carolina, it forms one of the most vivid parts of the fossilized English language on the eastern seaboard of the United States. The variety of English spoken on Tangier is not threatened with extinction. The speech of the young people is as strong and distinctive as their grandparents'. It will surely last into the twenty-first century.

Two years after the Jamestown landing, another ship, the *Sea Venture*, on its way to supply the first Virginians, was wrecked on an island over five hundred miles due east of Charleston, South Carolina. This was the spot known to Sir Walter Ralegh as "a hellish sea for thunder, lightning and storms", to Shakespeare, whose *Tempest* was inspired by the incident, as "the vex'd Bermoothes", and to the twentieth century as the apex of the "Bermuda triangle". Three survivors from the wreck of the *Sea Venture* were joined three years later, in 1612, by a shipload of settlers who set about establishing Bermuda, the second English colony in the New World. In 1648 a breakaway group of religious dissenters sailed south from Bermuda to the Bahamas, further extending the spread of English. Even today there are many similarities between the English spoken on all these islands.

There was always a free-booting, profiteering side to these Virginian expeditions, much in keeping with the spirit of the age. But only a few years after the English language came to the New World, quite a different emigration, notably from London and East Anglia, began to take place in Massachusetts to the north, an emigration that was to temper the fire of the southerners with the cold rigour of the Puritan mind and its inflexible ideology.

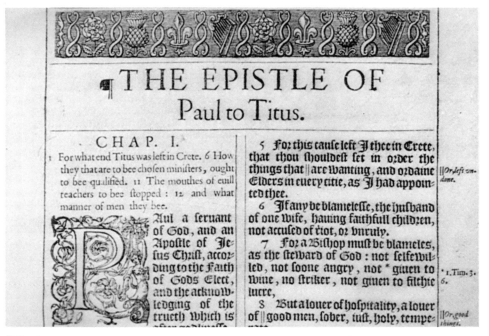

49 The First Edition of the King James Bible, 1611, probably the single most influential book ever published in the English language. Two issues of it were made in 1611, known respectively as the "He Bible" and the "She Bible" thanks to a misprint in Ruth iii.15.

THE AUTHORIZED VERSION

Elizabeth I, the queen to whom so many of these adventures were dedicated, died in 1603. In a surprisingly peaceful transfer of power, James VI of Scotland became James I of England. It was an event of momentous significance. The Elizabethans had initiated a renaissance in spoken and written English. Under the Jacobeans this achievement began to be standardized and disseminated throughout the British Isles, and spread overseas to the New World as the language of a unified nation. James became, at a stroke, the most powerful Protestant king in Europe, and he adopted, for the purposes of foreign policy, the title "Great Britain". The language of this enlarged state was now poised to achieve international recognition. Of all the ways in which James left his mark on the English language, none was to match the influence of the new translation of the Bible ordered in the second year of his reign.

In January 1604 James presided over a special conference at Hampton Court. This was a gathering of bishops and Puritan divines to discuss and reconcile religious differences. Out of their deliberations emerged a plan which would provide the English language with one of its great Renaissance masterpieces, a work whose impact on the history of English prose has been as fundamental as Shakespeare's: the Authorized Version of the Bible.

To understand the story of the King James Bible, we have to take a brief look at the earlier history of the Bible in English. The story is one of martyrdom and repression. It starts with John Wyclif's translation of the scriptures in the 1380s, for which he was denounced as a heretic. The orthodox view was that to make the Bible accessible to the common people would threaten the authority of the Church, and lead the people to question its teaching. A scandalized contemporary wrote: "This Master John Wyclif translated from Latin into English – the Angle not the angel speech – and so the pearl of the Gospel is scattered abroad and trodden underfoot by swine." This sentiment was echoed by the seventeenth-century philosopher Thomas Hobbes who sourly observed: "After the Bible was translated into English every man, nay, every boy and wench that could read English, thought they spoke with God Almighty and understood what he said." So Wyclif and his dissident Lollard movement were rigorously suppressed. Similarly when William Tyndale published his translation of the New Testament from the Greek in 1525, he entered into a conflict with Church and State that eventually brought him to the stake. Translating and publishing God's word in the language of the people was as revolutionary an act as, in the eighteenth century, advancing the proposition that states should be ruled by democracy not kings.

In 1534, the English Reformation reached a turning-point when Henry VIII defied the Pope and broke with the Roman Church. The following year, Coverdale, Tyndale's disciple, published his vernacular translation of the Bible. In retrospect, these were also turning-points in the story of the English language. Several Bibles now began to appear in English. Between 1535 and 1568 no less than five major version were published – Matthew's, Taverner's, Cranmer's (the "Great Bible"), the Geneva, and the Bishops' Bible. All were immediate bestsellers, as Bibles are to this day, and were probably the most widely read texts of the sixteenth century, with an enormous influence on the spread of English.

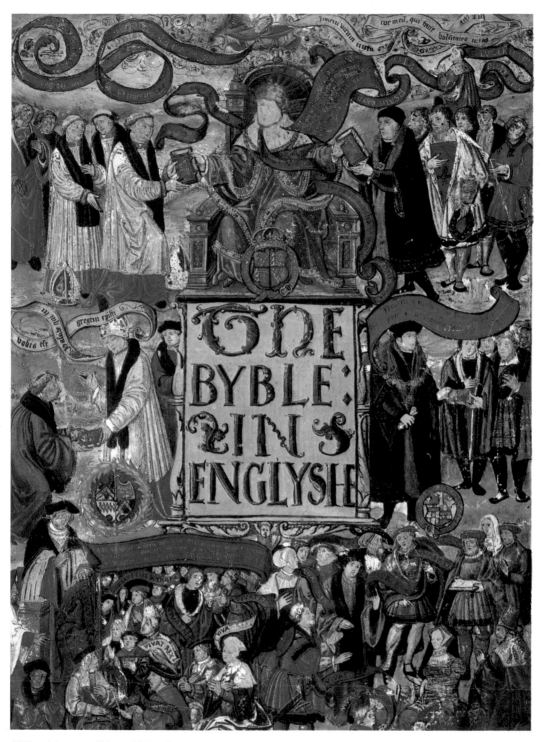

50 The title page of Henry VIII's "Great Bible", also known as "Cranmer's Bible", published in 1539.

Around the time that the last of these early Bibles, the Bishops' Bible of 1568, was published, a certain John Bois – whose mature years were dedicated to translating the Authorized Version – was just starting his education, learning Hebrew and Ancient Greek. Bois was born in 1560, just four years before William Shakespeare, and it is said that under his father's eye he had read the entire Bible in Hebrew by the time he was six years old. At fourteen he became a classics scholar at St John's College, Cambridge, passed through his examinations at record speed, and soon became a Fellow of the College.

John Bois was the sort of scholar people like to gossip about. It was said that he would rise at four in the morning to give classes in Greek, and would work until eight o'clock at night, always reading standing up. When his Fellowship expired he was offered a rectorship at Boxworth, a scattered hamlet a few miles to the north of Cambridge, on condition that he married the deceased rector's daughter. This he did, and moved out into the Fens, though he would often ride his horse into Cambridge to teach, reading a book as he went.

In 1604 Bois was forty-four, living quietly in Boxworth, a man with a brilliant scholarly reputation. At the Hampton Court Conference, Dr John Reynolds, President of Corpus Christi College, Oxford, proposed a definitive translation of the Bible to ameliorate the friction between the Anglicans and the Puritans. James I, the *rex pacificus*, gladly assented to the idea of "one uniforme translation", though he confessed he doubted whether he would "see a Bible well translated in English".

Progress was rapid. By June, it had been settled that there should be six groups of translators, two in Westminster, two in Oxford and two in Cambridge, each made up of at least eight scholars. It was perfectly natural that the brilliant John Bois should be recruited for one of the Cambridge committees. He was put in charge of translating the Apocrypha from the Greek. As it turned out, his was a level of scholarship that made him indispensable to more than one committee. Surprisingly, perhaps, for an age that was so familiar with Latin and Greek, the six committees were instructed to base their Authorized Version upon the previous *English* versions, translating afresh, but also comparing their work with the other vernacular Bibles, from Tyndale to Parker.

After six years' hard work, the six committees delivered their efforts to London for a final review. Each of the three scholarly centres provided two scholars to form the review committee. From Cambridge they sent John Bois and his old tutor, Dr Anthony Downes. For nearly nine months in 1610, these six scholars worked together on the final draft of the Authorized Version, refining and revising. They had a special brief from the Commissioners: they were to go through the text, re-working it so that it would not only read better but *sound* better, a quality for which it became famous throughout the English-speaking world. The translators obviously relished this priority. In their preface "To the Reader" they remarked, "Why should we be in bondage to them (words and syllables) if we may be free, use one precisely when we may use another no less fit, as commodiously?" It's an interesting reflection on the state of the language that the poetry of the Authorized Version came not from a single writer but a committee.

During these crucial nine months, before the publication of the Authorized Version in 1611, John Bois kept a diary. In the words of his biographer, "he, and he only tooke notes of their proceedings, which he diligently kept to his dying day". Miraculously, these notes survive in a contemporary copy and from them we can see how the six translators on the final committee honed the Authorized Version to perfection. In the First Epistle General of Peter, chapter two, verse three, there is a passage in which the key word is *pleasant*. Bois had several choices from previous versions:

> *Tyndale*: Yf so be that ye have tasted how pleasaunt the Lorde is . . .
> *Great Bible*: If so be that ye have tasted, how gracious the Lorde is . . .
> *Geneva Bible*: If so be that ye have tasted how bountifull the Lord (is).
> *Bishops' Bible*: If so be that ye have tasted how gractious the Lord is . . .
> *Rheims Bible*: . . . if yet you have tasted that our Lord is sweete.
> *Authorized Version*: . . . if so be ye have tasted that the Lord *is* gracious . . .
> *Bois's note*: or, how gracious the Lord is. (A variant proposed by another committee member.)

Not only does he make the right choice with *gracious*, he also makes the sentence sing.

If we compare the Authorized Version with Henry VIII's "Great Bible", the point is made even more forcefully. In the "Great Bible", in chapter 12 of Ecclesiastes, the preacher says:

> Or ever the silver lace be taken away, or the gold band be broke, or the pot broke at the well and the wheel upon the cistern, then shall the dust be turned again unto earth from whence it came, and the spirit shall return to God which gave it. All is but vanity saith the preacher, all is but plain vanity.

In the King James Version this becomes both clearer and more poetic:

> Or ever the silver cord be loosed, or the golden bowl be broken, or the pitcher be broken at the fountain, or the wheel broken at the cistern: Then shall the dust return to the earth as it was: and the spirit shall return unto God who gave it. Vanity of vanities, saith the preacher; all is vanity.

The King James Bible was published in the year Shakespeare began work on his last play, *The Tempest*. Both the play and the Bible are masterpieces of English, but there is one crucial difference between them. Whereas Shakespeare ransacked the lexicon, the King James Bible employs a bare 8000 words – God's teaching in homely English for everyman. From that day to this, the Shakespearian cornucopia and the biblical iron rations represent, as it were, the North and South Poles of the language, reference points for writers and speakers throughout the world, from the Shakespearian splendour of a Joyce or a Dickens to the biblical rigour of a Bunyan, or a Hemingway.

The King James Bible is still revered throughout the world. Bois is now almost forgotten. In 1628 the Bishop of Ely offered him a canonry at the cathedral, where he remained for the rest of his days while his country drifted slowly into civil war. He was unusually healthy and

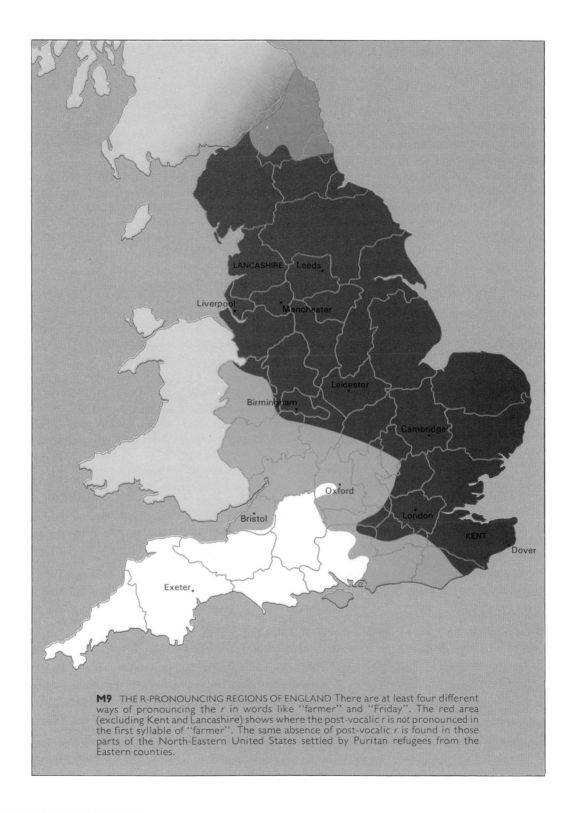

M9 THE R-PRONOUNCING REGIONS OF ENGLAND There are at least four different ways of pronouncing the *r* in words like "farmer" and "Friday". The red area (excluding Kent and Lancashire) shows where the post-vocalic *r* is *not* pronounced in the first syllable of "farmer". The same absence of post-vocalic *r* is found in those parts of the North-Eastern United States settled by Puritan refugees from the Eastern counties.

outlived a son, whose memorial plaque can still be seen in Ely Cathedral on one of the vast Norman columns in the nave. His biographer records that "after meat, he was careful, almost to curiosity, in picking and rubbing his teeth; esteeming that a special preservative of health. By which means he carried to his grave almost an Hebrew alphabet of teeth." He was buried in the cathedral on 6 February 1643.

The Lady Chapel of Ely is a superb example of the most ornate fourteenth-century church architecture and was richly decorated with stone carvings of saints and holy figures. But in 1539 every stone face, and there were literally hundreds, in the chapel was smashed by religious zealots. It was one of the earliest acts of defiance of the established church. By the turn of the century, this movement had developed into a new, revolutionary philosophy – Puritanism.

EAST ANGLIA AND THE PURITANS

The heartland of Puritanism was East Anglia. Oliver Cromwell himself had a small estate near Huntingdon; his New Model Army was raised, trained and financed in the East Anglian Fens; the university at Cambridge was as Puritan as Oxford was later to be Royalist. About two thirds of the early settlers in Massachusetts Bay came from the eastern counties.

51 James I spoke and wrote broad Scots, but his policy was to unite his two kingdoms with English.

52 Thomas Cranmer supervised the preparation of the *Book of Common Prayer*.

Throughout the seventeenth century, the villages and towns of these counties, from Lincolnshire in the north, to Essex in the south, and Bedfordshire and Huntingdonshire in the west, were to supply the New World with a ready stream of immigrants, country people with country skills who were already well adapted for the hard life of the pioneer. The speech-features of East Anglia that were transplanted to the place the Pilgrim Fathers named New England still linger in the rural parts of counties like Norfolk and Suffolk. Older people, especially, will say *noo* for "new", and when they say *bar*, *storm* or *yard*, the *r* is not sounded – quite different from Walter Ralegh's West Country burr.

The men and women from the middle and lower orders of East Anglia's towns and villages, who, encouraged by upper-class "promoters", crossed the Atlantic "to better themselves" were often Puritans, whose story now becomes the story of American English. Their motives were a tangle of idealistic, colonizing, self-interested, and religious ambitions. A minority, the Pilgrim Fathers, went to America to escape, in Andrew Marvell's words, "the prelate's rage". Their impulse to emigrate was both profoundly conservative, and profoundly religious. They hoped to find an austere wilderness where they could establish a Kingdom of God on the Geneva model. Other Puritans, men like John Winthrop and Roger Williams, were prompted by more commercial considerations of the kind that had excited Ralegh and the first Virginians. Williams, who believed that the state had no power over people's beliefs, established a liberal, tolerant society on Rhode Island quite different from the community founded by the stern ideologues of Massachusetts.

When the *Mayflower* set sail from Plymouth on 16 September 1620, the largest group on board came from East Anglia. Among their number was a young man from Fenstanton named John Howland who had been baptized in the desecrated chapel of Ely Cathedral. He and the other Pilgrim Fathers crossed the Atlantic in sixty-five days. John Howland fell overboard – family legend says he was drunk – but was miraculously rescued. Five people died. The pilgrims hoped to make a landfall in Virginia, but thanks to poor navigation, they landed at Cape Cod. In one of the finest and earliest examples of prose written in America, William Bradford, the *Mayflower*'s historian and the first Governor of the Massachusetts colony, described their situation:

> Being thus passed the vast ocean, and a sea of troubles . . . they had now no friends to welcome them, nor inns to entertain or refresh their weather-beaten bodys, no houses or much less townes to repaire to . . . it was muttered by some that if they got not a place in time they would turn them and their goods ashore [and return] . . . But may not and ought not the children of these fathers rightly say – Our Fathers were Englishmen which came over this great ocean, and were ready to perish in the wilderness, but they cried unto the Lord, and he heard their voice and looked on their adversities.

What happened to their English voices on this long sea journey and in the years that followed? There were almost thirty different communities from all over England represented on the *Mayflower*, a situation repeated on most of the subsequent transatlantic crossings. For many on board, we must suppose that it would be their first experience of another accent, another kind of English. The sea voyage across the stormy Atlantic provided a kind of language melting pot in which the regional differences of speech began to intermingle. In the settlement that followed the voices of Kent and Yorkshire and Devon, as well as those of the East Anglian majority, blended together to mark the beginnings of American English.

One group of New Englanders who make a professional study of English country speech are the members of the "living history" community at Plimouth Plantation. This is a 1627-style village, fenced in by a stockade, just overlooking the Atlantic Ocean, and barely three miles from the place – Plymouth Rock – where the Pilgrim Fathers finally landed in 1620. The members of the community live in the village and keep up an unshakeable pretence that today is the year 1627. They cook simple meals over open wood fires, they build and rebuild their 1620-style houses with the tools of the period, forging their own nails, hewing their own wood and mixing their own plaster. The women on the "Plantation" spin and weave and sew in the traditional manner, and all the members of the community – who adopt the names and characters of well-known Pilgrim Fathers – make a serious attempt at speaking the English of the 1620s.

53 The first settlers in the New World recorded the pidgin English they heard around them: "Umh, umh, me no strawmere fight Engis mon, Engis mon got two hed . . . if me cut off one hed, he got nodon . . ."

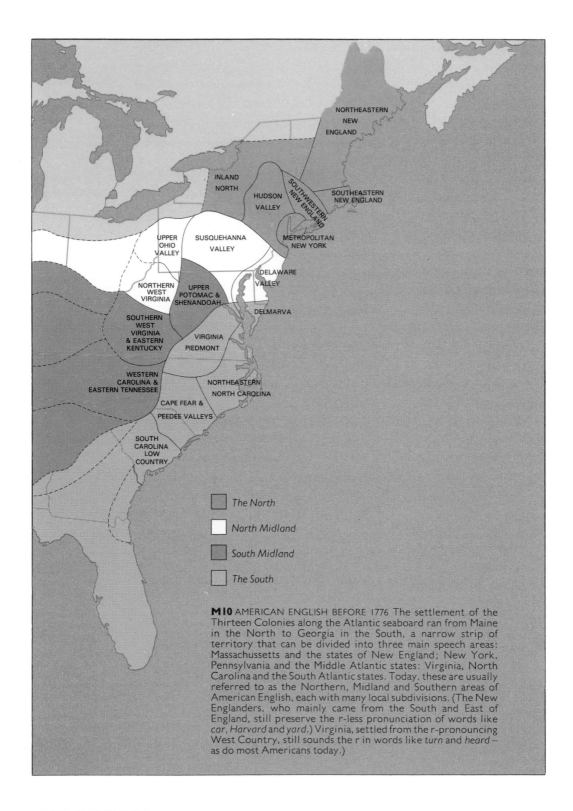

M10 AMERICAN ENGLISH BEFORE 1776 The settlement of the Thirteen Colonies along the Atlantic seaboard ran from Maine in the North to Georgia in the South, a narrow strip of territory that can be divided into three main speech areas: Massachussetts and the states of New England; New York, Pennsylvania and the Middle Atlantic states: Virginia, North Carolina and the South Atlantic states. Today, these are usually referred to as the Northern, Midland and Southern areas of American English, each with many local subdivisions. (The New Englanders, who mainly came from the South and East of England, still preserve the r-less pronunciation of words like *car*, *Harvard* and *yard*.) Virginia, settled from the r-pronouncing West Country, still sounds the r in words like *turn* and *heard* – as do most Americans today.)

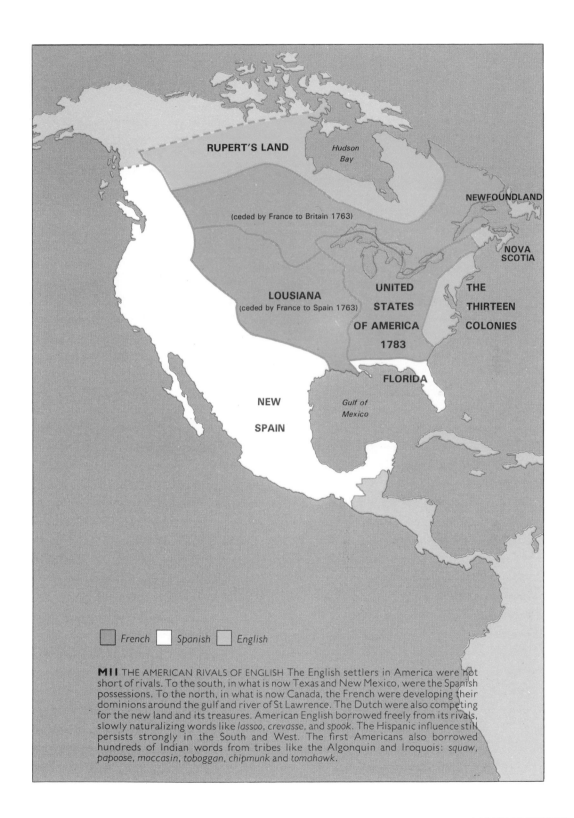

RUPERT'S LAND

Hudson Bay

NEWFOUNDLAND

(ceded by France to Britain 1763)

NOVA SCOTIA

LOUSIANA
(ceded by France to Spain 1763)

UNITED
STATES
OF AMERICA
1783

THE
THIRTEEN
COLONIES

NEW

SPAIN

FLORIDA

Gulf of Mexico

◼ French ◻ Spanish ◼ English

MII THE AMERICAN RIVALS OF ENGLISH The English settlers in America were not short of rivals. To the south, in what is now Texas and New Mexico, were the Spanish possessions. To the north, in what is now Canada, the French were developing their dominions around the gulf and river of St Lawrence. The Dutch were also competing for the new land and its treasures. American English borrowed freely from its rivals, slowly naturalizing words like *lassoo, crevasse,* and *spook.* The Hispanic influence still persists strongly in the South and West. The first Americans also borrowed hundreds of Indian words from tribes like the Algonquin and Iroquois: *squaw, papoose, moccasin, toboggan, chipmunk* and *tomahawk.*

Len Travers, who plays the part of Miles Standish, emphasizes the East Anglian roots of the English spoken in New England:

> Some people pick up their dialects rather quickly. Some of them have a natural advantage. For instance, if a New Englander is going to play an East Anglian they have a natural advantage, and find the dialect easier to pick up. Whereas if they must portray someone from "Zummerzet" they find that a bit more difficult to do because they must now pronounce their rs, which they never have done before.

To understand the momentous nature of the first English voyages to America, we have to appreciate the forlorn position of these weary travellers in a strange landscape without a single familiar reference point. We have to imagine a world in which all languages were foreign, all communications difficult, and even hazardous.

"BROKEN ENGLISH"

One of the first surprises for the Plymouth settlers was the appearance of Indians speaking "broken English". William Bradford's *History of Plimouth Plantation* reports that, "about 16th of March [1621], a certain Indian came boldly among them and spoke to them in broken English, which they could well understand but marvelled at it . . . At length they understood by discourse with him, that he was not of these parts, but belonged to the eastern parts where some English ships came to fish, with whom he was acquainted and . . . amongst whom he had got his language." Merchant trading ships plying the east coast of America between tiny English settlements like Jamestown and Plymouth, and the first Black slaves (arriving the year before the *Mayflower*), both helped to spread varieties of pidgin English among the Indian tribes.

The appearance of pidgin English in Massachusetts is a fascinating reminder of the chameleon-like character of the language. Just as the Saxon English, confronted by the Norse languages, adapted their speech, so the settlers of Roanoke, Jamestown and Plymouth, confronted by the need to communicate with Indians who could not speak a word of English, also adapted theirs. This process was probably accelerated by a genuine admiration for the Indians' speech. William Penn, the founder of Pennsylvania, wrote: "I know not a Language spoken in *Europe*, that hath words of more sweetness and greatness, in *Accent* and *Emphasis*, than theirs." Quite quickly, American English became enriched by what the settlers called "wigwam" words.

Wigwam itself is an Algonquin word, and it first appears in English in 1628, barely seven years after the Plymouth landing. It was eventually joined by about fifty American Indian words of which the most famous include vital descriptions of unfamiliar trees like *hickory*, fruits like *pecan*, animals like *chipmunk*, *moose* and *terrapin*, shellfish like *quahog*, and foods like *hominy* and *pemmican*. There were also the descriptive words from the Amerindian culture that have passed into English like *totem*, *papoose*, *squaw*, *moccasin*, *tomahawk*, and, from the far north, *igloo* and *kayak*.

The process whereby an Indian word became Standard English was often curious and tortuous. The animal we now know as a *racoon* was first recorded by Captain John Smith in 1608 as *raughroughouns*. By 1610, Virginians were talking about *aracouns*, and in due course the first syllable was dropped to give us the word we have today. The same process occurred to other Indian words, moving from the pidgin to the standard. *Scuppernong* meaning a yellow muscadine grape is first recorded as *askuponong*. *Opossum* became *possum*. *Skunk* began life as *segankn* or *segongw*. *Squash* (the fruit) was first recorded as *isquontersquash* and *squantersquash* from the Narragansett word *askutasquash* meaning "vegetables eaten green".

Some borrowings from the American Indians had very interesting histories. *Pow-wow*, for instance, was adopted very early to mean a priest or medicine man. Within fifty years it was used to mean a ceremony in which magic was practised, together with feasting and dancing. A hundred years later, it had moved closer to its present English meaning and was used to describe an Indian council. After that it became generalized to refer, colloquially, to a conference or get-together of any kind.

The story of *mugwump* also shows how words can have lives of their own. It came from *mugquomp*, a Natick Indian word meaning "great chief" (the Massachusetts Bible used it to translate *duke* in Genesis xxvi, 15). After that, the word gained a more jokey meaning and in 1884 it was used by Republican Party supporters of James G. Blaine to ridicule the breakaway Republicans who had thrown in their lot with Grover Cleveland, the Democratic nominee. In fact, the joke went against them because Cleveland won. Since then, *mugwump* has been used, often approvingly, in American politics to denote an Independent – but also derisively of a politician who straddles an issue or is ready to support either side.

Picturesque words from the Indian languages have also been joined by phrases and catchwords of assorted Indian derivation. In our own time, business executives might talk about going "on a scalp hunt" or "smoking a pipe of peace", and refer to their wives putting on "warpaint". Further in the past, *fire-water*, for "whisky", is apparently a translation of an Algonquin word. *Indian file* and *Indian summer* have obvious Amerindian meanings. Devotees of cowboy westerns will recognize *play possum*, *bury the hatchet* and *go on the warpath*.

The first settlers also scattered their new country with thousands of Indian place-names (much as Australia bears the marks of its Aboriginal culture). Twenty-six states have Indian names from Massachusetts to the Dakotas. Take rivers alone: there is Restigouche and Miramichi in New Brunswick; Penobscot, Kennebec, Merrimac and Connecticut in New England; Passaic and Raritan in New Jersey; and further south, Susquehanna and Potomac.

"NEW WORDS, NEW PHRASES"
The whole colonial experience in the New World had a dramatic effect on the English language. Nearly two hundred years after the first settlement of the United States, Thomas Jefferson, who took a more than amateur interest in the English language, explained that "new circumstances . . . call for new words, new phrases, and the transfer of old words to new

objects". Like the Roanoke settlers, the pioneers had a strange new landscape to explore and describe. After the first landings, they went inland along these rivers, through *bluff*, *notch*, *gap*, *divide* and *clearing* – all words that took on new meanings at this time. As they travelled, they came across new flora, which they began to cultivate: *hickory*, *live oak*, *sweet potato*, *eggplant*, *squash*; and fauna: *bullfrog*, *groundhog* and *garter snake*. The first Americans had a new way of life. Words like *backwoodsman*, *squatter*, *prairie*, *clapboard*, *popcorn*, *bobsled* and *sleigh* all reflect these new experiences, and give us a vivid impression of life in early America. So much for novelty. There was also "the transfer of old words to new objects". The English name *robin* was applied to the American red-breasted thrush; *turkey* was attached to a quite distinctive American bird; and *corn* (which in England is a generic term for all kinds of cereal crop) described a grain known in England as *maize*.

The English colonists in New England brought their language and usages with them, and British visitors to the United States today often note the unmistakable sixteenth- and early seventeenth-century characteristics still evident in American English, preserving features that are, to British ears, distinctly archaic. Americans use *gotten* in place of "got", a usage that was common in England until the late eighteenth century. They use *mad* in the sense of "angry", as Shakespeare did. "Sick" in England tends to refer to nausea; in America it retains its older sense of illness in general. *Platter*, for "dish", now largely unknown in England, is still common in the States. The old word *fall*, for "autumn", is often noticed. The American *I guess* goes back to Chaucer.

The English colonists in New England also brought with them the place-names from the old country. So, we find Bath in Maine; Brentwood and Croydon in New Hampshire; Danby and Maidstone in Vermont; Andover, Leominster (pronounced quite differently) and Salisbury in Massachusetts; Colchester and Norwich in Connecticut; Exeter in Rhode Island; and a whole slew of East Anglian place-names like Boston, Bedford, Braintree, Cambridge, Lincoln and Yarmouth. And of course there was the American impulse to make things new. In addition to twelve New Londons, there are eight New Bostons, four New Baltimores, five New Bedfords, and six New Richmonds.

THE SOUND OF AMERICAN ENGLISH

Once all these different varieties and patterns of speech up and down the eastern seaboard were thrown together into the melting pot, what did the first speakers of American English sound like? Initially, each community would have retained its English speech patterns and, as we have already seen, the flat *a*, common throughout England until the eighteenth century, has been preserved in the United States in words like *fast*, *dance*, *path*, *can't*, *half* and so on. Quite quickly, however, the process known as "accent levelling" would have started to merge the distinctive speech characteristics of, say, an emigrant from East Anglia and an emigrant from the West Country, into American English. This "levelling" would have been quickened among their children, the next generation, who would have had no direct exposure to English accents. The making of a new variety of English would have been further accelerated by encounters with all kinds of pidgin English among Dutch, French, and German settlers. In his memoirs, the Bostonian Alexander Hamilton describes a visit to Albany, the state capital of New York. Approaching the city he found: "The devil a word but Dutch was bandied about . . . and in general there was such a medley of Dutch and English as would have tired a horse."

Gradually, out of this chaos, an American pronunciation emerged, now recognized and imitated the world over. The *a* was mainly flat. Where the English now tend to introduce the sound *ah*, in the Midland states and towards the West, the *r* was generally pronounced after a vowel, as in *lorrd, carrd, herrd* – harking back to the century of origin. The *o* in words like *not, top, hot* and *lot* was flat not rounded, a characteristic of British English that died out in the eighteenth century. Words ending in *ile*, like *missile, fertile, sterile*, softened the emphasis on the last syllable becoming *missal, fertal, steral*. The emphasis on certain syllables of certain words shifted. In England it is de*tail* and re*search*; in America it is de*tail*, and *re*search. The English say *sec'ret'ry* and *nec'ess'ry*; in America all the syllables are accented. The English say *adver'tisement* and *labor'atory*, never *advertise'ment* or *lab'ratory*. The English speak quickly; the Americans tend to be more deliberate; the English tend to use a greater variety of tone; Americans tend to a certain monotony. It is as much the variety of tone as the different pronunciation of words that makes English speech so different to American ears.

DAGOES, CAJUNS AND YANKEES

The English were not the first in America. It was the Spanish, after all, who, in 1492, had commissioned the Genoa-born Cristoforo Colombo (whom we call Christopher Columbus) to seek out a westerly route to the East Indies. His discovery of the New World was a happy accident. The continent itself was named after the Italian navigator Amerigo Vespucci. Even before the Armada, the Spanish had introduced the horse and the cow to the land they called New Spain, known today as the states of Arizona, California, New Mexico and Texas. It was contact with Spanish, French and Dutch rivals that contributed to the unique flavour of American English.

English explorers had clashed with Spanish *conquistadores* from the days when America was still believed to be "the Indies", and when the Caribbean was still called "the Spanish Main". The first English colonists in North America soon encountered their Spanish rivals in well-established settlements from Florida to Santa Fé, and it was from here that English acquired such everyday words as *barbecue, chocolate* and *tomato*, once exotic borrowings from people the American English called *dagoes* (from the common Spanish name Diego) who had themselves borrowed them from Caribbean and South American Indian tribes. The Spanish influence in American life and language has persisted: many of America's nearest neighbours like Cuba, Mexico and Puerto Rico are Spanish-speaking, and so were important dependencies like the Philippines. To this day, American English has borrowed more words from Spanish – like *enchilada, marijuana, plaza, stampede* and *tornado* – than from any other language, and the list is growing year by year.

The French influence on English in America came later, and arrived from two very different sources. In the North and West, as the English pushed further inland, they soon came across French explorers, trappers, traders and missionaries who held all the strategic points along the two great North American rivers: the St Lawrence in the North and the Mississippi in the Mid-West. These were roughneck frontiers, a place of *toboggans* and *caribous* (two words adopted from the Indians by the French), or with a strange topography to which only French words like *bayou*, *butte*, *crevasse* and *levee* could do justice. Here the explorer would rely heavily on the local *depot* and might keep his *cents* and *dimes* carefully in a *cache*.

To the south, there was French New Orleans which provided quite a different influence. The capital of the state of Louisiana, named after Louis XIV in 1682, this was one of the most sophisticated cities in the New World. It had a theatre, a distinctive cuisine, fine architecture and a strong musical tradition – in 1808 it introduced grand opera to the United States. From the New Orleans tradition, Americans derive food words like *brioche*, *jambalaya* and *praline*. From the prairie, the well-known American *gopher* comes from the French *gaufre*, "honeycomb", apparently a reference to the animal's digging pattern. With typical American linguistic vigour this word was later extended to mean the free matches at cheap restaurants, i.e. the ones that customers were allowed to *go for*. This, in turn, developed into *gopher* or *gofer*, meaning someone employed as a *gopher*, i.e. to "go for" coffee, cigarettes, taxis, newspapers, etc. *Chowder*, familiar to all visitors to the eastern seaboard of the United States, appears to have come from the Breton *chaudière*, meaning a cauldron, and came from Nova Scotia. *Picayune*, originally the name of a small coin, was gradually extended to anything trifling.

Conflict between British and French colonists also produced one of the linguistic curiosities of Louisiana: the Cajuns. After the British captured the French colony of Acadia in 1716 (now Nova Scotia) they forced the French settlers to pledge allegiance to the British crown. Those who refused were deported in 1755, mainly to Louisiana where *Acadian* became *'Cadian* and finally *Cajun*. The Cajun dialect is called *Bougalie* possibly meaning *bogue talk*, a corruption of *bayou talk*, which is perhaps appropriate: *bayou* was one of the first French words to enter the lexicon of American English, in 1763, and has been used ever since to mean a creek or a marshy inlet, both of which abound in Louisiana.

Before the British settlers struck west, they fanned out up and down the east coast of North America. In 1664, they seized a town then known as New Amsterdam, and forced the Dutch to exchange it for the whole of Dutch Guiana, now Surinam, in what was perhaps one of the worst trade-offs in history. New Amsterdam was renamed New York, but Dutch influence remains in the place-names of New York City (Breukelyn, Haarlem and Bronck's) and in the vocabulary of contemporary American speech. If you have a *waffle* for brunch, or *coleslaw* with your dinner, or a *cookie* with your coffee, you are using Dutch American. If you ride through the *landscape* in a *caboose* or on a *sleigh*, if you find your *boss* or neighbour *snooping* and accuse him of being a *spook*, you are also using words that came to America from the Netherlands. And if you're a *Yankee* (what the Mexicans call a *Yanqui*) it's possible you should thank the Dutch. If you tell the boss he is talking *poppycock*, you are using a perfectly acceptable Victorian expletive, which comes from the Dutch *pappekak*, meaning "soft dung".

Boss is a typically American word, with enormous cultural overtones. What is interesting is that it comes into the language by two routes. In Black American English it means "superlative"; a *boss chick* is a "fine girl". This usage is also found in the Surinam creole, Srana Tongo, presumably thanks to the Dutch who moved there after the loss of New Amsterdam. The growth of the noun form of *boss* was explained by the nineteenth-century American novelist, James Fenimore Cooper. He noted that White domestic servants who wanted to avoid the word "master" or "massa", the form of address used by the Blacks, would turn to "boss" as a less demeaning alternative.

The first English settlers in North America encountered the Spanish, the French and the Dutch as colonial rivals. The Germans, on the other hand, were America's first non-colonizing immigrants, fleeing from religious persecution at home. The German migrations began as early as 1683 when settlers, mainly from the kingdom of Bavaria in the south-west of Germany, began to reach Pennsylvania. These new arrivals developed a hybrid language of their own, a compromise between their own speech and the dominant English of Pennsylvania. This is now known as Pennsylvania Dutch (*Deutsch*) and it survives to this day in the Lehigh, Lebanon and Berks counties of Pennsylvania. The reason for the persistence of Pennsylvania Dutch is its association with the Amish and Mennonite sects, religious separatists living austere country lives in devotion to their strict faith.

In the generation after the first landing at Plymouth Rock, about two hundred ships came from England to the North-East. By the time Charles I had been executed by Cromwell and the Puritans, there were perhaps some 250,000 residents in the region, mainly from London and East Anglia. Towards the south, the settlement at Jamestown continued to flourish, attracting adventurers from all over England: political refugees, Royalists, Commonwealth soldiers, deported prisoners, indentured servants, and many Puritans. Here, the accent-levelling process was accelerated by the wide variety of population, in terms both of class and of geography.

Both these settlement areas have one characteristic in common: they were mainly colonized by pioneers from the south-western and eastern parts of England. But the making of American English is by no means just a tale of English emigration. In the Middle Atlantic state of Pennsylvania there was a new, rowdy element of English speakers, hard-bitten, land-hungry frontiersmen from Scotland and the Ulster settlements of Northern Ireland. And further south, in Charleston, named after Charles II, there were, in addition to a thriving population of Irish and Scots-Irish emigrants, boatloads of Black slaves from Africa and the Caribbean, many of them speaking pidgin English. In the end, American English was to be influenced by these and many other peoples, in a series of vital blood transfusions.

54 Robert Burns wrote some three hundred and fifty songs, including "Auld Lang Syne", the unofficial Scottish national anthem.

4

THE GUID
SCOTS TONGUE

Scots is one of the oldest, richest and most interesting varieties of English, with a pedigree that dates back to the Anglo-Saxon invasions of the sixth and seventh centuries. The words and the music of the Scots are celebrated throughout the world. Most English-speaking people can recognize a Scots voice, and "Auld Lang Syne" is the international anthem of nostalgic reunion. The Scots who settled in New Zealand, Australia, Africa, the United States, Upper Canada and Nova Scotia have left a rich scattering of Scottish family and place-names. In America alone there are eight Aberdeens, eight Edinburghs, and seven Glasgows. One hundred towns beginning with Mac (or Mc) range from McAdams, Mississippi, to McWilliams, Alabama. In New Zealand Scots roots are commemorated in Dunedin, Hamilton, Invercargill; in Australia, in places like Perth, Waverley and Blair Athol. At home the Scots tongue (as it is known) has been largely neglected. The revival of its poetry is often treated as artificial. Today, you will hear a Scots accent throughout the country, but the language of Scottish newspapers, Scottish government and Scottish education is Standard English. The Older Scottish Tongue has lost its place as a written language. This chapter tells the story of its fate, or *weird*, as they used to say in Scotland, and the role it played in shaping world English.

The age of television takes the idea of Standard English – British or American – almost for granted. In London or New York, the evening network news is read in a way that would be intelligible to virtually any English speaker in the world. The rule of Standard English goes further. Television stations in Aberdeen, Scotland, or Boone, North Carolina, or Sydney, Australia, will broadcast a version of the international standard with a Scottish, an Appalachian or an Australian accent. Compare the *Glasgow Herald* with the *Melbourne Age* or the *Los Angeles Times*: the style will vary, but the English is virtually indistinguishable. If Scots news broadcasters still used the Older Scottish Tongue rather than Standard English, a bulletin might go something like this:

> Yet anither industry gangs agley wi the lorry drivers' strike. Want o' flour has gard the backsters renege on their promise tae keep breid counters thrang this winter. A Backsters Union spokesman said his men wer sweert tae stop work, but there wes nocht they could dae.

Snell winds hae wrocht havoc in aa the westlan airts o' Scotland the day. Glesga folk especially had a guid wheen broken lums tae thole. And while the West chittered in the cauld sough o' the wind, the North-East was smoored wi cranreuch an snaw.

Sport: An while Rangers is haein' a sair fecht tae regain their European Cup form, their faes in the neest roun, F.C. Cologne, had a dawdle o' a gemme the nicht, blouterin' fower goals past Eintracht Frankfurt.

And that's the news in Scotland the nicht.

Why is Scots no longer the written language of Edinburgh or Glasgow? And why is Standard English dominant throughout the British Isles? Historically, the answer lies in the South, in seventeenth- and eighteenth-century London. It was from here that the English crown, consolidating its rule throughout a barely united kingdom, encouraged the spread of southern English at the expense of regional varieties. And it was here that English first became refined and standardized as the *de facto* language of power and learning – to the permanent disadvantage of alternative regional varieties of English like Scots. Before we follow the story of the Scots tongue at home and abroad, we must look briefly at developments in the English of the South.

"THE CORRUPTIONS IN OUR LANGUAGE"

When Charles II came to the English throne, when the United States were still known as the Thirteen Colonies, and even when Australia was still the largely unexplored Van Diemen's Land, the idea of Standard English, spoken or written, was still in its infancy. England was a society with several competing speech varieties, of which Scots was one. The suggestion that there was a "right" way of speaking would have seemed strange to most people. Even the notion that there should be a "right" way of spelling was foreign to many letter writers and printers, as the uneven spelling of their books and papers demonstrates.

Shakespeare and his contemporaries had experimented with the English language as no other writers before or since. There was an air of childish innocence in the ease with which they broke the rules and made the language sing. After such a virtuoso performance, a new mood began to prevail. The writers of the late seventeenth and early eighteenth centuries had boundless admiration for their Elizabethan predecessors, but they believed that the situation had got out of hand. The English language, perhaps like the mass of English society itself, was unruly and unrefined. "How barbarously we yet write and speak," exclaimed the poet Dryden, voicing a common view. The language, it was thought, should be sent to school. But how? From the Restoration in 1660 to the publication of Samuel Johnson's *Dictionary* in 1755, this was one of the most serious issues facing the literary establishment. It is a debate that lives on to the present day in the correspondence pages of newspapers.

One of the main impulses behind the search for order was the need to assimilate the scientific and political revolutions of the seventeenth century. These had swelled the vocabulary of English almost beyond recognition. The scientific revolution in England reached its high point with Isaac Newton's theory of gravity. Newton was a member of the Royal Society, founded in 1662 primarily as a forum for scientific discussion. But not all its members and their interests were strictly scientific. In 1664, it was reported that:

> There were persons of the Society whose genius was very proper and inclined to improve the English tongue. Particularly for philosophic purposes, it was voted that there should be a committee for improving the English language; and that they meet at Sir Peter Wyche's lodgings in Gray's Inn once or twice a month, and give an account of their proceedings, when called upon.

Science was one model. Latin – still the language of mathematics and theology – with its regular grammar, spelling convention and systematic style, was another. Again and again during the next hundred years or so, English writers would look back to Latin for inspiration and authority. John Dryden, the finest English stylist of his time, admitted that he sometimes had to translate an idea into Latin to find the correct way to express it in English! Latin was the great example of a language that had lasted, precisely because it was ordered. To write in English, on the other hand, seemed to be inviting oblivion. The poet Edmund Waller spoke for many writers when he observed:

> *But who can hope his line should long*
> *Last, in a daily changing tongue?*
> *While they are new, Envy prevails;*
> *And as that dies, our language fails ...*
>
> *Poets that Lasting Marble seek,*
> *Must carve in Latin or in Greek;*
> *We write in Sand ...*

55/56/57 Sir Isaac Newton found most clarity in Latin. Men of learning looked to France for a means "to purifie our Native Language from Barbarism or Solecism" – an Academy, an idea discussed by the Royal Society.

58 Dr Samuel Johnson was born in Lichfield, the son of a bookseller. His life was spent in "Grub Street" and on his death he was immediately buried in Poets' Corner, a measure of his reputation.

Such were the fears and complaints of the literary men of the time. But what was the solution? Some looked abroad for inspiration, to Italy and France. The Italians had purified their language by publishing a dictionary specially commissioned by an Academy. Closer to home, Cardinal Richelieu had established the Académie Française with a specific charter, "to labour with all possible care and diligence to give definite rules to our language, and to render it pure, eloquent and capable of treating the arts and sciences".

The idea of an English Academy, canvassed throughout the seventeenth century, never got off the ground. The Royal Society's "committee for improving the English language" did meet. The diarist John Evelyn produced an ambitious proposal, including a "Lexicon or collection of all the pure English words by themselves", but the plans were shelved. From time to time, the idea of an Academy would be revived. In 1697, Daniel Defoe proposed that with an Academy to decide on right and wrong usage, "it would be as criminal to coin words as money". Perhaps precisely because the model was so obviously French, it remained only a gleam in the eye. At the turn of the century, however, one writer in particular addressed himself to the issue of standards in English. The need for control has never since been argued with such force and eloquence. Jonathan Swift focused his hatred of change and his fear of progress in a series of letters and pamphlets on the condition of the English language. Taken together, these writings amount to the greatest conservative statement for English ever put forward.

Swift, who was born in Dublin in 1667 of a well-known Royalist family, had literary connections from the start. He went to school with the playwright Congreve; Dryden was a cousin. His early writing, according to Dr Johnson, provoked Dryden to comment, "Cousin Swift, you will never be a poet." Today he is renowned as the author of *Gulliver's Travels*. When, in the first decade of the eighteenth century, he turned his formidable powers against the state of the English language he was devastating.

> From the Civil War to this present Time, I am apt to doubt whether the Corruptions in our Language have not at least equalled the Refinements of it; and these Corruptions very few of the best Authors in our Age have wholly escaped. During the Usurpation, such an Infusion of Enthusiastick Jargon prevailed in every Writing, as was not shook off in many Years after. To this succeeded that Licentiousness which entered with the *Restoration*, and from infecting our Religion and Morals, fell to corrupt our Language . . .

59 John Dryden was one of the first to demonstrate the *naturalness* of English prose.

60 Jonathan Swift's fears for the English language have been echoed by every subsequent generation.

Among the characteristics of eighteenth-century speech which he deplored was the tendency that still survives to shorten words that should, he believed, retain their full dignified length, *rep* for "reputation", *incog* for "incognito". These abridgements did not last, but *mob* for "mobile" did. Swift would certainly have objected to *taxi, bus* and *phone*. He considered any abridgement of verbs – *rebuk'd, disturb'd* – as "the disgrace of our language". He detested vogue words, especially when they crept into church. Young preachers, he says, "use all the modern terms of art, *sham, banter, mob, bubble, bully, cutting, shuffling* and *palming*".

Swift was concerned that the language would be so corrupted that in a few years English usage, replaced by another set of vogue words and phrases, would become unintelligible.

> The Fame of our Writers is usually confined to these two Islands, and it is hard it should be limited in *Time*, as much as *Place*, by the perpetual Variations of our Speech . . . if it were not for the *Bible* and *Common Prayer Book* in the vulgar Tongue, we should hardly be able to understand any Thing that was written among us an hundred Years ago: Which is certainly true: For those Books being perpetually read in Churches, have proved a kind of Standard for Language, especially to the common People.

Swift's finest statement of his position on English is made in a letter to Robert Harley, Earl of Oxford and leader of the ruling Tory Party, published in 1712 under the title *A Proposal for Correcting, Improving and Ascertaining the English Tongue*. Swift proposed the only sure remedy against "Manglings and Abbreviations" and against the innovations of "illiterate Court Fops, half-witted Poets, and University Boys" – an English Academy. His ideas were never adopted. The notion of a prescriptive society of this kind ran counter to the amateur tradition of English literary scholarship. Swift, a well-known Tory, found his *Proposal* attacked on purely political grounds. Finally, his patron's Tory ministry fell in 1714 on the death of Queen Anne. But his fears have been echoed, in one form or another, by every successive generation.

Another aspect of Swift's diatribe strikes a familiar chord: the chaos of English spelling.

> Another Cause (and perhaps borrowed from the former) which hath contributed not a little to the maiming of our Language, is a foolish Opinion, advanced of late Years, that we ought to spell exactly as we speak; which beside the obvious Inconvenience of utterly destroying our Etymology, would be a thing we should never see an End of. Not only the several Towns and Counties of *England* have a different way of Pronouncing, but even here in *London*, they clip their Words after one Manner about the Court, another in the City, and a third in the Suburbs; and in a few Years, it is probable, will all differ from themselves, as Fancy or Fashion shall direct: All which reduced to Writing would entirely confound Orthography. Yet many People are so fond of this Conceit, that it is sometimes a difficult matter to read modern Books and Pamphlets; where the Words are so curtailed, and varied from their original Spelling, that whoever hath been used to plain *English*, will hardly know them by sight.

Swift's complaint was not new, but by the eighteenth century it had become pressing. The gap between spoken and written English which had perplexed William Caxton had become wider than ever. For the aristocracy, the convention of spelling as you spoke produced words like *sartinly* (certainly), *byled* (boiled), *gine* (join), *agane* (again), and phrases like *jest agoing to be married*, *most people thinks*, and *I don't see no likelyhood of her dying*. The situation had become further complicated by the work of bad scholars who, convinced by false etymologies, had changed words like *iland*, *sissors*, *sithe*, *coud* and *ancor*, into *island*, *scissors*, *scythe*, *could* and *anchor*. Now, more than ever, the educated Englishman – especially one who was unsure of his position in society – needed a dictionary.

DR JOHNSON'S DICTIONARY

There had, of course, been English dictionaries in the past, the first of these being a little book of some 120 pages, compiled by a certain Robert Cawdray, published in 1604 under the title of *A Table Alphabeticall*, "of hard vsuall English wordes" compiled, he said, for "Ladies . . . or any other unskilfull persons". Like the various dictionaries that came after it during the seventeenth century, Cawdray's tended to concentrate on "scholarly" words; one function of the dictionary was to enable its student to convey an impression of fine learning. Beyond the practical need to make order out of chaos, the rise of dictionaries is associated with the rise of the English middle class, keen to ape their betters and anxious to define and circumscribe the various worlds to conquer – lexical as well as social and commercial. It is highly appropriate that Dr Samuel Johnson, the very model of an eighteenth-century literary man, as famous in his own time as ours, should have published his *Dictionary* at the very beginning of the heyday of the middle class.

Johnson was a poet and critic who raised common sense to the heights of genius. His approach to the problems Swift (and others) had been worrying about was intensely practical and typically English. Rather than have an Academy to settle arguments about language, he would write a dictionary; and he would do it single-handed. Johnson signed the contract for the *Dictionary* with the bookseller Robert Dodsley at a breakfast held at the Golden Anchor near Holborn Bar on 18 June 1746. He was to be paid £1,575 in instalments, and from this he took money to rent 17 Gough Square in which he set up his "dictionary workshop".

James Boswell, his biographer, described the garret where Johnson worked as "fitted up like a counting house" with a long desk running down the middle at which the copying clerks could work standing up. Johnson himself was stationed on a rickety chair at an "old crazy deal table" surrounded by a chaos of borrowed books. He was helped by six assistants (five Scots, one an expert in "low cant phrases", and an Englishman), two of whom died while the *Dictionary* was still in preparation.

The work was immense. Writing in about eighty large notebooks (and without a library to hand) Johnson wrote the definitions of more than 40,000 words, illustrating their many meanings with some 114,000 quotations drawn from English writing on every subject, from the Elizabethans to his own time. He did not expect to achieve complete originality. Working to a deadline, he had to draw on the best of all previous dictionaries, and to make his a work of heroic synthesis. In fact, it was very much more. Unlike his predecessors, Johnson treated English very practically, as a living language, with many different shades of meaning. He adopted his definitions on the principle of English common law – according to precedent. After its publication, his *Dictionary* was not seriously rivalled for over a century. And some of its definitions have become famous.

> *Lexicographer* – A writer of dictionaries, a harmless drudge.
> *Patron* – One who countenances, supports, or protects. Commonly a wretch who supports with insolence, and is paid with flattery.
> *Pension* – An allowance made to anyone without an equivalent. In England it is generally understood to mean pay given to a state hireling for treason to his country.
> *Whigs* – The name of a faction.

The distinctive wit of the *Dictionary* and its definitions has obscured its remarkable clarity.

> *Heart* – The muscle which by its contraction and dilation propels the blood through the course of circulation . . . It is supposed in popular language to be the seat sometimes of courage, sometimes of affection.

61 James Boswell was a Scot whose *Life of Samuel Johnson* is one of the masterpieces of English biography.

62 James Murray, the inspiration behind "the greatest dictionary of any language in the world", the *OED*.

OATS. n. ſ. [aɒen, Saxon.] A grain, which in England is generally given to horſes, but in Scotland ſupports the people.

It is of the graſs leaved tribe ; the flowers have no petals, and are diſpoſed in a looſe panicle : the grain is eatable. The meal makes tolerable good bread. *Miller.*

The *oats* have eaten the horſes. *Shakeſpeare.*

It is bare mechaniſm, no otherwiſe produced than the turning of a wild *oatbeard,* by the inſinuation of the particles of moiſture. *Locke.*

For your lean cattle, fodder them with barley ſtraw firſt, and the *oat* ſtraw laſt. *Mortimer's Huſbandry.*

His horſe's allowance of *oats* and beans, was greater than the journey required. *Swift.*

OA'TTHISTLE. n. ſ. [*oat* and *thiſtle.*] An herb. *Ainſ.*

OBAMBULA'TION. n. ſ. [*obambulatio,* from *obambulo,* Latin.]
* The act of walking about. *Dict.*

To OBDU'CE. v. a. [*obduco,* Latin.] To draw over as a co-vering.

No animal exhibits its face in the native colour of its ſkin

HEART. n. ſ. [ƿeoþc, Saxon; *hertz,* German.]
1. The muſcle which by its contraction and dilation propels the blood through the courſe of circulation, and is therefore conſidered as the ſource of vital motion. It is ſuppoſed in popular language to be the ſeat ſometimes of courage, ſometimes of affection.

He with providence and courage ſo paſſed over all, that the mother took ſuch ſpiteful grief at it, that her *heart* brake withal, and ſhe died. *Sidney.*

Thou wouldſt have left thy deareſt *heart* blood there,
Rather than made that ſavage duke thine heir,
And diſinherited thine only ſon. *Shakeſp. Henry VI.*

Snakes, in my *heart* blood warm'd, that ſting my *heart.* *Shakeſpeare's Richard II.*

Our battle is more full of names than your's,
Our men more perfect in the uſe of arms,
Our armour all as ſtrong, our cauſe the beſt ;
Then reaſon wills our *hearts* ſhould be as good. *Shak. H. IV.*

I thank you for my veniſon, maſter Shallow.

63/64 Two entries in Johnson's *Dictionary* exhibiting his wit, his clarity and his prodigious scholarship. It was the subtlety of definition and the wealth of illustrative quotation that gave the work its authority.

The twelve definitions for a tricky word like *thought* display the fluency and accuracy of a great mind:

1. The operation of the mind; the act of thinking. 2. Idea; image formed in the mind. 3. Sentiment; fancy; imagery. 4. Reflection; particular consideration. 5. Conception; preconceived notion. 6. Opinion; judgement. 7. Meditation; serious consideration. 8. Design; purpose. 9. Silent contemplation. 10. Solicitude; care; concern. 11. Expectation. 12. A small degree; a small quantity.

After many vicissitudes the *Dictionary* was finally published on 15 April 1755. It was instantly recognized as a landmark throughout Europe. "This very noble work", wrote the leading Italian lexicographer, "will be a perpetual monument of Fame to the Author, an Honour to his own Country in particular, and a general Benefit to the Republic of Letters throughout Europe." The fact that Johnson had taken on the Academies of Europe and matched them (everyone knew that forty French academicians had taken forty years to produce the first French national dictionary) was cause for much English celebration. Johnson's friend and pupil, the actor David Garrick, summarized the London view:

And Johnson, well arm'd like a hero of yore,
Has beat forty French, and will beat forty more.

Johnson had laboured for nine years, "with little assistance of the learned, and without any patronage of the great; not in the soft obscurities of retirement, or under the shelter of academic bowers, but amidst inconvenience and distraction, in sickness and in sorrow". For all its faults and eccentricities his two-volume work is a masterpiece and a landmark, in his own words "setting the orthography, displaying the analogy, regulating the structures, and ascertaining the significations of English words". It is the cornerstone of Standard English, an achievement which, in James Boswell's words, conferred stability on the language of his country".

In his Preface to the *Dictionary*, Johnson addresses himself to Swift's idea of "fixing" the language. He scorned the idea of permanence in language. To believe that, he said, was to believe in the elixir of eternal life.

> Those who have been persuaded to think well of my design, require that it should fix our language, and put a stop to those alterations which time and chance have hitherto been suffered to make in it without opposition. With this consequence I will confess that I have flattered myself for a while; but now begin to fear that I have indulged expectation which neither reason nor experience can justify. When we see men grow old and die at a certain time one after another, from century to century, we laugh at the elixir that promises to prolong life to a thousand years; and with equal justice may the lexicographer be derided, who being able to produce no example of a nation that has preserved their words and phrases from mutability, shall imagine that his dictionary can embalm his language, and secure it from corruption and decay, that it is in his power to change sublunary nature, and clear the world at once from folly, vanity, and affectation.

Then he takes issue with Swift's idea for an Academy on the French model:

> With this hope, however, academies have been instituted, to guard the avenues of their languages, to retain fugitives, and repulse intruders; but their vigilance and activity have hitherto been vain; sounds are too volatile and subtile for legal restraints; to enchain syllables, and to lash the wind, are equally the undertakings of pride, unwilling to measure its desires by its strength. The *French* language has visibly changed under the inspection of the academy . . .

The *Dictionary*, together with his other writing, made Johnson famous, and so well-esteemed that his friends were able to prevail upon George III to offer him a pension. From then on, he was to become the Johnson of folklore. James Boswell, who was responsible for much of the legend, was a Scot. Early on in their strange relationship, Johnson had remarked that he would like to visit the islands of the Hebrides, places which seemed to him, he said, as remote as "Borneo or Sumatra". In the autumn of 1773, ten years after the first mention of this "very romantick fancy", when Johnson was sixty-three and Boswell thirty-two, the two men set off on the great high road to the North.

A TOUR OF THE HIGHLANDS AND ISLANDS

The Scotland through which they journeyed was a divided nation, linguistically and politically. The Scots in the Lowlands were adopting the English of the South, a process we shall explore in more detail shortly. Johnson noted the decline of "the Scots tongue" here with a Sassenach's satisfaction:

> The conversation of the Scots grows every day less unpleasing to the English; their peculiarities wear fast away; their dialect is likely to become in half a century provincial and rustick, even to themselves. The great, the learned, the ambitious, and the vain, all cultivate the English phrase, and the English pronunciation.

Edinburgh, where Boswell and Johnson began their historic tour, was at the dawn of a golden age of achievement – the age of Robert Burns the poet, David Hume the philosopher, Adam Smith the economist, Robert Adam the architect, and later Thomas Telford the engineer. But in the Highlands, which had been Gaelic-speaking for centuries, the people of the clans were in a wretched condition.

In 1746, the same year that Johnson started work on his *Dictionary*, Bonnie Prince Charlie's failed Jacobite uprising had brought Highland pride to its lowest ebb. The defeated clans who had risen against the Hanoverian dynasty were ruthlessly anglicized in the wake of the Duke of Cumberland's victory at Culloden. The traditions of the Highlanders were put under severe attack. Johnson noted:

> There was perhaps never any change of national manners so quick, so great, and so general, as that which has operated in the Highlands, by the last conquest, and the subsequent laws. We came thither too late to see what we expected, a people of peculiar appearance, and a system of antiquated life... Of what they had before the late conquest of the country, there remain only their language and their poverty. Their language is attacked on every side. Schools are erected, in which *English* only is taught, and there were lately some who thought it reasonable to refuse them a version of the holy scriptures, that they might have no monument of their mother-tongue.

65 ''Bonnie Prince Charlie'', the ''Young Pretender''.

66 After Culloden, according to Johnson, ''the clans retain(ed) little of their original character''.

The isolation of the Highlanders began in Scotland itself. Gaelic-speaking, fierce, clannish and remote, their ancestral roots lay not in Scotland but across the sea in Ireland. They were outsiders in their own country. James I had once referred to them as "utterly barbarous". The Lowlanders often called them "Irish", unwilling to consider them Scottish. Before the '45, they were known chiefly for their military prowess. After the '45 they were smashed: forbidden to carry firearms, forbidden to wear Highland dress and play the pipes, governed by Lowland lawyers sitting in Edinburgh. The Society for Promoting Christian Knowledge and its missionary schools took the teachings and the English of the Church of Scotland into the glens. As Johnson remarked, Gaelic *mores* were rapidly undermined. "The religion of the Islands is that of the Kirk of Scotland. The gentlemen with whom I conversed are all inclined to the English Liturgy." The Gaelic language probably persisted strongly among the peasantry (when Dorothy Wordsworth visited Loch Lomondside in 1803, it was still the language of the ordinary local conversation), but among the clan chieftains, English was beginning to gain ground.

Johnson, an astute observer, noted something remarkable about the English of the Highlanders: it was not very Scottish in tone.

> By subsequent opportunities of observation, I found that my host's diction had nothing peculiar. Those Highlanders that can speak English, commonly speak it well, with few of the words, and little of the tone by which a Scotchman is distinguished. Their language seems to have been learned in the army or the navy, or by some communication with those who could give them good examples of accent and pronunciation.

Boswell and Johnson first headed north to Inverness and then crossed over to Glenelg and the islands of Skye and Raasay. Even then, the Gaelic tradition of the Highlands was threatened on all sides. Today there is virtually nothing left. All these places have become fully anglicized by schools and roads and tourism. Only in the remote Outer Hebrides, for instance on the windswept island of Barra, can we still catch a flavour of what has been lost.

Barra is a good six hours in the ferry from Oban. Its tiny population (about 1300 inhabitants) is certainly influenced by the English of the airwaves, but down in the post office, or in the harbourmaster's cabin overlooking Castlebay, English is still a foreign language, virtually unknown before the advent of the regular ferry. John MacDonald, the harbourmaster, uses Scots Gaelic most of his working life. "English is like a foreign language to me, before I went to school. It was very little English we spoke at home. It was after we went to school that we learnt the English."

John MacDonald's lilting sing-song is nothing like the popular idea of a Scots accent. Outsiders – people "without the island", as the locals say – sometimes think the Highlanders sound Irish. This is not surprising: much of Highland culture comes from Ireland, including the kilt, the bagpipes and even the Irish surname prefix "Mac". Father Colin MacInnes, the local priest, dedicates part of his life to the preservation of the Celtic traditions. He teaches

67 Castlebay on the island of Barra. Scots Gaelic still survives in the Outer Hebrides.

the local children the old Highland game of shinty – a kind of hockey – which is very like the Irish sport of hurling. Father MacInnes points out that Highlander and Irishman sound similar because they share a common language, Gaelic, with the same rhythms and many of the same constructions. The Gaelic background gives English on Barra a fine, musical lilt. "I think the English spoken here", says Father MacInnes, "is a beautiful, sweet-sounding, rolling, soft type of English . . . It is a very comforting sound compared to the harshness, the whiskied, fast-moving accents you get in the cities and towns."

Even in a place as isolated as Barra the local language almost certainly faces extinction, swamped by a tidal wave of English. The children of Barra speak a mixture of Gaelic and English at play and at home, but if they were to seek a future in the outside world it would depend on English. Father MacInnes does his best to keep the local culture alive:

> We are like all minority groups, a small freshwater loch being invaded by a
> huge ocean which flows in. If you don't prevent that flow, it is natural that
> the fresh water will be contaminated.

Scots Gaelic has been a persecuted language for two hundred years. Highlanders have never forgotten that the Jacobite Revolt was used as a pretext to impose the English way of life. As Father MacInnes puts it:

> After Culloden, the laws that were enacted were ordained really to destroy
> the way of life, the language and the customs of the Highlanders and
> Islanders. The Highlander wasn't permitted to practise his language. He
> wasn't permitted to wear his native dress . . . He wasn't permitted to be
> educated through the medium of Gaelic. Consequently, it made it very
> difficult for the Gaelic culture to survive.

The Highland clearances stripped the land of its Gaelic-speaking population, leaving deserted farms and broken crofts to remind visitors like Boswell and Johnson of what had been lost. By the turn of the century, a rising population and the economic crisis had turned the Highlands into a society on the edge of catastrophe. For many, there was no choice but to leave. Even in Johnson's day, there was a steady flow of emigration overseas: "He that cannot live as he desires at home, listens to the tale of fortunate islands, and happy regions, where every man may have land of his own, and eat the product of his labour without a superior."

It is impossible to calculate how many Highlanders crossed the Atlantic after the '45 in search of a better future, but there is no doubt that emigration to North America became a torrent. The Highland clearances left their mark on the character of the English spoken in parts of Canada. The story of Nova Scotia is typical. Heavy migration by crofters who had been forced off the land in Scotland changed the ethnic character of Nova Scotia quite suddenly. A 1767 census shows a total population of about 13,000, a mixture of Acadians (French), Germans, Dutch, New Englanders, Irish and free Blacks. There were only 173 Scots. In 1773, the ship *Hector* sailed from Greenock with 200 Highland farmers. There were eleven stormy weeks across the North Atlantic in a rotting ship from whose bulwarks pieces of wood could be picked by hand, but a Scottish piper kept their spirits up and piped them ashore at Pictou. As the clearances of the Highlands quickened, thousands of Scots followed. Their legendary hardiness was sorely tested by the dense forests, the bitter winters and the marauding Indians. But they prospered, and by 1851 some 35,000 had made the difficult journey and had become a major force in the life of the colony that now deserved its new name, New Scotland. The province still cherishes its Scottish roots. The annual Gatherings of the Clans for Highland games are a major tourist attraction. The province proudly sports its own official Nova Scotian tartan. In Halifax, there are prominent statues to Robert Burns and Sir Walter Scott, and a piper sounds the changing of the Highland Guard on the Citadel commanding the harbour. The Highland traditions of fiddling and hurling flourish, and Nova Scotian English has the lilt of the Highlands.

Within the British Isles, there was another escape route for the Highlander: the British Army. Highland regiments have fought some of Britain's toughest battles, from Waterloo to the Falklands. Callum Keene and John Northcote are both Highland lads from Oban, brought up in Gaelic-speaking families. Enlisted in the Argyll and Sutherland Highlanders, they are living examples of the way in which British institutions have swallowed up the Celtic traditions of old Scotland. The language of command in the regiment has always been English and even their Scottish mates – city-educated, English-speaking Lowlanders – mock their lilting Highland accents. They refer to Keene and Northcote by the derogatory term *teuchter* (meaning "highlander"; the *eu* is pronounced as in *feud*).

Callum Keene remembers the experience of enlisting in the Argylls only too well:

> When I came down from the Highlands, I spoke with a really broad
> Highland accent, and they all started saying: Where are you from? I says,

Well I'm from Oban. And they seemed to say: He's a teuchter. They were taking the mickey out of me. I says to myself, Well I'm going to have to change my accent because I don't like getting slagged all the time.

Both Keene and Northcote were forced by their mates to adopt the speech of the majority, and when we spoke to them their accents were almost indistinguishable from their Lowland comrades', though they were quite capable of demonstrating what they had lost. Callum Keene describes the process: "Gradually, as time went on, I picked up the Lowland dialect. If I was talking to you in my old accent, I'd be talking more like a Highlander, a teuchter." John Northcote still has a pride in his roots – and regrets the loss. "To me, I feel a teuchter's a real Scottish Highlander. Glasgow and that, they're just Lowlanders. I wish I still had my old lingo."

The Highlanders have stood watch over British possessions on British territory from Edinburgh to the Ganges. Driven from their lands, they were forced to learn the language of their old enemies and, by a final irony, carried it for them to the four corners of the world – from Sydney to Saskatchewan. All that is left of the fighting clans are the great names – Campbell, Cameron, Macdonald, and Macleod. The original Gaelic of so many Jacobite ballads longs for the return of the Bonnie Prince, but of course he'll never come. His people are in exile. Their words have been translated into the English of the English-speaking world, and only their music lingers. The Highlanders came from the Scotland of legend – misty glens, skirling bagpipes and hunting tartans. But there is another Scotland, a Scotland that spoke Scots, not Gaelic. They too had what Samuel Johnson called "this epidemick desire of wandering" – the Lowland Scots.

THE OLDER SCOTTISH TONGUE

The Scots of the Lowlands was originally a northern variety of English brought there by the Angles who landed in Northumbria and who occupied the south-eastern parts of Scotland in the seventh century. In those days they were one of five different ethnic groups who invaded northern Britain during the Dark Ages: the Picts; the Britons; another Celtic people from Ireland calling themselves the *Scotti*; and finally, the Norse (Norwegians). Each of the five spoke a distinct language, each was warlike, each occupied a distinct geographical area. By the tenth century, largely thanks to the efforts of the *Scotti*, the kingdom was more or less unified, and was mostly Celtic-speaking. In 1057 Malcolm Canmore killed a certain Macbeth in a fight for the Scottish throne. After William of Normandy's invasion of England in 1066, Malcolm welcomed northern-English speakers to his court (refugees from William's Harrying of the North), and later married an English princess, Margaret. The tradition of welcoming immigrants from the South continued into the twelfth century: King David I granted extensive lands to Anglo-Norman families like the Bruces, Comyns and Balliols, or to the Breton families like the Stewarts, and even to Fleming families, notably the Douglases. Most important of all, for the development of Scots, David I introduced the *burgh* (a colony or town surrounding a castle) to Scotland. These English-speaking burghs marked the

68/69 John Northcote and Callum Keene were brought up in Gaelic-speaking families. Outnumbered by Lowlanders in their regiment, and teased for their Highland accents, they have had to adopt Lowland Scots.

beginning of what was to become Scots English (the Northern English of Scotland, later known as Scots).

David I established some fourteen burghs, including Aberdeen, Dundee, Edinburgh and Perth, English-speaking trading settlements in a polyglot society of Celts, Northerners and even some Flemings. The Scottish court, like the English, was Anglo-Norman, or, in the words of the chronicler, "French in race and manner of life, in speech and in culture." The ordinary people of the burghs, on the other hand, spoke neither French (though French was known as far north as Beauly, near Inverness), nor Gaelic – they were English. As William of Newburgh wrote around the year 1200, "The fortified places and burghs of the Scottish Kingdoms are known to be inhabited by English."

These royal burghs were the foundation of Lowland Scots and its culture: it was in these towns that Gaelic speakers gave up their language in favour of Scots. Gradually, the frontier between Scots and Gaelic was formed along the edge of the Highlands, a division that persists (along a line of geography) to the present. More than a few Gaelic words have entered the English vocabulary, topographical words like *bog* and *inch*, and *whisky* (from the Gaelic *uisce beatha*, meaning "water of life"). Gradually, in the records, we see a familiar process taking place: the English vernacular creeps in when the scribe is lost for an appropriate Latin word to describe the Scots reality. *Croft* makes its first appearance in this way.

Then, just as the conditions for the marriage of Scots and English seemed to be ideal, the two kingdoms, far from drawing closer together in politics and language, came to blows. Scotland, led first by Wallace and then by the celebrated Robert Bruce, fiercely resisted Edward I's attempts to annex Scotland. For more than a century there was bitter border warfare. In the words of an old saying, "Scotland was born fighting."

While Chaucer and Caxton (and many others) were enlarging the currency of the London-based southern standard, there was, in the North, a process at work that was making the Scottish language and literature as distinctive as, say, Danish from Swedish, or Portuguese from Spanish. This language, which comes to us in poetry, memoirs, sermons, letters and diaries, is known as the Older Scottish Tongue. The golden age of Scots literature is conventionally dated from 1376 (the year of John Barbour's poem "The Bruce") to 1603 (the Union of Crowns). It produced, at one level, the singers from the medieval tradition of anonymous popular poetry who now reached new heights of lyrical invention in ballads like "Sir Patrick Spens".

> *The king sits in Dunfermlin town*
> *Drinking the blood-red wine:*
> *Oh where will I get a good sailor*
> *To sail this ship of mine?*

In the court, there were the great *makars*, poets like Dunbar whose "Celebrations" is quite the equal of its English contemporaries. (In this verse, "quhois" is Scots for "whose".)

> *In bed at morrow, sleiping as I lay,*
> *Me thocht Aurora with hir cristall ene*
> *In at the window lukit by the day*
> *And halsit me, with visage paill and grene;*
> *On quhois hand a lark sang fro the splene,*
> *"Awalk, luvaris, out of your slomering,*
> *Se how the lusty morrow dois up spring."*

Sadly, the achievement was short-lived. As early as the middle of the sixteenth century we find even so Scottish a figure as the Calvinist John Knox being accused of having forgotten his "auld plane Scottis". What was happening?

In essence, by a process that dates back as far as Chaucer, Gower and Lydgate, Scottish culture was being influenced by (and then imitating) its English rival. English literature became increasingly popular with the Scots. English books and pamphlets found their way into the libraries of the great Scottish houses, and the brilliance of English poetry (Spenser, Shakespeare, Marlowe, Jonson, Donne) continued to provide Scottish writers with new models to imitate and compete with. Compare Dunbar with the way a later Scots poet, William Drummond of Hawthornden, abandons his native voice in favour of a southern one:

> *I know that all beneath the moon decays*
> *And what by mortals in this world is brought*
> *In times great periods shall return to nought*
> *That fairest states have fatal nights and days.*

The decisive blow to the possibility of a Scots language was James VI's move to London in 1603 to take up the English crown. James, son of Mary, Queen of Scots, spoke and wrote broad Scots, but when he left Holyrood House and moved south, he adopted the ways of the South. The Scottish court, which had nurtured Scots literary life for centuries, went with him. Now all official documents were in English, and the Scottish aristocracy discovered that to get on at Court they had to have a command of London English. Scottish peers began to send their children to English tutors and schools, a practice that continues to this day.

The story of the Maitland family captures this experience in miniature. An Anglo-Norman family, the Maitlands first came to Scotland in the twelfth century. The family seat, Thirlestane, in the heart of the Lauder valley, is one of the strategic castles on the road to Edinburgh and has been fought over for eight hundred years. There were Maitlands fighting for Scotland at Bannockburn and Flodden Field. One ancestor is the subject of the Scots ballad, "Auld Maitland". Another early Maitland spoke Scots so broad it was said that his tongue was too big for his mouth. A third was Lord Chancellor under James VI and went with him to London when he inherited the English crown. The present owner of Thirlestane, Captain the Honourable Gerald Maitland Carew, is as Scottish in ancestry as he could be. Yet there is not a trace of Scots in his speech. Most people would say that he spoke good "upper-class English". He explains why:

> My ancestors have been politicians at Westminster, and a lot of the family
> have been educated in the South, and that is why we speak the Queen's
> English.

He says that he finds Scots "a very rich language and I love listening to it". But he can't speak it. "I'm very bad at putting on accents." And just as ambitious Scots used to take lessons to lose what were called "marks of rusticity", the two Maitland Carew boys, Edward and Peter, will go to a boarding school in the South.

"A BIBLE IN VULGARE LANGUAGE"

The second and final blow to the Scots tongue came from an institution even more influential than the Court, the Church of Scotland, the Kirk. It was Scots law (1579) that every householder worth 300 merks had to possess "a bible and psalme buke in vulgare language". And when, a year later, the Scots did print their own edition of the Bible in Scotland, it was not in Scots, but it was a reprint of the English Geneva Bible. A generation later, James I ordered that every church in Scotland should conduct its Sunday service using the newly translated Authorized Version of the Bible. Thanks to the emphasis placed by the Kirk on Bible study, English was presented with a powerful weapon to penetrate even further into Scotland.

Fraser Aitken, a true Scot, is the minister in Girvan, Ayrshire. For three hundred and fifty years his predecessors have used the King James Version of the Bible, and when he preaches it is not in Scots but in Standard English with a Scots accent. Fraser Aitken calls the domination of the Authorized Version "a major blow to the Scots language, and it's a great shame", he adds, "that a Scottish translation has not been available up until now." William Lorimer's translation of the New Testament is a recent, belated triumph for Scots. Finally published in 1983, it was an immediate bestseller and has been popular with Scots churchgoers ever since. When Fraser Aitken reads the Lorimer version in church:

It's met with a very favourable reaction, although there are those who prefer the King James Version to be read because that to them is the Bible they've been so used to since their childhood days ... People listen more attentively because they're picking up words they haven't heard for a long time ... On the whole they understand the gist of the passage. The words they can't understand are few and far between.

Lorimer's version (using twelve varieties of Scots) demonstrates the range and vigour of Scots prose:

As he gaed yont the gate frae there, he saw a man caa'd Matthew sittin at his dask i the Towbuid, an he said til him, "Fallow me"; an he rase an fallowt him.
Efterhin he was i the houss, lyin at the buird, an belyve a guid wheen tax-uplifters an siclike outlans cam ben an lay doun aside Jesus an his disciples. Whan the Pharisees saw it, they said til his disciples, "What for taks your Maister his mait wi tax-uplifters an siclike outlans?"

In the Lorimer *New Testament* only the Devil speaks Standard English.

Fraser Aitken, who speaks in a classic middle-class Scots accent, is keen to preserve the old Scottish words: "It would be a great shame if they died out. They are part of Scottish tradition and heritage ... we want to keep these things and pass them on to the generations who come after us." Aitken is aware that he is probably fighting a losing battle.

Throughout the seventeenth century, the process of anglicization went on in the kirk and the home. Among the educated, English was now the familiar language, larded with occasional Scotticisms like *a glisk*, *to ken*, *the flitting*, *to mind of* something, and *Sunday's night*. In Lowland Edinburgh, social life was patterned on the London coffee houses. England – stable, prosperous and refined – was the model that many Scots did their best to imitate. The first president of the Fair Intellectual Club complimented her fellow blue-stockings on their English, noting "how difficult it is for our country people to acquire it". She added: "What a shame it is that ladies who value themselves for wit and politeness should be ignorant of their mother tongue!"

In the years after the '45, the vogue for English speech led to hostility towards Scots, especially among the educated. In 1752, the philosopher David Hume published a small collection of Scottish usages together with their admired English equivalents, obtained, as he put it, from the "best authors". For the Scots *proven*, the English say "proved", for *park*, "enclosure", for *learn*, they say "teach", and so on. Hume belonged to the most famous of the literary clubs, the Select Society. Around 1761 it changed its name to the Society for Promoting the Reading and Speaking of the English Language, and in the same year it invited the Irish actor Thomas Sheridan to Edinburgh to teach elocution. About three hundred leading citizens came to hear an attack on "marks of rusticity" and the Scottish vowel in words like *battle* and *habit*. It was said of Hume, whose admiration for things English was inordinate, that he died confessing not his sins but his Scotticisms.

The Lowland Scots capitulated to English largely out of choice. From the eighteenth century on, it was always "the great, the learned, the ambitious and the vain" who would imitate English. The Scottish tongue survived, but in diminishing ways, mainly through collections of dialect verse and occasional booklets (for schools) of Scottish texts. Here and there, in such volumes, one can catch the difference between "polite" and "broad" pronunciation. The preface of one textbook attacks Scots speakers who "to avoid cawvalry, bawank", say "kevalry, benk" and "fearing to say Scoatland, mincingly pronounce Sketland". Away from a centre of fashion like Edinburgh, the "Scots tongue" survived in the songs and conversation of the country people, and it was the Ayrshire countryside that gave Scotland her most famous poet, Robert Burns, the author of "Auld Lang Syne".

FROM BURNS TO LALLANS

Burns was born in the village of Alloway, near Girvan, in 1759. He grew up on the land, living the hard life of a farmer, an experience which inspired poems like "The Twa Dogs", "Halloween" and "To a Mouse". Burns, Dr Johnson's near contemporary, was an immensely likeable, charming man, with a taste for women and good living. After the success of his poems (published, he claimed, to raise money for a passage to Jamaica), he moved to Edinburgh and became something of a literary lion. His farm failed, and he lived on his writing and his pension as an exciseman. Most of his compositions now were songs, either new or adapted; "A Red, Red Rose", "Scots Wha Hae", "Comin' thro' the Rye", "The Banks of Doon", and "Mary Morrison". His hard living and a weak heart got the better of him and he died in 1796, only 37 years old.

Burns was educated in the Standard English of the day, in the words of his teacher, "the *Spelling Book*, the New Testament, the Bible, . . . and *Fisher's English Grammar*". Throughout his life he was capable of writing and speaking formal English. A contemporary reported that the philosopher Hume had a stronger Scottish accent than the poet. But for all his education, Burns was of peasant stock, close to the land, its customs and its people. It was his genius, in an age of slavish imitation, to draw on the despised Scottish tradition, half folk ballads and half Court poetry. Burns fused the two streams together into songs and satires of unrivalled colour and eloquence.

He is the poet of eating, drinking and wenching. The marvellous unforced Scots lyricism of a song like "Rigs o' Barley" is exhilarating and joyous:

> *I hae been blythe wi' comrades dear;*
> *I hae been merry drinking;*
> *I hae been joyfu' gath'rin gear;*
> *I hae been happy thinking:*
> *But a' the pleasures e'er I saw*
> *Tho' three times doubl'd fairly*
> *That happy night was worth them a',*
> *Among the rigs o' barley.*

With some regional exceptions (Shetland, Buchan and a few rural areas) Scots is a language you hear in its full richness only when Burns (or Lorimer) is quoted. It was Burns' great achievement, in the tradition of his predecessors, poets like Ramsay and Fergusson, to give his nation a voice and give the Scots tongue back its pride. When the Scots celebrate "the immortal memory" on Burns Night, they are honouring the writer who showed them that it is the loyalty to Scots language and culture that is, for an assimilated people, the best and most lasting assertion of Scottish nationalism.

Burns is remembered as the final flowering of a glorious literature. After his death, the process of anglicization that Johnson had witnessed took hold. For subsequent generations, the Scottish tongue was "dying", and their celebration of the past had the nostalgic air of an elegy. One Scotsman, a Lowlander, who felt the decline of his country keenly, and who helped to revive an international interest in Scottish culture, was Sir Walter Scott, famous throughout the world as the storyteller of Old Scotland. Scott's popularity hangs round him now like a millstone. But almost more important than how he wrote was what he wrote about. For later Scots writers like Robert Louis Stevenson, he established the tradition of rediscovering Scottishness through literature, and through the Scots tongue.

Scott looked to the great Scottish cultural achievements of the past, the poetry, the ballads and the folk songs, for an authentic expression of Scots pride. He was obsessed by the Jacobite Uprising as the turning-point in Scotland's fortunes: the subtitle of his first novel,

70 Sir Walter Scott gave inspiration to a revived Scottish nationalism.

71 Robert Louis Stevenson, whose work includes Scots ballads like "Sing me a song of a land that is gone".

Waverley, begun in 1805, was "'Tis Sixty Years Since" – since the '45. He was a traditionalist who looked back longingly to Scotland's lost independence. His work gave inspiration to a revived Scottish nationalism. In 1802–3, he published three volumes of ballads, many collected from his favourite Border country, many, like "Auld Maitland", reproduced for the first time. He concluded his Introduction with the significant remark that "it has been my object to throw together, perhaps without sufficient attention to method, a variety of remarks, regarding popular superstitions, and legendary history, which if not now collected, must soon have been totally forgotten".

> By such efforts, [Scott continued] feeble as they are, I may contribute somewhat to the history of my native country; the peculiar features of whose manners and character are daily melting and dissolving into those of her sister and ally. And, trivial as may appear such an offering, to the *manes* of a kingdom, once proud and independent, I hang it upon her altar with a mixture of feelings, which I shall not attempt to describe.

The Minstrelsy of the Scottish Borders was the first book to which Scott put his name and it was followed by bestselling narrative poems like the *Lay of the Last Minstrel*. Soon, however, trumped by Byron in the public's affection, he turned to prose. The Waverley novels made Scott's name and his reputation synonymous with his country's, so much so that he supervised the visit of George IV to Scotland in 1822. In the last years of his life unexpected bankruptcy forced him into literary overproduction, but the finest of his novels, *Ivanhoe*, *The Heart of Midlothian*, *Rob Roy* and *Quentin Durward*, had been written, finding enormous audiences throughout Europe and even further afield. An American commentator wrote that "The appearance of a new novel from his pen caused a greater sensation in the United States than did some of the battles of Napoleon."

Robert Louis Stevenson was born a generation after Scott's death, but we can see a literary approach that takes its inspiration from the Scots tongue Stevenson heard all about him. He writes in the preface to *Underwoods*:

> I simply wrote my Scots as well as I was able, not caring if it hailed from Lauderdale or Angus, from the Mearns or Galloway; if I had ever heard a good word I used it without shame; and when Scots was lacking, or the rhyme jibbed, I was glad (like my betters) to fall back on English.

Stevenson also attempted to indicate Scots pronunciation by his spelling:

> *Frae nirly, nippin', Eas'lan' breeze,*
> *Frae Norlan' snaw, an' haar o' seas,*
> *Weel happit in your gairden trees,*
>   *A bonny bit,*
> *Atween the muckle Pentland's knees,*
>   *Secure ye sit.*

72 William Laughton Lorimer devoted the last years of his life to *The New Testament in Scots*.

73 Hugh MacDiarmid, writing in "Lallans", was a leader of the 20th-century Scottish literary renaissance.

In the twentieth century, a revival of interest in Lallans – "plain braid Lallans" – a literary cocktail of Scots mixed from a variety of sources, past and present, has produced the poetry of Hugh MacDiarmid (the pseudonym adopted by C. M. Grieve). MacDiarmid chose Lallans partly out of patriotic motives, and partly because, he argued, a Scot can write creatively only in the language of his childhood and experience. His poem "Empty Vessel" begins:

> *I met ayont the cairney*
> *A lass wi' tousie hair*
> *Singin' till a bairnie*
> *That was nae langer there.*

Today, a magazine like *Lallans* keeps alive the idea of a Scottish Standard, but even here there is no escaping the pressures of Standard English. A recent issue had a paragraph headed "Scots in Jeopardie", appealing for help to complete the *Dictionary of the Older Scottish Tongue*. Perhaps more significant, its note to subscribers is printed not in Scots but in Standard English.

At the popular level, too, there are still a few authentic reminders of the Scottish folk tradition that inspired the Scottish writers of the past. Stanley Robertson, now a fish filleter in Aberdeen, is the son of a travelling people. He was brought up in the Aberdonian heartland of Broad Scots – the Doric accent – where *loons* are boys and *quines* are girls. He is a traditional

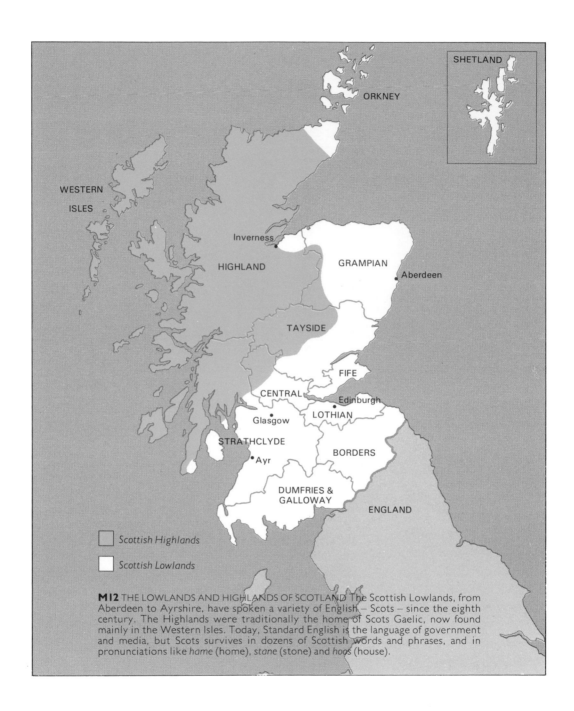

M12 THE LOWLANDS AND HIGHLANDS OF SCOTLAND The Scottish Lowlands, from Aberdeen to Ayrshire, have spoken a variety of English — Scots — since the eighth century. The Highlands were traditionally the home of Scots Gaelic, now found mainly in the Western Isles. Today, Standard English is the language of government and media, but Scots survives in dozens of Scottish words and phrases, and in pronunciations like *hame* (home), *stane* (stone) and *hoos* (house).

storyteller whose "Jack Tales" have a pedigree that stretches into the mists of the Scottish past. He knows more Scots ballads than any man alive. His memory is a treasure trove of Scots folklore and language and he still remembers how he first heard the "Jack Tales" from his family:

74 In 1608, James I encouraged the Scottish Lowlanders to establish plantations in the north of Ireland. It was not a peaceful settlement for long: Protestants and Catholics were soon at war.

> My people bein' travellers fae different parts o' the country . . . they had this great wealth o' tradition an' folklore. An' fan they were oot in the country, because there was nae other distractions, ye hed the great opportunity o' bein' close with the tradition . . . The story was telt every night. Nae just one, but maybe two or three. An' the beauty of the story was, ye see, some night we'd hear the same story telt three of four times.

Scots like this is preserved in the speech of Aberdeenshire and the working-class districts of the big cities like Glasgow, but its survival as a literary form is self-conscious and artificial. The majority of the Scots speak standard English with a Scottish accent, and write Standard English occasionally flavoured with a word like *loch*, *burn* or *brae*.

Yet Scottish influence ranges the English-speaking world. The "Jack Tales" that Stanley Robertson tells, and the ballads that his parents used to sing, are known not only in Scotland, but also across the water in Ulster, and further afield still in the blue hills of Appalachia. For centuries the Scots had fought and traded and intermarried with the people of Ulster, barely twenty miles across the Irish Sea, and when James I went south to London he gave his former Scottish (now his British) subjects a new incentive to emigrate: land.

THE SCOTS IN IRELAND

In a series of measures designed to break the rule of the Celtic chiefs in Ulster, James confiscated the lands of the Lords of Tyrone and Tyrconnel and granted territory in the North to English and Scottish planters. Scotland, being nearer to Ulster and more poverty-stricken, provided the bulk of the new tenants. Besides, the Presbyterian Lowlanders hoped to find in Ulster the religious freedom they were denied at home. So, in the first decades of the seventeenth century, the Lowland Scots set sail for Ulster and the life of the pioneer. In total some 200,000 Scots migrated to Northern Ireland. In turn, some two million of their descendants migrated to America, during the eighteenth, nineteenth and even the early part of the twentieth century.

The Scots-Irish (see Notes p. 359) transformed the province. Formerly backward, it now became the most prosperous part of Ireland. The new settlers acquired a reputation for hard bargaining, thrift and even meanness that persists to this day: they are said to have short arms and deep pockets. Their migration occurred, as we have seen, at a point when Scots and English had become remarkably divergent, perhaps almost as divergent as Swedish and Danish. So the Scots brought to Ulster a language that was very different from the English that was being imported from the South and Midlands. In Ulster, the Scots outnumbered the English six to one and in language, as in everything else, their influence was decisive.

The Scots who crossed to the coast of Antrim and settled in towns like Ballymena believed that they had come to the promised land. It is said that when they landed in Ulster they fell on their knees and prayed to the Lord – and then they fell on the natives and preyed on them. Back home in Scotland, these Ulster settlers were considered to be, as some put it, " the scum of the earth", and crossing the Irish Sea was seen as the last mark of a despicable rogue.

From the start, the speech of the settlers was isolated in a sea of Irish. Theirs was not a peaceful settlement. Towns like Londonderry became walled fortresses in a state of war with the Gaelic-speaking Irish. The never-to-be-forgotten siege of Derry in 1689 gave the language a new phrase: No Surrender. The fighting tradition of the Scots lived on, and even today a simple language map of Northern Ireland shows the Scots-Irish element separated from the rest of the community.

One of the most distinctive Scots-Irish localities is the country around the market town of Ballymena. Here a kind of Scots is spoken that is possibly more archaic than much that is spoken in Lowland Scotland itself. G. B. Adams, who has made a study of the speech customs of the region, has recorded a typical exchange in a country farmhouse:

> "Jammie, you're an oul baachelor, A hear. It's a wundher ye navver merried."
> "Oh you're aa wraang there, Joahn, A'm no an oul baachelor, A'm a weeda-maan. Aye, ma wife deed wheen we were jist a year married, wheen harr waen was boarn."
> "Weel, Jammie, A'm soary tae hear thaat, but it's a wundher ye navver merried again."

The transplanting of Scots English to Ulster broke its contact with the homeland. As we have already seen with English in America, the effect of the separation was to preserve older forms of Scots in the new settlement, forms that have in some cases died out back home. In parts of rural Ulster as in Central Scotland, words like "bone" and "stone" have remained *bane* and *stane*. The *v* in a word like "give" is dropped, making *gie*. Many other pronunciations seem to come from the lines of a Burns poem: *saft* for "soft", *lea'* for "leave", *ba'* for "ball", *tap* for "top", and *seek* for "sick". The familiar "How now brown cow?" becomes *Hoo noo broon coo?*

The Scots-Irish also preserve some very Scottish vocabulary. Professor John Braidwood, who is compiling an Ulster-English dictionary, has some examples of these, "You hear words like *hain* – hain is to use a thing sparingly, to save it up ... *Blate* is shy, rather backward in coming forward. *Sprachle* is to clamber awkwardly. You hear *cassie*, a cassie is the paved yard in front of a farm. Or you hear *fornent*, meaning opposite. The Ulster Scots are very fond of *fornent*. You hear *gunk* – for disappointment. A *quare gunk* is a right disappointment."

Professor Braidwood tells a story that captures the special richness of the Ulster "Scots-Irish" English:

> There's a nice wee story of Sammy. Sammy was a bachelor, middle-aged, "frae Crossgar" as they say here, and he married a great big sowdie woman – a big hefty woman. As he went to bring his bride home (on his cart), a wag on the side of the road shouted, Hey Sammy, will ye bring her all haim in ane laid [will you bring her all home in one load]. That's a big sowdie o' a woman. All beef to the heels like a Millingar heifer.

One unmistakable mark of the Scots-Irish is their ancestral ability to pronounce what Braidwood calls "a good strong *ch*" – as in words like *loch*, names like *McMachan*, and Gaelic place names like *Ahoghill* (pronounced achockle) and *Aughacully* (pronounced ochacully).

Both Ahoghill and Aughacully are in the Braid Valley near Slemish Mountain, where St Patrick used to graze his sheep. Scots farmers have worked these Irish fields for three hundred years. The Scottishness of these settlers became a byword in the province. When Irish speakers came to learn English in places like Belfast or Londonderry, they said they were going "to lift the Scotch". Another story tells of some Donegal Irish apologizing to a traveller for not speaking English. As the tale goes, they said to him: "It's the Irish we speak among ourselves, but we hae enou' Scotch to speak to your honour." This, of course, is broad Ayrshire of the Burns variety. The farmers in the Braid Valley have names like McBurney, Hamilton, Cruickshank and Logan. Every week or so they take their calves to the Ballymena Cattle Auction, driving through the Irish lanes with their Irish place-names. Their speech is full of Scots words: *yin* for "one", *geyly* for "almost", and *a wee colour mair* for "a drop of whisky".

Travelling through Ulster in the 1980s, there is no escaping the security measures: checkpoints, control zones in towns, jeeps, roadblocks and policemen in bullet-proof jackets.

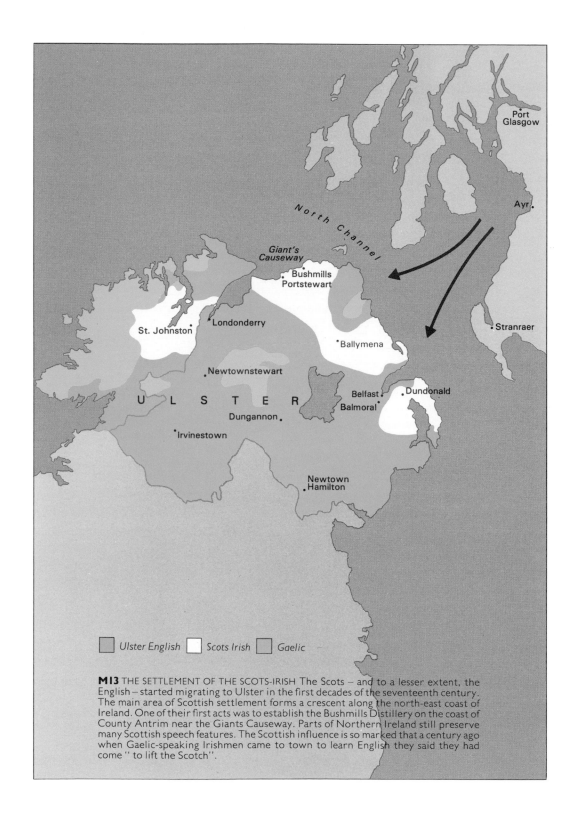

Port
Glasgow

Ayr

North Channel

Stranraer

Giant's
Causeway

Bushmills
Portstewart

St. Johnston

Londonderry

Ballymena

U L S T E R

Newtownstewart

Belfast
Balmoral

Dundonald

Dungannon

Irvinestown

Newtown
Hamilton

☐ Ulster English ☐ Scots Irish ☐ Gaelic

M13 THE SETTLEMENT OF THE SCOTS-IRISH The Scots — and to a lesser extent, the English — started migrating to Ulster in the first decades of the seventeenth century. The main area of Scottish settlement forms a crescent along the north-east coast of Ireland. One of their first acts was to establish the Bushmills Distillery on the coast of County Antrim near the Giants Causeway. Parts of Northern Ireland still preserve many Scottish speech features. The Scottish influence is so marked that a century ago when Gaelic-speaking Irishmen came to town to learn English they said they had come " to lift the Scotch".

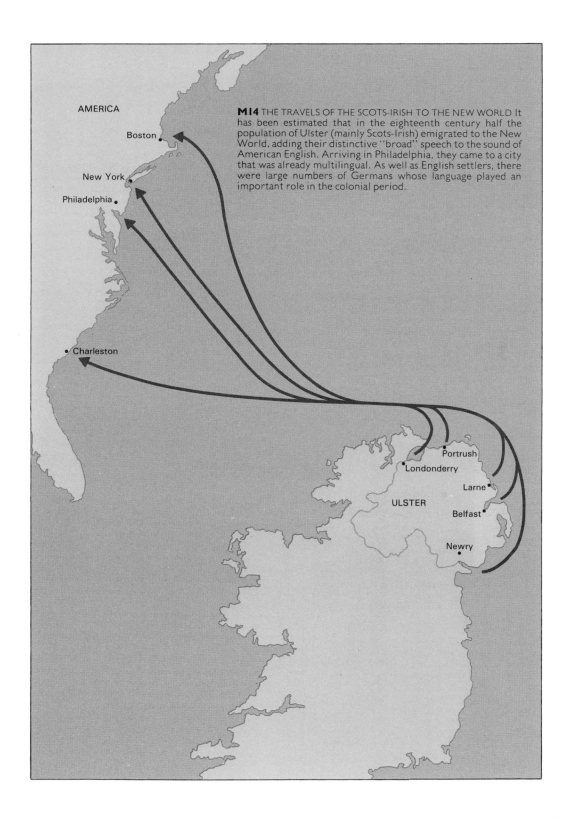

AMERICA

Boston

New York

Philadelphia

Charleston

M14 THE TRAVELS OF THE SCOTS-IRISH TO THE NEW WORLD It has been estimated that in the eighteenth century half the population of Ulster (mainly Scots-Irish) emigrated to the New World, adding their distinctive "broad" speech to the sound of American English. Arriving in Philadelphia, they came to a city that was already multilingual. As well as English settlers, there were large numbers of Germans whose language played an important role in the colonial period.

Portrush
Londonderry
Larne
ULSTER
Belfast
Newry

The Scots-Irish are at war with the Irish – as they always have been. In the seventeenth and eighteenth centuries they trampled on the native Irish Catholics (whom they despised) and struggled to assert their claims against the ruling English (who despised them). They became characteristically energetic and pugnacious, with a natural and inbuilt frontier mentality, ready to take on all comers.

About a hundred years after the first Ulster settlements, the conditions became more hostile. Rising rents, bad harvests and religious discrimination combined to set the Scots-Irish on the move again. Typically undaunted, they set off to the new frontier – the colonies of North America. In the 1720s, some 50,000 sailed across the Atlantic, the first of many succeeding generations of Scots-Irish to try their fortunes in the New World, from Charleston to Montreal. By the year of Independence, 1776, it has been calculated that almost half of Ulster had crossed the Atlantic, and that one in seven of the colonists was Scots-Irish.

THE AMERICAN PLANTATIONS

The fair prospect of America was a powerful stimulus to these waves of emigration. Relatives would write home with inviting accounts of the opportunities of the New World. Two Presbyterian clergymen reported, in 1729, that numbers of Ulstermen had received "many letters from their friends and acquaintances who have already settled in the American Plantations, inviting them to transport themselves thither, and promising them liberty and ease as the reward of their honest industry . . ."

The five emigrant ports – Belfast, Londonderry, Newry, Larne and Portrush – were busy with the America trade, especially when shipping agents were out looking for business. It is reported that shipworkers (in 1729) "send agents to markets and fairs and [circulate] public advertisements through the country to assemble the people together, where they assure them that in America they can get good land to them and their posterity for little or no rent". Many of the poorest share croppers needed no further inducement, and would be willing to cross the Atlantic as indentured servants, being offered for hire in the New World, a class just above the Black slaves.

At first, the Scots-Irish headed for New England, where they were not well received. The native New Englanders found the latest arrivals intolerant, violent, unruly and poverty-stricken. "These confounded Irish", complained the surveyor general of Boston, "will eat us all up." They were encouraged to head south towards Pennsylvania, with its economic opportunities and religious toleration. The state capital, Philadelphia, and its river, the Delaware, became the main entry-point for the majority of the Scots-Irish. In 1760, Benjamin Franklin, who was right about most things, estimated that the city was one-third English, one-third German – and one-third Scots (meaning Scots-Irish). It was this last third who were to become, in the words of Theodore Roosevelt "the kernel of the distinctively and intensely American stock who were the pioneers of our people in their march westward".

At first Philadelphia welcomed them for their frontier toughness – local Pennsylvania officials believed they would be ideal for keeping the French and the Indians at bay. James

Logan, the state secretary of Pennsylvania, himself from Ulster, enthusiastically granted a chunk of land to a group of Scots-Irish to establish the new American frontier town of Donegal.

> At the time we were apprehensive from the Northern Indians ... I therefore thought it prudent to plant a settlement of such men as those who formerly had so bravely defended Londonderry and Enniskillen as a frontier against any disturbance.

Logan soon doubted his own judgement. The Scots-Irish were nothing but trouble. "A settlement of five families from the North of Ireland gives me more trouble than fifty of any other people." He was infuriated by their "audacious and disorderly habit" of claiming squatters' rights on "any spot of vacant land they fancied".

At odds with the English, they moved inland – through German country. The Pennsylvania Dutch, who had first come here in the 1680s, traded words and customs with their Scottish and English neighbours. The language picked up words like *hex* meaning "a spell", and food words like *sauerkraut*. The Scots settled briefly, for a generation – the cemeteries of Pennsylvania recall typical Scots family names like Agnew, Hamilton and Taggart. Many Scots-Irish now became absorbed into the life of the new society, mixing with their English and German neighbours. As their children grew up young Americans, the distinctive accents of all three ethnic groups became merged into one variety of American speech. With their love of music and song, the Scots-Irish borrowed the dulcimer from their German neighbours and, for defence against a harsh climate, German-style log-cabins.

The Scots-Irish who did not settle pushed on south through the Cumberland Gap towards the hills of Appalachia. On the frontier, they bore the brunt of Indian hostility. They tended to live isolated lives in backwoods settlements. It was a harsh, pioneering existence, but they had become well suited to it. They were fierce, clannish and unruly. It is said that they were overfond of whisky. With their long rifles and coonskin hats, Scots-Irish frontiermen, like the legendary Davy Crockett, acquired a ferocious reputation as Indian fighters. Great boasters and compulsive storytellers, they had a keen ear for a striking phrase. Davy Crockett described himself as, "Fresh from the backwoods, half-horse, half-alligator, a little touched with snapping turtle, can wade the Mississippi, leap the Ohio, ride a streak of lightning, slide down a honey locust and not get scratched." Their descendants are found in the remoter parts of the Appalachian mountains.

The Scots-Irish brought with them a rich oral culture: aphorisms, proverbs, superstitions and an ability to turn a striking phrase – *mad as a meat axe, dead as a hammer, so drunk he couldn't hit the wall with a handful of beans*. It was the frontiermen who first spoke of someone with *an axe to grind*, or someone who *sat on the fence* when he should perhaps *go the whole hog*. Their rhymes and ditties came from the traditions of Scotland and Ireland. Their ballads, such as *Edward*, tell the stories of their ancestors, and the tunes of the Scottish Lowland ballads of the sixteenth and seventeenth centuries have been an important influence in the making of American country music.

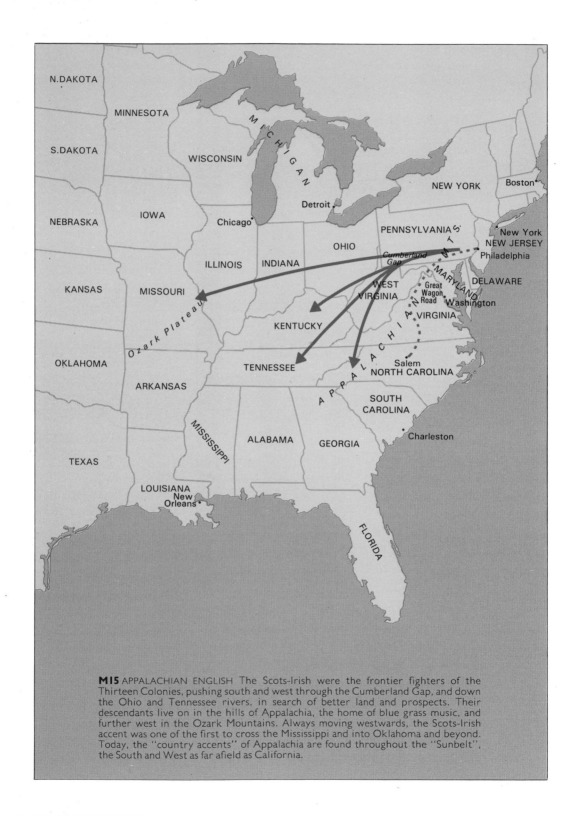

M15 APPALACHIAN ENGLISH The Scots-Irish were the frontier fighters of the Thirteen Colonies, pushing south and west through the Cumberland Gap, and down the Ohio and Tennessee rivers, in search of better land and prospects. Their descendants live on in the hills of Appalachia, the home of blue grass music, and further west in the Ozark Mountains. Always moving westwards, the Scots-Irish accent was one of the first to cross the Mississippi and into Oklahoma and beyond. Today, the "country accents" of Appalachia are found throughout the "Sunbelt", the South and West as far afield as California.

75/76 Willard Watson is an old "moonshiner" from Appalachia: "If you drink a pint of moonshine whiskey . . . you couldn't hit the wall with a handful of beans."

The Appalachian mountains are the home of the hillbillies, old-time American Whites, whose traditional speech – *afeared*, *damnedest* and *plum right* – is sometimes, mistakenly, thought to be a relic of Elizabethan English. Two of the most typical of these old mountain people are the storyteller Ray Hicks and his wife, Clara, who live up in the mountains, some ten miles from Boone, the centre of the Appalachian region. This is Clara describing how to find their house:

> When you're starting here, you come in a plane as far as you can go, then you get in a car and ride as far as you can run. Then you get down and crawl as far as you can come. Go that-a-way, then you straighten up, and then you find the house. It's an old-timey one. It looks haunted, but it's really not.

Ray Hicks grew up in this house. He is celebrated in the region as a teller of the traditional "Jack Tales", which the Scots brought with them and which Stanley Robertson still tells in Aberdeen. Local people come from miles around to hear him talk, and the rhythms of his speech are vital source material for anyone who wants to study Appalachian English. (In this extract, Ray Hicks pronounces the *w* in a word like "sword" making *sward*.)

> So Jack he heeard a racket up in the attic of the log cabin, and directly he's a-watchin', and down come six black devils, a-swingin' down through the skirtle hole they call it, and these six little black devils had a sword apiece. They was at him with them swords, and Jack was a-jumpin' around thar, and he saw a sack over in the corner. So he jumped over and he grabbed it, and he said: Whickety-whack, come down in this sack.

Professor Cratis Williams, who has been called "the father of Appalachian studies" and has devoted years to a study of the speech in that region, considers that the Appalachian people are "the best storytellers in the world", a tradition he attributes to their Scottish past.

> The Appalachian people love stories. Even when they're in a hurry, they'll stop to hear stories. Children and old people too, when they're relaxed, love to hear long stories . . . The best stories in the Appalachian tradition are told in the dialect.

According to Williams, the talk of these hills is now a jumble of Scots-Irish, English and German. But from the beginning, the Scots-Irish in the Appalachians were especially noted for their speech. In the advertisements of the time, their speech was called "broad", as distinct from the Irish who spoke with "the Brogue on his Tongue". English words borrowed into Pennsylvanian German often show archaic forms which could have come from the Scots-Irish: *chaw* for "chew", *ingine* for "engine" and *picter* for "picture". Writers of the time knew what they were describing. The Reverend Jonathan Boucher, writing in the 1800s, says that it was one of the four distinctive "dialects" remaining in the States – "the Scotch-Irish, as it used to be called, in some of the back settlers of the Middle States".

Many examples of Scots-Irish usage prevail to this day – words like *bonny-clabber* for curdled sour milk (an anglicization of the Irish Gaelic *bainne clabair*) and *flannel-cake* for a thin wheat cake. *Sook, sookie,* or *sook cow* is the local cry farmers use to summon the herd and comes from the Old English *sūcan* meaning "to suck". The famous Southern *you-all* is a Scots-Irish translation of the plural *yous*. The use of *all* in this context, and in contexts like *who-all was there?* and *tell me, what-all you did?*, is typical both of Ulster and of the (largely southern) states of America.

Most famous of all, perhaps, is the Scots-Irish use of the word *cabin* to refer to the log houses of the frontier. *Log cabin* is first recorded in 1770 referring to the buildings of Virginia, and it is clear that the Scots-Irish, who lived in such buildings (borrowing the design from the German Americans), spread both the name and the building method, until the term entered American folklore.

Cratis Williams says that the distinctive marks of contemporary Appalachian English are clear enough. The word "there" becomes *tharr*, "bear" becomes *barr* and "hair" is *herr*.

> No one says *hair* the way we do. That's because of the strong influence of the *r* . . . Instead of saying *hair* or *hayre* as other Americans would do, we say *herr* . . . We continue to omit the final *g*. Strictly speaking, we don't really omit it, we never did get around to putting it on. And we continue to use the Middle English *a-* in front of *ing* words. So we go *a-huntin'* and *a-fishin'* . . . Outsiders are sometimes impressed by hearing us say *Hit* for *it* . . . *Hit* and *it* can both appear in the same sentence. If the word is stressed, it's *hit*. If it's not stressed, then it's *it*. One would never say, "I've never heard of *hit*." One would say, "I've never heard of it. *Hit's* something new to me."

The continuities that Cratis Williams describes are vividly sustained in the talk and lifestyle of an old-timer like Willard Watson. Somewhere in the hills – he wouldn't want the taxman to find out where – Willard Watson distils "moonshine whiskey" the traditional way, next to a stream. There's an old Appalachian saying that the English settlers built a house, the Germans built a barn, and the Scots-Irish built a still – to make what they called their "mountain lightning". In the words of Willard Watson, who pronounces *pint* as "parnt":

> A pint is enough, and a pint is just about too much. If you drink a pint of moonshine whiskey, you won't know where the sun went down or where it come up. Get you where you couldn't hit the wall with a handful of beans.

Willard Watson is now in a minority, but throughout West Virginia, Kentucky, Tennessee and the Ozarks, the Appalachian speech tradition has strong, unshakeable roots. The tobacco farmers of the Boone district, who still prefer to use horses for ploughing their steep upland fields, do not talk as broad as Ray Hicks or Willard Watson, but they would never be mistaken for a New Englander or a Westerner. And if their children stay on in these parts, they too will speak with their parents' accents, talk of *baccer* for "tobacco", and say perhaps that so-and-so is *plum crazy* or *plum right*. The strength of this tradition is now reinforced by the fashion for American "country" style – in music, talk and dress. Today, the ballads of the Scots-Irish that travelled here during the eighteenth century are imitated and reproduced from Arkansas to Alberta, by singers like Dolly Parton and Kenny Rogers who have internationalized a style that was once confined to the hills.

The popularity of country music is only the latest example of the Scots-Irish influence on American life. After expanding the frontier southwards and westwards, the Scots-Irish became the shock troops in the War of Independence, accounting for half of the rebel army, according to one British general. George Washington is said to have remarked that "with these men" he would make his "last stand for liberty". They made other important contributions to the history of the United States. Some were soldiers like Stonewall Jackson. Many American presidents are of Scots-Irish stock: Andrew Jackson, James Buchanan, Chester A. Arthur, James K. Polk, Ulysses S. Grant, Grover Cleveland, Benjamin Harrison, William McKinley and Woodrow Wilson. Today, about twenty million people, some 10 per cent of the American population, can claim Scots-Irish ancestry.

The pioneering of the English language in the New World by the Scots and the English proceeded apace. When a Scottish academic, John Witherspoon, went to America towards the end of the eighteenth century to become president of the College of New Jersey (later Princeton University), he was so struck by the "Americanisms" he heard all around him that he presented a series of papers on the subject. He noted the use of *mad* for "angry", of *bamboozle* for "swindle", the use of contractions like *ain't*, *can't* and *don't*, mistakes like *lay* for "lie" and *knowed* for "knew", and pronunciations such as *winder* for "window". In due course, some of these usages became part of American English. But not before a third set of immigrants had made their mark on the English of the Thirteen Colonies: the Irish.

77 James Joyce. In *The Portrait of the Artist as a Young Man*, his hero Stephen Dedalus says that he will "forge in the smithy of my soul the uncreated conscience of my race".

5
THE
IRISH QUESTION

English is not the native language of Ireland, though the English themselves often speak as if it were. In Britain, the Irish literary achievement – the long roll-call of names that includes Spenser, Congreve, Swift, Sheridan, Wilde, Yeats, Synge, Shaw, Joyce, Beckett and Heaney – has become assimilated into the tradition of English writing. In the United States, St Patrick's Day is an important occasion, and in recent times three presidents have made calculated pilgrimages to their ancestral villages in Ireland. The island and its people exert such a powerful hold over the American imagination that about forty million citizens claim Irish descent, a figure the census authorities know to be inflated. Indeed, Ireland occupies an almost mythic place in the English-speaking world. The soft music of the Irish voice is admired by speakers of British or American English everywhere. Many people say they prefer the Irish accent to all others. Together with the Scots, their speech is one of the most widely recognized varieties of English in the world. The Irish are renowned for their gifts as storytellers, admired for the lyrical constructions of their daily talk and teased for what some call "Irish logic". The story is told of the railway station at Ballyhough. It had two clocks which disagreed by some six minutes. When an irate traveller asked a porter what was the use of having two clocks if they didn't tell the same time, the porter replied, "And what would we be wanting with two clocks if they told the same time?"

There are many ironies to the English colonization of Ireland. Politically, Ireland is a trauma. English armies have trampled on Irish sovereignty for over eight hundred years and have shed much blood there. Culturally, the Irish are the traditional butt – as above – of "Irish jokes": envied for their eloquence, they are almost in the same breath scorned for their "stupidity". In England, as we have seen, the Anglo-Saxons and the Celts hardly mixed. In Ireland, the strange and sometimes tragic fusion of their two languages has made a culture, spoken and written, that is one of the glories of the English language. The story of English in Ireland throws up many questions: what is the source of our fascination with the Irish voice? Why *is* Irish literature in English so impressive? And, most elusive of all, what has been the exact influence of the Irish on the English language itself?

The popular shrine of this fascination with the Irish and their language is Blarney Castle in County Cork. The gift of eloquence, or "the Blarney", is widely believed to be an Irish quality, one that is much prized, and every year thousands of tourists come to Cork "to kiss the Blarney stone". Some say that the legend of Blarney begins with Queen Elizabeth I. According to the apocryphal story, the castle was then occupied by Cormac MacCarthymore, a local chieftain, a man with a great gift for talk and prevarication. Elizabeth, probably with good reason, regarded his loyalty as doubtful and called on him to surrender his castle. MacCarthymore, so the story goes, replied, via Elizabeth's favourite the Earl of Essex, with speeches of great flattery that he was, of course, just about to do as his queen desired. But nothing happened. Elizabeth repeated her demand, and received the same response: he would when he could, but there were one or two matters of great urgency and importance he had to attend to first. This was MacCarthymore's way of avoiding the issue. Eventually, after many such exchanges, the frustrated queen is said to have exclaimed, "It's all Blarney – he says he will do it, but he never means to do what he says," or, according to another version, "Blarney, Blarney, I will hear no more of this Blarney!" Today, "Blarney" means finding the right speech in an extraordinary situation, when you don't have a word prepared. It is a kind of impromptu eloquence.

The legend of the Blarney stone, like so many supposed Gaelic myths, did not flourish until the nineteenth century, and the origins of the stone itself are veiled in mystery. Some say it was the stone of Jacob's Dream, and that the prophet Jeremiah brought it to Ireland. Another story tells that it was originally part of the Stone of Scone (on which English monarchs are traditionally crowned), and was given to the lord of Blarney by Robert Bruce after the Battle of Bannockburn. Whatever the truth, the stone itself is found on one of the castle's parapets. To kiss it, the visitor has to lie on his back and be lowered head downwards over the edge of the wall.

The present owner of the castle is Sir Richard Colthurst, whose family have lived in Ireland since the end of the sixteenth century when one of his ancestors, who participated in Sir Walter Ralegh's expedition there, was granted land. In the present owner's words, they "have never married out of Ireland". The Colthurst family history is typical of the English experience in Ireland before 1800: vastly outnumbered by the native Irish population, the Anglo-Irish in their castles and mansions were scattered islands of English in a sea of Gaelic.

"THE PAGAN SPEECH"
The Gaelic tradition is Ireland's well of inspiration. W. B. Yeats, whose work was steeped in it, once wrote:

> *I have no speech but symbol, the pagan speech I made*
> *Amid the dreams of youth.*

This "pagan speech" was the language of Old Ireland. Later the victim of English invasion and oppression, this remote Celtic society exhibited great confidence in the eighth and ninth centuries, raiding and settling the neighbouring shores of Scotland, Cornwall and Wales, the parts of old Britain not conquered by the Anglo-Saxons. (According to legend, St Patrick, who introduced Christianity into Ireland, was himself an escaped Welsh slave.) In the tenth century, the golden age of Irish saints and scholars, the culture of the island achieved a glorious perfection, a misty landmark at which later generations would gaze nostalgically.

In 1171, Henry II came to Ireland in the aftermath of a landing by his Anglo-Norman knights, the first English king to do so. This visit marked the beginning of English domination. At the time, the all-pervasive Celtic culture rapidly gaelicized the majority of the first Englishmen to settle in Ireland, so they became more Irish than the Irish themselves. The power of the Irish language is demonstrated by the so-called Statutes of Kilkenny (1366) which specified, with a rather desperate severity, that all Englishmen in Ireland should use English surnames, speak English and follow English customs – or forfeit their lands. As those who try to impose language by statute discover, the law was ineffective. The status and prestige of the native tongue rose even more in the 1550s, when Roman Catholic opposition to the Reformation championed Irish Gaelic against Protestant English. In 1578, an English Lord Chancellor reported that "all English, and the most part with delight, even in Dublin, speak Irish, and greatly are spotted in manners, habit and conditions with Irish stains". By the turn of the century, English in Ireland had almost died out. A scandalized visitor to Ireland observed that, "The English Irish and the very Cittizens (excepting those of Dublin where the Lord Deputy resides) though they could speake English as well as wee, yet Commonly speake Irish among themselues, and were hardly induced by our familiar Conversation to speake English with vs."

For the next two hundred years, the Protestant English and the Ulster Scots were at odds with the ruling families, as the planters competed with the native Irish. It was a bitter conflict with consequences that persist to the present. Until the Act of Union in 1803, which made Ireland part of the United Kingdom, Irish Gaelic was inextricably associated with Roman Catholicism, English with the Protestant supremacy. Even today the language war is not over. The rhetoric of the IRA graffiti is often in Gaelic: a phrase like "Vote Sinn Fein" is two thirds Irish. It is said that Protestants and Catholics still use language against each other, and that the pronunciation of the letter h ("aitch" for Protestants; "haitch" for Roman Catholics) has been used by both the IRA and the UDR to determine the fate of their captives. (Another well-known contemporary shibboleth is the Roman Catholic use of "Derry" in contrast to the Protestant "Londonderry".)

Following the ascendancy of English power throughout the eighteenth century, the English language was dominant, at least in the cities and towns, where it flourished among the ambitious classes in particular. The story is told of Richard Hennessy, the son of a prosperous Roman Catholic family who later became renowned as French brandy distillers. Hennessy was born in County Cork. In 1740, at the age of twenty, he went to fight with the Irish Brigade in France. (As readers of Thackeray's *Barry Lyndon* will remember, there were Irish regiments fighting for France, Prussia and Russia until the Napoleonic Wars.) Only then did

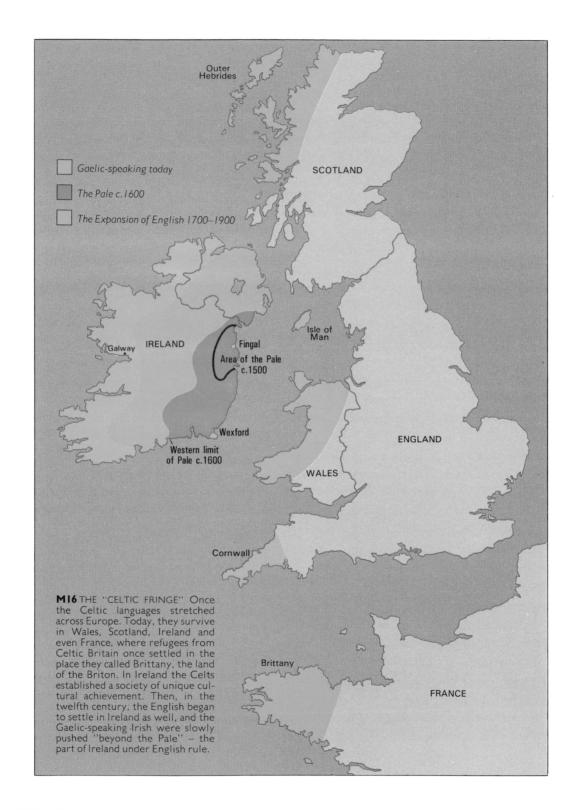

Outer
Hebrides

SCOTLAND

☐ *Gaelic-speaking today*

▨ *The Pale c.1600*

☐ *The Expansion of English 1700–1900*

IRELAND

Galway

Fingal
Area of the Pale
c.1500

Isle of
Man

Wexford

Western limit
of Pale c.1600

ENGLAND

WALES

Cornwall

Brittany

FRANCE

M16 THE "CELTIC FRINGE" Once
the Celtic languages stretched
across Europe. Today, they survive
in Wales, Scotland, Ireland and
even France, where refugees from
Celtic Britain once settled in the
place they called Brittany, the land
of the Briton. In Ireland the Celts
established a society of unique cultural achievement. Then, in the
twelfth century, the English began
to settle in Ireland as well, and the
Gaelic-speaking Irish were slowly
pushed "beyond the Pale" – the
part of Ireland under English rule.

78 The Gaeltacht, Co. Glenbeigh. Less than one per cent of the population still speaks Irish Gaelic.

79 Launching a curragh in County Mayo. *Curragh* and *coracle* share the same Gaelic root.

he learn to speak Irish Gaelic. A hundred years earlier such ignorance of his "mother tongue" would have been unthinkable.

The Irish ruling class were quite pragmatic about their anglicization: they wanted to influence their English overlords. There were, for instance, many English-speaking Irishmen in the independence movement of the 1790s. In 1803, after the Act of Union, the Englishness of the Anglo-Irish aristocracy became more distinctive and (like the Scottish aristocracy two hundred years earlier) they began to have their children educated in England. Generations of co-existence between the Irish and Anglo-Saxon traditions, at times more or less peaceful but always mutually suspicious, had made a kind of English unique in the story of the language. Unlike our account of other varieties of English, it is not enough simply to speak of Irish English. Scholars distinguish between Anglo-Irish (the English of those whose ancestral mother tongue is English) and Hiberno-English (the English of those whose ancestral mother tongue is Gaelic), and we shall use both terms. Fundamentally, of course, the chief influence on English in Ireland was Irish Gaelic, the language of the Irish Celts, part of a family of Gaelic languages stretching from Scotland to Brittany.

THE GAELIC FACTOR

On the west coast of Ireland, in County Mayo, there is a surviving tradition of Irish poetry that symbolizes this marriage of Irish Gaelic and English. Pat Linney, now in his seventies, lives in a cottage on the edge of the little village of Rossport. A copybook Republican, he composes his poems looking at the *greeshy* (embers) of his *turf* (peat) fire. What he calls his "obsessional brain" thinks in Irish, but he gives alternate verses in English. The twenty-two verses of his "History of Ireland" have all the typical alliterations, poetic cliché, and internal rhyme-schemes of the Irish oral tradition. The English version, each stanza ending with the traditional "long line", opens:

Ireland's history is painful reading,
Each page and chapter relates her woe,
Of her loving children died as martyrs,
And then thousands slaughtered by the Saxon foe.

The subjugation of this lovely nation,
Was the theme and aim of the rootless foe . . .

This part of County Mayo is still a place of superstition and folklore, remote from tourism and the twentieth century. There are the remains of prehistoric forests and fairy mounds in the peat-bogs. People talk of ancestors as if they were neighbours, and of three-hundred-year-old events as if they happened yesterday. Here it is not hard to understand how the Gaelic past transformed the invading English so completely. In Celtic Ireland, language was passed from generation to generation on the lips of storytellers (*sean chaithe*) like Pat Linney. The stories were often collected from wandering beggars, and eagerly awaited by the villagers. Traditionally, stories and poems were told at night, mainly during the long winter, from harvest-time to spring. "I have heard", wrote one traveller, "of a man who fell asleep by the fire and found a story going on when he woke next morning."

The marriage of Gaelic and English constructions, as in sentences like "He's in bed with the leg", or "I do be living in Dublin" or "He is after writing", is the chief characteristic of Irish speech. It is well illustrated by a conversational sentence describing the marriage of a young couple who had courted each other at the church gate: "'Tis an aise to the gate they to be married," which could be translated into "Did you know that for years before they were married, they used to meet at the wooden gate?" The Hiberno-English sentence is a more or less direct translation of the Irish "Is mór an suaimhneas don gheata iad a bheith pósta," which rendered literally in Standard English comes out as a wooden and almost meaningless, "It's a relief to the gate that they're married."

It is the unEnglishness of Hiberno-English that supplies its fascination to the English. The distinguished creolist Loreto Todd, who spent most of her childhood in Coal Island, County Tyrone (itself an anglicization of *Tír Eoghain*, Land of Owen), describes the collision of the two languages from her own experience. She recalls farmers at the local market saying "There's a great buying on the cows the day", and – more intelligibly – of a woman who made a dress without a pattern, "She made it out of her head." She notes that there are "Gaelic words which are quite widely used in Tyrone, especially among the old people". One that we are all familiar with is *banshee*. This has no English equivalent. "Literally, it means 'fairy woman', i.e. *bean* (woman) *sí* (fairy). In my area, *banshee* is associated with a little white-haired woman who has the ability to transform herself into a white cat." Another Tyrone word is *keeny*, meaning "to cry, in a wailing way". "It comes from *caoine*, 'wail' . . . and it is associated with the idea of death. If a child cries in a particular way he may be told: 'Will you whisht that keenying. You'll keeny a death in the house.'"

Loreto Todd believes that "much idiosyncratic Anglo-Irish speech behaviour which is caricatured in films, plays and novels can be traced back to the influence of Gaelic". The most famous "Irishism" is the use of *after*.

> In Tyrone when I say: "I'm after doing that", I mean "I have just done that". Some English people misunderstand this construction, thinking that it refers to the future ... Almost certainly, the reason for this construction is that, in Gaelic, one may use the same word *indiaidh* in the sense of English *after*, as well as in forming verbal constructions.

Another typical usage borrowed from the Gaelic is "destroyed". A Tyrone woman, caught in a downpour, might say: "I'm destroyed! My coat's totally destroyed."

Tyrone English has many of the other typical marks of the Gaelic influence. There are local constructions like *sevendable* for "wonderful" (literally, "seven-double", i.e. doubly lucky). There is the use of four kinds of present tense (*I go to school, I am going to school, I be going to school* and *I do be going to school*), each with a different shade of meaning. There is the famous Irish reluctance to say "yes" or "no", partly to do with not wishing to sound rude or abrupt, and partly because in Gaelic there are no specific terms for "yes" or "no". The closest Irish comes to "yes" is a word like *maise* (indeed) or *cinnte* (sure). Loreto Todd gives an example of the Irish aversion to the strong affirmative:

> Let's say that I asked someone if he would like to sing. If he answered "yes" I would feel he was agreeing out of politeness or a sense of duty. If he said "I would" I would know that his agreement was a little more enthusiastic, but I would only be certain of his wholehearted participation if I heard:
> "Indeed I would."
> "I would indeed/surely."

The absence of Standard English models in most of Ireland contributed to two very typical aspects of Irish English. First, in some words, the stress syllable is different from Standard English: *disci'pline* instead of *di'scipline*, *lame'ntable* instead of *la'mentable*, and *archite'cture* instead of *a'rchitecture*. The second (found in Dublin especially), is a tendency towards malapropism, the habit (named after Mrs Malaprop, the character in R. B. Sheridan's play, *The Rivals*) of selecting words whose choice is often slightly, and ludicrously, inappropriate – "an allegory on the banks of the Nile". In the Dublin of Sean O'Casey's plays, for instance, the word *formularies* is used instead of "formalities", and *declivity* for "proclivity". In the countryside, too, there are folk etymologies that give us *windystool* for "windowsill", *rosy dandrums* for "rhododendrons" and *piano roses* for "peonies". Standard English speakers can find this amusing, or charming, or, xenophobically, evidence that the Irish are under-educated. In fact – as we will see with Black English – malapropism is the linguistic product of British colonialism. These are the "mistakes" made by people forced to become fluent in a language that is not theirs.

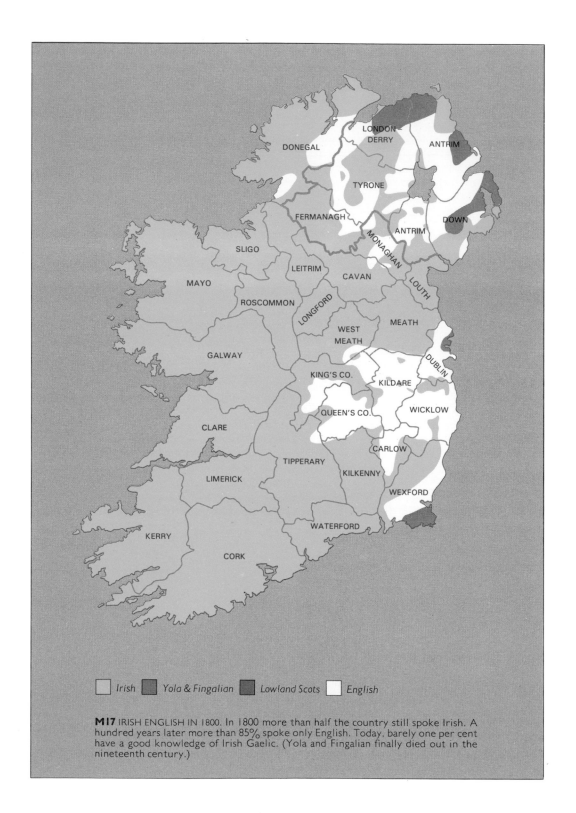

Irish ☐ Yola & Fingalian ■ Lowland Scots ■ English ☐

M17 IRISH ENGLISH IN 1800. In 1800 more than half the country still spoke Irish. A hundred years later more than 85% spoke only English. Today, barely one per cent have a good knowledge of Irish Gaelic. (Yola and Fingalian finally died out in the nineteenth century.)

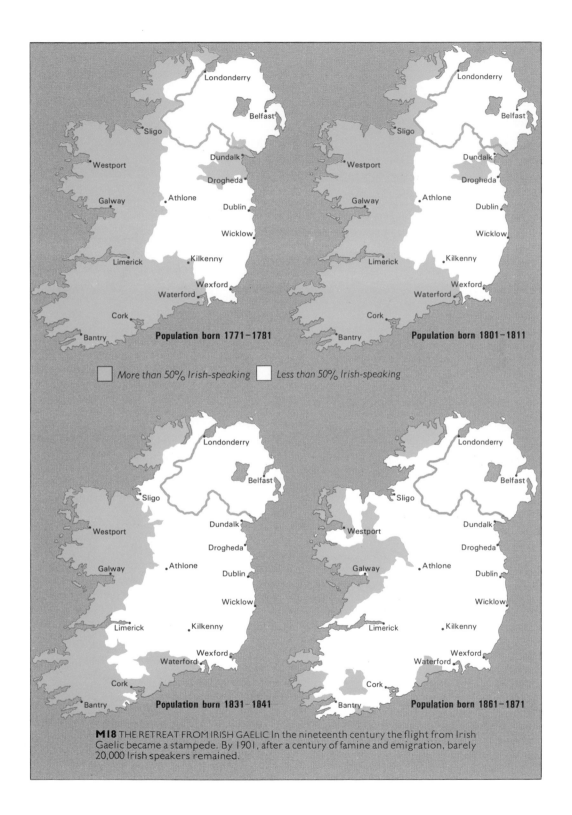

Population born 1771–1781

Population born 1801–1811

☐ More than 50% Irish-speaking   ☐ Less than 50% Irish-speaking

Population born 1831–1841

Population born 1861–1871

M18 THE RETREAT FROM IRISH GAELIC In the nineteenth century the flight from Irish Gaelic became a stampede. By 1901, after a century of famine and emigration, barely 20,000 Irish speakers remained.

In a remarkable way the Irish have made English their own, and have preserved qualities of speech and writing that many Standard English speakers feel they have lost. Why is this? Partly, it is the result of the centuries of isolation suffered by the island, which is a powerful factor in arresting language evolution. Partly it is to do with the sense of English being a *learned* language for the Irish, and with the eight centuries of interbreeding between the Celtic and the Anglo-Saxon traditions. Partly it is to do with the dispossessed nature of Irish society, and with what the Irish poet Tom Paulin has called "the romantic, unfettered existence of Irish-English". Unlike the Scots and the English, the Irish have never had a dictionary of Hiberno-English. Many words and phrases commonly used in Ireland are not to be found in any Standard English or American lexicon. The condition of English in Ireland (mirroring the politics) is still Elizabethan. It is unrepresented, non-standard, and it has no official voice. The Elizabethans were "eloquent before they were grammatical", and the same is true of the Irish: their English lives on the lips of ordinary people and in the minds of the Irish writers who can use it and play upon it without hindrance. In the fusion of the two traditions, Anglo-Saxon and Celtic, it is sometimes said that Irish Gaelic was the loser. The language was certainly transmuted into English, but it found, in another language, ways of expressing the cultural nuances of Irish society, of making English in its own image.

"THE IRISH BROGUE"

The strange co-existence of Irish and English and the comparative isolation of the English-speaking community in Ireland created a variety of English of special fascination during the seventeenth and eighteenth centuries. Throughout the eight hundred years of its contact with England, Gaelic-speaking Ireland, isolated from many of the influences that helped to transform English on "the mainland", has shown a remarkable power partly to fossilize, and partly to reinterpret the English language. Just before Henry II set foot in Ireland, a company of English, led by a group of Anglo-Norman knights, had settled in and around Wexford on the south coast of Ireland. Anglo-Norman names like Devereux and Parle are still common in the area. The English spoken by these families became known as *Yola* – a version of their word for "old" – and survived as a local curiosity until the middle of the nineteenth century. Even in Elizabethan times, the Wexford Yola was regarded as antique, "the dregs of the olde auncient Chaucer English", as one writer put it. Another sixteenth-century traveller noted that "to this day they generally speake oulde English". This is the Yola rendering of the Lord's Prayer:

> Oure vaader fho yarth ing heaveene, ee-hallowet bee t'naame. Thee kingdomw coome, thee weel be eedoane, as ing heaveene, zo eake an earthe. Yee ouze todeire oure deilye breed . . .

Not all traces of this strange speech have been lost. Even now, the Wexford region sustains an extraordinarily rich vocabulary, part Anglo-Norman English, part Gaelic. A "parsnip" is a *neape*, an Old English word that would not be strange to a Scotsman today.

The next important English settlement of Ireland occurred in the sixteenth and seventeenth centuries, with Elizabeth I's and then Oliver Cromwell's campaigns there. The English spoken in Ireland still preserves many Elizabethan traits. Shakespeare, for instance, would probably have sounded slightly Irish. His plays have several "Irish" rhymes: *ease–case*, *grease–grace*, *steal–stale*, and *sea–play*. More than this, Elizabethan English and Irish English share a delight in language for its own sake.

The way in which Irish English retains an older form of English is demonstrated by Alexander Pope, the English poet and satirist, who composed a famous couplet which rhymes *tea* with *tay*, as the Irish do to this day:

> *Here thou, great* ANNA! *whom three realms obey,*
> *Dost sometimes counsel take – and sometimes Tea.*

Several other rhymes in Pope's work depend on pronunciations we should now consider "Irish": *full–rule*, *ear–repair*, and *reserve–starve*. Later still, the English poet William Cowper, who died in 1800, composed a now-familiar hymn which relies on the rhyming of *way* and *sea*:

> *God moves in a mysterious way,*
> *His wonders to perform;*
> *He plants His footsteps in the sea,*
> *And rides upon the storm.*

The best account of what was happening to English in Ireland comes from Pope's contemporary, Dr Jonathan Swift, the gloomy Dean. A native Dubliner, Swift wrote two burlesque pieces entitled *A Dialogue in Hibernian Stile* and *Irish Eloquence* in which he satirized the English spoken in and around his home town. The two speakers in the *Dialogue* are landowners. They speak English, but in the space of fifty lines they use no fewer than seventeen Irish words. Some sentences are strongly influenced by the Gaelic:

> Pray how does he get his health? (What kind of health does he enjoy?)

and

> It is kind father for you. (You have inherited that tendency from your father.)

and

> I wonder what is gone with them. (I wonder what has happened to them.)

One well-established borrowing from Irish Gaelic, used by Swift, was *bother*. (Perhaps the most startling Irish innovation – precisely because it is so simple and now so common – is a word that was first mentioned by Lord Chesterfield in 1755, who wrote a letter to his son: "I am what you call in Ireland, and a very good expression I think it is, *unwell*." The special interest of this word is that it is made from native English elements, without anything in Gaelic to suggest it.)

Elsewhere, Swift attacks not only the usages of the Anglo-Irish, but also their pronunciation:

> How is it possible that a gentleman who lives in those parts where the *townlands* (as they call them) of his estate produce such odious sounds from the mouth, the throat, and the nose, can be able to repeat the words without dislocating every muscle that is used in speaking, and without applying the same tone to all other words, in every language he understands; as it is plainly to be observed not only in those people of the better sort who live in Galway and the Western parts, but in most counties of Ireland? ... What we call the Irish *brogue* is no sooner discovered, than it makes the deliverer, in the last degree, ridiculous and despised; and, from such a mouth, an Englishman expects nothing but bulls, blunders and follies.

The word *brogue* itself is a perfect reproduction of the sound of the Irish word for "shoe" (*bróg*). In other words, the Irishman was said to speak with "a shoe on his tongue" – a phrase that persists in Irish Gaelic to the present. The meaning of *brogue* (first used in 1689) is elaborated on by the actor Thomas Sheridan in his *General Dictionary of the English Language*, in which he discusses the "mistakes" made by "well-educated natives of Ireland". The first and most general tendency is one that has survived to this day. Irishmen, Sheridan writes, pronounce words like "tea", "sea" and "please", as *tay*, *say* and *plays*. In addition Sheridan mentions *pahtron* for "patron" (to which we can add *dahta* for "data" and *stahtus* for "status"), and one that has vanished, *cawm* for "calm".

The "brogue" that Sheridan was trying to express is almost impossible to describe, but it has to do with a certain breathiness and aspiration of consonants and with a "vowel harmony" partly inherited from Irish Gaelic. It was first acquired by the Anglo-Irish gentry from the English of the native Irish. It became so distinctive perhaps because the Irish rarely, if ever, had the benefit of learning from a speaker of Standard English. The children of the gentry would have spent much time in the company of Irish servants. The late-Victorian childhood of Douglas Hyde, the first President of Ireland, illustrates this process. Hyde had a virtually bilingual education, and during his teens kept a diary (in Irish) which gives a good insight into the life of Anglo-Irish children in Ireland over the centuries. He describes how he, his two brothers and his father used to sit up in the kitchen with their servant, Seamus.

> Seamus Hart and the Master, Oldfield, Arthur and myself in the kitchen with a good fire in the grate. We sit down and drink a few glasses of punch or grog. Seamus tells us stories and we drink plenty, and go to bed drunk, or at least merry.

Below the level of the gentry (who would occasionally travel to England), most Irishmen acquired their English from non-Standard speakers. The so-called "hedge schools" were self-perpetuating educational backwaters in which the teachers of English acquired their expertise from their Irish predecessors. Even the English of the landlords – as we have seen from Swift – was influenced by the speech of their servants, stewards, grooms and gardeners, many of whom would be expressing Irish Gaelic phrases in English translations. As early as 1600, a contemporary play records the speech of perhaps the first "stage Irishman", with the pronunciation of *shecretary* for "secretary" and *blesh* for "bless", both derived from the Gaelic treatment of the *s* sound in English (in Irish Gaelic an *s* followed by an *i* or an *e* is pronounced *sh*).

By the end of the eighteenth century, the "brogue" was sufficiently well known for a man who had never been to Ireland to hold forth on the subject. It is, of course, Dr Johnson (whose friends included the poet and playwright Oliver Goldsmith, one of several Irishmen in the literary London of the time) who announces, apropos Irish pronunciation, that:

> A small intermixture of provincial peculiarities may, perhaps, have an agreeable effect, as the notes of different birds concur in the harmony of the grove, and please more than if they were all exactly alike. I could name some gentlemen of Ireland, to whom a slight proportion of the accent and recitative of that country is an advantage.

The conversation, recorded by Boswell on 28 March 1772, turned to a discussion of Thomas Sheridan's pronouncing dictionary. Johnson was sceptical about it, recalling that when he had started work on *his* dictionary, "Lord Chesterfield told me that the word *great* should be pronounced so as to rhyme to *state*; and Sir William Yonge sent me word that it should be pronounced so as to rhyme to *seat*, and that none but an Irishman would pronounce it *grait*." In other words, agreement about correct pronunciation was a will o' the wisp.

This discussion holds many fascinating clues for the language detective. The disagreement between Chesterfield and Yonge, "two men of the highest rank", about the pronunciation of the word *great* demonstrates how precisely Irish English has preserved one of several key English pronunciations that were in transition in Johnson's day. In the long run, of course, it was Chesterfield's *grait* that was to triumph over Yonge's *greet*.

80 Thomas Sheridan, an actor who lectured successfully in Dublin on English pronunciation.

Johnson's contemporary, the orator and philosopher Edmund Burke, was another Irishman whose "brogue" would have been familiar in London. The two centuries since the Elizabethan settlement of Ireland had given rise to some of the most remarkable literature in the English canon, from Edmund Spenser's *Faerie Queene* to Burke's *Reflections on the Revolution in France*. It has been suggested that the continuing predominance of Irish literary achievement – a characteristic that still flourishes in both the North and the South – comes from a heightened linguistic consciousness, a greater awareness of the genius and resources of the English language. This awareness may have been fostered in those who were brought up in Ireland by their contact with a form of English notably different from Standard English.

Heavily gaelicized and distinctly archaic, English in Ireland has always had a character of its own, but there is some question about its regional variations. There is broad agreement that, even before the Elizabethan and Jacobean settlements, the speech of Ulster was always different from that of the other provinces.

In the South, in the provinces of Leinster, Munster, Connacht and Meath, there are some who say that English in Ireland is remarkable for the absence of regional variation. Others argue that although the similarities are perhaps more noticeable than the differences, a careful study distinguishes some important contrasts between the Hiberno-English of the town and the country. One essential distinction is between the Irish English of the cities (notably Dublin and Cork) and the speech of the countryside. It is also said that a more standard form of English, based on the speech of the Dublin school and college system and on the broadcasters of Radio Telefís Éireann (RTE), is emerging in the capital. The Irish themselves will tell you that they can distinguish all kinds of regional variation (at least three in Kerry alone, according to one informant), and will comment especially on the distinctiveness of the English around Cork contrasted, say, with the English spoken in Dublin. As we shall see elsewhere, such fine tuning occurs in all speech communities and often misses the broad, overall homogeneity identified by the outsider.

IRISH GALORE

Ever since the first English and Scots planters settled in Ulster at the beginning of the seventeenth century, the Irish have left their homeland in ever increasing numbers. Ironically, it was the Irish who were to help spread English, the language of their oppressor, to parts of the globe where previously it was virtually unknown. *Irish* is an Old English word; *galore* is Gaelic. Both have been claimed for the English dictionary, but because Irish has assimilated to English culture so completely, it is sometimes easy to overlook and undervalue the extent of the Irish contribution to the story of English, chiefly because it is often so hard to detect. There is, however, one exception, the island of Newfoundland, whose inhabitants preserve a kind of Irish English that is almost indistinguishable from the real thing two-and-a-half thousand miles away.

Newfoundland lies off the coast of Labrador at the mouth of the St Lawrence river, commanding the North Atlantic sea lanes to Canada. In winter, it is shrouded in mist and menaced by ice. In spring, rogue icebergs drift serenely past the island's massive cliffs. When the mist lifts, the landscape is reminiscent of the west coast of Ireland. The island's Gaelic name, *Talav-An-Easg*, means "land of the fish", and traditionally the people of Newfoundland are fishermen. Recently, the oil industry has established a major prospecting base in the capital, St John's, a large town which many visitors, listening to the local people, would mistake for Dublin or Waterford.

Newfoundland was actually the first English-speaking colony in the New World, founded by Sir Walter Ralegh's half brother, Sir Humphrey Gilbert, in 1588. In the early days, the settlement was a seasonal one. Fishermen would sail out from Ireland and the English West Country for the summer cod-fishing season, returning home before the harsh winter. Throughout the seventeenth century, a slow migration of English shipowners gradually developed the community on the island. In a pattern repeated throughout the New World, most of their servants were Irish, far outnumbering their masters. Quite quickly, Irish-English became the socially dominant language in St John's, not least because the English tended to absenteeism while the Irish stayed put. By the end of the eighteenth century, one visitor made the following observation:

> As this Island has been inhabit'd for such a number of years and was peopled by British and Irish, you frequently meet with Familys whose Grandfathers were born in Newfoundland. These are what I call the Natives. They speak English but they have a manner peculiar to themselves – the common people lisp . . . they would on answering my enquirys say – "Yes, *dat* is the way" or "O No, we *tant* do it so; but *den* we do it the other way, *tafter* we bring it home because it is *taffer*."

The scattering of the islanders along the craggy, inaccessible shoreline has confirmed a number of strong local variants. As well as the Irish, who are based on the South Avalon Peninsula, there are the West Country communities (with strong Dorset and Devonshire accents) to the north of the island. The fur trade on the east of the island was dominated by the Scots, who have left traces of their speech behind. Among the Irish, there has been very little accent levelling or mixing. Unlike those who went to New England and rapidly participated in the already-established town life there, the Irish in Newfoundland returned to their village ways, living in communities of two or three hundred people. They earned their living from the sea, mainly in the salt-fish business, and there was no incentive to travel further than the nearest salt-fish factory. Besides, in the winters they would be cut off for weeks at a time by blizzards. For these reasons, the English of Newfoundland and that of contemporary Kilkenny, for example, are remarkably similar. Pronunciation, stress, sense and traditional customs are repeated again and again. The definitive *Dictionary of Newfoundland English*, recently published, contains many Irish words, like *froster* (a nail or cleat on a horse's hoof to prevent slipping on the ice), *maneen* (a boy who acts the part of a man) and *sulick* (the liquid obtained from cooking meat or fish).

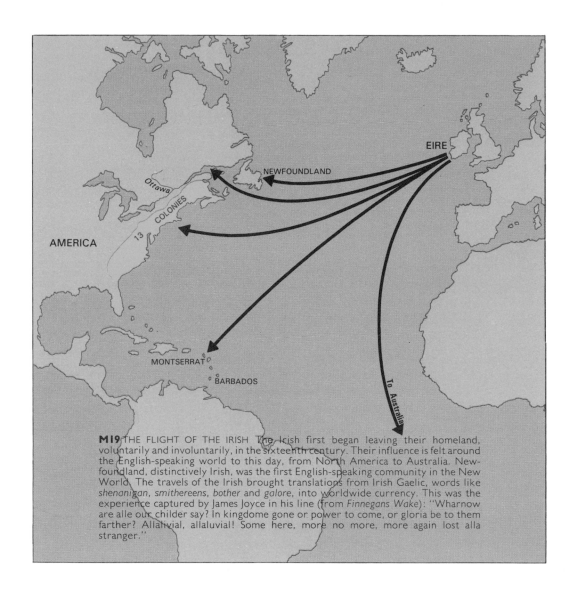

EIRE

NEWFOUNDLAND

Ottawa

COLONIES

13

AMERICA

MONTSERRAT

BARBADOS

To Australia

M19 THE FLIGHT OF THE IRISH The Irish first began leaving their homeland, voluntarily and involuntarily, in the sixteenth century. Their influence is felt around the English-speaking world to this day, from North America to Australia. Newfoundland, distinctively Irish, was the first English-speaking community in the New World. The travels of the Irish brought translations from Irish Gaelic, words like *shenanigan*, *smithereens*, *bother* and *galore*, into worldwide currency. This was the experience captured by James Joyce in his line (from *Finnegans Wake*): "Wharnow are alle our childer say? In kingdome gone or power to come, or gloria be to them farther? Allalivial, allaluvial! Some here, more no more, more again lost alla stranger."

81 The Irish settled all over North America. Newfoundland still preserves much Irish culture.

82 Poor whites in Barbados are known as "redlegs".

The Avalon Peninsula is the heart of the Irish community in Newfoundland. Towards its tip is the little community of St Shott's, typical of so many villages on the island. It has about two hundred and fifty inhabitants, fifty wooden houses, one small school, one church, and two village stores. In the words of Regina Myrick, who runs one of these, St Shott's "is really one giant family". The men of the village prepare their boats in the spring, fish from June to August, and spend the rest of the year looking after their houses, and hunting duck, moose, caribou and partridge. The area is very rugged and known locally as a graveyard for ships.

The St Shott's settlement dates back to at least the 1800s, and everyone speaks broad Hiberno-English. We were greeted in one household with a self-conscious parody: "Welcome, my sweet fellow, would you be after having some tea?" On Sunday, everyone goes to church. The only other local entertainment is the St Shott's home video, which is rented from Regina Myrick, together with the latest cassette. This ancient community is, like many in Ireland itself, slowly losing its traditional isolation. There is no doctor: serious illness has to be treated in St John's, three hours away. Children above the age of fourteen are bussed out to bigger schools up the coast. Brighter children who want to get on will gravitate towards St John's. Here, as around the world, we believe that the threat to the variety of English does not come (as many have suggested) from the all-pervasive presence of radio and television, but from the accent-levelling and mixing effects of improved roads and schools.

Newfoundland is simply the earliest and best-preserved of all the Irish communities scattered round the world. There are many others – cities, islands, parishes, wards – the result of a migration that goes back to 1600, the end of Elizabeth I's long reign. For the next three hundred years, almost everyone in Ireland had good reason to look beyond their homeland for a better place to be. Not all were voluntary travellers. One of the strangest settlements with Irish (and English) roots is the White community in another island, Barbados.

History has charged the English with using Barbados as a dumping ground for Black slaves. In fact, they first used the island as a place of penal exile for Whites. A Jesuit priest who visited the island in 1634 noted that "some few Catholiques here be, both English and Irish". Oliver Cromwell used it as an internment camp for prisoners taken during his battles in Ireland. In September 1649, reporting the storming of Drogheda, he wrote to the Speaker of the English Parliament: "When they submitted, their officers were knocked on the head; and every tenth man of the soldiers killed; and the rest shipped off for the Barbadoes." This wholesale transportation of some 12,000 men gave rise to a new verb, "to barbadoes". A letter of 1655 describes Cromwell as "a terrible Protector ... He dislikes shedding blood, but is very apt 'to barbadoes' an unruly man – has sent and sends us by hundreds to Barbadoes, so that we have made an active verb of it: 'Barbadoes you'."

Initially, these involuntary exiles, now known as *redlegs*, worked as indentured servants and were treated almost as badly as the Blacks. In due course, they were joined by Scottish rebels from the Highlands and, after the failure of the Duke of Monmouth's rising in 1685, by West Country Englishmen. With the passage of time, some of these luckless Barbadians became "poor Whites", and today their descendants live in a small, impoverished community in the St Martin's bay parish, speaking a kind of English which is indistinguishable from that of the Blacks.

Wilson Norris, who is descended from some of the first Whites on Barbados, lives down by the beach. He earns a precarious living fishing, in his own words, "for pilchards, runts, bear fish, leathercoats, foggies and rock fish". At night, he goes out with a lantern and hunts for lobsters and crabs in the shallow water. His talk is pure "Bajan" (Barbadian English). When questioned about his "redleg" ancestry, he becomes evasive. In a predominantly Black society the poor White minority is widely despised. The traditional Barbadian scorn for the "redlegs", he says, "don't bother me". But his denial carries only partial credibility.

The influence of the Irish—names and place-names—is also found on the island of Montserrat, "the emerald isle of the Caribbean". The Irish came here fleeing religious persecution in neighbouring St Kitt's and in Virginia. In 1643, an Irish priest, Father O'Hartegan, wrote of "French, English and Irish, all of which are used freely in that part of the world". The centre of the island has a valley named Glenmór, the Irish for "big valley". The first Irish planters here – men with family names like Riley and Sweeney – came of their own free will. After Cromwell, they were joined by involuntary exiles like those on Barbados. When the first slaves came from West Africa, some of the Irish took Black wives and mistresses, giving rise to the so-called "Black Irish" community on the island.

Back home, for all the tension between England and Ireland, there was a long-established tradition of seasonal visiting of the English "mainland" by migrant Irish workers. It is a custom that has survived on the west coast until the present. Pat Linney, the poet of Rossport, worked on the land in England for about thirty years. The Irish storyteller John Henry, who lives in a nearby village, worked on the potato farms of Lincolnshire, and many of the men of Mayo are well acquainted with the fields of East Anglia.

The Irish also played a vital part in the English settlement of Australia – as involuntary exiles once again. There are few reliable figures, but it is estimated that in 1851, while 60 per cent of all Australians had come from England, just over 30 per cent were from Ireland. The songs tell a similar story. Many of the most famous hark back to the memory of Ireland. "Oh! I am a shamrock," cries the convict in "The Île de France". The hero of "The Wild Colonial Boy" was "born in Castlemaine", and the narrator of "If We Only Had Old Ireland Over Here" begins, "I was dreaming of old Ireland and Killarney's lake and fells."

The Irish who went to Australia were enthusiastic exiles, in the words of one writer, growing "fat and saucy as soon as they exchange their rags and potatoes ... for our fine climate and Bushfare". After the horrors of economic depression and potato famine, Australia was a land of plenty, and many Irish persuaded their friends and families to follow. The story is told of one Irish convict girl who, having served her statutory seven years, returned to Dublin but then committed another crime solely for the purpose of re-emigrating at government expense. As the judge read out her sentence, the girl exclaimed to the court: "Hurrah for old Sydney and the skies over it!"

The Irish in Australia brought a complex hatred of England with them that has lasted – in a more developed form – to the present. Much later in the nineteenth century, the celebrated bushranger Ned Kelly, one of the legendary figures of Australian history, gave vehement expression, voiced in his valedictory *Letter*, to the question: why should men obey the laws of England, under which so many Irishmen were starved to death? It goes on, with a sadly garbled eloquence:

> more was transported to Van Diemand's [*sic*] Land to pine their young lives away in starvation and misery among tyrants ... were doomed to Port McQuarie Toweringabbie Norfolk island and Emu Plains and in those places of tyranny and condemnation many a blooming Irishman rather than subdue to the Saxon yoke were flogged to death and bravely died in servile chains ...

To trace the Irish influence in Australian speech and writing is almost, if not totally, impossible. The famous Australianism *sheila* is probably Irish, and so, it is said, are colloquialisms like *to nick, to nobble, to peg out* and *to take a rise out of someone*. Another typical Australianism, *barrack*, meaning "to support someone vociferously against others" probably comes from an Ulster English word meaning "to be boastful of one's fighting prowess". Many Australians believe (a touch romantically) that there *is* an Irish influence in Australian English, even if it is hard to pin down. One aspect of Australian life, Australian Rules Football (known to its detractors as "aerial ping-pong"), is not only based on Gaelic football, but has always had players of Irish ancestry. Australian Rules Football has also encouraged a sportswriting tradition that has all the eloquence associated with the Irish. In 1906, we find "Centre" describing the exploits of a star player in the "Football Notes" of the *Melbourne Age*:

> Mallee Johnson, the white-headed boy who strides across the sward in $3\frac{1}{2}$ steps, added still more shine and polish to his already brilliant career. His

passing was poetic. He brought down aces and bowers from nowhere like the Heathen Chinee. He rang the bell every time. He cakewalked down the aisle. Whether soaring into the clouds, striding gaily round the lawn, on the blob, or guarding the citadel, one of the loveliest features of the scenery was Mallee's genial smile shining in the sun. He took the biscuit. To put Mallee in charge of the Swanston Street crossing is like using a razor to chop firewood. He should be guarding the Appian Way or the Milky Way or directing the traffic in the Land of the Bubbling Ale . . . Carlton.

Which looks suspiciously like Blarney. (The phrase "white-headed boy" is a direct translation of the Irish Gaelic for "a favourite".)

Australian English also preserves at least three Irish English usages that suggest a greater Irish influence in the making of Australian English (see chapter eight) than has, at times, been allowed: the second person plural pronoun *youse*; the grammatical construction *Come here till I kiss you*; and, perhaps most persuasive of all, the use of *must not* (as in *He mustn't have seen me – he didn't stop*), which is unknown in England – except in Liverpool. In the nineteenth century, as we shall see, Merseyside became the focus of a massive Irish immigration, and the Irish diaspora of the seventeenth and eighteenth centuries was eclipsed by a social cataclysm which scattered the people of Ireland to the four winds and from which Irish Gaelic has never recovered.

THE NATURALIZATION OF IRISH ENGLISH

In 1800, out of a total population in Ireland of about five million, Irish was the mother tongue of perhaps two million; one-and-a-half million spoke only English, while a further one-and-a-half million were bilingual. Irish Gaelic, "the pagan speech", was still the language of the majority, though not, perhaps, the most influential. In the next one hundred years, this supremacy was to be dramatically overthrown. The English language in Ireland became so naturalized that it appeared to be indigenous. The figures tell the story. By 1901, English was the sole language of 85 per cent, and the Irish Gaelic culture had become almost totally submerged. Only a mere 21,000, living in the poorest and remotest parts of the country, especially the West coast, spoke Irish and were ignorant of English. As one old fellow said to the writer J. M. Synge, one of the leaders of the Irish revival, in 1902, "Now all this country is gone lonesome and bewildered and there's no man knows what ails it." (In Ireland today, Gaelic is threatened with extinction. In 1986, there are only a handful of monoglot Irish speakers, and fewer than 100,000 Irish citizens have a good knowledge of Irish. In fact, some pessimistic commentators predict that by the year 2000 Irish Gaelic will have become a dead language, remaining, in Seamus Heaney's words, only "mythically alive".)

After the Act of Union in 1803, without official backing, Irish Gaelic went into decline, owing its survival mainly to the traditional support of the Roman Catholic church. Education, now in the hands of English administrators, meant learning English. Even the leaders of the independence movements, men like Daniel O'Connell, believed that in order to advance the campaign for an independent Ireland, the rank and file had to learn the language of the enemy. O'Connell was said to have delivered a speech in Irish on only two occasions – when he thought there were police spies present.

The slow erosion of Irish was matched by the great social crises of the nineteenth century which annihilated the Gaelic-speaking communities. One million died in the terrible famine; millions more fled abroad. Almost more important than the famine itself was the fear of another one. Irish parents encouraged their children to learn English and to leave in ever larger numbers for England, Australia and, above all, the United States. The land was seen as cursed, and there was a tragic and almost universal rejection of things Irish. During the darkest moments of the Victorian age, the reality of everyday life in Ireland was so intolerable the Irish felt that only an escape into the English way of life and language would solve their problems. What has been called "the mass flight from the Irish language" was enforced in the national schools by a series of frightening educational measures. Gaelic-speaking children were punished with wooden gags, and subjected to mockery and humiliation. Brothers were encouraged to spy on sisters. Under the regime of the tally-sticks, the child would wear a stick on a string round its neck. Every time the child used an Irish Gaelic word, the parents would cut a notch in the wood. At the end of the week, the village schoolmaster would tally up the notches and administer punishment accordingly. There was only one end in view: the eradication of Irish. The schools became the instrument of suppression, just as, ironically, they are today the chief promoters of Gaelic.

The new railway network spreading out from Dublin and Belfast extended the influence of the English-speaking towns. By mid-century the damage had been done. The census figures of 1861 tell a chilling tale. Of the Irish population aged between two and ten years, less than 2 per cent were monoglot Irish speakers. There were now more Irish abroad than at home. The future was an English-speaking one, and for many it was to lie overseas: in America, the English "mainland", and throughout the British Empire.

For the leaders of the movement for Irish independence the replacement of the language of the oppressor by a return to Gaelic was a symbolic aim. (Éamon De Valera once said that he would willingly give up all he knew of English to speak Irish properly.) In 1921, with the emergence of the Irish Free State, Gaelic was acclaimed a national language, and promoted within the educational system. Today it is taught in schools as a second language and, though the majority know it about as well as most English know French, Gaelic has become a focus of cultural and ethnic loyalty, a symbol for Ireland. In the Dail, the Irish have a phrase for the customary nod at the Celtic past, the *cúpla focal*, "the couple of words". Politicians are advised to start their speeches with the *cúpla focal*.

THE IRISH REVIVAL

The flight of the Irish from their homeland left the countryside devastated. In the West, especially in the Gaeltacht, the landscape today is one of ruined cottages, desolate peat bogs and abandoned villages. In the far west of Mayo is a small village called Kilgalligan with a special place in the story of English in Ireland. Until the European Economic Community began to subsidize the region, life here was harsh. The villagers' holdings were so small they could barely support a potato-patch or grow enough hay for a cow and a few sheep. The people of Kilgalligan still live in small stone crofts, a hundred yards from the high cliffs of Mayo where the Atlantic rollers break. Half a mile to the south, some fishing boats and three or four curraghs wait by a small jetty. Stretching inland is a great strand of beach where the villagers used to hold donkey races. This, runs the speculation, is the true setting for one of Ireland's most famous plays, a monument to the marriage of Gaelic and English, *The Playboy of the Western World* by J. M. Synge.

Synge, who could speak and read Irish Gaelic, was a leader of the remarkable resurgence in Irish writing associated with the names of Sean O'Casey, James Joyce, and W. B. Yeats at the turn of the century. It was probably Yeats who first began to see the extraordinary possibilities of the new idiom at his disposal. The forced marriage between Irish and English had, after a century of calamity, produced a soft-spoken, lyrical kind of English that seemed almost ready-made for literature. According to Yeats himself, it was he who, meeting Synge in Paris, urged his friend to rediscover the treasures of Irish English.

> I said: "Give up Paris, you will never create anything by reading Racine, and Arthur Symons will always be a better critic of French Literature. Go to the Aran Islands. Live there as if you were one of the people themselves;

83 The Great Famine. One million died. Enfeebled by hunger, the living lay with the dead. Government inspectors found frozen bodies "half devoured by rats". Gaelic-speaking Ireland was overwhelmed.

express a life that has never found expression." I had just come from Aran, and my imagination was full of those grey islands where men must reap with knives because of the stones.

So Synge went, and he kept an intimate record of his visit, which he published, together with some of his own photographs, in 1907. The *Journal* is rich with description of the tone, cadence and rhythm of the Irish speech. He describes one girl "brooding and cooing over every syllable she uttered".

> She plays continual tricks with her Gaelic in the way girls are fond of, piling up diminutives and repeating adjectives with a humorous scorn of syntax. While she is here the talk never stops in the kitchen.

Describing his own experiences among the Irish peasantry Synge has many interesting observations to make about their language. He re-asserts the parallels between Elizabethan English and the Irish English of his own experience. "It is probable that when the Elizabethan dramatist took his ink horn and sat down to his work he used many phrases that he had just heard, as he sat at dinner, from his mother or his children. In Ireland, those of us who know the people have the same privileges." In the same autobiographical vein, Synge offers some insights into the dedication of his working methods, revealing in a memorable passage that he "got more aid than any learning could have given me from a chink in the floor of the old Wicklow house where I was staying". He would lie there, he wrote, and eavesdrop on "what was being said by the servant girls in the kitchen".

It was among the Aran islanders that Synge found the inspiration for *The Playboy of the Western World*. According to one old man with whom he had many conversations, there was "a Connaught man who killed his father with the blow of a spade when he was in a passion, and then fled to this island and threw himself on the mercy of some of the natives with whom he was said to be related. They hid him in a hole . . . In spite of a reward which was offered, the island was incorruptible, and after much trouble the man was safely shipped to America."

In his play, Synge transforms both the story and the speech of the Aran islanders. The story of Christy Mahon, the man who says he has killed his Da, becomes a metaphor for the Blarney itself, and the speech of Christy, Pegeen and the Widow Quin becomes the quintessence of Irish English. As the play unfolds, and with it Christy's lying pretensions, his speech becomes a kind of poetry:

> rising up in the red dawn, or before it maybe, and going out into the yard as naked as an ashtree in the moon of May, and shying clods against the visage of the stars till he'd put the fear of death into the banbhs and the screeching sows.

When Christy's father, who is very much alive, finally appears in the village, the Widow Quin tries to make out he is mad for claiming Christy as his son. The father replies in an Irish

English of unrestrained splendour:

> Oh, I'm raving with a madness that would fright the world!... There was
> one time I seen ten scarlet divils letting on they'd cork my spirit in a gallon
> can; and one time I seen rats as big as badgers sucking the lifeblood from
> the butt of my lug; but I never till this day confused that dribbling idiot
> with a likely man. I'm destroyed surely...

The play was a controversial success at the Abbey Theatre in Dublin. When it was
published in 1907, Synge wrote a special preface emphasizing the authenticity of his research
and the accuracy, as he saw it, of the play's dialogue. There were, he said, "one or two words
only that I have not heard among the country people of Ireland". In fact, he believed he had
probably not done justice to his material:

> Anyone who has lived in real intimacy with the Irish peasantry will know
> that the wildest sayings and ideas in this play are tame indeed, compared
> with the fancies one may hear in any little hillside cabin in Geesala, or
> Carraroe, or Dingle Bay.

Synge pays a special tribute to his fellow countrymen. "In countries where the imagination of
the people, and the language they use, is rich and living, it is possible for a writer to be rich
and copious in his words, and at the same time to give the reality, which is the root of all
poetry, in comprehensive and natural form." Probably there was an element of myth-making
in Synge's closing words, but they are stirring none the less:

> In a good play every speech should be as fully flavoured as a nut or apple,
> and such speeches cannot be written by any one who works among people
> who have shut their lips on poetry. In Ireland, for a few years more, we have
> a popular imagination that is fiery, and magnificent, and tender;...

84 W. B. Yeats. He did as much as any writer to revive
an interest in Ireland's Celtic past.

85 J. M. Synge. According to another Irish writer,
George Bernard Shaw, "The Playboy's real name was
Synge..."

Synge's close attention to the spoken idioms of his people was soon overshadowed by an even greater Irish writer: James Joyce. Perhaps no writer since Shakespeare has so transformed our idea of the language – from the outside. In *A Portrait of the Artist as a Young Man*, Joyce describes how, when his hero's Irish vocabulary is corrected by the dean of college (who is English), Stephen Dedalus remarks in frustration that "the language in which we are speaking is his before it is mine". From *Dubliners* to *Ulysses*, the writings of James Joyce teem with the Irish English of his native Dublin. He once claimed that if the city was ever destroyed, it could be re-created from the pages of his fiction. In fact, he left Dublin for good in 1904 at the age of twenty-two, declaring that Ireland is "the sow that eats her farrow". His long exile was European, but his work is a monument to the English language in Ireland and, more than any other writer, his work universalized the Irish experience. In 1923, as part of the long preparation for *Finnegans Wake*, he kept a notebook of the commonplace Hiberno-English phrases used by his wife, Nora Barnacle, later published as *Scribbledehobble*. The turns of Nora's speech that Joyce scribbled in his notebook included delightful sentences like "He looked at the time", "A knock came to the door", "Can't believe a word out of his mouth" and wifely questions like "Will I do as I am?" For the Irish critic, David Norris, Joyce's writing "caught the flavour and intonation of the Dublin accent better than any other writer, particularly the conversation of pubs". It was also alert to the everyday collision between Irish sensibility and the English language:

86 Millions emigrated. "The Irishman looks on America", wrote one contemporary, "as the refuge of his race . . . The shores of England are farther off in his heart's geography than those of Massachusetts or New York."

Ulysses is a great experiment in language, but it is outclassed by the joyful experiment of *Finnegans Wake*. Joyce revenges himself for the taking away of the Irish language by the English, for this linguistic exploitation. After eight hundred years of occupation, he takes the English language, and smashes it up into smithereens, and hands it back and says: This is our revenge. He makes the character, Shem, boast that he will "wipe alley english spooker, or multiphoniaksically spuking off the face of the erse".

Joyce's experiments with language were partly inspired by his European exile. For many Irish, their escape lay in the West – in the United States.

THE LAND OF YOUTH

One of the oldest Celtic tales, still told and remembered in the remoter parts of the Gaeltacht, narrates the adventures of a young Irishman in the fabled west, in *Tír na nÓg*, the "land of youth". Like Christy Mahon in *The Playboy of the Western World*, the Irish had been looking hopefully to America, the New World, the Land of Youth, for centuries. They were among the first to emigrate to the Thirteen Colonies. The indentured Irish servant became such a familiar figure in the American South that by the end of the seventeenth century three states, Maryland, Virginia and South Carolina, had passed laws limiting the immigration of Irish servants.

Statistically, the Irish accounted for a very significant part of the population, perhaps as many as 400,000 by 1790, the largest non-English community in the States. By this time, the Irish in the New World had become a remarkably mixed society. During the War of Independence, they fought on both sides, and were equally praised by both for their prowess. Sir Henry Clinton, the ill-fated British commander-in-chief, proposed to stiffen his demoralized troops from "that source whence the rebels themselves drew most of their best soldiers – I mean the Irish". A few years later, in 1784, a speaker in the Irish parliament complained that "America was lost by Irish emigrants."

During the nineteenth century, a staggering total of 4.7 million Irishmen arrived in the United States fleeing the catastrophes at home. The idea of America permeated Irish society to an extraordinary degree. "Wasn't it a great thought Columbus had," one peasant was said to have observed, gazing out over the Atlantic, "to find out America? For if there wasn't America, the Island wouldn't stand a week." Villages on the west coast still remember "the America Wake", the lamentations attending a departure to the New World.

What was the effect of these English-speaking Irish arrivals on the English of the new United States? What traces, if any, of the English spoken by the first Irish in America can be recognized today? One reason why it is hard to identify the Irish influence is because Irish and American English have many characteristics in common. Both, as we have seen, acquired their distinctive vocabularies and accents from seventeenth-century English, and though the language has evolved further in America than it has in Ireland, there are still important points of contact. Benedict Kiely, an Irish novelist who has written on language, recalls once being told in Virginia that he had a southern accent: "When I asked why that outrageous statement should be made I was asked to repeat the names of God and of Carolina. The explanation was simply that into the Carolinas, Virginia, Georgia and so on, a lot of people with Ulster vowel sounds had once come, grabbing the land and hunting the red men. The red men are as good as gone. Some of the Ulster vowel sounds remain. There's a county I've heard of in Alabama where some of the people have, by and large, a Tyrone accent."

Some details of American speech are almost certainly derived from the Irish, mainly in grammar, syntax and pronunciation. Irish immigrants introduced the typical American *I seen* for "I saw", and also perhaps the use of the hypercorrect *shall* where "will" is the more usual form. In Irish Gaelic, there is no indefinite article: the Irish tended to use the definite article where earlier Americans would not. They would say "She is in *the* school", not "She is in school." Or they might say, "He is on *his* vacation", not "He is on vacation." And when we hear an American say *belave* not "beleeve", or *jine* not "join", or *applesass* not "apple sauce", these are all fragments of the Irish retained in American speech. Perhaps the most famous Irishism is the Gaelic-inspired plural of "you", *yous*, still authentically found on the lips of Irish American policemen – "the cops" – in New York and Boston.

The Irish were, apparently, an unusually literate group of immigrants: by mid-century, 75 per cent were able to read and write English, which supports the evidence for the decline of Irish Gaelic in Ireland itself. More and more were learning English in preparation for their new life across the Atlantic. All the same, a number of Irishisms appear to creep into American speech. *Shenanigan*, meaning "trickery, or mischief" is first recorded in America in 1855, and comes from the Irish Gaelic *sionnachuighim* meaning "I play the fox, I play tricks". Or does it? One authority believes the word to be American Indian. Another folk etymology gives a contraction of the Irish names, Sean Hannigan. Some experts claim that *smithereens* comes from the County Mayo anglicization of the Irish *smidirin*, meaning "a small fragment", but others argue that it comes from the English regional word, *smithers*, to which the Irish added a diminutive. Some say that *brash* is a borrowing from Irish, and also the all-American *buddy*, from the Irish *bodach*, meaning "a churl", but the *Oxford English Dictionary* claims it as an American nursery corruption of *brother*. The phrase "strong-arm tactics" may derive from the Irish word for violence, a word whose literal English translation is "with strong arm", but that too is disputed; so is *shebang*, meaning "a temporary shelter or hovel", said to come from the Anglo-Irish *shebeen*, "an illegal drinking establishment", in turn derived from the Gaelic *seibe*, "a mug". (The phrase "the whole shebang" is an Americanism of 1879.) Even *shanty*, which allegedly comes from the Irish *sean-tigh* (pronounced "shan tee"), meaning "old house", has a controversial etymology. One expert believes that "people don't like to admit Gaelic etymologies"; another considers that "from a sociological point of view it's very interesting to speculate about why Irishmen are so keen to derive ordinary English words from Irish". The socio-political realities of the Irish question suggest that we are never likely to fathom Irish influence in American English.

Derivations aside, the dictionary tells us that the word *shantytown* was first used in 1882 and originally referred to the shacks that were built alongside American railroads by Irish navvies working on the transcontinental railroad. In Boston, *shanty Irish* was a derogatory term for Irish families like the Kennedys, the first of whom, Patrick, arrived penniless in Boston in 1848 and earned his living as a cooper. The pejorative *Paddy* dates as far back as 1748. The *paddy waggon* (police van) was coined in the 1920s, originating in cities – like Boston – where many of the policemen were Irish. The Irish were always believed to be unruly and aggressive. *To get one's Irish up* is an American phrase meaning "to get angry". An *Irish hoist* meant "a kick in the pants".

Traditionally, the Irish in America worked as labourers or servants or soldiers. The Americanism *biddy*, meaning "a servant girl", is thought to come from the abbreviation of the common Irish name, Bridget. The better-educated became clerks, priests or school-teachers. As in England, an important part of the American literary tradition is Irish. The playwright Dion Boucicault, the novelist F. Scott Fitzgerald, and perhaps the greatest of them all, Eugene O'Neill, are all of Irish descent. The Irish provided much of the leadership of the American Roman Catholic church, as well as of big-city politics, and the labour unions. They showed an intensely political nature. Charles Dickens, visiting New York in 1867, wrote that "the general corruption in respect of local funds appears to be stupendous . . . The Irish element is acquiring such enormous influence in New York City, that when I think of it, and see the large Roman Catholic cathedral rising there, it seems unfair to stigmatize as 'American' other monstrous things that one also sees."

The place of Ireland in American political life is perhaps demonstrated by the visits of three presidents with Irish ancestry. John F. Kennedy's visit there was a genuine (though politically astute) pilgrimage, which drew huge crowds on a scale that his successors, Nixon and Reagan, never matched. Richard Nixon's one day stop-over, on his way home from a world tour, had the element of chicanery so often associated with him. Embassy officials had to scour the countryside for genuine relations (living or dead) and finally came up with a certain Thomas Milhous (his great-great-great-great grandfather on his mother's side) who had emigrated to Pennsylvania in the early eighteenth century. The visit was not a success: the authenticity of the Milhous ancestry was disputed, the village Nixon finally visited was daubed with IRA slogans, and Nixon flew home after the briefest of ceremonies. Ronald Reagan's visit in 1984 (the year of his re-election campaign) was similarly contrived. Controversy surrounded the identification of the presidential forebear: some claimed that the man's name was Ryan not Reagan, others (notably the Reagan look-alike from County Cork, Miles O'Regan) argued that the wrong ancestor had been selected. Either way, Irish enthusiasm for the visit (during which Reagan sipped gingerly at a pint of Guinness in the village pub named after him) was muted and the camera crews hoping to film crowds thronging the president's entourage for his campaign commercials were disappointed.

As these visits suggest, the impact of the Irish on the English of America is probably more a matter of the heart than of the tongue. Closer to Ireland itself, there are those parts of

87 John F. Kennedy riding into O'Connell Street in June 1963 with the President of Ireland, Éamon De Valera. In the background is the Dublin landmark, the Parnell monument, inscribed in English and Gaelic.

industrial England that have had continuous contact with the work-hungry Irish. Victorian Manchester had its "Little Ireland" near the River Medlock. London still has its Irish communities in Kilburn, Wapping and Hammersmith, where you can buy the full range of Irish newspapers, from the *Munster Express* to the *Tipperary Star*, as easily as the *Mirror* or the *Daily Telegraph*. And there is one region of England whose speech – famous the world over – has been transformed by generations of travel between the two countries: Liverpool and the Merseyside, the port where the Irish landed from Dublin.

THE MERSEY SOUND

The accent of Liverpool and Merseyside is known as Scouse, a unique city voice that finally resounded in the ears of the world in 1962/3 with the astonishing popular success of The Beatles. Unlike most of the English varieties we have described, Scouse is a late flower, a nineteenth-century accent, created in part by the flood of Irish immigrants who came to Lancashire during the height of the industrial revolution. The "Mersey sound" is also extremely localized, confined to the city of Liverpool, to its suburbs, and to the towns facing the city across the river Mersey. The Irish characteristics in Scouse include *youse* for the plural of you, *tree* for "three", and *dat* for "that". The Irishness of Scouse extends to some characteristic Protestant/Catholic differentiations. John Lennon, from a Roman Catholic family, would pronounce a word like "early" as *airly*, quite differently from Cilla Black, a Liverpudlian singer from a Protestant background, who would say something like *urrly*. Scouse is also famous for its distinctive adenoidal quality and for the rising inflection which differentiates it from the other Northern accents. Sentences (such as "I don't like it") tend to rise at the end where in Standard English they tend to fall.

The close and long-standing links between Dublin and Liverpool are typified by the ferry, the British and Irish Steamship line, which plies backwards and forwards on the seven-hour crossing. In the summer season it ferries tens of thousands of tourists; in the winter, a more regular Irish clientele: the Dublin supporters of the Everton and Liverpool football clubs. Each weekend, if these clubs have a home match, several hundred fans will take the Friday night boat from Dublin to Merseyside, watch the game on Saturday afternoon, and return to Dublin on the Saturday night ferry. The closeness of the links between the two cities extends to the football teams as well. Both Everton and Liverpool have, over the years, had many Dublin players in their teams. In the 1980s, Liverpool, once the gateway to the United States and the British Empire, has come to share Ireland's fate: economic decline mixed with cultural achievement. The unemployment rate on Merseyside generally has risen beyond 25 per cent. At the same time, writers like Willy Russell and Alan Bleasdale, and a new generation of bands, Frankie Goes to Hollywood, for example, give the city a special place in contemporary English culture.

For the present generation in the Republic of Ireland and the United Kingdom, the English of Ireland is a loaded speech. In the words of the Irish critic Seamus Deane, "the problem of Irish English is that everything in this country, from accent to pronunciation, to place names to the name of a city – all of these things carry a political charge". In the British public mind, it represents the language of the IRA bomber, the RUC reservist and the Noraid propagandist, of Gerry Adams MP, and the Reverend Ian Paisley. Paradoxically, Irish–English is also the best-loved regional accent. The love-affair with the music of the Irish voice is demonstrated by the remarkable success in Britain of several Irish broadcasters, the most notable of whom is Terry Wogan. "My accent, since you ask," he is quoted as saying, "is the bourgeois of Dublin." He describes his accent as "the crucial fact about me ... a Lancashire voice can upset Yorkshire people, but an Irish voice doesn't upset any English regions". A fellow BBC broadcaster, another Irishman, Anthony Clare, has summarized the success of Terry Wogan: "He is the classic Irish talker – mocking, self-deprecating, playing with words, attacking his betters, getting the boot in, but doing it in a way which would be thought aggressive from an English person ... You could accuse him of really saying very little, which again is very Irish. 'Mind you, now, I've said nothing.' That's a phrase you hear all the time in Dublin."

The success of Wogan and his Irish broadcasting colleagues is partly to do with the absence of class or regional connotations in their speech. But it is also open to speculation that the English especially enjoy listening to their language spoken by an Irishman for folk-memories of the lost speech-riches of the past. The poet Louis MacNeice expressed something of this in his *Autumn Journal* when he asked "Why do we like being Irish?"

Partly because
It gives us a hold on the sentimental English
As members of a world that never was,
Baptized with fairy water;

For the Irish, the English language is both the voice of an historic enemy, and also the voice of contemporary Irish poets like Seamus Heaney and Tom Paulin. Even the poets, some of whom have occasionally professed a remoteness from the politics of Ireland, are now caught up in the bitter and continuing arguments about the future of the language. One group of writers, that includes both Heaney and Paulin, calling itself Field Day, has adopted a programme that plans to redefine and re-explore the frame of reference in which English in Ireland is debated. For Heaney, the language question raises fundamental questions of national self-confidence:

> Your language has a lot to do with your confidence, your sense of your place and authority ... So to speak your own language [Irish English] and to get a trust in the pronunciation and in the quirks of vocabulary, and so on, is to go through a kind of political re-awakening ... That applies in all colonial or post-colonial situations: you have it in the Caribbean, and you had it of course in America.

In the words of Tom Paulin:

> We aim, if we can, to transcend the great gaps that there are between different political ideologies and obvious religious antagonisms by saying, Yes, there are two main traditions in this country and they are both to be attended to and nurtured ... They are both important, each on its own is somehow inadequate, but the two playing together, rather than fighting together, in a state of creative tension, could produce a really rich and interesting cultural life.

Paulin himself has published a pamphlet arguing the urgent need for "A Dictionary of Irish English". Until then, Paulin argues, English in Ireland will be like Irish society, "a living, but fragmented speech" with "untold numbers of homeless words, and an uncertain or derelict prose."

There are some "homeless words" throughout the Celtic Fringe: in Scotland, in Wales, and even in the areas of "language death" like Cornwall and the Isle of Man. It has been the fate of all these communities to find a means of self-expression through an alien tongue, and over the centuries much breath has been spent and much ink spilt lamenting this fact. But this cultural domination rather pales in significance when we consider what happened to the culture and languages of West Africa as a result of the slave trade.

88 This crude caricature, published in Philadelphia in the 1830s, demonstrates some of the long-standing traditions of Black American English.

6

BLACK
ON WHITE

Philadelphia is a city with one of the oldest free Black communities in the United States. In the 1830s, more than two hundred years after the first slaves were shipped to America, an anonymous Philadelphian cartoonist published a series of crude satires aimed at the pretensions of the local Black middle class. In a way that now seems profoundly racist, the artist caricatured Black imitations of White society – the musical evening, the tea party, and so on. He also represented what he took to be Black speech. "Shall I hab de honor to dance de next quadrille wid you, Miss Minta?" asks a bewigged partygoer. Yet for all their prejudice, these cartoons provide solid evidence of a long-standing, distinctive and separate Black English tradition (recognized, though misunderstood, by the Whites), with its own rules of grammar and pronunciation, its own roots and heritage.

In the past, such use of English was often thought to be lazy, or ungrammatical, or even to suggest an inferior intelligence. Now it is gradually being recognized as just another variety of English, neither worse nor better than the way English is spoken by Scots or New Yorkers or Londoners or Sydneysiders, with as much right to exist as any other variety of English. Yet it remains controversial even within the Black community. For some, it is an authentic means of self-expression for Black English speakers throughout America and the world. For others, who prefer the norms of Standard English, Black English represents the disadvantaged past, an obstacle to advancement, something better unlearned, denied or forgotten.

The cruel process that brought Africa into collision with European culture has enriched the English language with everyday words like *voodoo*, *tote*, *banjo*, *juke*, and *banana*. We also owe familiar phrases like *to bad-mouth*, *a high five* and *jam session*, and expressions like *yum-yum* and *nitty gritty* to the African speech traditions. Ironically, even *Sambo*, hated by the Black community as a racial stereotype, has three West African derivations. And beyond the obvious influence of words and phrases, the culture of Black English – from Negro spirituals to rock'n' roll – is permeated by its African past.

The story of the Blacks in history is surrounded by controversy and polemic. The story of their language – the nerve-end of politics – is no exception. No other form of speech in the history of the English language has been so deplored, debated and defended. Its stigma is ironic: Black English itself was the product of one of the most infamous episodes in the history of our civilization, the slave trade. Today, Black English speakers are members of a scattered family that includes African pidgins, Caribbean creole, the English of the southern states of America and the Black English of the post-colonial British Isles.

Three hundred and fifty years ago their ancestors lived in the hinterland of what is now Sierra Leone, Nigeria, Ghana and the Ivory Coast, in West Africa. They would have spoken one of several hundred local languages, including Hausa, Wolof, Bulu, Bamoun, Temne, Akan, and Twi. The first English they would have heard – and it has become the basis of Black English to this day – would have been from the sailors of the slave ships, many of whom started their journey from the old English trading ports like Liverpool and Bristol.

THE ATLANTIC TRIANGLE

For 150 years, Bristol was the apex of a trading triangle that was one of the most ruthless in the history of capitalism. British ships laden with cheap cotton goods, trinkets and Bibles sailed from Bristol and Liverpool for the west coast of Africa. They exchanged their cargo for a shipload of Black slaves who were then transported on the notorious Middle Passage, the second leg of the journey, to the sugar-bowl of the Caribbean, where they were sold to plantation owners and set to work as house servants or in the fields. Meanwhile, the same ships, laden with sugar, rum and molasses, returned to their home port, registering substantial profit for their merchant-owners. Before the British parliament finally abolished the slave trade in 1807, every leg of the journey contributed to the making of a completely new kind of English.

Bristol is now a busy provincial city and the once-crowded port, teeming with vessels, "all shipshape and Bristol fashion" as the phrase went, has been taken over by tourism. The great merchants' houses and Regency crescents are splendid reminders of the city's former prosperity. The famous Bristol "nails" on which so much business was transacted (giving us *cash on the nail*) still stand, but there is, of course, no monument to the human cargo on which these riches were based. For a memorial to the slaving past, you have to go to the outskirts of Bristol to the village of Henbury. There, in the graveyard of St Mary's Church, is the tomb of one Scipio Africanus, a young slave who died here at the age of eighteen. The epitaph on the gravestone is a poignant memorial to the mingling of English and African culture.

> *I who was Born a Pagan and a Slave*
> *Now sweetly Sleep a Christian in my Grave*
> *What tho my hue was dark my Saviour's sight*
> *Shall change this darkness into radiant light.*

Nothing is known of Scipio Africanus (a witty classical allusion that suggests the gulf between Blacks and Whites). As his name suggests, he, or his family, came from Africa. He, or his mother, or grandmother, would have spoken an African language. Here, in England, handsomely buried by an affectionate White owner, he would have spoken English, perhaps with the accents of his master.

THE MAKING OF PIDGIN ENGLISH

The making of Black English probably began even before the slave ships arrived on the west coast of Africa. The kind of English spoken on the ships at that time would have been highly idiosyncratic. Even if the captain was English, many of his crew would have been foreign. The sailors, who it is fair to assume would have worked on many ships for many masters, would almost certainly have been familiar with the Mediterranean sea-going lingua franca, Sabir, a language which evolved in the Mediterranean basin to cope with multi-ethnic crews. Sabir, which dates from the Crusades and survived to the nineteenth century, had strong Iberian roots, and this may well explain why West African pidgin English contains words like *pickaninny* and *savvy*, words that have a Mediterranean origin (*pequino* is the Portuguese for "small" and *savez-vous* is French for "do you know?"). The Portuguese had already been trading in West Africa for 200 years. The mixture of European languages from which the West African Blacks formed a means of communication with the European intruders, was described by one contemporary who wrote of Sierra Leone that, "Most of the *Blacks* about the bay speak either *Portuguese* or lingua franca (i.e. Sabir), which is a great convenience to the Europeans who come hither, and some understand a little *English* or *Dutch*."

There is much confusion about the term *pidgin*. The word itself comes from the Chinese pronunciation of the English word *business*. (It was a form of English used between the English and the Chinese in seaports in China and the Straits settlements in the nineteenth century.) Technically, a "pidgin" is an auxiliary language, one that has no native speakers. In other words, it is a speech-system that has been formed to provide a means of communication between people who have no common language. When a "pidgin" (English, French or Portuguese) becomes the principal language of a speech community – as on the slave ships – it evolves into a *creole*. Imagine two slaves who have met on a ship. The children of these pidgin-speaking slaves who have been brought up to speak their parents' pidgin as a native language, then develop it into a creole. (The word "creole" seems to have come from the Portuguese *crioulo*, meaning a slave born in a master's household, a house-slave.) This is how the English-based Caribbean creole of Barbados, Jamaica and the other English-speaking islands of the West Indies has developed. (Haitian creole is derived by the same process from the pidgin of the French slave trade.)

It is a misconception to imagine that a pidgin is a debased form of speech without rules. A pidgin will always have its own way of constructing a sentence. What is different about a pidgin is that usually it dispenses with the difficult or unusual parts of a language, the parts that speakers from a great variety of language backgrounds would find strange or hard to learn. We have seen in chapter two that this is what the Saxons and Danes did to English in the ninth century, and this is the reason why Black English, whose distant ancestor is the English pidgin of the slave ships, has two simplifying characteristics:

1. The omission of verbs like *is*, as in: *You out the game.*
2. The dropping of present-tense inflections, as in: *He fast in everything he do.*

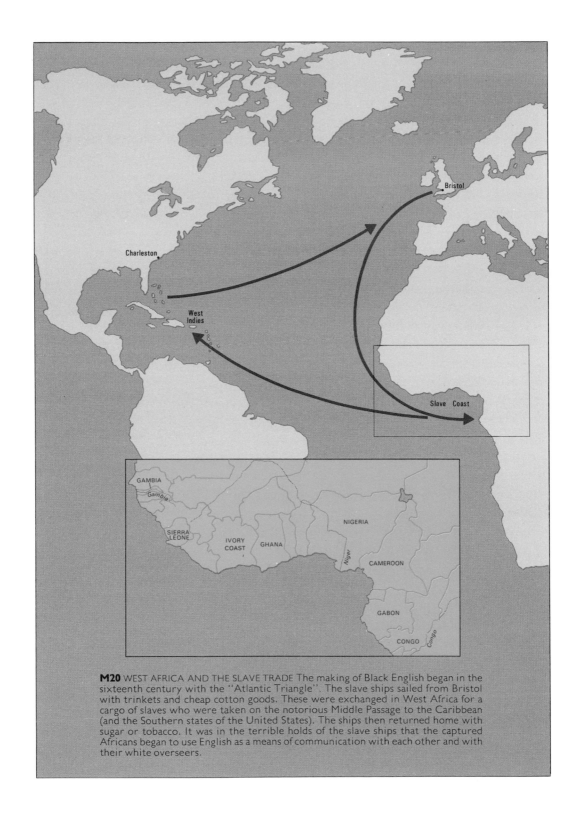

M20 WEST AFRICA AND THE SLAVE TRADE The making of Black English began in the sixteenth century with the "Atlantic Triangle". The slave ships sailed from Bristol with trinkets and cheap cotton goods. These were exchanged in West Africa for a cargo of slaves who were taken on the notorious Middle Passage to the Caribbean (and the Southern states of the United States). The ships then returned home with sugar or tobacco. It was in the terrible holds of the slave ships that the captured Africans began to use English as a means of communication with each other and with their white overseers.

89 The Slave Ship (*Slavers throwing overboard the dead and dying, typhoon coming on*) by J. M. W. Turner captures the horror of the slave trade.

Black English also has useful refinements that Standard English lacks, for instance the use of *be* to signify a stable condition in a sentence like: *some of them be big*. In Black English, *he working* means that "he is busy right now". On the other hand, *he be working* means that "he has a steady job".

The roots of pidgin English are controversial, and the early literature is patchy. No one disputes, however, the fact that the idea of pidgin-like English (*sicky-sicky* and *workee* for "sick" and "work") was recognized from the middle of the sixteenth century. Christopher Marlowe puts a kind of pidgin into the mouth of Barabas in his play *The Jew of Malta*. "Very mush", he says, "Monsieur, you no be his man?" Shakespeare's "'Ban, 'Ban, Ca-Caliban" is perhaps another kind of pidgin. By the beginning of the eighteenth century, the concept was sufficiently well established for Daniel Defoe to put it in the mouth of Man Friday in *Robinson Crusoe* without any special explanation. In America, the first record of pidgin comes from Cotton Mather during a heated argument about inoculation against smallpox among the people of Boston. Mather, who favoured the practice, interviewed some Bostonian slaves in the early 1700s and discovered that they had brought inoculation methods with them from Africa. "These Africans", he wrote, "all agree in One Story ... People take Juice of Small-Pox; and *Cutty-skin*, and Putt in a Drop; then by and by a little *Sicky-sicky*."

Adding uncertainty and confusion to our picture of pidgin English is the world-famous pidgin spoken in the Pacific, which we have become used to hearing in the televised speeches of the Pope or of Prince Charles to Melanesian and Polynesian islanders. It has not always been easy to trace the connection between this and the West African pidgin. The explanation for this confusion is quite simple. West African pidgin English was partly developed on board ship. Maritime expansion from the sixteenth to the nineteenth centuries would have taken the same ships, and sailors, as far afield as the China Seas, Hawaii and Melanesia. It was this maritime trade that developed different kinds of partly related pidgin across the globe.

In the 1940s, a pioneering fieldworker and scholar, Robert A. Hall, studied the pidgin English of what is now Papua New Guinea, a richly endowed territory for anthropologists. The result of Hall's work was the codification of Papua New Guinea pidgin as a written form. This anthropological activity, together with the special socio-political condition of Papua, helped to focus the world's attention on this exotic variety of English. Only recently has similar attention been focused on the pidgins of West Africa, whose origins are far earlier, dating directly from the slave trade.

"THE TOWER OF BABEL"

When the slave ships arrived in West Africa, the need for a pidgin occurred immediately. The slaves, from many different language backgrounds, had to communicate with each other and with their overseers. There is plenty of evidence that the slave masters broke up the various tribes to minimize the risk of rebellion. As Captain William Smith wrote in *A New Voyage to Guinea* in 1744, by "having some of every Sort on board, there will be no more Likelihood of their succeeding in a Plot, than of finishing the Tower of Babel".

The conditions under which this new English emerged were horrendous. The captured Africans were brought to the coast in columns, loaded with heavy stones to prevent escape, and forced to march sometimes hundreds of miles to the sea. At the ports they were penned into "trunks" for the inspection of buyers. Here, the death rate was one in five. Outside in the harbour, the slave captains waited to ferry their purchases on board. One of them, Captain Newton, who later became active in the anti-slavery movement, passed the time composing the famous hymn "How Sweet The Name of Jesus Sounds!"

On board, the Blacks were packed in like animals. They could not sit upright or lie full length. Once a day, they were brought up for exercise and to allow the sailors a chance to "clean the pails". When the weather was bad, they remained incarcerated. No place on earth, observed one writer, concentrated so much misery as the hold of a slave ship. Many more died. When they reached the West Indies or America, the survivors were brought up on deck to be sold. Their purchasers examined them for defects, pinched the skin, and sometimes tasted the perspiration to see if their blood was pure. Finally, the slave was branded on the chest with a hot iron.

By the time they left the slave ship, the Blacks would have become familiar with quite a range of pidgin English. *In extremis*, as they were, there would have been every incentive to form a new speech community, the first step in the painful rebuilding of a shattered world. So pidgin English, borrowed from the sailors, became the slave lingua franca. In French-controlled Louisiana, pidgin French fulfilled the same role.

In Sierra Leone to this day there are some remarkable continuities with the past. The Great Scearcies river, like the Congo and the Niger elsewhere, is still one of the country's main trading routes, plied by ferries and river traders for hundreds of miles along its length. On the banks, the multilingual villages of tribal Africa have a traditional way of life stretching back to the days when the Portuguese first explored this coast. One of the words for "White man" is still *oporto*, the name of a city in Portugal. Sierra Leone, like most African countries, is a rich patchwork of local languages. In the little kingdom of Paramount Chief Bai Sheborah Somanoh "Anlanth" II, barely a hundred square miles in extent, there are four major and two minor languages.

Chief Anlanth II travels his kingdom accompanied by a group of praise-singers who extol his virtues wherever he goes, a tradition that was first noticed by English travellers in the seventeenth century. The Chief explains: "Dey sing in praise of me for my good work to raise de standard of living within de entire chiefdom." On his own account, he is deeply respected by his people as a wise talker, as "a man of words". The reverence for the spoken word, from the west coast of Africa to the ghettos of Philadelphia, is a phenomenon that underlies the entire development of Black English. When the villagers gather to hear Chief Anlanth's wisdom, they burst into spontaneous song when they approve of his advice, a custom that is preserved in the Black church communities of the American South. The Chief describes how his people react to his speeches (using the characteristic Black English pronunciation of *dey* for "they" and *de* for "the"):

> When dey accept part of your speech to be de truth traditionally dey throw in a song in praise of what you have said ... dey praise me to be a wise paramount chief, because I could see things from afar.

The Chief himself can speak English, and also any of the languages of his kingdom. When he visits Mambolo, an upriver trading post since the first Portuguese traders landed in 1462, he negotiates with riverboat captain Issa Fofone for the shipment of some cement in a language descended from the first English pidgins.

CHIEF:	Tomorrow when you go Freetown, I want you to bring cement back for me.
ISSA FOFONE:	All right, sir.
CHIEF:	Because de road transport business don't work correct. But how much for de bag for [must I] pay?
ISSA FOFONE:	How many bag, sir?
CHIEF:	I get hundred and fifty bags which I want you to bring back for me ...

Issa Fofone travels up and down the river every day of his working life. He speaks four African languages, but Sierra Leone creole is probably the most efficient form of communication. When he casts off from the riverbank at Mambolo, his crew summons the passengers from among the villagers with cries of "Gotta go Freetown, gotta go Freetown, now, now, now." In a complicated language situation, pidgin – and its descendant Krio (see chapter nine) – is a vital means of communication. It was a process like this that spread pidgin English up and down the rivers of Africa by the early 1700s. Most Africans will know at least three languages. They are among the most accomplished linguists in the world. On the Great

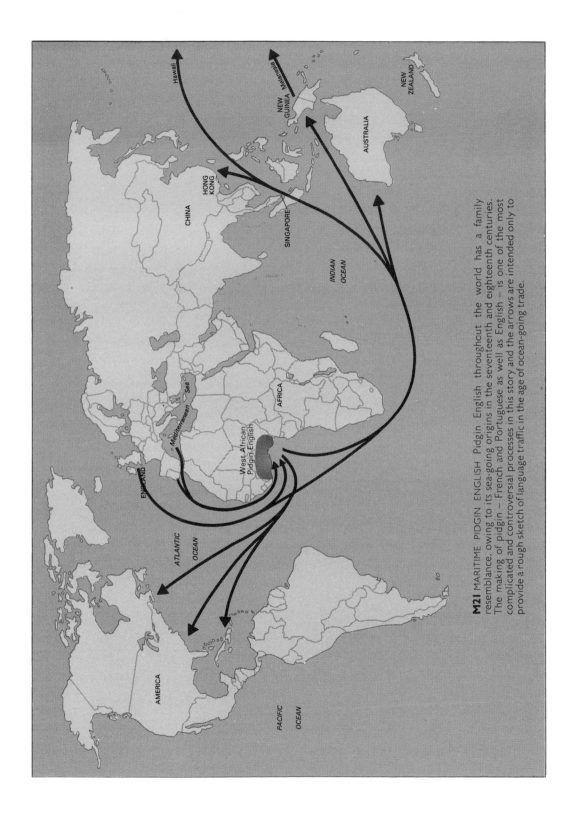

M21 MARITIME PIDGIN ENGLISH Pidgin English throughout the world has a family resemblance, owing to its sea-going origins in the seventeenth and eighteenth centuries. The making of pidgin – French and Portuguese as well as English – is one of the most complicated and controversial processes in this story and the arrows are intended only to provide a rough sketch of language traffic in the age of ocean-going trade.

Scearcies, six languages are spoken. On a river like the Congo, it may be as high as one hundred and sixty.

The English used by Issa Fofone shows signs of other European influence. "Much" is *beaucoup*, "burnt" is *bonni-bon*, "plenty of them" is *all dem plenty*. *Wait for water small* means "wait for the water for a little while". Steering between the treacherous sandbanks of the river, Issa Fofone instructs his steersman with pidgin-English cries of *Go small-small* ("go very slow"). Like any pidgin-derived English, this African creole has its own elaborate rules. *Him go* means "he goes"; *him done go* means "he went"; *him binna go* means "he was going".

CARIBBEAN CREOLE

The slave ships began crossing the Atlantic to the West Indies and to the ports of Georgia and South Carolina (then British colonies) at the beginning of the seventeenth century – the age of Shakespeare and the Authorized Bible. It is clear that by the eighteenth century Black English was established on the plantations of the South. It was also known – but not quite as fixed – wherever else in North America the slaves were brought, including Nova Scotia, New York and Massachusetts.

At the same time, down in the islands of the Caribbean, the arrival of first the Whites, and then the thousands of Black slaves caused an extraordinary transformation of the region's social and linguistic geography: the making of Caribbean creole. In retrospect, it is as though the Caribbean was a vast language laboratory. The tiny Carib and Arawak Indian population, once native to the region, speaking their own languages, and influencing Spanish with words like *cannibal* that have finally passed into English, were savagely obliterated. In their place, creolized forms of the invading European languages have emerged. Into the fertile and sugar-rich islands came Whites and Blacks in unequal proportions to exploit their potential, the former speaking English, French or Spanish, the latter a mixture of African languages and English, or perhaps even Portuguese, pidgin. From this meeting of Europe and Africa

90 The beginnings of Black English lie on the rivers of Africa, the Congo, the Niger and the Scearcies.

91 Paramount Chief Bai Sheborah Somanoh "Anlanth" II travelling his kingdom in Sierra Leone.

emerged a Caribbean English that is the next link in the chain that makes up the family of Black English.

Some aspects of the English that is spoken within the arc of the Windward and Leeward Islands still remain little known. At the extreme western edge of the Caribbean, for instance, on the Miskito Coast of Nicaragua, a variety of English survives that has only now been brought to the ears of the world by the crisis in Central America. The Miskito Indians who are interviewed about Nicaraguan politics by American network reporters use a variety of English that has evolved from a unique collision of languages: the speech of seventeenth- and eighteenth-century British settlers, their African slaves, the Indians themselves, and later the Spanish-speakers who seized the area at the end of the nineteenth century.

Miskito English has been isolated from the mainstream of the language for nearly two centuries, but although it has evolved its own linguistic system, its vocabulary is clearly English-based. Many of the words it has borrowed are nautical, regional (especially North Country and Scots), or now obsolete in Standard English. We can see at a glance that this variety of English is not unlike the pidgins of West Africa:

> A no wahn a ting tu du wid yu bika yu kom . . . lang taym an yu no kom luk fu Titi. Hu iz dis, Pap? (I want nothing to do with you because you have not come for a long time to see Titi. Who is this?)

Moving east, we find that the Caribbean, despite an appearance of uniformity, is fragmented in other ways. Each island has its own strong loyalties and traditions. Even the islands of the former British West Indies are not a federation, either politically or linguistically. Cuba and the Dominican Republic are Spanish; Haiti is French; Trinidad, the birthplace of the novelist V. S. Naipaul, is heavily influenced by Spanish, French creole and immigrant Indian traditions. The most English of the islands are Antigua, Jamaica and, above all, Barbados, whose eastern shores face across the ocean towards Africa.

Sometimes called "Little England", Barbados was settled in the 1620s. The island owes its prosperity to the development of the sugar industry in the 1640s and the settlement of slaves from the west coast of Africa to work the plantations: it was the first main port of call for the slave ships. It is said that the unruly slaves from the least domesticated tribes were progressively shipped up the claw of the West Indies, until they finally reached Jamaica. In any case the Barbadians – or Bajans as they are sometimes called – still have a reputation for well-spoken respectability, and Bajan creole is much closer to Standard English than Jamaican creole. The Caribbean writer George Lamming is a Barbadian whose first novel, *In the Castle of My Skin*, explores the subtle relations between Blacks and Whites in Barbados. He describes the similarity of Black and White Barbadian speech:

> One of the curious things about Barbados is that given the same region . . . there is great proximity in accent, and intonation between Black and White . . . If I hear a voice next door . . . I would recognize that was a Barbadian

speaking. I would not be too sure at first hearing whether that was a White Barbadian or a Black Barbadian.

Lamming has his own summary of the mixed language roots of Barbados:

> There will certainly be an element of Irish and Scots and English, greatly influenced of course by the African syntax and vocabulary which has been brought here.

Lamming can remember from childhood some of the distinctive Africanisms that survive on the island:

> You speak of people who are making a *bassa bassa*. A *bassa bassa* is a Twi word, but what it really means is a noise ... Teachers would use that. "Don't make any *bassa bassa* in this classroom."

Barbados itself, barely twenty-one miles long, is still almost wholly devoted to sugar which, next to tourism, is its main source of income. The plantation boundaries remain much as they always have. To the north of the capital, Bridgetown, stretches a long plain on which there are many plantations dating back to the 1640s, fringed with hills and majestic royal palms. Much of the fertile ground is devoted to sugar cane. One such hilly plantation is Dukes, about ten miles from Bridgetown. The earliest map of Barbados, published in 1657 by Richard Ligon, shows a Duke Plantation though it is not clear if the reference is the same. Dukes – which is still worked for sugar – is presently owned by Eddie Edgehill and his wife Vanessa. Both can trace their ancestry back to the first settlement of the island. Their story (and the story of the Black workers on their estate) expresses much of the Caribbean experience and the development of the English language.

The Edgehills are White. Vanessa and Eddie have two sons, a White estate manager, and several Black servants. From the top of its hill, Dukes itself has a fine view of much of Barbados, including Bridgetown. Many of the locals have worked for what they call "Edgehills" for many years. The sugar fields are sown and harvested in a four-year cycle, with "cropover" occurring in May each year. The Black workers who have devoted their lives to working on Dukes include three old men with special memories of the old days: Winston Daniel (known as "Sir Winston"), Leslie Barker (known as Michael) and Garfield Ford. The Winston Daniel family includes eleven children. One of the sons works on the buses in London. Part of the family is in Toronto. The old men, talking among themselves in the fields, use a Caribbean creole that is difficult if not impossible for a Standard English speaker to follow. Their boss, Eddie Edgehill, can not only follow what is being said, but quite naturally uses the same language.

> On the plantations you tend to speak a simple and rather plain language and it's broken English sometimes. You do this for the purpose of getting them

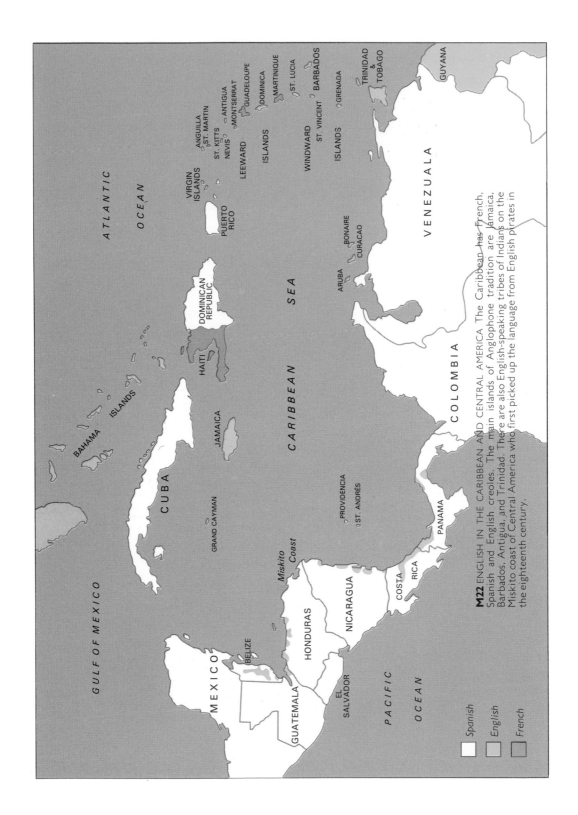

GULF OF MEXICO

ATLANTIC OCEAN

BAHAMA ISLANDS

MEXICO

BELIZE

GUATEMALA

EL SALVADOR

HONDURAS

NICARAGUA

COSTA RICA

PANAMA

PACIFIC OCEAN

CUBA

GRAND CAYMAN

Miskito Coast

JAMAICA

PROVIDENCIA

ST. ANDRÉS

HAITI

DOMINICAN REPUBLIC

PUERTO RICO

VIRGIN ISLANDS

ANGUILLA

ST. MARTIN

ST. KITTS

NEVIS

MONTSERRAT

ANTIGUA

GUADELOUPE

LEEWARD ISLANDS

DOMINICA

MARTINIQUE

ST. LUCIA

ST. VINCENT

WINDWARD ISLANDS

BARBADOS

GRENADA

TRINIDAD & TOBAGO

GUYANA

VENEZUALA

COLOMBIA

ARUBA

BONAIRE

CURACAO

CARIBBEAN SEA

M22 ENGLISH IN THE CARIBBEAN AND CENTRAL AMERICA The Caribbean has French, Spanish and English creoles. The main islands of Anglophone tradition are Jamaica, Barbados, Antigua, and Trinidad. There are also English-speaking tribes of Indians on the Miskito coast of Central America who first picked up the language from English pirates in the eighteenth century.

Spanish

English

French

206/THE STORY OF ENGLISH

92 British and American slavers, trading up river, introduced the English language to Africa in the sixteenth century.

to understand you better. You get into the habit of using words and phrases which are not strictly correct but they influence your language, and you end up speaking what we call Bajan.

Eddie Edgehill has a great loyalty to his native variety of English. And like all the inhabitants of the West Indies, he can distinguish one islander from another:

> I don't think that speaking in Bajan is an incorrect way. I just use it as a different way. You know, we talk of islanders coming from Trinidad, or people coming from other islands as speaking another language altogether. They're speaking English but they're putting different stresses, as they do in places like Jamaica. Bajans themselves sometimes don't understand it although they're not far away from that particular country.

He has no difficulty in recognizing the African roots of some Caribbean English: "White Bajans are certainly influenced by Africans, by the Black people, and vice versa of course." Eddie Edgehill notices a feature of his own speech habits that is not unusual for anyone who has to communicate with a different variety of English: "I become more of a Bajan as soon as I'm talking to my brothers, or people in the field, or Michael in the plantation. But when I'm sitting at a professional desk I'm slightly more English."

Today Caribbean creole has developed far beyond its pidgin English roots (see chapter nine). To recapture the early days of Black American English, the place to visit is the southern United States, especially South Carolina. It was to Charleston, a city that was known as the slave capital of the South, that many of the slaves were brought. Those that survived the terrible Middle Passage would have been unloaded on Sullivan Island, a swampy, low-lying strip of land opposite the main harbour in Charleston, a place that has been called the "Ellis Island for Blacks". Soon they would have been sold off and shipped inland to the big plantations. But some remained. On the Sea Islands of the South Carolina coast a kind of Black English – a creole known as Gullah – is preserved to this day. Gullah is probably closer than any other American variety of Black English to the original creole English of the New World, and the lost pidgin English of the slave ships.

"AN ECHO OF PLANTATION TALK"

Gullah, still spoken by about a quarter of a million Blacks, has survived here chiefly thanks to the peculiar geography of the islands. Lying close to Charleston, they were near a slave port that flourished well into the nineteenth century. Constantly resupplied with new arrivals, they were also, until the early years of this century, cut off from the outside world. The Blacks lived self-sufficient lives on these islands, growing their own crops in the fertile soil and fishing for crabs, oysters and red snapper out of the thousands of creeks and inlets. Like the Cornish fishermen on Tangier Island in the Chesapeake Bay, theirs was a self-contained language community whose speech-patterns became partially ossified.

The most important quality of Gullah is still its African roots. In 1949, Lorenzo Turner's trailblazing study, *Africanisms in the Gullah Dialect*, established once and for all that Gullah talk retained as many as 6000 Africanisms. Janey Hunter, now seventy years old, has experience through her parents of the old slaving times. She grew up on Jenkins' Plantation, Charleston, and now lives on Johns Island. She has fourteen children, one hundred grandchildren and twenty-eight great-grandchildren. She says:

> Thank God 'em be here. And I love all 'em, allus love the children. I ain't bring 'em up all the way that I come up, but I bring them part of the way how I was raised.

To White ears, Janey Hunter's speech is strongly reminiscent of the Uncle Remus stories she still repeats to her grandchildren. Her way of life owes much to the old traditions:

> There was no radio, no record player, no newspaper to read, so our parents teach us all different kinda games, and learned us religious songs of the Bible.

She draws a distinction between the way she talks and the way her parents used to talk, and she is very decided about the roots of the Sunday hymns sung at the Wesleyan United Methodist Church:

> I would say: Well, go and bring me some water. Old people say: Gal, go fetch me some water. I thirsty . . . We music is slavery music. We was made by the hand and the feet. That's the way we make our music – clap and shout.

The African past is still vivid for Janey Hunter:

> This was our home, Africa. That's where all this Gullah language comes from, Africa . . . Many Africa word. Dere. That's Africa word. We may say *here*, but they say *dere*.

Janey Hunter knows her reasons for speaking Gullah in her everyday work:

> I keep my Gullah language too, 'cos I love it, and that's me. I can speak other language, but I love my Gullah language. If you disown that, you're disowning your parents . . .

Like many rural varieties of English, Gullah is thought by some of those who speak it to suggest inferiority. Janey Hunter describes the way in which Gullah speakers will try to disguise their speech:

> A lot of old people know Gullah language, 'cos that' all they've ever speaken all their life. But they feel like people look down on them now when they speak Gullah language . . . They feel like the young people take 'em for fun. They come and say: Why you speak so bad? See, I don't know what she talk about.

The argument about the African nature of Gullah and Black English brings us back to politics. Before the 1960s, there was a profound reluctance on the part of Whites to admit any slave-contribution to the making of American English. White American dialectologists preferred to argue that the usages of Black English came from *British* regional speech, especially from East Anglia and the West Country! Even the master himself, H. L. Mencken, author of *The American Language*, wrote, "The Negro dialect, as we know it today, seems to have been formulated by the song-writers for the minstrel shows; it did not appear in literature until the time of the Civil War . . . it was a vague and artificial lingo which had little relation to the actual speech of Southern Blacks."

After Turner published his study, this preposterous theory became impossible to maintain. With politics still in the forefront, the battleground of the argument shifted. It was argued that Gullah was a freak, an isolated language phenomenon limited to the Sea Islands. Gullah, it was said, had nothing to do with the English of other American Blacks. But the difficulty with this argument was that a close study of Gullah shows that it is remarkably similar to Krio and the other English creoles, with deep historical roots. Only now, in the 1980s, do most American linguists accept that there is a continuum in the varieties of Black English which runs from the Krio of Sierra Leone to Caribbean creole to Gullah to the modern Black English of the United States.

The African element in the English spoken by the slaves on the plantations – known as Plantation Creole – was sustained for some time, since some African languages, Wolof in particular, were spoken quite widely in the southern states during the eighteenth century. At least one or two slaves on each plantation knew – and probably were admired for knowing – an African language. Slave advertisements from the seventeenth and eighteenth centuries indicate the presence of Wolof speakers. Others refer to the quality of the English spoken. Phrases like "speaks English though somewhat Negroish" and "speaks rather more proper than Negroes in general" occur regularly. Slavery was a part of everyday life. In England, Samuel Johnson had a much-loved Black servant, Francis Barber, an ex-slave. Many famous Americans had slaves. Indeed, one of Benjamin Franklin's sale notices advertised: "A likely Negro wench, about 15 years old . . . [has] been in the country above a year and talks English."

By the end of the eighteenth century, the linguistic situation among the Black slave communities on the plantation had excited enough literary comment for it to be clear to us today that Gullah was not an isolated example, but a forerunner of Black English. One British visitor bought a slave named Richmond from a plantation in North Carolina and represented his speech, an early instance of *coppin' a plea*, as follows:

> Kay, massa, (says he), you just leave me, me sit here, great fish jump up into de canoe, here he be, massa, fine fish, massa; me den very grad; den me sit very still, until another great fish jump into de canoe; but me fall asleep, massa, and no wake till you come; now, massa, me know me deserve flogging, cause if great fish did jump into de canoe, he see me asleep, den he jump out again, and I no catch him; so, massa, me willing now take good flogging.

The same visitor noted that: "Many of the others also speak a mixed dialect between the Guinea and the English." And Benjamin Franklin himself attempted a version of Black

93 Janey Hunter is a Gullah speaker in an almost forgotten community on the coast of South Carolina.

94 African fishing traditions survive in the Sea Islands.

English in his *Information for those Who Would Remove to America*:

> Boccarorra [a form of *buckra*, "White man"] make de Black Man workee,
> make de Horse workee, make de Ox workee, make ebery thing workee; only
> de Hog. He, de Hog, no workee; he eat, he drink, he walk about, he go to
> sleep when he please, he libb a gentleman.

By the time Benjamin Franklin was caught up in the American Revolution, there were slave communities from Massachusetts to Georgia. The majority in the South were now speaking a wide range of English. The latest arrivals from Africa would know only pidgin English. Those who had been shipped from the West Indies and those who had been born on a plantation would speak Plantation Creole. If they were house slaves they would, in the words of the advertisements, speak "very proper English". In the North, and away from the influence of the plantations, where the Black population was heavily outnumbered, the Blacks were more rapidly assimilated linguistically than in the South. Gradually, the memory of their African languages faded. It was the children who were chiefly responsible for this. The social pressure in their playgrounds was towards English. If a mother called her child in from play, she might, if she was a first generation slave, use her native African tongue. The child would respond in the language of its peers – Plantation Creole.

"THE NEGRO DIALECT"
By one route or another words and phrases from various West African languages passed into American speech. There are also the words and phrases that emerged from nearly 250 years' experience of slavery itself. There were a handful of slaves in 1619, half a million in 1772 (half of them in Virginia and South Carolina), and four million when the Civil War began. Slavery made its own traditions of speech and vocabulary, and the memory of both is still fundamental to Black American English.

The slaves themselves were called *Negroes*, or *Blacks*, or, euphemistically, *servants*. Phrases like *slave labour* and *slave driver* come from the plantations. *To sell down the river*, now generally used to mean taking advantage of someone, and to treat them badly for personal gain or advantage, comes from the 1830s. It was a way of punishing a slave to sell him to a sugar-cane plantation owner on the Lower Mississippi, where, everyone knew, the slave conditions were generally the worst. Mark Twain's Nigger Jim was always afraid they would sell him down the river.

> Well, you see, it 'uz dis way. Ole Missus – dat's Miss Watson – she pecks on
> me all de time, en treats me pooty rough, but she awluz said she wouldn' sell
> me down to Orleans. But I noticed dey wuz a nigger trader roun' de place
> considable, lately, en I begin to git oneasy.

As the nineteenth century unfolded, so-called "Nigger English", and later the "Negro dialect", became widely recognized among both Blacks and Whites. Among the former, there is a neglected tradition of "Invisible Poets" from George Moses Horton, "the Coloured Bard of North Carolina" (born *c.* 1797), to Daniel Webster Davis (1862–1913), whose poem "Wey Down Souf" is typical of early Black English literature:

> O, de birds ar' sweetly singin',
>   'Wey down Souf,
> An' de banjer is a-ringin',
>   'Wey down Souf;
> An' my heart it is a-sighin',
> Whil' de moments am a-flyin'
> Fur my hom' I am a-cryin',
>   'Wey down Souf.

Daniel Webster Davis is doubly interesting. He offers a two-page glossary of the terms used in this poem.

Fhar: fair	*Peckin'*: impose upon
Ho'oped: helped	*Reggin'*: reckon
Huccum: how come	*Shorz*: sure as

Among the Whites, the popular literature of the period made free (and often accurate) use of Black English, for example in *Uncle Tom's Cabin* by Harriet Beecher Stowe, and in the famous Uncle Remus Stories.

> One day atter Brer Rabbit fool 'im wid dat calamus root, Brer Fox went ter wuk en got 'im some tar, en mix it wid some turpentine, en fix up a contrapshun wat he call a Tar-Baby, en tuck dish yer Tar-Baby en he sot 'er in de big road, en den he lay off in de bushes fer ter see wat de news wuz gwinter be.

95 Joel Chandler Harris, author of the *Uncle Remus Stories*.

Joel Chandler Harris, their author, exemplifies the close relationship between plantation owners and slaves: his stories are creole tales from the plantations, but he himself was White, which, as Mark Twain records, caused great disappointment among his fans. "Undersized, red-haired and somewhat freckled . . . it turned out", wrote Twain, "that he had never read aloud to people, and was too shy to venture the attempt now." Twain considered this a shame, because "Mr Harris ought to be able to read the Negro dialect better than anybody else . . . in the matter of writing it he is the only master the country has produced." And Twain, a master of authentic American dialogue, knew what he was talking about.

In the Introduction to *Uncle Remus* Harris draws an interesting distinction between what he called "the dialect of the cotton plantations as used by Uncle Remus, and the lingo in vogue on the rice plantations and Sea Islands of the South Atlantic states". He also pays tribute, in the style of the day, to the rich tradition he was attempting to preserve:

> If the language of Uncle Remus fails to give vivid hints of the really poetic imagination of the Negro; if it fails to embody the quaint and homely humor which was his most prominent characteristic . . . then I have reproduced the form of the dialect merely, and not the essence.

The entry of Black English into the mainstream of American life began with the Brer Rabbit stories. Later it was to sustain its place there through minstrel shows, vaudeville, music hall, radio and finally the movies.

Slavery itself had worried Americans ever since the Revolution. Thomas Jefferson, with his usual prescience, had seen that when the slave states of the South and the free states of the North competed to join the Union, there would be trouble. "This momentous question, like a firebell in the night, awakened and filled me with terror. I considered it at once as the knell of the Union." After Britain abolished the trade and then emancipated its West Indian slaves, the United States had to decide whether or not they would do likewise. North and South were at odds. Abraham Lincoln expressed the greatest fear of all in a speech made at Edwardsville, Illinois, in 1858:

> When . . . you have succeeded in dehumanizing the Negro, when you have put him down and made it impossible for him to be but as the beasts in the field . . . are you quite sure that the demon you have roused will not turn and rend you?

Linguistically speaking, the effects of the Civil War and the liberation of the slaves on the spread of Black English were comparatively slight in the short run. Most Southern Blacks stayed on or near the plantations, and not until the industrialization of the North and the mass emigration to the cities in the early twentieth century did Black English enter a new phase. In the South, it continued to flourish and, perhaps most controversial of all, to influence the accent and vocabulary of White Southerners.

"THE THICK NEGRO SPEECH OF THE SOUTHERNERS"

The assumption of White superiority over Blacks, even in language, died hard. As late as 1935 it was perfectly orthodox to publish books with titles like *The Relation of the Alabama – Georgian Dialect to the Provincial Dialects of Great Britain* and to argue that the special language forms of the Blacks came from the Whites, not the other way round.

Even today, the question is still a disputed topic in the South. Professor J. L. Dillard, who has devoted much of his life to the study of Black English, remarks:

> It is highly controversial to say that Southern White English has been influenced by Black English. The Southern Whites often resent that. Yet if you look at the map it's rather striking that what we call the Southern dialect survives exactly where the Confederate states were, and where slavery was *the* institution.

Dillard goes on to highlight some of his reasons for his assertion:

> There are details of pronunciation, for example, in Southern White English which match Black English and even match Africanisms. Take the so-called plosive consonant – the pronunciation of *beel* rather than *bill* – which is characteristic of Black English. This plosive consonant exists in African languages. It's not characteristic in Northern White English, and there has never been any dialect like that reported in England.

Dillard's claims are not as radical as, at first sight, they sometimes have seemed. There had always been voices of commonsense when it came to the issue of Southern White talk. In 1885 one observer – declaring his prejudices – unabashedly wrote:

96/97 The Blacks who lived in the slave quarters of the great estates had a significant effect on the speech of their White masters. Charles Dickens noted that Southern women spoke like their Black slaves.

It must be confessed, to the shame of the White population of the South, that they perpetuate many of these pronunciations in common with their Negro dependants; and that, in many places, if one happened to be talking to a native with one's eyes shut, it would be impossible to say whether a Negro or a White person were responding.

Once again, we have to rely on the testimony of visitors to the United States. In 1849, Sir Charles Lyell noticed how Black and White children on the plantations were being educated together. In his *A Second Visit to the United States of North America*, he wrote:

> Unfortunately, the Whites, in return, often learn from the Negroes to speak broken English, and in spite of losing much time in unlearning ungrammatical phrases, well-educated persons retain some of them all their lives.

The plantations of the deep South became the cradle of a new ingredient in American culture. The English of the slaves was having a decisive effect on the English of their White Anglo-Saxon masters. The Southern accent of the United States would almost certainly have been quite different without the influence of the Blacks. The influence of Black English was felt in the fields (where slave and overseer would mix), in the house (where master and mistress used Plantation Creole to communicate with their house-slaves); but above all, it was found in the nursery. Up to the age of about six years, Black and White children grew up together, played together, and learned together. In these crucial years of their development the Whites were often outnumbered by the Black slave children. Furthermore, all the nursing – as any reader of Southern literature knows – was done by Blacks. As early as the mid-eighteenth century it was reported that, "the better sort, in this country, particularly, consign their children to the care of Negroes . . ."

98 Martha de Wies, the daughter of a man born into slavery, uses Black English words like "tote".

99 Mary Shepherd, the cook at Middleton, uses Black English like "I writes", and "they gone".

100/101 White plantation children, nursed by Black "mammies" and mixing with Black "play-children", grew up speaking Plantation Creole. Southern families sent their boys away to school to learn "good English".

Charles Dickens, on a tour of the United States, noticed that it was the Southern women whose speech was most influenced. A closer and better-informed set of observations come from the *Journal of Residence on a Georgia Plantation in 1838–39*, a fascinating social document kept by the famous British actress Fanny Kemble, after her marriage to a plantation owner. She reports with some alarm that her daughter was beginning to pick up the local speech, described by her as "the thick Negro speech of the Southerners".

> The children of the owners, brought up among them (the slaves), acquire their Negro mode of talking – slavish speech surely it is – and it is distinctly perceptible in the utterances of all Southerners, particularly of the women, whose avocations, taking them less from home, are less favourable to their throwing off this ignoble trick of pronunciation than the varied occupation and the more extended and promiscuous business relations of men.

Southern boys from good families, in contrast, were usually sent away to White schools, often in the Northern states. From the age of six or seven they were separated from Black talk and educated in race hostility to the Blacks. The women remained on the plantations, rearing children, coping with the servants, and mixing with the house slaves. The reasons for the acquisition of Black English characteristics in Southern speech are many. One – among children – was simply imitation. Fanny Kemble wrote of four-year-old Sally that:

> Apparently the Negro jargon has commended itself as euphonious to her infantile ears, and she is now treating me to the most ludicrous and accurate imitations of it every time she opens her mouth. Of course I shall not allow this to become a habit. This is the way the Southern ladies acquire the thick and inelegant pronunciation which distinguishes their utterances from the Northern snuffle, and I have no desire that S— should adorn her mother tongue with either peculiarity.

The mingling of Black and White American culture is illustrated by the story of the Charleston writer Du Bose Heyward. A White Southerner, Heyward was descended from one of the signers of the Declaration of Independence, Thomas Heyward. In 1915 he published a novel based on some of the famous Black characters of his native Charleston. His novel, which became a bestseller, was *Porgy*. The story goes that up in New York, the young composer George Gershwin, celebrated for his *Rhapsody in Blue*, was looking for a suitable subject for an American folk opera. Sometime in 1926 a friend lent him a copy of *Porgy* for light reading. Gershwin at once saw its potential and set about trying to acquire the rights. As it turned out, the novel's very success stood in his path: there were plans for a play, which appeared in 1927. Finally the way was clear, and in 1934, Gershwin and Heyward spent the summer together working in a seaside cottage at Folly Beach just outside Charleston. Heyward and Ira Gershwin worked on the lyrics. George Gershwin immersed himself in the culture of the Gullah-speaking Blacks, especially their spirituals and songs. The opera he composed that year is full of the sound of Black music, Black rhythms and Black English.

Summertime an' the livin' is easy,
Fish are jumpin' an' the cotton is high.
O yo' Daddy's rich an yo' Ma is goodlookin'
So hush little baby don' yo' cry.

THE BLACKS MOVE NORTH

The half century between the Civil War and the First World War saw the American Blacks catapulted from slavery to legal equality, then snapped back into a state almost as degrading as slavery. At the end of the Civil War, four million slaves were freed, and an old English legal phrase, "civil rights", entered the American lexicon. Congress rapidly passed further legislation granting full citizenship and the guarantee of the right to vote to the freed slaves. The avenging zeal of the Republican administrations of these years meant that by 1867 there were more Southern Blacks registered to vote than Whites, while Congress had twenty-four Black congressmen. (The Congress elected in 1984 had only twenty.)

All these gains were lost as White Southerners wore down the North. Once the last Federal troops were withdrawn, the South hit back, passing "Jim Crow" laws to abridge the rights of Blacks. The word *segregation* became part of the vocabulary of discrimination, as did *uppity*, a White Southern word for Blacks who did not know their place. Thus did language signal social and political change. The final blows to the freed Blacks came in the 1880s and 1890s when the Supreme Court attacked the Civil Rights Act as "unconstitutional" and sanctioned segregated ("separate but equal") education. Decades of second-class citizenship lay ahead.

Their new subjugation helped drive a great Black migration to the North. After the First World War and the surge in manufacturing, there were even more potent economic reasons for the Blacks to leave the South. Black language and culture began to have a major impact on White American speech and life, which began a massive appropriation of Black words and styles. In music, the Blacks have given us *jazz*, the *blues* and *rock 'n' roll*; in dance, the

102 Black emigrants on the road to Kansas in the nineteenth century. Despite emancipation in 1865, most Blacks did not migrate to the North until the 1920s.

cakewalk, the *jitterbug*, and *break dancing*; and in slang, the street talk and *jive-talk* of *cool*, *heavy* and *doing your own thing*, the essential vocabulary of letting your hair down and having a good time.

In the 1920s and 1930s, Blacks living in the cities in large numbers were seen by most White Americans as stereotypes – maids, cooks, waiters, porters, and minstrels. Partly this reflected the socio-economic reality; and partly it showed the influence of vaudeville, radio and the talkies. It was through the entertainment business that many Southern Blacks fought their way out of the ghettos, and out of the poverty-ridden South, working their way, like the New Orleans jazzmen, all the way up the Mississippi to Chicago and finally New York. (The stereotype was by no means entirely accurate. Harlem in the 1920s underwent a cultural renaissance, symbolized by the work of the poet Langston Hughes, and the flourishing there of a sophisticated Black middle class.)

The social and linguistic parallels between Blacks in America and East End Cockneys in Britain are striking. While the socio-political muscle of Black Americans is obviously far greater, the two groups have a lot in common. Both were outsiders in their own society; both had an immensely rich and vital cultural tradition, expressed in speech and song; both found a form of self-expression through the entertainment business (and sport, especially boxing), and both suffered considerable stereotyping in radio, film and later television. Both Blacks and Cockneys have contributed some of the most vivid words and phrases to the language. Both are exceptionally good at describing the nuance of personal relationships, of feeling (anger and love), and of good times. The language of both societies is spicy, racy (as the English say) and, for those on the outside, connotes a mild rebellion. This is why both the American and British middle classes have adopted some of the terminology – *mate*, *man*, *cool*, *hip*, *wotcha* – as a form of relaxation, a form of linguistic dissidence (see chapter eight).

One pervasive Black stereotype among Whites was that Blacks had "rhythm": a conviction that Whites insisted on ever since slaves had danced "Jim Crow jigs" in the 1730s or performed the juba dance for the astonished plantation overseers. Minstrel shows, coming out of this tradition, dated back to the 1840s, and after the emancipation a succession of musical styles (and words) had their origin in Black culture – the *spiritual* in 1866, the *blues* in 1870, *ragtime* in 1896, *boogie woogie* in the 1920s, *jive* in the 1930s, *rhythm and blues* in the 1950s, and *soul music* in the 1960s.

Like almost everything else in the story of Black English, the musical tradition began on the plantations. The slaves' lives were restricted in many ways, but they *were* free to hold religious gatherings. Spirituals, Black English versions of White Christian religious sentiment, began not only as acts of religious devotion, but also as coded messages amongst an oppressed people.

> *I ain't never been to heaben but Ah been told,*
> *Comin' fuh to carry me home,*
> *Dat de streets in heaben am paved wif gold,*
> *Comin' to carry me home.*

Steal away to Jesus was an invitation to a gathering of slaves; *Judgement Day* was the day of the slave uprising; *Home*, *Canaan* (the promised land) and *Heaven* were all veiled allusions to Africa. A spiritual that talked of a fellow slave "a-gwine to Glory" was actually making a reference to one who had successfully boarded a repatriation ship bound for Africa. Nat Turner, a slave preacher, inspired by a vision of Blacks and Whites in battle, made the greatest use of hymns as covert propaganda. When his famous revolt in 1831 was crushed and he was jailed in Courtland, Virginia, the place became known among Blacks as *Jerusalem*. Nat Turner became one of the first martyrs of Black liberation. After his execution, the Negro spiritual tended to lose its revolutionary associations and become a vehicle for Black Christian devotion. But the tradition of double meanings in songs had been established and was to flourish in later flowerings of Black music.

The subversive use of religious songs was just part of an understandably subversive attitude among speakers of Black English toward the language of their masters. Even today, in the right context *ugly*, meaning African-looking, can mean "beautiful"; *bad* (pronounced *baa-ad*) can mean "very good"; *mean* can denote "excellent". There were other kinds of codes used on the plantation:

> Sometimes while loading corn in the field, which demands loud singing,
> Josh would call to Alice, a girl he wanted to court on the adjoining

plantation, "I'm so hongry want a piece of bread"; and her reply would be "I'se so hongry almost dead." Then they would try to meet after dark in some secluded spot.

In the mid-1870s all these elements – double meanings, covert sexuality, Black liberation, African rhythms – came together in what was then the most vital centre of Black American culture, New Orleans. The name they gave to the new music was *jazz*. Originally, the word was used by Blacks to mean *to speed up*. The specific etymology of the word has never been pinpointed, but most scholars believe that it is of West African origin. By 1913 the word had moved into the mainstream of American culture, with both Blacks and Whites using *jazz* to mean a particular type of *ragtime* music with a syncopated rhythm. By the end of 1917, the year the "doughboys" sailed for Europe to fight the Kaiser, jazz music and jazz bands were the talk of the town in New York, London and Paris.

The jazzmen brought with them their own Black English vocabulary. *Uptight* is a famous (though controversial) example. Originally it was associated with readiness: "I got my boots laced up tight – and am ready to go places." Too much preparation, however, could kill the spontaneity needed for the greatest jazz performance, so a player who won't improvise easily becomes *uptight*. Early jazz was *hot* (frenetic), but when this word was over-exploited by the Whites, it was considered best to develop *cool* (which may, ironically, have come from *White* West Coast jazz bands of the 1950s).

One of the greatest of the early jazzmen was the legendary Jelly Roll Morton. His real name was Ferdinand Le Menthe, but as leader of the Red Hot Peppers he became simply Morton, a milestone figure in the history of jazz. Upstaged during one performance by a Black comedian (who introduced himself as "Sweet Papa Cream Puff right out of the bakery shop"), Morton had gone one better and announced himself as "Sweet Papa Jelly Roll, with stove pipes in my hips and all the women in town dyin' to turn my damper down". Food words like "cookie", "cake", "pie" and "angel-food cake", all hidden expressions for sex, permeate Black English,

103 The Cotton Club was at the centre of the Harlem night-club scene, an important influence on White American English.

104 Ferdinand Le Menthe, better known as Jelly Roll Morton.

but this was the ultimate sexual braggadocio. Few words in the Black English lexicon have more sexual evocation than *jelly roll*.

> *Jelly roll, jelly roll ain't so hard to find,*
> *There's a baker shop in town makes it brown like mine.*
> *I got a sweet jelly, a lovin' sweet jelly roll.*
> *If you taste my jelly it'll satisfy your worried soul.*

In the African language Mandingo, *jeli* is a minstrel who gains popularity with women through skill with words and music. In the English creole of the Caribbean, *jelly* refers to the meat of the coconut when it is still at a white, viscous stage, and in a form closely resembling semen. In English, *jelly* and *jelly roll* are both items of food. In *Look Homeward, Angel* by Thomas Wolfe, a novel published in 1929, the newsboy Eugene Gant, trying to collect his debts, has this conversation with a Black customer who cannot pay:

> "I'll have somethin' fo' yuh, sho. I'se waitin' fo' a White gent'man now.
> He's gonna gib me a dollar." . . .
> "What's – what's he going to give you a dollar for?"
> "Jelly Roll."

On the street, *jelly roll* had many associated meanings, from the respectable "lover, or spouse", to the Harlem slang of the 1930s, "a term for the vagina".

"MR HEPSTER'S JIVE TALK DICTIONARY"

Harlem in the 1920s and 1930s was the pinnacle of Black city life and it was to Harlem that the jazzmen ultimately gravitated. Cab Calloway, Count Basie, Duke Ellington and Louis Armstrong all ended up there, playing in clubs like the Cotton Club and Leroy's. In those days, the Whites travelled *uptown*, as they put it, to see the shows. Or, as the Blacks put it, "came down from Sugar Hill" – the heights overlooking the west side of Harlem where all the *sugar* (money) was. Albert Murray, whose syncopated autobiography, *South To A Very Old Place*, celebrates both his youth and the roots of Black culture, has defined thirty-two meanings of the word *soul*. He also has vivid memories of Harlem's heyday:

> Leroy's was at the corner of 135th Street and Fifth Avenue. That was a very
> exclusive club and was mainly for uptown people. Only very special people
> who knew somebody very important in Harlem got a chance to go there. On
> the other hand, Edmond's which was on Seventh Avenue near where
> Small's is now, was a sort of mixed club. It was patronized by a number of
> downtown clientele.

The downtowners who came uptown would have been called *jazz babies* or *flappers* if they were women, and a *jazzbo* or *sheik* (after Rudolph Valentino's starring role in *The Sheik*, 1921), if they were men. The fascination of White "flappers" and "sheiks" with Black music

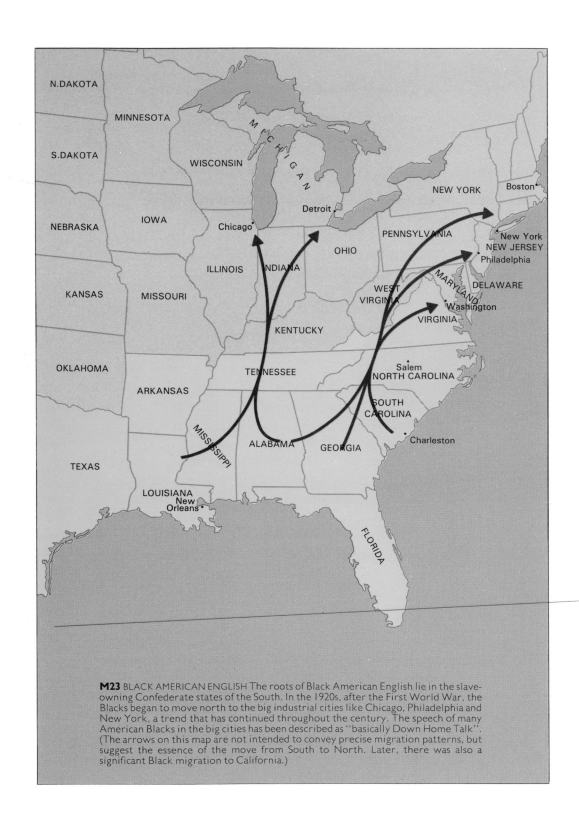

M23 BLACK AMERICAN ENGLISH The roots of Black American English lie in the slave-owning Confederate states of the South. In the 1920s, after the First World War, the Blacks began to move north to the big industrial cities like Chicago, Philadelphia and New York, a trend that has continued throughout the century. The speech of many American Blacks in the big cities has been described as "basically Down Home Talk". (The arrows on this map are not intended to convey precise migration patterns, but suggest the essence of the move from South to North. Later, there was also a significant Black migration to California.)

and lyrics carried much of the private code of the jazz players into the mainstream of American English.

The language of the jazz players was known as *jive talk*. In the words of Albert Murray:

> Jive talk was really the talk of the world of entertainment, and people who frequented the world of entertainment, and people who imitated entertainers. It was called "hip talk" or "hip", the language of hipsters . . . it reflected the jargon of music, of the stage, of the night clubs and of sports mainly.

Albert Murray was born in the South and emigrated to the North, where the money and the future were. He is unequivocal about the roots of jive talk.

> It's derived from down home speech . . . It's the Southern musician moving into the North which made the difference. Although normally people in the North show the great influence of Irish and Jewish people in their talk, the other great influence would be the speech of Southern musicians . . .

The significance of jive talk is probably best explained through the figure of Cab Calloway, one of the most popular jazzband leaders in Harlem during the heyday of the uptown night-clubs. He wasn't a musician like Count Basie or Duke Ellington, he was a front-man, an entertainer who sang "Jive talk is the lingo the jitterbugs use today" and used it as a kind of comic patter. Cab Calloway even had a song about it, called "Mister Hepster's Jive Talk Dictionary".

> *What's a hepcat? A hepcat is a guy*
> *Who knows all the answers, and I'm telling you why . . .*
> *He's a high-falutin' student*
> *Of the Calloway vocab.*
>
> *What's the twister to the slammer?*
> *The twister is the key*
> *That opens up the slammer*
> *To my chicken fricassee.*
>
> *If you want to learn the lingo:*
> *Jive from ABC to Zee,*
> *Get hip with*
> *Mister Hepster's Dictionary.*

Some of Cab Calloway's phrases – and he is only one example – have passed into the language. According to Albert Murray, "He would say 'All you hip to the jive . . . hip, hip, hip'. He had a lot of old phrases which he would just repeat over and over, phrases like 'I'm beat to my socks', 'it's far out', 'it's groovy', 'it's grooving', 'send me' he'd say. 'A solid sender' was an outstanding person. 'A hip chick' was a beautiful woman."

When we list the words and phrases that have passed into the language, the importance of jive talk is inescapable. This list is Cab Calloway's and dates from 1938. In Calloway's words, "the first glossary of words, expressions, and general patois employed by musicians and entertainers in New York's teeming Harlem".

A hummer: exceptionally good	*Joint is jumping*: the place is lively
Beat: exhausted	*Latch on*: take hold, get wise to
Beat up: sad, tired	*Mellow*: all right, fine
Cat: musician in a swing band	*Out of the world*: perfect
Chick: girl	*Pad*: bed
Groovy: fine	*Riff*: musical phrase
Have a ball: to enjoy yourself	*Sharp*: neat, smart
Hip: wise, sophisticated	*Solid*: great, swell
Hype: build up for a loan, wooing	*Square*: an unhip person
a girl, persuasive talk	*Stache*: to hide away, to secrete
In the groove: perfect, no deviation	*Too much*: term of highest praise
Jam: improvised swing music	*Yeah, man*: an exclamation of assent

Jive talk soon caught on generally. The downtown clientele – the flappers and sheiks – who went to the Cotton Club would slip the new words and phrases into their conversation to show how smart and up to date they were. The journalists who reported the jazz scene would drop the same words and phrases into their columns for the same reason. Language moves fast when fashion drives it. Then, once the same entertainers and musicians began to get exposure on radio and later television, their vocabulary reached an even larger audience.

At the same time, other White performers who wanted to be in on the vogue would imitate the language of the clubs – "'beat me Daddy' is quite passé, if you're sent the Harlem way" they sang. By the 1940s, we find Helen O'Connell, a big-name White singer with Jimmy Dorsey's band, performing songs to the refrain, "Hey, man, that's groovy".

Way up town
There's a riff that's going round,
And all the cats have got it down
Because it's solid and in the groove.

In the lingo of hi-de-ho,
When the Harlem rhythm flows,
Here's the way to say, Yes I know:
'Man, that's groovy.'

At the centre of Harlem, the clubs and the bands, was the greatest of them all, Louis Armstrong. His influence on jive talk, and the breadth of his audience, makes him one of the key figures in this part of the story. Albert Murray remembers him for phrases like "hip cats" and "daddy-o":

He was the veritable Prometheus of Jazz ... the invention of it as a sort of national language was [due to] Louis. He was not the father of jive talk but he was the most important single individual in the development of jive talk from the world of entertainment into the mainstream of American speech.

The jazzmen had a relatively small, if influential, circle of admirers. It was the phonograph and radio which introduced the talk of the clubs to a national audience, in particular the radio show *Amos and Andy*, which had developed from a vaudeville act. Ironically, its creators and performers were two White comedians named Gosden and Correll. Albert Murray has a vivid recollection of its influence:

At its height the *Amos and Andy* show was by far the most popular program in the United States. In every community things used to stop. Just as we all stopped for the news, everybody used to stop for *Amos and Andy*. Even movies used to stop. There was hardly anybody who didn't know what Andy said or Amos said on a given day.

The recurrent theme of the show was the idea that Amos and Andy would go north and "make a lot o' money". Here they discuss getting on the road to a fortune with the "Fresh Air Taxi Company of America, Incorpulated".

ANDY: De thing we gotta do is to git in some kind o' bizness so we kin work fo' ourselves.

AMOS: I was talkin' to Sylvester today an' he say dat he knows where we kin git a open car – but it ain't got no top on it.

ANDY: Ain't got no top on it, huh?

AMOS: No, he say it ain't got no top on it – dat's de trouble.

ANDY: Wait a minute – I got a idea.

AMOS: Whut is it, whut is it – 'splain it to me.

ANDY: We kin start sumpin' new – be diff'ent dan anything else in de country – we kin clean up a fortune – make barrels o' money – be millionaires – have de biggest comp'ny in de world ... We'll buy dat automobile an' start up a comp'ny called de Fresh Air Taxi Comp'ny.

The popularity of the show ensured imitation. Murray remembers that "People would imitate the words and also the rhythms of speech. You could hear all kinds of people, Irish truck drivers, for instance, saying 'Holy Mackerel, Andy'." Later, the show became a television performance, with Black actors taking the original Amos and Andy roles, further enlarging the influence of the idiom.

In the heady, post-war atmosphere of the 1950s, the story of Little Richard, self-styled father of rock 'n' roll, reiterates the experience of the Harlem jazz kings. Born in Macon, Georgia, the former Richard Pennyman began to make a name for himself in Atlanta in the 1950s. His first national hit was "Tutti frutti". The original lyrics, in the sex-coded tradition of much Black culture, ran as follows:

Tutti frutti, good booty,
If it don't fit, don't force it,
You can grease it, make it easy.

Suitably doctored, with lines like "She runs to the east and she runs to the west/But she's the girl that I love the best", this lyric climbed to the top of the charts – where it was promptly "covered", first by Elvis Presley, and then by the Tennessee heart-throb, Pat Boone, both of whom outsold Little Richard.

The talk of the jazzmen also became the cult slang of the White *hippies* (from *hip*, of course) in the 1960s. *Cool* we have already explained. *For kicks, rip off* and *hang-up* also have Black roots. *Rock 'n' roll*, for White culture a musical term, is a sexual one for Blacks: "My baby rocks with me one steady roll." Much of the vocabulary of the drug culture was also borrowed from the Blacks. *Stoned* was borrowed from the Black use of the traditional "intensifier" in phrases like *stone blind* and *my stone friend*. The hippy use of *man* (and sometimes *dude*) and *roach* is Black English. Even *busted*, as in *to get busted* (arrested by the police) has its antecedents in the Black underworld. *Heavy*, meaning "serious", "arcane", "profound", has deep Black roots, and was adopted by The Beatles in the lyric "She's so heavy".

It is one of the many ironies of this story that it was British not American imitators of Black musical slang who finally achieved the re-integration of some elements of Black English into American talk. The greatest impact of Black music on the young popular musicians of the late 1950s and early 1960s occurred not in New York or Chicago, but in Liverpool and London. Pop groups like The Beatles and The Rolling Stones responded with the most enthusiasm to the possibilities of rock 'n' roll, and rhythm and blues. They borrowed – probably to an extent still unrecognized – from the music and the language of the Blacks. So it was that the Americans Black English slang of *cool* and *heavy* was introduced to White Americans by British musicians who had started their careers in the old slave-port of Liverpool.

Alongside the Black entertainers of the 1930s were the sportsmen. Sport was another way of getting out of the ghetto. Jesse Owens, who dominated the Berlin Olympic Games of 1936, Joe Louis, the world heavyweight boxing champion, and Jackie Robinson, the first Black major-league baseball player, were among the lucky few. Most Blacks lived segregated, economically depressed lives in which they had the worst of everything: jobs, pay, housing, schooling and opportunity.

"I HAVE A DREAM"
Within the Black community, Black English has continued to flourish in its own way. Horace Williams – known as "Mr Spoons" – has been shining shoes most of his life. He plies his trade with rhyming talk:

Step up on the stand
And get the best shine in the land.

If you don't like your shine, you get you money back
But if you don't pay, you get your head cracked.
That's the business of the boot-black.

Mr Spoons' prestige among Philadelphia Blacks comes from his versatility with language – he is part of a longstanding oral tradition that is virtually unknown outside the Black community. Like Chief Anlanth II in Sierra Leone, he enjoys the traditional respect paid to the "man of words". His own experience mirrors the story of twentieth-century Blacks in miniature. His parents were share-croppers in the deep South. He himself was born in South Carolina, and grew up with virtually no formal education. In his youth he witnessed lynchings and mob violence. To escape the poverty and intolerance he came north, to Philadelphia. In due course he found his vocation:

> I told my aunt, I said: I'm gonna sing a song . . . . I got a tin lid – you know a
> bucket lid . . . and I started playing:
>
> > *There's a hill far away*
> > *in a land big and gray*
>
> This is how I started writing.

Mr Spoons, who still accompanies himself on the spoons or the pickle jar, explains the inspiration for what he calls his "po-ems".

> There's a lotta times you see things you wanna say and you can't say them.
> Then you feel as if you sing 'em in a poetic way, a musical way, whatever . . .
> You can present it to whomever you want to hear it.

105 Accompanying himself on the spoons or the pickle-jar, Horace Williams, "Mr Spoons", improvises poems about the Black predicament.

106 Martin Luther King in 1965: "We want all our rights."

Mr Spoons sings about many aspects of Black life. His subjects can be funny, or bawdy, or autobiographical. They tend to rhyme. But he can also be angry. One of his finest poems – many lines long – is about Civil Rights.

> *There just ain't no justice here for the Black man.*
> *How then can that be but wrong.*
> *You see they closed most of the schools to us down here,*

107 The March on Washington, 1963.

108 The "man of words" tradition inspired the rhyming repartee – "Float like a butterfly, sting like a bee" – of Cassius Clay, now Muhammad Ali.

And we pay taxes but afraid to vote.
Now, Father, where is that great constitution that the so-called
White man wrote?

The Civil Rights movement gained momentum after the Second World War. Black veterans who had risked their lives for the United States felt that the White community owed them equal opportunities, especially as post-war prosperity began to raise national expectations, particularly among the more assertive children of city-dwelling migrants from the South. By the late 1950s, the Civil Rights leadership was symbolized by Martin Luther King. In 1963, at the climax of a "March on Washington", standing in front of the Lincoln Memorial, he made the speech which will stand as long as the English language itself.

> I say to you today . . . that in spite of the difficulties and frustrations of the moment I still have a dream . . .
>
> I have a dream that one day on the red hills of Georgia the sons of former slaves and the sons of former slave owners will be able to sit down together at the table of brotherhood . . .
>
> I have a dream that my four little children will one day live in a nation where they will not be judged by the color of their skin . . .
>
> Let freedom ring from the mighty mountains of New York . . . When we let it ring from every village and every hamlet, from every state and every city, we will be able to speed up that day when all of God's children, Black men and White men, Jews and Gentiles, Protestants and Catholics, will be able to join hands and sing in the words of the old Negro spiritual, Free at last, Free at last, thank God Almighty we are free at last!

With the Civil Rights movement, "Black" became the key word, replacing "Negro". People started to talk and write about *Black English*, *Black history*, *Black studies*, *Black theatre*, and *Black power*. To this movement we owe words like *sit-in*, *blood brother*, *soul*, *backlash*, *bussing*. To this period, too, we owe *nitty gritty*, which became a vogue term in about 1963, a synonym for "brass tacks". The Black militants would say "let's get down to the nitty gritty". No one is sure of its origin, but it may have referred to the gritlike nits (the eggs of head lice) that are so hard to get out of the hair and scalp, well known to ghetto dwellers and rural Southerners who seldom had hot running water and proper bathing facilities. Another word which took on a new meaning at this time was *rap*. Interestingly the word has meant "a rebuke" or "blame" in England since 1733. In America, *to take the rap* means "to take the blame", and *not give a rap* (meaning "don't give a damn") dates from the 1880s. But in the 1960s, *to rap* was used by Blacks to criticize Whites, to demand Black rights and finally, by extension, "to talk". The word was soon adopted by streetwise White teenagers who still use it as a synonym for conversation. Once again, White America appropriated elements of Black English.

Black English acquired its label from the Civil Rights movement (and later from the pioneering work of William Labor, William Stewart and J. L. Dillard). Recognition was much slower – and much more controversial. The battleground was the education system.

Some Black activists argued that if Black English was a variety of the language with its own norms and rules, then the schools should make allowances for Black English-speaking children. You have recognized the political and social rights of the Blacks, they said, now you must recognize their language rights. (The same debate is now taking place in the *British* Black and Asian communities.) The battlelines were immediately confused because many educated middle-class Blacks refused to reject Standard American English. Parents and teachers found themselves wondering whether they wanted their children educated in a way that would disadvantage them socially and economically for the rest of their lives.

Constance Clayton, the Black superintendent of schools in Philadelphia, eloquently expresses this point of view:

> I consider Black English as a dialect of a particular ethnic group – the Blacks. I consider it incorrect English. I would want an understanding of it, an appreciation of it, as we would for other dialects . . . but we should never lose sight of the need to provide for our young people access to Standard English, which is really a gateway for them to the broader community.

At the heart of the education debate was the fear that to encourage Black English would be to foster the spirit of the ghetto. "I know of no company or corporation", says Constance Clayton, "which hires you on the basis of your ability to speak Black English." To benefit fully from the American way of life, she argues, Blacks (among other ethnic groups) have to speak its language:

> I have yet to find Black English as being beneficial in filling out a job application. Somehow those questions are not phrased in Black English . . . That's a very valid reason for the utilization and understanding of Standard English. If a person is interviewing you for a job, I think if you said, "I've come to *aks* you for a job", rather than "*ask* you for a job" I think the potential employer might be somewhat confused.

The upshot of the Black English debate, which raged throughout the 1970s, was a landmark court decision in Detroit in 1979. In July that year the Ann Arbor school district became the first American school system ordered by the courts to take the Black English of the schoolchildren into account when planning the curriculum. In his summing-up, the judge gave a remarkably succinct description of our story:

> All of the distinguished researchers and professionals testified as to the existence of a language system, which is part of the English language but different in significant respects from the Standard English used in the school setting, the commercial world, the world of the arts and science, among the professions, and in government. It is and has been used at some time by 80 per cent of the Black people of this country and has as its genesis the transitional or pidgin language of the slaves, which after a generation or two became a creole language. Since then it has constantly been refined and

109 Breakdancing. The streets of the ghetto have been one of the recent word-factories of English, on both sides of the Atlantic.

brought closer to the mainstream of society. It still flourishes in areas where there are concentrations of Black people. It contains aspects of southern dialect and is used largely by Black people in their casual conversation and informal talk.

To this day, the status of Black English remains a flashpoint in the continuing debate about Black rights.

One prominent member of the Black community in the United States who has benefited from the eradication of the Black English characteristics in his speech is the Mayor of Philadelphia, Wilson Goode, who was born in a country district of North Carolina. When he ran for office in Philadelphia, he took language lessons to eradicate all traces of Black American English from his speech. The *Philadelphia Inquirer* reported that during his election campaign, "Goode still continues to try to overcome the idiosyncrasies of his regional North Carolina accent. Despite the speech lessons, Goode still drops his *t*s and *s*s, and makes words like 'specific' sound more like 'pacific'. Yet he can rally crowds, and sometimes inspire." To succeed in White Society, Mayor Goode has had to learn to talk White.

Ironically, just a few blocks away from the Mayor's office, in the Black district of North Philadelphia, an alternative tradition flourishes on the street with the vigour and freshness we can now see is typical of the Black contribution to the language. The "Scanner Boys" are the fast-talking, breakdancing sensation of the neighbourhood. Their street talk is *funky-fresh*, and their leader, Prince (or "Prince of the Ghetto"), is respected as the best talker in the gang. Prince describes their vocabulary, much of which is already making its way into the talk of White children in Britain as well as the United States: *funky-fresh* for "excellent", *fierce* for "good", *crib* for "your house", *maxing* for "relaxing", *chill* meaning "to cold shoulder", *biting* meaning "copying", and *jonesing* meaning "wanting something really badly".

More sophisticated – in the "man of words" tradition – is the street rapping of a young Black like Perrey P. Like the paramount chief, like Mr Spoons, Perrey P's skills are oral:

> Well, me myself, I don't write 'em. There's different people that write their raps throughout the city, state, world, whatever. I myself, I just make 'em up outa my head as I go along.

And like the preacher, or the mayor, even Perrey P has a message for people that he wants to express: "Message rap is basically on a subject that you use. It might be the streets, it might be war."

> *Synthetics, genetics, command your soul,*
> *Trucks, tanks, laser beams*
> *Guns, blasts, submarines,*
> *Neutron, B-bomb, A-bomb, gas*
> *All that stuff will kill you fas'.*

Perrey P's talk is in the tradition of Black English from the slave plantations to the ghettos: it has its own highly developed norms and codes:

> When you say regular English, you say somethin' like: I really like that. You might say: Well that's nice. Instead of saying this, they (the Blacks) say: That's fresh . . . You go up to 'em and say: We can go battle. When you say "battle" you're getting on . . . When you say: "you down by law", that means real good.

Perrey P, self-styled "voice-master", can improvise like a ghetto Homer for up to fifty minutes at a stretch. At a Philadelphia block party, he and "Grandmaster Tone", sing of the street in a rhythm emphasized by the accompanying disco:

> *Hiding on the corner*
> *Of a dark avenue,*
> *'Cos you didn't have nothing*
> *Better to do . . .*
> *Always have fun,*
> *Always on the run,*
> *Can't rap now*
> *Till I see the sun . . .*
> *You see twenty dollars*
> *Laying on the ground*
> *Try to pick it up*
> *But it moved across town*
> *You see an old lady*
> *Walking down the street . . .*
> *Perrey P won't you help me*
> *Rap to the beat . . .*

Chief, preacher, mayor, rapper – in one sense, there's no distinction: they are all part of the same tradition. In Africa, in the Caribbean, in the Deep South, and in the great cities of the North, the magical use of the spoken word is still reverenced among all classes of Blacks. In the past, White society has resisted the idea, but there is now no escaping the fact that theirs has been one of the most profound contributions to the English language.

Walt Whitman once wrote that English was not "an abstract construction of dictionary makers" but a language that had "its basis broad and low, close to the ground". This is a sharp reminder that the best of English comes from a wide range of sources – Black and White. Whitman was also the self-proclaimed poet of all America, one of the first voices of a distinctively *American* English.

110 Richard Wright and James Baldwin. The work of Black American writers has suggested new potentialities for the English language.

111 Mark Twain's masterpiece, *The Adventures of Huckleberry Finn*, was at first judged to be in appallingly bad taste; now it justifies his claims to be "the American Chaucer".

7
PIONEERS!
O PIONEERS!

The English language* has always been one of the battlegrounds of Anglo-American rivalry, a fascinating window on to the tensions of the "special relationship". Divided by a common language, each generation has made the enjoyable discovery that the English of England is different from the English of America, arguing or joking about it according to the mood and politics of the time. As early as 1735, the settlers' word *bluff* (meaning "a bank or cliff") was under attack as "barbarous English". As pioneers, the first Americans had to make up many new words, some of which now seem absurdly commonplace. *Lengthy*, which dates back to 1689, is an early Americanism. So are *calculate*, *seaboard*, *bookstore* and *presidential*. Even an original mind like Benjamin Franklin allowed his usage to be criticized by the philosopher David Hume, admitting that *colonize* "I give up as bad", while *unshakable* "I give up as rather low". *Antagonize* and *placate* were both hated by British Victorians. As members of a multiracial society, the first Americans also adopted works like *wigwam*, *pretzel*, *spook*, *depot* and *canyon*, borrowing from the Indians, Germans, Dutch, French and Spanish. It was these kinds of new usages that Samuel Johnson referred to in his famous complaint about "the American dialect, a tract of corruption to which every language widely diffused must always be exposed".

As the United States grew in power and influence, the louder were the cries of pain from the old country. The magazine *Punch* wrote that "if the pure well of English is to remain undefiled no Yankee should be allowed henceforth to throw mud into it". Among Americans, there was exasperation at the superior airs of their British cousins. The statesman John Hay, having witnessed his ambassador in London, exclaimed: "How our Ambassador does go it when he gets a roomful of bovine Britons in front of him . . . I never so clearly appreciated the power of the unhesitating orotundity of the Yankee speech, as in listening – after an hour or two of hum-ha of tongue-tied British men – to the long wash of our Ambassador's sonority."

For all the fury of the early British attacks, many of the changes in language that fueled these complaints have evolved – in both countries – only during the last two hundred years.

---

*Observant readers will notice, to their pain or pleasure, that this chapter has adopted American spellings.

In 1776, the spoken English in both countries was essentially the same. A contemporary diarist reported that the Americans "in general speak better English than the English do. No country or colonial dialect is to be distinguished here." A conversation between George Washington and Lord North would probably have produced only a handful of noticeable contrasts in vocabulary and accent. In 1986, no one who eavesdropped on a conversation between President Reagan and Prime Minister Margaret Thatcher would be in any doubt about their respective nationalities.

"THE AMERICAN LANGUAGE"

The American Revolution marked the turning-point in the making of this new, American kind of English. The rebels wanted to announce their separation from the old country in every department of life. In 1782 the citizens of the new Republic were proudly christened *Americans*, and in 1802 the United States Congress recorded the first use of the phrase, "the American language". One of the signers of the Declaration of Independence, John Witherspoon, the Scottish academic whose comments on the English of America were noted in chapter four, described what we can now see as the first stirrings of American English:

> I have heard in this country, in the Senate, at the bar, and from the pulpit, and see daily in dissertations from the press, errors in grammar, improprieties and vulgarisms which hardly any person of the same class in point of rank and literature would have fallen into in Great Britain.

The men who gathered in Philadelphia to sign the Declaration of Independence had a more than amateur interest in words and, like so many national leaders (from Alfred the Great to Winston Churchill), they understood the power of language to shape national consciousness. The words of the Declaration itself, a clarion call to freedom, are also a monument to the measured English of the Age of Reason:

> When in the course of human events it becomes necessary for one people to dissolve the political bands which have connected them with another, and to assume among the Powers of the Earth, the separate and equal station to which the Laws of Nature and of Nature's God entitle them, a decent respect to the opinions of mankind requires that they should declare the causes which impel them to the separation.
> We hold these truths to be self-evident: that all men are created equal; that they are endowed by their Creator with certain unalienable rights, that among these are life, liberty and the pursuit of happiness . . .

Thomas Jefferson, the Virginian lawyer, who at the age of thirty-three was chiefly responsible for drafting the Declaration of Independence, was fascinated by words. Not surprisingly for a man who designed his own house at Monticello, his own writing desk and his own telescope, he liked to invent words. *Belittle* was one of his most famous, much ridiculed in London at the time. He also lent his approval to the new currency terms like *cent* and *dollar*. Jefferson had a

112 The American and British English of Roosevelt and Churchill respectively was unmistakable. George Washington and Lord North would have had accents more in common.

philosophical understanding of the process of language change:

> There are so many differences between us and England, of soil, climate, culture, productions, laws, religion and government, that we must be left far behind the march of circumstances, were we to hold ourselves rigorously to their standard ... Judicious neology can alone give strength and copiousness to language, and enable it to be the vehicle of new ideas.

His policy of "judicious neology", or invention, was, like so many of the policies that he and his fellow rebels adopted, self-conscious, the work of a man who knew he was, so to speak, inventing a nation.

Benjamin Franklin, who taught himself to read and write by copying essays from *The Spectator*, was a printer who set up shop in Philadelphia at the age of seventeen. He was obviously proud of his trade. On his tombstone there is the simple legend "Benjamin Franklin, Printer". Franklin took a tireless interest in the world around him – he organized the first fire brigade, he founded the United States' first free public library, he was among the first to wear spectacles, he invented the Franklin stove. At heart a printer, he became intrigued by the chaotic spelling conventions of the English language and, typically enough, proposed its reform. In 1768, he published a paper entitled *A Scheme for a New Alphabet and a Reformed Mode of Spelling*, and went so far as to have a special type cut to put his ideas into effect. His plan was not adopted, but it was to have a profound influence on America's great lexicographer, Noah Webster. Franklin was the godfather, if not the midwife, of such spelling differences as *honor* for "honour", *theater* for "theatre", *plow* for "plough" and *curb* for "kerb", a familiar cause of Anglo-American linguistic friction.

For Jefferson, Franklin, John Adams, and the other leaders of the American Revolution,

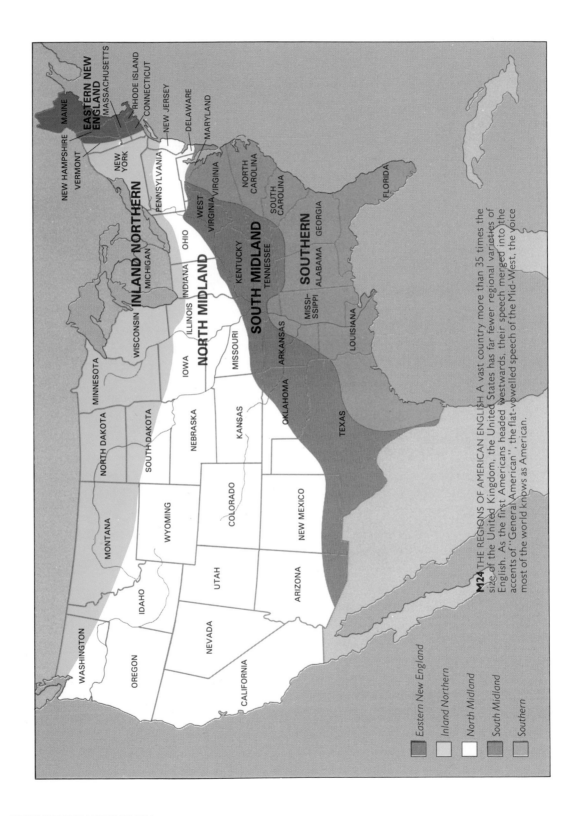

M24 THE REGIONS OF AMERICAN ENGLISH A vast country more than 35 times the size of the United Kingdom, the United States has far fewer regional varieties of English. As the first Americans headed westwards, their speech merged into the accents of "General American", the flat-vowelled speech of the Mid-West, the voice most of the world knows as American.

EASTERN NEW ENGLAND
MAINE
MASSACHUSETTS
RHODE ISLAND
CONNECTICUT
NEW HAMPSHIRE
VERMONT
NEW JERSEY
DELAWARE
MARYLAND
NEW YORK
PENNSYLVANIA
WEST VIRGINIA
VIRGINIA
NORTH CAROLINA
SOUTH CAROLINA
FLORIDA
OHIO
INLAND NORTHERN
MICHIGAN
INDIANA
KENTUCKY
TENNESSEE
SOUTH MIDLAND
SOUTHERN
GEORGIA
ALABAMA
MISSISSIPPI
WISCONSIN
ILLINOIS
NORTH MIDLAND
MISSOURI
ARKANSAS
LOUISIANA
IOWA
MINNESOTA
NORTH DAKOTA
SOUTH DAKOTA
NEBRASKA
KANSAS
OKLAHOMA
TEXAS
MONTANA
WYOMING
COLORADO
NEW MEXICO
WASHINGTON
IDAHO
UTAH
ARIZONA
OREGON
NEVADA
CALIFORNIA

Eastern New England
Inland Northern
North Midland
South Midland
Southern

American English was the proud badge of independence, a language with a future.

> English [wrote Adams in 1780] is destined to be in the next and succeeding centuries more generally the language of the world than Latin was in the last or French is in the present age. The reason for this is obvious, because the increasing population in America, and their universal connection and correspondence with all nations will, aided by the influence of England in the world, whether great or small, force their language into general use . . .

Language nationalism like this inspired the recommendation the American Continental Congress made in 1778, that when the French minister visited the new Republic and its legislature, "all replies and answers" to him should be put "in the language of the United States" (not in French, not in British English).

Others went further. According to the Marquis de Chastellux, who traveled with George Washington in the 1780s, some Americans "propose introducing a new language; and some persons were desirous, for the convenience of the public, that the *Hebrew* should be substituted for English . . ." Other patriots proposed to revenge themselves on England by adopting French. One or two hot-headed legislators even toyed with the idea of adopting Greek. This proposal was rejected on the grounds that "it would be more convenient for us to keep the language as it was, and make the English speak Greek".

Part of the problem for the new Americans was that theirs was already a polyglot society. Many of the country's leaders, while recognizing the advantages of a national standard, also wanted to recognize the linguistic diversity of the new nation. Jefferson, for instance, advised his daughters to learn French to gain access to scientific progress. Benjamin Rush, another republican leader, championed German in particular and multilingualism in general. It was, he argued, more democratic.

The voices of reason argued that English was the obvious first language of the new United States. This was an unavoidable fact. In 1790, when the first census was taken, four million Americans were counted, and 90 percent were descendants of English colonists. But what kind of English? Hardly the English of the oppressor, "the turgid style of Johnson, the purple glare of Gibbon" as Benjamin Rush put it. No, English in America should be "improved and perfected". But how?

John Adams had a familiar answer to this now-familiar problem: an Academy. Paraphrasing Jonathan Swift, but also drawing on his experiences in Europe, he suggested that a United States Academy would provide for the study of all languages in the Union, while promoting American English as a public institution. English, as he saw it, was the way for the new republic to spread its ideals round the world. Just as a constitution was necessary to prevent a government becoming corrupt, so an Academy was necessary to sustain the purity of the language. He rejected the idea of establishing a new language. "We have not made war against the English language, any more than against the old English character." As he saw it, English would be exploited to advance the cause of America.

> You must know [he wrote a friend] I have undertaken to prophesy that
> English will be the most respectable language in the world and the most
> universally read and spoken in the next century, if not before the close of
> this. American population will in the next age produce a greater number of
> persons who will speak English than any other language, and these persons
> will have more general acquaintance and conversation with all other nations
> than any other people . . .

The result of his plan would be national glory: "England will never have any more honor, excepting now and then imitating the Americans." It is impossible not to catch the note of glee in his voice, but the Congress found his plans too sweeping and the issue was left – in the spirit of pluralism – to individual pressure-groups, like the Philological Society.

The extent to which the English language became a political issue is illustrated by a curious procession that took place through the streets of New York on 23 July 1788. The occasion was the ratification of the new American Constitution. The demonstrators included all classes, professional men, tradespeople and laborers. "In the procession", recalled one of the participants, "an association of young men, of which the writer was one, called the Philological Society, carried through the streets of New York a book inscribed *Federal Language*." The coat of arms they carried emphasized the strong desire of many Americans to break with British English and its eighteenth-century classical traditions. "Argent three tongues, gules, in chief; emblematic of *language*, the improvement of which is the object of the institution. Chevron, or, indicating firmness and support; an *eye*, emblematical of *discernment*, over a pyramid, or rude monument, sculptured with Gothic, Hebrew, and Greek letters. The Gothic on the *light* side, indicating the *obvious* origin of the American language from the Gothic . . ." The words are Noah Webster's.

NOAH WEBSTER

The most famous of all American dictionary-makers and a tireless champion of American English, Noah Webster was as influential in the story of American English as George Washington was in the narrative of the American Revolution. From his *Dissertations on the English Language* in 1789 to his great monument of 1828, *An American Dictionary of the English Language* (referred to today simply as *Webster's*), his work, like Samuel Johnson's, is a landmark.

Webster was born in Hartford, Connecticut, and, like many of the American revolutionaries, turned from law to teaching as a means of making his living. It was one of those career changes that transform a man's life. Britain was at war with the colonies, and schoolbooks, traditionally imported from London, were in short supply. Besides, in Webster's view, they were unsatisfactory. So, very much in the spirit of the New World, he set about filling the gap. Between 1783 and 1785, while still in his twenties, Webster published three elementary books on English, a speller, a grammar and a reader, to which he gave the grandiose title *A Grammatical Institute of the English Language*. The "Blue-Backed" *American Speller* turned out to be a runaway bestseller, selling over eighty million copies in

Webster's lifetime (second only to the Bible, with which it was often marketed by Webster's salesmen). It was Webster's intention, as he put it, "to introduce uniformity and accuracy of pronunciation into common schools". As early as 1782, a commentator on the uniformity of American speech had attributed this to "a process which the frequency of, or rather the universality of, school-learning in North America must naturally have assisted". The use to which the *American Speller* was put in schools is explained by the reminiscences of a New England newspaper proprietor:

> It was the custom for all such pupils [those who were sufficiently advanced to pronounce distinctly words of more than one syllable] to stand together as one class, and with *one voice* to read a column or two of the tables for spelling. The master gave the signal to begin, and all united to read, letter by letter, pronouncing each syllable by itself, and adding to it the preceding one till the word was complete. Thus a–d *ad*, m–i *mi*, *admi*, r–a *ra*, *admira*, t–i–o–n *shun*, *admiration*. This mode of reading was exceedingly exciting, and, in my humble judgment, exceedingly useful; as it required and taught deliberate and distinct articulation . . .

The success of the *American Speller* gave Webster, on a royalty of one cent per copy, more than enough to live on, and he now devoted the rest of his life to the zealous championing of the cause of the American language, its spelling, its grammar and its pronunciation. The story is told, by an old printer recalling his apprenticeship, of the day "a little pale-faced man came into the office and handed me a printed slip, saying 'My lad, when you use these words, please oblige me by spelling them as here: *theater*, *center*, etc.' " It was Noah Webster traveling about the printing offices and persuading people to follow his "improved" conventions.

In 1789, Webster published his *Dissertations on the English Language*, announcing a fiery, almost evangelical, commitment to the separation of American English from its parent:

> Several circumstances render a future separation of the American tongue from the English necessary and unavoidable . . . Numerous local causes, such as a new country, new associations of people, new combinations of ideas in arts and science, and some intercourse with tribes wholly unknown in Europe, will introduce new words into the American tongue. These causes will produce, in a course of time, a language in North America, as different from the future language of England, as the modern Dutch, Danish and Swedish are from the German, or from one another . . .

It was not enough to let history take its course. Americans had to act. "Our honor", Webster wrote, "requires us to have a system of our own, in language as well as government." In 1806, Webster published his first *Dictionary*, the next step in his program to standardize the American language, and continued to call for the "detachment" from English literary models: "There is nothing which, in my opinion, so debases the genius and character of my countrymen, as the implicit confidence they place in English authors, and their unhesitating submission to their *opinions*, their *decision*, and their *frowns*."

The culmination of Webster's efforts came with the publication of his *American Dictionary of the English Language* in 1828, larger than Johnson's by about a third and containing much American usage. But perhaps a lifetime of effort, and a year spent in England, had mellowed him. In the preface to this, his monument, he noted that, "The body of the language is the same as in England, and it is desirable to perpetuate that sameness." Despite its now honored place in the history of American English, the first Webster's sold only 2500 copies and he was forced to mortgage his home to bring out a second edition. The rest of his life was dogged by debt and he died in New Haven, Connecticut, in 1843 with much of his effort unrecognized and unapplauded.

In retrospect, Webster's influence on American spelling was enormous. It is to him that Americans owe *color* for "colour", *wagon* for "waggon", *fiber* for "fibre", *defense* for "defence", and *tire* for "tyre". The distinctive pattern of American speech, the due emphasis given to each syllable in a word can, in part, be attributed to the influence of Webster's spelling bees and to his maxim: "A good articulation consists in giving every letter in a syllable its due proportion of sound, according to the most approved custom of pronouncing it; and in making such a distinction, between syllables, of which words are composed, that the ear shall without difficulty acknowledge their number." (This maxim gives American English *sec-ret-ary* instead of the British *secret'ry*. Similarly, the English pronunciation of a word like *waistcoat* was, as readers of Dickens will remember, *weskit*. Especially for the ease of immigrants acquiring English for the first time, Webster's pronunciation guide gives the word its full value, *waist-coat*.)

The precise extent of Webster's influence on American speech rhythms will always – like so much language history – remain controversial. No one disputes, however, the remarkable uniformity of much American speech, particularly beyond the eastern seaboard. Even in the

113 Benjamin Franklin had a special interest in English spelling and was the first American to propose its reform.

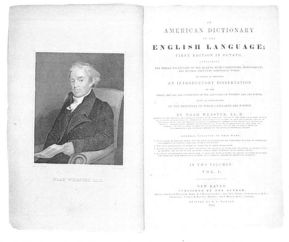

114 Noah Webster's dictionary aimed to eradicate English pronunciation, indicating "fore-head" instead of "forrid". American speech is still more measured than English.

East, there was nothing like the patchwork of local variation known in Britain. The actress Fanny Kemble, professionally trained to listen to the spoken word, observed during her tour of the eastern United States that: "The southern, western, and eastern states of America, have each their strong peculiarities of enunciation, which render them easy of recognition." Roughly speaking, her remarks still hold good, and it was these large speech areas which were mistaken for uniformity.

The speech of the North-East, whose origins we have already traced, was usually clipped and tended to elide the *r*. New Englanders are recorded as saying r'*ally* for "really", *un'neath* for "underneath", and *pooty* for "pretty". In the South, according to the novelist Thomas Low Nichols, "speech is clipped, softened and broadened by the Negro admixture". Southerners tended to retain the traditional English *a-doing*, dropping the final *g*. They are also recorded as saying *wunst* for "once", *hoss* for "horse", and *aks* for "ask", a pronunciation possibly adopted from the Blacks. Toward and beyond the Mississippi, American speech grew richer and stronger. "It is certain", wrote Nichols, "that men open their mouths and broaden their speech as they go West." He described how the Westerner "walks the water, out-hollers the thunder, drinks the Mississippi, calculates that he is the genuwine article, and that those he don't like ain't worth shucks". As Mark Twain reported it, from his own experience, the talk of the frontier, even at a funeral, was renowned for stepping high and wide: "One of the boys has passed in his checks and we want to give him a good send-off, and so the thing I'm on now is to roust out somebody to jerk a little chin-music for us and waltz him through handsome."

These vast speech regions, in which almost all people were broadly intelligible to each other, contrasted very favorably, for Americans, with what they took to be the many and incomprehensible regional varieties of British English. For many commentators, it was this contrast that suggested the remarkable "uniformity" of American speech. In 1828, the novelist James Fenimore Cooper, famous for *The Last of the Mohicans*, wrote: "In America, while there are provincial and state peculiarities, in tone, and even in the pronunciation and use of certain words, there is no patois. An American may distinguish between the Georgian and the New-Englandman, but you [his British audience] cannot." Cooper went on to identify perhaps the main reason for this leveling of accent: the flood of immigrants arriving in the USA from Europe: "The distinctions in speech between New-England and New-York, or Pennsylvania, or any other State, were far greater twenty years ago than they are now. Immigration alone would produce a large portion of this change."

Many nineteenth-century travelers to the United States also commented on the nasal quality and drawl of the American voice, characteristics about which some Americans feel defensive to this day. The Victorian novelist, Captain Marryat, author of *Mr Midshipman Easy* and other schoolboy classics, traveled widely in the States, and noticed that: "The Americans dwell upon their words when they speak – a custom arising, I presume, from their cautious, calculating habits; and they have always more or less of a nasal twang." Marryat also noted with obvious fascination another aspect of American speech which endured on the lips of a star like Gary Cooper. "There are two syllables – *um, hu* – which are very generally used by the Americans as a sort of reply, intimating that they are attentive, and that the party may proceed with his narrative; but, by inflection and intonation, these two syllables are made to express dissent or assent, surprise, disdain, and a great deal more ..." Marryat confessed he found the *um* and the *hu* to be useful expressions and admits to having acquired a taste for them himself. The hostility of British visitors to American English undoubtedly bred a certain defensive arrogance among those who were not afraid or ashamed of "the American twang". One traveler reported that, "not an American, let him be Yankee or Southerner, from the banks of the Hudson or the Mississippi, but flatters himself that he speaks more correct English than we illiterate sons of the mother isle ..."

CANADIAN ENGLISH

Every revolution – and the American Revolution was no exception – has its casualties. The Loyalists, those who had backed the British, were driven into exile partly by mob violence and partly by a desire to protect their investments. Some went to England, some to the West Indies, but the majority fled north to Canada, and settled in the part that is now Ontario. This was the beginning of a separate Canadian English.

The Ontario Loyalists were late arrivals but, west of Quebec, they dominated the making of modern Canada, and their speech has become the basis for what is called General Canadian, a definition based on urban middle-class speech, not rural variants (some of which diverge quite sharply from the norm). From this point of view Canadian English is another regional variant of North American English, but one which spans almost the whole continent instead of occupying just one region. As many observers have noted, "the most surprising thing" – to quote one of them – "about the English currently spoken in Canada is its homogeneity ... It is certain that no Ontario Canadian, meeting another Canadian, can tell whether he comes from Manitoba, Saskatchewan, Alberta, or British Columbia – or even Ontario, unless he asks." As in so many other aspects of Canadian individuality, you have to look carefully for the subtleties that make Canadian speech distinctive. In language, as in national character, Canadian identity often seems understated and unhistrionic beside the boisterous American giant across the border.

Canadian English is usually defined by the ways in which it differs from what American or British observers consider their norm. American visitors at first think how British the Canadian vocabulary sounds (*tap, braces,* and *porridge,* instead of "faucet", "suspenders" and "oatmeal"). The British think how Americanized the Canadians have become (they hear *gas, truck* and *wrench* for "petrol", "lorry" and "spanner"). The British have been making these observations for a long time. A Dr Thomas Rolph, traveling in Upper Canada (now Ontario) in 1832, complained:

> It is really melancholy to traverse the Province, and go into many of the common schools; you find a herd of children instructed by some anti-

British adventurer, instilling into their young and tender minds sentiments hostile to the parent state . . . and American spelling-books, dictionaries and grammar, teaching them an anti-British dialect, and idiom, although living in the Province, and being subjects of the British Crown.

Considering the bombardment by American English from everywhere south of the 3000 mile border, it is remarkable that Canada's twenty-five million people should have preserved national characteristics as distinct as they are, and perhaps even more remarkable that the regional differences in Canadian English have not yet been snuffed out by the influence of American English.

Canadian English is difficult to distinguish from some other North American varieties without the tools of the phonetician, yet it is instantly recognizable to other Canadians, if not to the rest of the English-speaking world. In a crowd, where the Englishman or the Australian could not, the Canadian with a good ear will easily spot the other Canadian among the North Americans.

The differences are mainly of vocabulary and pronunciation. There is no distinctive Canadian grammar. Until recently most of the books Canadians read were American or British, and the grammar and spelling reflect that. Canadian English uses elements of both, retaining more of the formality of Standard British English. Canadian spelling preserves some British forms (*colour*, *theatre*), but not all (*aluminum*). Canadians live with compromises like "tire centre". The Canadian humorist Stephen Leacock once wrote, "In Canada we have enough to do keeping up with the two spoken languages without trying to invent slang, so we just go right ahead and use English for literature, Scotch for sermons and American for conversation."

Among the original Canadian idioms, perhaps the most famous is the almost universal use of "eh?" This has become such a national tic that a lighthearted but accurate treatment of popular Canadian speech is entitled *Canajan, eh?* This is its dissertation (using its own phonetic spelling) on the various uses of "Eh":

> I'm walking down the street, eh? (Like this, see?) I had a few beers en I was feeling priddy good, eh? (You know how it is.) When all of a sudden I saw this big guy, eh? (Ya see.) He musta weighed all of 220 pounds, eh? (Believe me.) I could see him from a long ways off en he was a real big guy, eh? (I'm not fooling.) I'm minding my own business, eh? (You can bet I was.)

And so on. Canadians have been avid chroniclers of their own distinctive variety of English. *A Dictionary of Canadianisms on Historical Principles* identifies some 10,000 words and expressions with Canadian origins, words like *kerosene* and *chesterfield* (sofa), and ice-hockey terms like *face-off*, *blue-line* and *puck*.

It is primarily in pronunciation that Canadian English asserts its distinctiveness, and has done from earliest times. Canadian pronunciation also reflects the continuing schizophrenia of a people struggling for national identity against two strong influences. So a recent "Survey

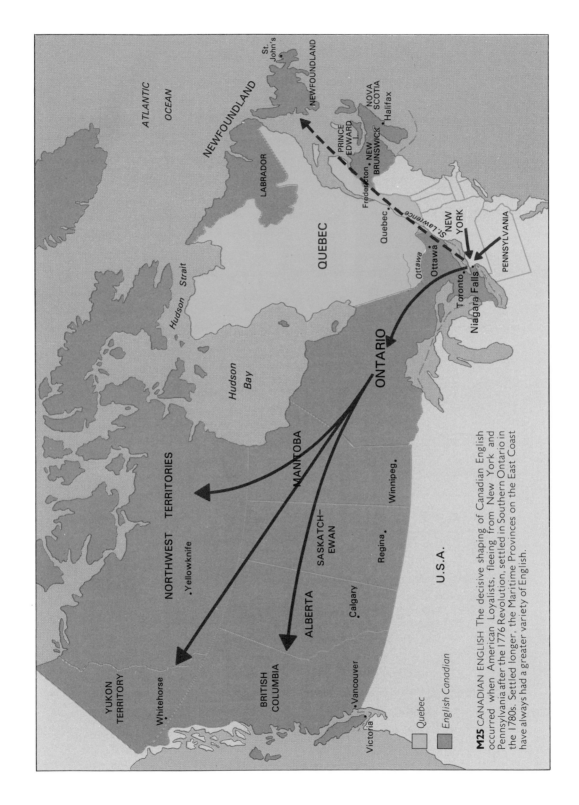

M25 CANADIAN ENGLISH The decisive shaping of Canadian English occurred when American Loyalists, fleeing from New York and Pennsylvania after the 1776 Revolution, settled in Southern Ontario in the 1780s. Settled longer, the Maritime Provinces on the East Coast have always had a greater variety of English.

Quebec

English Canadian

ATLANTIC OCEAN

NEWFOUNDLAND

St. John's

NEWFOUNDLAND

NEWFOUNDLAND

LABRADOR

PRINCE EDWARD

NOVA SCOTIA

Halifax

Fredericton . NEW BRUNSWICK

QUEBEC

Quebec .

St. Lawrence

NEW YORK

PENNSYLVANIA

Ottawa

Ottawa .

Toronto .

Niagara Falls

ONTARIO

Hudson Strait

Hudson Bay

MANITOBA

Winnipeg .

NORTHWEST TERRITORIES

. Yellowknife

SASKATCH-EWAN

Regina .

ALBERTA

Calgary .

U.S.A.

BRITISH COLUMBIA

. Vancouver

YUKON TERRITORY

Whitehorse .

Victoria .

of Canadian English" found that about three-quarters of Canadians use the British *zed* rather than the American *zee*. But more than three-quarters of Canadians said they use the American pronunciation of *schedule*, *tomato* and *missile*, while 58 per cent use the British pronunciation for *progress* and *new*. In earlier days, some Canadians would have been content to have it thought that they sounded British or American, depending on where they lived. In 1936, Stephen Leacock wrote:

> We used to be ashamed of our Canadian language, before the war, and try to correct it and take on English phrases and say, "What a ripping day", instead of "What a peach of a morning", and "Ah you thah?" instead of "Hello, Central", and "Oh! rather!" instead of "O-Hell-Yes". But now since the Great War put Canada on the right level with the Portuguese and Siamese and those fellows who come from – ah! one forgets the names, but it doesn't matter – I mean, made Canada a real nation – we just accept our language and are not ashamed of it. We say "yep!" when we mean "yep!", and we don't dare try to make out it's "yes", which is a word we don't use; and if we mean "four" we say so and don't call it "faw".

The snobbish affectation of English sounds barely outlived Leacock. It has been replaced by a desire just to sound Canadian. This pattern of a people being pulled in two cultural directions is not just the result of recent influences. The differences between American and Canadian speech were well enough known by the 1830s to be a source of humor to the Nova Scotian writer Thomas Chandler Haliburton. His character Sam Slick, an itinerant Yankee clock pedlar, says, "they all know me here to be an American citizen by my talk".

The most obvious and distinctive feature of Canadian speech is probably its vowel sound, the diphthong *ou*. (Thus *out* rhymes with *boat*, so that a phrase like "out and about in a boat" emerges as "oat and aboat in a boat".) There is a deeply held belief that this trait comes from Scotland, but this is a myth. The Scottish *oo* is really quite different from the Canadian *ou*. Professor Jack Chambers believes that it was an independent development in Canadian English.

> The *ou* in "house" and "about" begins with the vowel sound in *hut* and *but*, whereas the *ou* in "houses" and "bough" begins with the vowel sound in *hot* and *bought*. The difference in the two *ou* sounds is systematic, and known to linguists as Canadian Raising. Because of it, Canadians have a different *ou* sound in *house* and *houses*, and in *lout* and *loud*.

There is, according to Chambers, a characteristic of pronunciation that can be traced to Pennsylvania: the merger of the two vowels in words like *cot* and *caught*, *don* and *dawn*, *offal* and *awful*. When Canadians pronounce these word-pairs they sound identical. Professor Chambers has also demonstrated that, in the big cities especially, the younger generations of Canadians are adopting American pronunciations, and that here, at any rate, a distinctive Canadian speech identity is threatened. Like other colonial varieties of English, Canadian

English is the result of a language melting pot that resolved into a standard accent. The process was vividly described in the mid-nineteenth century by a settler in South Ontario:

> Listening to the children at any school, composed of the children of Englishmen, Scotchmen, Americans and even Germans, it is impossible to detect any marked difference in their accent, or way of expressing themselves.

If Canadian English lacks the roustabout adventurousness of American English, it is because its character owes so much to the people who settled there after the American Revolution, called "Loyalists" by the British, but "Tories" by the Americans. Like other aspects of Canadian culture, it is torn between the push-pull of the British and American models.

In the nineteenth century, American English, bursting at the seams with new energy and new experiences, left Canadian English far behind. Wave upon wave of new Americans were now flooding in from Ireland, Germany, Italy and, in due course, Central Europe. At the same time, the most adventurous among them were pushing westwards, pioneering the new frontier. Walt Whitman, the poet of this new America, captured the essence of this new enthusiasm:

> *Come my tan-faced children,*
> *Follow well in order, get your weapons ready,*
> *Have you your pistols? have you your sharped-edged axes?*
> *Pioneers! O Pioneers!*
>
> *For we cannot tarry here,*
> *We must march my darlings, we must bear the brunt of danger,*
> *We the youthful sinewy races, all the rest on us depend,*
> *Pioneers! O Pioneers!*

"GO WEST, YOUNG MAN! GO WEST!"
Go West was originally an Elizabethan expression meaning "to die" or, like the sun, "to disappear into an unknown abyss". In the early days of America, it was used to refer to the frontiersmen who went into Pennsylvania, Ohio and Illinois and disappeared. Later, the American cowboy used the phrase *gone west* to refer to someone who had deserted his family or left his job, usually in search of a new and better start. The doughboys of the First World War used *gone west* to describe a fellow soldier who went AWOL (absent without leave). Ironically, it was the Hollywood cowboys who restored the phrase to its original Elizabethan sense of "to die".

"Gone west" is one phrase among many that entered the mainstream of the English language from the American frontier. Throughout the nineteenth century, the very notion and definition of the West kept changing. When Charles Dickens visited America, he went no farther than St Louis, nine hundred miles short of the Rocky Mountains, announced that he had seen the West, and declared it to be a fraud. A generation later, Oscar Wilde lectured his way round America and ended up drinking gold miners under the saloon tables of the Wild West. As the frontier expanded, its language changed with each new environment.

In the first part of the nineteenth century the vast American continent offered so many obstacles to travel that the easiest way to the West was along the great broad Mississippi, running up from New Orleans to St Louis, then the heart of the country. The Mississippi is 2340 miles long and has 250 tributaries, including the Ohio and Missouri rivers. It takes its name from the Chippewa Indian *mici sibi* (big river), but it is more than that. The river was a way of life. It ferried settlers, farmers and merchants; it prompted the development of the *steamboat*, or *paddlesteamer*. Together with its mighty tributaries, it was the cargo route for cotton, sugar, tobacco and slaves; it brought prosperity to scores of cities and towns, Pittsburgh, Cincinnati, Louisville, Kansas City, Minneapolis, St Louis, Memphis, Baton Rouge and, of course, New Orleans. Mark Twain, the river's greatest admirer, its pilot, poet and immortalizer, wrote:

> When I was a boy, there was but one permanent ambition among my comrades in our village [Hannibal, Missouri] on the west bank of the Mississippi River. That was, to be a steamboatman. We had transient ambitions of other sorts, but they were only transient. When a circus came and went, it left us all burning to become clowns; the first Negro minstrel show that ever came to our section left us all suffering to try that kind of life; now and then we had a hope that, if we lived and were good, God would permit us to be pirates. These ambitions faded out, each in its turn; but the ambition to be a steamboatman always remained.

Small or large, the river steamboats, floating palaces of the Mississippi, carried the notorious *river gamblers*, from professional poker players exploiting the traveling fat-cats from the plantations, to the freebooting conmen who preyed on the poorer deck passengers, or *standees* as they were known. Gambling was ubiquitous. In *The Domestic Manners of the Americans*, Mrs Frances Trollope, the mother of the novelist Anthony Trollope, reported that, "No boat left New Orleans without having as cabin passengers one or two gentlemen whose profession it was to drill the fifty-two elements of a deck of cards to profitable duty."

The gambling game *par excellence* was poker. The word itself comes from a three-card game (known to the French as *poque*) which swept through America's frontier society like a religion. Betting became so much a part of the American way of life in the more remote parts of the Union that the phrase "You bet" soon became the standard affirmative. Mark Twain tells the story of a Westerner who has been instructed to bring a newly widowed wife the news of her husband's death. "Does Joe Toole live here?" he asks. She nods. "Bet you he don't!" replies the man.

The French origins of poker – present in usages like *ace* and *deuce* – were soon forgotten, especially when the Westerners evolved their own variant, *stud* poker (one card down, the other cards up). As the wild men of the West carried the game far and wide, so phrases like *put up or shut up*, *I'll call your bluff* and *passing the buck* entered the language. (The buck was the buckhorn-handled knife placed in front of the dealer and passed by a player who did not care to deal the next hand.) *Deal* itself, a word with a long pedigree, now acquired a whole new resonance, spawning a family of phrases, from *square deal* to *new deal*, to *fair deal* to *raw deal* and *big deal!* Once the cards had been dealt, the quality of *bluffing* became an important factor in the game. By the middle of the century, *bluff* was synonymous with poker, and the best way to win was to have a *poker face* and to hope that *the cards weren't stacked against you*. Such gambling terms are now common in English. We talk about having *an ace up one's sleeve*, and we boast that we will *up the ante*, we say of someone that he has *hit the jackpot*, or *loaded the dice*, or *thrown in his hand*, or *played both ends against the middle*, that he *wouldn't follow suit* and preferred to *play a wild card* when perhaps he should have recognized that *the chips were down*.

The frontier drink was whiskey, (or *joywater*, or *firewater* or *corn juice*) and was made not, as in Britain, from barley, but from corn (maize or Indian corn) or rye. Whiskey, neat or mixed, was the staple of frontier life. The legendary Davy Crockett once proposed that "Congress allows lemonade to the members and has it charged under the head of stationery – I move also that *whiskey* be allowed under the item of fuel." From the first, American *bartenders* liked to experiment and innovate. *Cocktail* makes its first appearance in 1806 and, from then to now, the cocktail has been as American as a dry martini – in Mencken's memorable phrase, "The only American invention as perfect as a sonnet." The early history of the word "cocktail" is shrouded, as so often, in mystery, but some believe that, like some other Americanisms it may have an African pedigree. In the Krio of Sierra Leone, *kaktel* means "scorpion" – a creature with a sting in the tail.

At the frontier itself, whiskey was traded unmixed and often used to corrupt the local Indians. Congress tried to regulate the worst excesses of the liquor trade, but the pioneers turned to *bootlegging* (the whiskey would be sold illegally to the Indians in a flat bottle that

115 "A riverboat", Mark Twain once wrote, "is like a wedding cake – without the complications."

116 American English owes many striking phrases to the Mississippi riverboat gambling man.

could literally be carried in the leg of a boot). *Bootleg*, in the sense of an unauthorized sale, has now become part of the language, with phrases like *bootleg album*.

As the West developed, so did its famous watering-hole, the *saloon*, a word derived from the French *salon*, which made its first appearance in the 1840s. It was introduced by settlers who liked its association with fashion, elegance and politeness, but rapidly degenerated so that by the end of the century Oscar Wilde could remark of a London hostess that she had intended to open a *salon* but had inaugurated a *saloon*. The *saloon*, or *bar-room*, or even *groggery* was, like the riverboat, the hub of much social activity and the vocabulary and phrasing of the bar has remained part of English ever since, from *bender* (bending the elbow) to *taking it straight*.

Looking back on the effect of the frontier, H. L. Mencken once remarked that this was "the Gothic age of American drinking as of American word-making". The men of the West certainly developed a remarkable range of vocabulary: *discombobulate* (to confuse), *hornswoggle* (to swindle), *squablification* (quarreling), *lallapalooza* (an extraordinary person or thing) and perhaps best of all *absquatulate*, meaning "to go away" or "to skedaddle", itself a colorful borrowing from Scots Gaelic.

The frontier was always changing. In the Far West it was often hard to define: the states of Texas, Arizona, Nevada, Utah and California were simply part of northern Mexico, happy hunting grounds for any brave adventurer who wanted *to stake a claim*. The shock-troops of the frontier were the beaver trappers, or mountain men, who, until the trade collapsed in the 1830s, scoured the Rocky Mountains for beaver pelts. Nothing illustrates better the characteristic habit of American English to use jargon as metaphor than the adoption of the word *beaver*. Beaver had always been at the center of the North American fur trade from the early 1600s, and in parts of New England a man's worth might be reckoned in beaver skins (just as they were later reckoned in buck skins, or *bucks*). The beaver became a well-known and fashionable kind of fur-trimmed hat and the news that the Rockies were "running over with beaver" gave a new lease of life to the trade. Phrases like *eager beaver* and *work like a beaver* also echo this frontier experience.

After the beaver trade collapsed many of the old trappers and scouts found new business as guides when Oregon fever swept the Mississippi in the early 1840s. But this latest migration was nothing compared to what was to follow. For in 1848 there was suddenly a reason for every adventurous Yankee to head out to the West lickety-split. The reason? *Gold fever* – a phrase that had entered the language at a gallop the year before.

"TO SEE THE ELEPHANT"

The Gold Rush was one of the most remarkable phenomena ever to sweep the United States. In the words of the New York *Herald*, "All classes of our citizens seem to be under the influence of this extraordinary mania ... Poets, philosophers, lawyers, brokers, bankers, merchants, farmers, clergymen – all are feeling the impulse and are preparing to go and dig for gold and swell the numbers of adventurers to the new El Dorado." The Gold Rush was unique: it was essentially for city people, lily-fingered Easterners who, knowing nothing of the land, hoped to go out West, get rich quick, and come home "with a pocket full of rocks". In one year alone, 1849, a hundred thousand of them, young men in their twenties mainly, headed for California – and all of them were stunned by the experience.

They had a phrase for it, now forgotten. They used to say that they had been *to see the elephant*. In the 1840s almost no one in America had seen an elephant and when the leading circuses of the day introduced these fabulous beasts into their act they proved an immensely popular attraction. The story goes that a farmer set out with his wagon and his market goods for the local fair, announcing to all and sundry at home that he was going "to see the elephant". On his way to the fair, the farmer and his horse meet the circus coming into town. When his horse sees the elephant, it rears up, overturns the wagon, spills the goods, and bolts. The now ruined farmer trudges wearily home. When his family ask him what has happened, he replies sadly, "I saw the elephant." For the Forty-niners, the phrase came to mean experiencing a catastrophe, or having a shock, and above all being matured by reality. Many, for whom "seeing the elephant" was a regular experience, found it difficult to express what they were going through. "It is impossible for me to give you an account of the interesting incidents that occur on this route," one doctor wrote to his wife, "but when I have an opportunity I will give you enough to satisfy you that 1849 will ever be a memorable epoch in the history of our country. Neither the Crusades nor Alexander's expedition to India can ever equal this emigration to California."

Astonished by the adventure, separated from their loved ones, alone in a vast and hostile wilderness, the Forty-niners responded like city people – they wrote about it. They published books by the hundred, they kept diaries by the thousand, and they scribbled uncountable numbers of letters home. They were the first – and the last – frontiermen to have the education and the inclination to describe what they saw and heard. What is more, once they arrived in the Sierra goldfields, they had the leisure to write: very few returned home within the year as they had planned. Like many wars, the Gold Rush was a literary and a public event with a wide popular appeal. Shipped East by letter and newspaper, the phrases and the vocabulary of the West passed swiftly into the language. Several gold-rush words from California and other goldfields are now part of everyday speech:

bonanza:	originally a Spanish word meaning fair weather.
diggings:	the place where the prospectors mined for gold, abbreviated to *digs*.
el dorado:	the name of the legendary Indian Kingdom of Gold sought by the Spanish in the sixteenth century.
pan out:	the gold would be *panned* in a river, it was accumulated by *panning out*, which came to mean, generally, to produce, to be successful.

prospector:	this was first recorded in 1846, derived from a *prospect*, a promising place to search for gold.
stake a claim:	the process of establishing exclusive rights to mining land, a phrase which goes back, referring to land generally, to the earliest days of White America.
strike:	the Californian Gold Rush spawned a whole family of *strike* phrases – *strike it rich, big strike, lucky strike.*

Founded by free-spending adventurers, California became the thirty-first state in the Union in 1850, taking its name from a Spanish word meaning "an earthly paradise". The new state developed in a sudden flurry of extraordinary riches and excitement. In the words of the song, "The miners came in '49, The whores in '51, And when they got together, they produced the native son." Places like Bonanza, Prompt Pay, Croesus Extension, Bread Winner, Gold Coin, We Got 'Em and Big Wampush express eloquently the notion of get-rich-quick to which the happy-go-lucky new population of the Golden State subscribed.

117/118 The Gold Rush stimulated a massive emigration to the West. Americans, one commentator noted, "moving frequently from place to place . . . are not so liable to local peculiarities either in accent or phraseology".

"THE REAL McCOY"

In the long history of the American frontier, the Gold Rush was something of a freak, a story of overnight riches (or disaster) that ran counter to the experience of most pioneers. Those who came to settle the land and live on it, generation by generation, had to find a way of life less precarious than the fur trade, and less solitary and dangerous than prospecting, a way of life that suited the peculiar climate and geography of the Far West. We are talking, of course, of the true Westerner, the *cowboy*, a word that first appeared in print, in its present sense, in 1877, although it had a British meaning, "a boy who tends cattle", first recorded in 1725.

The legend of the cowboys began ten years earlier, in the spring of 1867, when the as-yet-uncompleted transcontinental railroad ran a branch line to Abilene, Kansas. It was here that a 29-year-old livestock trader from Chicago named Joseph McCoy had an idea that put millions of dollars in his bank account and his name into the dictionaries. His plan was simple. Having bought most of the town for a princely $4250, he set about bringing the cows from the high grasslands of southern Texas up to the new railhead to ship them back to feed the cities of the North and East. He at once advertised for ranchers and cow-handlers to bring the half-wild longhorns from Texas up the Chisholm Trail to his new railway cattleyards. To do this, he offered $40 a head, ten times the going rate. As the story goes, a hundred days after McCoy first posted his offer, the first herds arrived from the South, two and three thousand at a time. McCoy had bragged that he would deliver two hundred thousand cattle in the first decade of business. He was wrong. In the first four years alone he shipped more than two million back to the East. His performance matched his advertising. He was, as he liked to say, "the real McCoy".

Soon there were at least 5000 cowboys on the Chisholm Trail and for twenty years (until the drought of 1886–7) the cowboy was king, leaving behind a rich legacy of words and phrases in American English. As a frontiersman dealing with Indians and Mexicans, he could speak pidgin English, using phrases like *long time no see* and *no can do*. The contact with Spanish-speaking horse-handlers brought a number of new words into American English: *rodeo*, *stampede* (from *estampeda*), *bronco* (Spanish: *rough, unruly*), *chaps* (short for *chaparejos*), *lassoo* (from Spanish *lazo*, a snare), *mustang, lariat, pinto, poncho, ranch* (*rancho* was the Spanish word for a soldiers' mess). Then, once the Chisholm Trail established Joe McCoy and the *cattle barons* (1874), the language became flooded with *cow*-terms: *cow camp, cowhand, cowboy song, cowpuncher, cowpoke* (or *bronco-buster, wrangler* or *range rider*), as well as *maverick*, named, it is said, after Samuel Maverick, a Texas pioneer, and mayor of San Antonio. Allegedly Mayor Maverick never branded his calves on his 385,000 acres, so that he could claim all unbranded cattle on the range. The word did not acquire its nonconformist connotation until 1901. Branded or unbranded, the calves were always vulnerable to what *Blackwood's Magazine* described, for its British readers, as "a gang of 'rustlers' – as the lawless desperadoes who abound in Arizona, New Mexico, and Texas are called". This now familiar meaning deprived *rustler* of its earlier connotation, "an energetic or bustling man", a role which, by one of those inexplicable processes of language change, has now been taken over by *hustler* ("an aggressive person seeking business success", 1886), except where – in American *red light districts* – it refers to prostitutes.

Phrases like *hot under the collar* and *bite the dust* are an everyday reminder of the powerful influence the cowboy has had on the English language. Perhaps this is because, of all the frontier heroes, the cowboy was the beneficiary of late nineteenth-century technology. The camera and the railroad exported the cowboy lifestyle and language back to the East so vividly that a New York dentist, Zane Gray, who was virtually ignorant of the real West, could create a believable picture of cowboy society from the information available to him in New York, thousands of miles from the range. But of all the peddlers of the cowboy myth, none was more successful than Bill Cody, "Buffalo Bill".

Cody's early years were packed with incident. At thirteen he was panning for gold, at fourteen he was riding for the Pony Express. Two years later he fought in the Civil War, and immediately afterward was hired to hunt buffalo to feed the railroad workers on the Kansas Pacific. His skill at shooting from the saddle of a galloping horse earned him his nickname. In 1876, he served as a scout to General Custer just before Little Big Horn, and two weeks after the battle led the retaliatory raid against the Cheyenne, killing and then scalping Chief Yellow Hand. Such is the stuff of legend, and Cody now set about bringing the legend before a growing American, and finally a European, audience. Cody formed the Wild West Show in 1883 and, as Wild West fever swept the English-speaking world, he became the toast of fashionable society on both sides of the Atlantic. Queen Victoria broke a seclusion of forty years to attend his show and was reportedly much impressed by the dignity of the Indian Red Cloud, who had become part of the act. Ten days later, after four European heads of state and the Prince of Wales had driven round the arena in the "Deadwood Stagecoach", and been ambushed by Indians, Buffalo Bill declared that "Four kings and a prince of Wales must beat a royal flush any time."

119 *Cowboy* is an old English word that found a new meaning in the American West. Much cowboy language was actually Spanish.

120 The beaver trappers coined the phrase "to work like a beaver".

FROM COAST TO COAST

Without the magical invention known to the Indians as "the Iron Horse", Buffalo Bill would never have left Wyoming. The transcontinental railroad, which so enriched McCoy and the cattle barons, also added its share of new words and phrases to the dictionary.

After the Civil War was over and the Union had been made safe, it became the American dream to unite the country in fact as well as in rhetoric. Eastern railroads stretched as far as Nebraska; in the West, there were tracks up and down California. Between them was a gap of some 1700 miles, and two companies, the Union Pacific and the Central Pacific, were feverishly laying down tracks to close it. Spurred on by government subsidy and commercial rivalry, the two companies set out to lay 1775 miles of track in three years, the Easterners across the prairie and through the Rockies; the Westerners through the Sierras and into Utah. The two teams met at a place they called Promontory Point on 10 May 1869. Bigwigs from both companies were ferried out for the ceremony – the driving of a golden spike into the last sleeper. In fact, when the Governor of California swung the hammer to do the deed, he missed. But it didn't matter. The news was already racing down the telegraph wire. In New York they fired a hundred-gun salute; in Philadelphia they rang the Liberty Bell; and in San Francisco, one of the newspapers cheekily announced the "annexation of the United States".

Steam was king and the railroad companies were a source of great fascination. Just as some airlines today have in-house nicknames ("Air Chance" for Air France, "Please Inform Allah" for PIA, and "Better Walk It Alone" for BWIA), so the railway companies would be known locally as "Take Your Parcels and Walk" (Texas, Pacific and Western) or "Damned Small Salaries and Abuse" (Duluth, South Shore and Atlantic). For all its magic, much of the railroad's terminology – *berth, purser, steward, fare, cabin, freight* – was simply nautical jargon, a borrowing that has been repeated by the airlines in our own time (*boarding, landing*). None the less, the railroad did bring some new words and phrases into the language. *Railroad*, as a verb, first meant to convict someone falsely (1877) and now has the generalized meaning of *coerce*. If you weren't *railroaded*, you might be *sidetracked*, a word which, by the 1890s, was widely used to mean to divert from the main issue, course or goal. And if you weren't *sidetracked*, it might still be necessary to go in for some *streamlining*. Two political terms, *on the gravy train* and *whistle stop tour*, became common currency during the presidential campaign of 1948 between Harry S. Truman and Thomas E. Dewey. The latter is credited with coining "whistle stop tour" on 8 October 1948, when he criticized his opponent for his remarks about the Congress made from the platform of his campaign train. The words *whistle stop* refer to a town too small for a scheduled stop. If passengers wanted to get on or off at such stations it was necessary to signal to the driver, who would acknowledge the request with two toots of his whistle. Other standard American English phrases with a railroad past include *to be in the clear, to make the grade, to have the right of way, to backtrack, to reach the end of the line*, and, of course, *to go off the rails*.

The coming of the railroad marked the end of the excitement and novelty associated with the frontier. One of the reasons why the influence of the railroad on the language was so restricted was precisely because it put the comforts of ordinary life on wheels. Railway journeys were short and not very disruptive. Even the crews might finish a working day back at their home base. Despite tales of Indian raiding parties whooping round the "Iron Horse" as it shuddered across the prairie, most train journeys were uneventful. There was neither the widespread gambling and the drinking of the riverboats, nor the hardship and the isolation of the Gold Rush. The railroad ushered in the age of technology, whose impact on language was of a different kind, as we shall see. The way in which the vigor and energy of frontier talk was returned to the East is perhaps symbolized by the emergence of two great Americans: Abraham Lincoln and Mark Twain.

"MARK TWAIN"

Most recent wars have given the English language many new words and phrases. The American Civil War, with which Lincoln's name is forever associated, appears to be an exception. Apart from the phrase *unconditional surrender*, first used by General Grant in 1862, the conflict had little lasting impact on the English of most Americans. But what the war between the States did do was to bring the people and the economy of the pioneering Mid-West into play for the first time in the history of their country. Both Lincoln and Twain were Mid-Westerners. When the farm boy from Illinois became president, the country ways of American speech and behavior seemed to many to have become united in the gangling figure of one man. But the direct simplicity of Lincoln's speech, remembered above all in the "Gettysburg Address", just two minutes of prose scribbled on the back of an envelope, and audible, according to eye-witnesses, only to those standing next to him, shows the new

121 In the United States and Britain the railroad (or railway) enjoys parallel vocabularies. In Britain, "grade crossings" become "level crossings", "switches" are "points", and "tracks" are "rails".

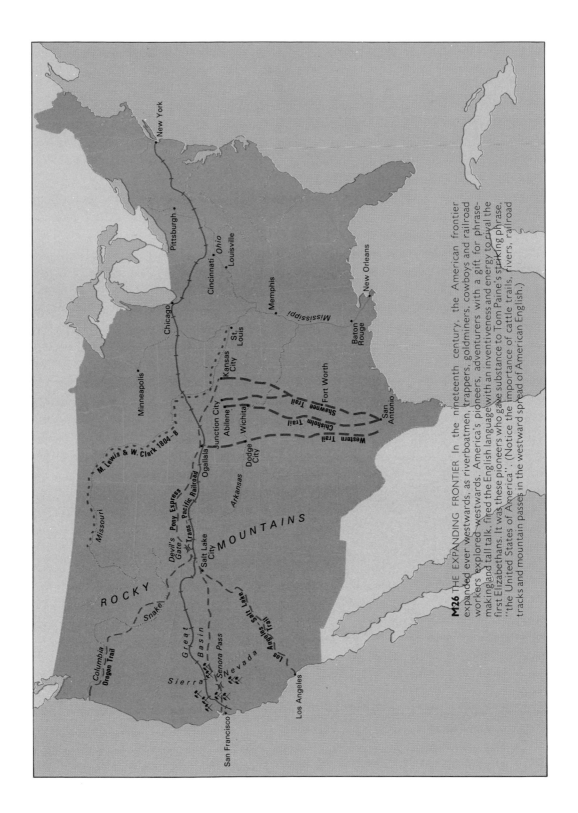

M26 THE EXPANDING FRONTIER In the nineteenth century, the American frontier expanded ever westwards, as riverboatmen, trappers, goldminers, cowboys and railroad workers explored westwards. America's pioneers, adventurers with a gift for phrase-making and tall talk, fired the English language with an inventiveness and energy to rival the first Elizabethans. It was these pioneers who gave substance to Tom Paine's striking phrase, "the United States of America". (Notice the importance of cattle trails, rivers, railroad tracks and mountain passes in the westward spread of American English.)

New York

Pittsburgh

Ohio
Cincinnati
Louisville

Chicago
Memphis
Mississippi

St. Louis
Kansas City

Baton Rouge

New Orleans

Minneapolis

Fort Worth
San Antonio

Junction City
Abilene
Wichita
Ogallala

Shawnee Trail
Chisholm Trail
Western Trail

M. Lewis & W. Clark 1804–6

Dodge City

Arkansas

Missouri

Devil's Gate
Pony Express
Trans - Pacific Railroad

ROCKY MOUNTAINS

Salt Lake City

Snake

Great Basin
Salt Lake
Los Angeles Trail

Columbia
Oregon Trail

Senora Pass
Sierra
Nevada

San Francisco

Los Angeles

maturity and confidence of American English:

> Four score and seven years ago our fathers brought forth on this continent a new nation, conceived in liberty and dedicated to the proposition that all men are created equal. Now we are engaged in a great civil war, testing whether that nation, or any nation so conceived and so dedicated, can long endure.

Then, on 16 December 1865, almost exactly a year after Lincoln's Second Inaugural, something happened to American literature and language for which it had been waiting, and from which it has never recovered. The New York *Saturday Press* published a story which began (in the form of a letter to Artemus Ward) as follows:

> In compliance with the request of a friend of mine who wrote me from the East, I called on good-natured, garrulous old Simon Wheeler and inquired after my friend's friend, Leonidas W. Smiley, as requested to do, and I hereto append the result.

The story was entitled "John Smiley and his Jumping Frog" (later known to literature as "The Celebrated Jumping Frog of Calaveras County") and it was by a young reporter from the West writing under the pen name of "Mark Twain". As Ernest Hemingway put it in *The Green Hills of Africa*: "All modern American literature comes from one book by Mark Twain called *Huckleberry Finn* ... It's the best book we've had. All American writing comes from that. There was nothing before. There has been nothing as good since."

Just as Lincoln united his country, so, in Mark Twain (or Samuel Clemens, as he was born), we find an American writer who could render the rhythms and vocabulary and tone of the American English vernacular in a way that was neither a parody nor a caricature but literature. With Twain, the oral achievements we have just described become literary. There are, besides, some striking similarities between Lincoln and Twain. Both were brought up at the frontier; both were from the lively middle of the American continent and both shared its ethos and beliefs – democratic, individualistic, egalitarian. Lincoln believed in the American people; Twain wrote about them, using their common speech. T. S. Eliot once wrote that Mark Twain was "one of those writers, of whom there are not a great many in any literature, who have discovered a new way of writing, valid not only for themselves but for others. I should place him ... as one of those rare writers who have brought their language up to date."

In *Life on the Mississippi*, Twain summarizes his early career:

> In due course I got my license. I was a pilot now, full-fledged ... Time drifted smoothly and prosperously on, and I supposed – and hoped – that I was going to follow the river the rest of my days, and die at the wheel when my mission was ended. But by and by the war came, commerce was suspended, my occupation gone.
> I had to seek another livelihood. So I became a silver-miner in Nevada;

next, a newspaper reporter; next, a gold-miner in California; next, a reporter in San Francisco; next, a special correspondent in the Sandwich Islands; next a roving correspondent in Europe and the East; next, an instructional torch-bearer on the lecture platform; and, finally I became a scribbler of books, and an immovable fixture among the other rocks of New England.

That was written in 1883, when he was forty-eight. Years later, toward the end of his life, describing his slow start in literature, he wrote to a correspondent: "I have been an author for twenty years and an ass for fifty-five."

Twain's early life epitomizes all the westward movements we have been describing. One of his early books, *Roughing It*, is full of what he called "the vigorous new vernacular of the occidental plains and mountains". For instance, we find him explaining that *heap* is "Injun-English" for "very much". He uses the language of the Californian prospectors when he explains to his reader that, "In mining parlance, the Wide West had 'struck it rich!'" Describing his experiences in the silver mines of Nevada, he remarks: "Slang was the language of Nevada. It was hard to preach a sermon without it, and be understood. Such phrases as 'You bet!' 'Oh, no, I reckon not!' 'No Irish need apply,' and a hundred others, became so common as to fall from the lips of a speaker unconsciously . . ." (Slang phrases that make their first appearance with Twain include: *dead broke, take it easy, to get even, gilt-edged* and *a close call*.)

In his work as a journalist he would have met pioneers from every part of the American frontier. As one reviewer of his first book, *Innocents Abroad*, noted, his work is "characterized by the breadth and ruggedness and audacity of the West". Twain himself described the publication of this celebrated travel book, an instant bestseller, as "the Turning Point of My Life". And it was the last link in the chain of events that made him the writer Mark Twain. He was famous; he was successful; he was well-off. Now, like many English and American

122 The young Mark Twain was among the first to experiment with the typewriter.

123 For Walt Whitman, the English language "befriends the grand American expression".

writers who have struck gold and found a public, he took to the lecture-circuit, talking about the travels abroad that make up *Innocents Abroad*. He promised, he said, to make his lecture "somewhat didactic. I don't know what didactic means, but it is a good, high-sounding word, and I wish to use it, meaning no harm whatsoever."

This is the authentic voice of the humorist, of a writer for whom the English language was a playground. Unlike his sober literary predecessors, the men of the eastern districts, Emerson, Thoreau, Hawthorne, and many others now forgotten, Samuel Clemens had an enormously wide experience of American life, of all classes of people in all kinds of occupation and mood. His work has a zest and gusto different from his predecessors'.

The two novels for which he is best known and with which American literature truly comes of age are *The Adventures of Tom Sawyer* and *Huckleberry Finn*. Once, forgetting that he himself had adapted it for the theater, Twain refused a dramatization of *Tom Sawyer* on the grounds that you cannot make a hymn into a play. This is a true valuation of both books, although *Huckleberry Finn* caused a scandal at its first appearance among the respectable reading public. They celebrate the lost worlds of childhood, the space and mystery of the American Mid-West, and the rich variety of American society. In *Huckleberry Finn* the voice of American speech comes through loud and clear from the first page to the last:

> You don't know about me without you have read a book by the name of *The Adventures of Tom Sawyer*, but that ain't no matter. That book was made by Mr. Mark Twain and he told me the truth, mainly. There was things which he stretched, but mainly he told the truth. That is nothing. I never seen anybody but lied one time or another, without it was Aunt Polly or the Widow, or maybe Mary. Aunt Polly – Tom's Aunt Polly, she is – and Mary and the Widow Douglas is all told about in that book, which is mostly a true book, with some stretchers as I said before.

So Huck Finn sets off down the great river that runs through the heart of America, and with him goes the runaway slave, Nigger Jim, making his bid for freedom. What is especially interesting about *Huckleberry Finn* for our purposes is the "Explanatory Note" that precedes the first chapter. Twain had already noted that: "The Northern word 'guess' . . . is but little used among Southerners. They say 'reckon'." He now sets out a complete prospectus for his use of "dialect", with a characteristic Twain coda:

> In this book a number of dialects are used, to wit: the Missouri Negro dialect, the extremest form of the backwoods Southwestern dialect, the ordinary "Pike County" dialect, and four modified varieties of this last. The shadings have not been done in a haphazard fashion or by guesswork, but painstakingly and with the trustworthy guidance and support of personal familiarity with these several forms of speech.
>
> I make this explanation for the reason that without it many readers would suppose that all these characters were trying to talk alike and not succeeding.

Mark Twain wrote about the West. Samuel Clemens lived in the East, in a world far removed from the riverboats and open skies of the Mississippi, a world of gas companies and telephones. Twain was the writer who brought the newly forged American language back from the frontier to the teeming cities of the East Coast. By a quirk of history, the only writer to touch Twain when it came to expressing the naturalness and vitality of American speech was already making a name for himself among the more discriminating members of the East Coast poetry-reading public. This was Walt Whitman, who announced with typical gusto in 1855 that "The United States themselves are essentially the greatest poem."

The author of *Leaves of Grass* was one of the most photographed poets of his century, perhaps of all time. Whitman was a tireless self-promoter who would think nothing of writing his own reviews or co-authoring his own biography. Perhaps this was because he found success comparatively late in life. He was an Easterner, born on Long Island and raised in Brooklyn. He left school early and completed his education in the newspaper offices of Long Island and Brooklyn, rising through the ranks of the *Brooklyn Eagle* to become editor in 1846. (In later life, he liked to experiment with new spellings, and would render Canada as Kanada, a *K*-vogue that was also responsible for the spelling Ku-Klux-Klan.) But two years later, in the year of revolutions, he upped sticks in the American way and went south to New Orleans. Little is known of the next few years, but in 1855, at the age of thirty-six, he bursts on the scene as the author of *Leaves of Grass*. With typical brashness he sent an early copy to the great Ralph Waldo Emerson at home in Concord. The sage recognized his genius at once. "I am not blind", wrote Emerson, "to the worth of the wonderful gift of *Leaves of Grass*. I find it the most extraordinary piece of wit and wisdom that America has yet contributed." Few new writers could have had such a wonderful encomium as a send-off. But Emerson was right: here was a new voice that insisted on an audience.

> *I celebrate myself,*
> *And what I assume you shall assume,*
> *For every atom belonging to me as good belongs to you.*
>
> *I loafe and invite my soul,*
> *I lean and loafe at my ease . . . observing a spear of summer grass.*

His poetry expressed the new voice of America, or as he put it with characteristic immodesty:

> My Book and I – what a period we have presumed to span! those thirty
> years from 1850 to 1880 – and America in them! Proud, indeed may we be,
> if we have cull'd enough of that period in its own spirit to worthily waft a
> few live breaths of it to the future!

Whitman showed American writers and readers that it was not necessary to imitate English or European models. He encouraged those who came after to look at and write about their own society in their own way. He celebrated the United States; he was intoxicated by it.

He gave it a myth. "I hear America singing", he wrote, and traveled mightily to hear the songs. Where Twain came east, Whitman went out west. "What an exhilaration!" he wrote, looking back on his journey through the great states of Illinois, Missouri, Kansas and Colorado. His ambitions are clearly stated. He wanted, he said, to see "all those inimitable American areas fused in the alembic of a perfect poem, or other esthetic work, entirely western, fresh and limitless – altogether our own without a trace or taste of Europe's soil, reminiscence, technical letter or spirit". He was, in his own way, an American radical, and he found that the language was his ally in his quest:

> The English language befriends the grand American expression ... it is brawny enough and limber and full enough. On the tough stock of a race who through all change of circumstances was never without the idea of political liberty, which is the animus of all liberty, it has attracted the terms of daintier and gayer and subtler and more elegant tongues. It is the powerful language of resistance ... it is the dialect of common sense. It is the speech of the proud and melancholy races and of all who aspire. It is the chosen tongue to express growth faith self-esteem freedom justice equality friendliness amplitude prudence decision and courage. It is the medium that shall well nigh express the inexpressible.

When Whitman died, in Camden, New Jersey, in 1892 he was recognized throughout America as the poet, a pioneer in language, who had given his country its first lyrical voice and one that was uniquely American.

THE "HUDDLED MASSES"

Whitman's reputation was made in New York, now the first city of polyglot America. In the days of the American Revolution, Philadelphia had been the first city of the Republic. During the nineteenth century, partly because the city could not afford to be choosy about its inhabitants, partly because of the links with the new Erie canal, connecting Albany to Buffalo, and partly because it offered excellent berthing facilities, the port of New York became the entry point of one of the greatest migrations in history.

Decade by decade they came: the Irish fleeing from the potato famine in the 1840s; the Germans and Italians leaving Europe after the failure of the 1848 revolutions; the Central European Jews fleeing the persecutions of the 1880s. "We call England the Mother country", the humorist Robert Benchley once remarked, "because most us came from Poland or Italy."

Immigrant is an American word, coined in 1789, to refine *emigrant* (previously used in a double sense). Humanitarian idealism mixed with the need for a workforce to man the burgeoning American economy now made America the immigrant society *par excellence*. This was expressed in the famous lines of Emma Lazarus inscribed on the pedestal of the Statue of Liberty:

> *Give me your tired, your poor,*
> *Your huddled masses, yearning to breathe free,*

The wretched refuse of your teeming shore,
Send these, the homeless, tempest-tossed to me :
I lift my lamp beside the golden door.

Bad poetry, but good propaganda. As O. Henry, the American storywriter, once remarked of the Statue of Liberty, "It was made by a Dago ... on behalf of the French ... for the purpose of welcomin' Irish immigrants to the Dutch city of New York." The city remains an ethnic mosaic, especially in its foods: *liverwurst* from Germany, *goulash* from Hungary, *borscht* from Russia, *lasagne* from Italy, *Guinness* from Ireland, *lox* and *bagels* from Central Europe.

The impact of these huge invasions was less than might have been expected because most immigrants were anxious to enlist in American society as rapidly as possible. From the Gaelic-speaking Irish to the Yiddish-speaking Jews, they adopted English with enthusiasm, at least in public. (There were some discreet nudges in this direction from some American institutions: it was impossible, for example, to borrow foreign-language books from the New York Public Library.) At home, the older generation tended to cling to their mother tongue, and even today many American families are virtually bilingual. The experience of the immigrant children was quite different. Once again, as with the children of the Southern plantations, we find that in the schoolroom, and especially the playground, there were fierce pressures favoring the use of the American standard. The schools were the places where the immigrant children were rapidly Americanized by their playmates, and life was made intolerable, one imagines, for the child who had to use a foreign word rather than the English.

Among the most distinctive and serious-minded of the new arrivals were the American Germans. Since 1776 a total of some seven million Germans have come to the United States – some middle class (after 1848), some working class (after the Civil War). They lived in German cities like Cincinnati, Ohio, Milwaukee, Wisconsin, and St Louis, Missouri. Like earlier English immigrants, they remembered the Old World in the New: in the United States there are twelve Berlins; seven Germantowns; four Bismarcks; and five Fredericks. The Germans established themselves quickly: by 1860 there were twenty-eight daily German newspapers in fifteen cities. It is probably for this reason – a large, professionally successful, literate alternative culture – that American English acquired German words like *bummer* (*Bummler*, loafer), *check* (*Zeiche*, bill for drinks), *cookbook* (*Kochbuch*), *delicatessen* (*Delikatesse*, delicacies), *ecology* (*Ökologie*), *fresh* (*frech*, impertinent), *hoodlum* (German Bavarian word: *Hoadlum*, rowdy), *kindergarten*, *nix* (*nichts*, nothing), *phooey* (*pfui*), *rifle* (*riffel*, groove), *scram!* (Yiddish: *scrammen*), *spiel* (*spielen*, play), *yesman* (*Jasager*, yes-sayer). A further reflection of the distinctive German contribution to American society is the direct translation of German into English: *and how!* (*und wie*), *no way* (*keineswegs*), *can be* (*kann sein*), *will do* (*wird getan*) and even *let it be* (*lass es sein*).

Before the First World War, the Germans were a popular element in American society, renowned in the universities for their science, their philosophy and their pedantry. After the *Lusitania* was sunk in 1915 with the loss of 1200 lives, they became *Huns*, the *Boche* (from the French *al boche*: *al*-lemand ca-*boche* i.e. German blockhead), and finally, in the movies,

Jerries. This was borrowed from British troops in the trenches – the English slang word for a chamber-pot, "Jerry", was applied to the Germans because their coal-scuttle helmets looked like chamber-pots. The rash of anti-German feeling was reflected in a changing of names. Many Knoebels became Noble; many Shoens, Shane; and many Steins, Stone. *Sauerkraut* became "liberty cabbage", and *frankfurters* became "hot dogs". If you are an American and your name is Astor, Budweiser, Chrysler, Custer, Eisenhower, Frick, Heinz, Pershing, Rockefeller, Singer, Steinway, Studebaker or Westinghouse, then you are a member of the biggest and most longstanding non-British ethnic group in the United States.

The Italians, who followed the Germans, were of a different social class and status, as the abusive nickname *wop* suggests. There is an apocryphal story that the immigration authorities on Ellis Island would tag the new immigrants who arrived without proper papers with a label initialed WOP (without passport). The evidence that *wop* comes from *guappo*, a Neapolitan dialect word for a dandy, often used by Italians to refer to the Neapolitans, is rather more conclusive. Either way, the point is made: the Italians tended to be poor, often illiterate, peasants from the South. Between 1865 and 1920, as the age of the steamship brought cheap travel to more and more Europeans, more than five million Italians came to the United States, mainly to the great cities of the North-East. Soon – as in New York – every city had its *Little Italy*. Unlike the Germans, the less-educated Italians made a more complete adoption of American English. As a result, the influence of Italian words is mainly limited to food words like *pizza*, *spaghetti*, *lasagne*, *espresso*, *cannelloni*, *minestrone*, *parmesan*, *pasta*, *vermicelli*, *tortellini*, *macaroni*, *ravioli*, *broccoli*, and *zucchini*.

124 Generations of Europeans passed through Ellis Island and, after a medical examination, acquired a new *American* identity.

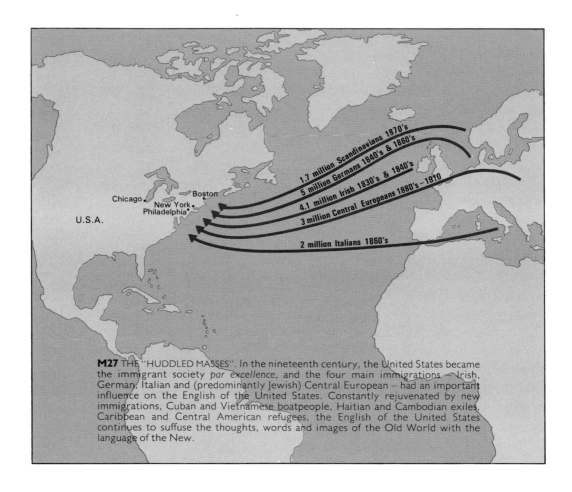

M27 THE "HUDDLED MASSES". In the nineteenth century, the United States became the immigrant society *par excellence*, and the four main immigrations — Irish, German, Italian and (predominantly Jewish) Central European — had an important influence on the English of the United States. Constantly rejuvenated by new immigrations, Cuban and Vietnamese boatpeople, Haitian and Cambodian exiles, Caribbean and Central American refugees, the English of the United States continues to suffuse the thoughts, words and images of the Old World with the language of the New.

There was, however, one Italian import whose vocabulary has had an influence on the language out of all proportion to its significance in the American-Italian community: the Mafia. Now treated as synonymous with organized crime (which it is not), the Mafia has added terms like *godfather, the family* and *capo* to the language. Hollywood's love affair with "gangster movies" has ensured a wide dissemination of criminal slang: *hoodlum, racketeer, rough house, hatchet man, doing the dirty work, hot seat* (originally "the electric chair"), *protection racket* and *loan shark*. The fact that these words – in the minds of many – now come with Italian accents, is to do with the power of the media not the Mafia.

For the real power of the media over the language, there is the story of our third group of European exiles: the three million East and Central European Jews who landed between 1880 and 1910. At peak times, as many as 15,000 per day would arrive on Ellis Island, "the isle of tears". Here the authorities checked the papers, the physical condition of the new arrivals, and then their material circumstances. Finally, each name was checked against the ship's papers. This was when many new Americans acquired a new identity at the hand of ill-educated immigration officials. Names like Ouspenska would become Spensky; Nisnyevich would become Nissen. Warned of this, some made the change in advance. One immigrant named Ostazzinski met a man named Frankelstein on the ship from Russia. Frankelstein, so the story goes, said: "Those immigration officials will change your name into O'Shaughnessy. You'd better change it. Take mine." But Ostazzinski thought Frankelstein too long, so he took half of it – and the family became Stein.

Many of the East and Central European Jews ended up on the Lower East Side of New York City, working in the garment trade. Like the Germans, theirs was a strong subculture within American society. In the 1890s, the Yiddish newspaper the *Jewish Daily Forward* (which survives to this day) had a circulation of a quarter of a million. Excluded from the more established avenues of advancement, many American Jews moved into the entertainment business – newspapers, magazines, vaudeville, and later radio, films and television. The spread of *Yinglish* (Yiddish and English) into the mainstream of the language is partly the result of the preponderance of Jewish Americans in the media of the United States, performers as well as executives. Thanks to stars like Woody Allen and Joan Rivers, the English-speaking world has learned about brazen *chutzpah*, the intrepid *kibitzer*, and the skulking *gonef*, all of which are now in the dictionary. As Leo Rosten, the champion of "Yinglish", remarks, "The foothold established on the hospitable shore of English may be glimpsed if you scan the entries beginning with *ch, k, sch, sh, y*." In recent years, they have been joined by a richly onomatopaeic family: *shlep* ("to drag, pull, lag behind"); *shtik* ("business"); *kosher* ("authentic, unadulterated, the 'real McCoy'"); *mensch* ("someone of consequence"); *momzer* ("a bastard, a mischievous, amusing person"); *nebbish* ("a nonentity"); *shlemiel* ("a simpleton"); *schmooz* ("friendly, aimless talk"); *schmuck* ("a fool, a jerk"); *shnorrer* ("a chiseler, a compulsive bargainer"); *shamus* ("a detective"); *meshuggener* ("a crazy man"); *schlock* ("a shoddy, cheap article"); and *yenta* ("a gossipy woman").

The collision of English and Yiddish has also given America such expressions as *Get lost*, *Give a look*, *He knows from nothing*, *If you'll excuse the expression*, *I'm telling you*, *I need it like a hole in the head*, *Enjoy!*, *Smart he isn't* and *I should worry*. Many of these expressions – and the sarcastic *schm* prefix: *Oedipus-schmoedipus* or *actor-schmactor* – first evolved in the burlesque theaters of the late nineteenth century, a place where the new arrivals could send each other up. W. C. Fields, Groucho Marx, Jack Benny, Bert Lahr and George Burns all grew up in this environment. The comic writer Milt Gross translated the immigrant English he heard on the Lower East Side in retold episodes from American history, "De Bettle From Bonker Heel" and "De Bustun Tippotty". This is his version of Christopher Columbus:

> C. Columbus – dot's I'm – und de woild is rond – Dees is Hindia und I was told to look opp a guy entitled Gonga Dink … Ha wot – dees is wot – ?? Dees is *America* – Yi Yi Yi – Queeck, boyiss, hev preented on de beezness cods – "Countinants deescovered – while you wiat – Eef you are plizzed tal de Quinn – If not tal oss."

At the turn of the century, Henry James, who was fascinated by these new immigrants, visited the Lower East Side. Reflecting on the impact of the new Americans on the language of which he was such a master, James observed that "whatever we shall know it for . . . we shall not know it for English", a point of view still shared by some conservatives. For better or worse, though, this was the America – brash, prosperous, polyglot but united – that came to Europe in the late spring of 1917 to help the Allies in their slogging-match war with the Kaiser.

"OVER THERE"

Woodrow Wilson, who had campaigned only a year before for a second presidential term on the slogan *He Kept Us Out of War!*, had finally made common cause with Great Britain and declared war on 6 April 1917. That same day the songwriter George M. Cohan, having read the headlines in the newspaper, sat down and wrote the number which brought the "doughboys" – as they were called – to Europe.

> *Over there, over there,*
> *Send the word, send the word, over there,*
> *That the Yanks are coming, the Yanks are coming*
> *The drums rum-tumming everywhere . . .*

The trenches were just another frontier for the American pioneers – two million of them in total, backed up by an American war industry totaling many millions more. For Britons and Americans alike, the war created a host of words and phrases many of which we still use regularly everyday: *bombproof, barrage, camouflage, civvy, convoy, dud, red tape, sabotage, shell shock, tank, no-man's-land, going over the top,* and *digging in.* Now, not for the first time, but more generally than ever before, speakers of British and American English could marvel at the differences in their two vocabularies: *checkers* versus *draughts, elevator* versus *lift, garbage* versus *rubbish, kerosene* versus *paraffin, lumber* versus *timber, mail* versus *post, pants* versus *trousers, sidewalk* versus *pavement, vacation* versus *holiday, wrench* versus *spanner,* and *zero* versus *nought.*

The entry of the United States into the First World War tipped the balance. It was over within eighteen months of Wilson's declaration – before a single American plane had been delivered to the front. Announcing that "the world must be made safe for democracy", Wilson set sail for the Peace Conference in Paris, the first American president to visit Europe while still in office. The point was made. America was a world power; American English a world language. That was 1919. By one of those timely coincidences, the same year saw a hell-raising American journalist publish the first edition of the book – a labor of love – which brings the story of the English language in America to a fitting climax. The book was *The American Language* and its author was H. L. Mencken, as powerful and influential in the United States as G. B. Shaw in Britain. A lifelong columnist with the Baltimore *Sun*, and the scourge of office-holders and frauds, Mencken would analyze and dissect anything that took his fancy, from The Average Man to The Immortality of the Soul – these are just two pieces

125 S. J. Perelman: part of the tradition of American Jewish humor.

126 H.L.Mencken liked to attack anglophile America's "marsh-mallow gentility".

from his own personal selection, *Chrestomathy*, a word that means "a collection of choice passages from an author or authors".

The word was a typical Mencken discovery. He was fascinated by the English language and wrote prodigiously about it. Alistair Cooke recalls supplying him with English equivalents for American cuts of meat, *rump* for "sirloin", and *best end* for "rib chops". When Mencken finally published the results of his inquiries into "the common tongue", his argument was as vigorous as his title. In the first edition, echoing Noah Webster, he stated that British English and American English were two separate languages on divergent paths. With every subsequent edition and its flotilla of critics, the case was modified, but even in the much revised Fourth Edition he was, like the first American revolutionaries, anxious to beat the drum for the language of which he was such a master:

> The American of today is much more honestly English, in any sense that Shakespeare would have understood, than the so-called Standard English of England. It still shows all the characteristics that marked the common tongue in the days of Elizabeth I, and it continues to resist stoutly the policing that ironed out Standard English in the seventeenth and eighteenth centuries.

Mencken's national pride is unmistakable. His was also a single-minded vision, an assertion of American superiority that paid no attention to other national varieties of English. The index of *The American Language*, for example, has only a handful of references to Australia, and none to New Zealand or South Africa. Within a generation, and at the end of another world war, these latest English voices were also demanding to be heard. When in 1945 an Australian writer named Sydney Baker published an account of his country's English, inspired by Mencken he called it *The Australian Language*. The age of the English *languages* was dawning.

127 The Voice of Australia: Dame Edna Everage a.k.a. Barry Humphries.

8

THE ECHOES OF
AN ENGLISH VOICE

In January 1788, at the height of the Australian summer, a fleet of eleven British ships anchored in Botany Bay after an eight-month voyage from the mother country. Just over a thousand people disembarked from this First Fleet, three-quarters of them convicts, sentenced for various crimes, large and small, to a seven-year term in the penal colony of New South Wales. This historic landing of Australia's founding fathers marked the beginning of a new phase in the world journey of English: the settlement of the British Empire.

In the next one hundred years, the English, the Scots and the Irish were to take their mother tongue to some of the furthest places on earth: to New Zealand, to the Cape colony in Southern Africa, to the country then known as Rhodesia, to India, the imperial jewel, to the island fortress of Singapore, to Hong Kong and the China Station, and to the Falkland Islands in the South Atlantic. To this day, Australian, New Zealand, and South African English in particular bear a distinct resemblance. Exported English in the nineteenth century had a common stock: these countries were all first settled by the same kind of people within roughly the same generation.

For many Victorians at home the adventures of explorers like David Livingstone in colonial Africa seemed comparable to the great exploits of Ralegh and the Elizabethans. Charles Kingsley, author of many books, including the famous *Westward Ho!*, wrote with typical enthusiasm of "brave young England longing to wing its way out of its island prison, to discover and to traffic, to colonize and to civilize, until no wind can sweep the earth which does not bear the echoes of an English voice".

Traders, soldiers, sailors, missionaries, settlers and explorers: in the years between the Battle of Waterloo (1815) and the outbreak of the American Civil War (1860), some seven million people left the British Isles, drawn or driven by a tangle of motives, personal, economic, or social. Many were the casualties of the industrial cataclysm that transformed Victorian society. About half went to the new United States, one and a half million to Canada, another million to Australia, and the rest were scattered across the globe from Tanganyika (now Tanzania) to Siam (now Thailand).

Colonial possessions meant colonial wars. Also scattered across the globe there were "the soldiers of the Queen", defending these new interests against the Burmese, the Pathans in

Afghanistan, the Maoris, the so-called Kaffirs, and the Zulus. Some of these Empire-builders were Irish, especially after the Great Famine of the 1840s, but most were English, from London and the industrial Midlands, and this was the dominant English voice that now began to echo round the world. It was, as the century unfolded, a voice that had two accents – in the idiom of class – "posh" (among officers and imperial civil servants) and "Cockney" (among the troops, or *Tommies*, as they became known).

"THE LONDON LANGUAGE"

In 1899, when the British Empire was at its height, George Bernard Shaw took his first shot at the pretensions of English speech in *Captain Brassbound's Conversion*. Although the play has been overshadowed by the later, and more successful, *Pygmalion*, it exhibits all Shaw's special fascination with the class geography of London talk. At the end of the published text Shaw addresses himself to perhaps the most famous characteristic of London talk, the silent or dropped "aitch".

> I should say that in England he who bothers about his *h*s is a fool, and he who ridicules a dropped *h* is a snob. As to the interpolated *h*, my experience as a London vestryman has convinced me that it is often effective as a means of emphasis, and that the London language would be poorer without it.

This "London language" has deep historical roots. The word *cockney* – from *coken-ay*, a cock's egg, an inferior or worthless thing – is as old as Chaucer, and the original use of Cockney had little to do with the idea of "bad English". In the sixteenth century, Cockney was simply the language of all Londoners who were not part of the Court, and was spoken by all sorts and conditions of people, craftsmen, clerks, shopkeepers and tradesmen. One of these, a funeral furnisher named Henry Machyn, kept a diary, and it is clear from the spellings he uses that he was talking "the London language". He left *h*s off words because he never heard people pronounce them. So "half" appears as *alffe*, and *Ampton* is Machyn's spelling of "Hampton". Many of his other spellings suggest Cockney: *frust* for "thrust", *farding* for "farthing", and *Fever stone* for "Featherstone". He would also add a *t* to make *orphant* and *sermont*. For the words we know as "chains", "strange" and "obtain", he wrote *chynes*, *strynge*, and *obtyn*. Henry Machyn's English had its roots in the Anglo-Saxon regions of East Mercia, East Anglia and Kent, the English of Shakespeare's Mistress Quickly, and later of Sam Weller in *Pickwick Papers*. It was the speech of the working Londoner.

The transformation of Cockney into the working-class speech of East London, and its gradual redefinition as "low", "ugly" or "coarse", occurred in the eighteenth century, the age of Samuel Johnson and "correct English". The same economic forces that created a market for dictionaries and books of etiquette transformed the City into the square mile of money and trade it is today. The old City dwellers – street traders, artisans, and guildworkers – were driven out. They took their distinctive accents to the docklands of Wapping and Shoreditch, and across the river to Bermondsey. They were joined by refugees from the now middle-class West End, as the new Georgian squares and terraces of Bloomsbury and Kensington displaced the working population. At the same time, the gathering momentum of the industrial revolution was depopulating the neighbouring countryside of Essex, Suffolk, Kent and Middlesex, sending tens of thousands of destitute farmworkers to the East End in search of work. These country immigrants now added their speech traditions to "the London language".

The situation of spoken English in London at the end of the eighteenth century was neatly summarized by Thomas Sheridan, whose definition of the Irish brogue and criticisms of Scottish "rusticity" we noted earlier:

> Two different modes of pronunciation prevail, by which the inhabitants of one part of the town are distinguished from those of the other. One is current in the City, and is called the cockney; the other at the court end, and is called the polite pronunciation.

That "polite pronunciation" was now coming much closer to the language the southern English middle class speaks today. In the words of a contemporary lexicographer, Standard English was now based on "the general practice of men of letters and polite speakers in the Metropolis". One of the most distinctive changes was the now widespread lengthening of the vowel in words like *fast* and *path*. The long *a* became, and has remained, one of the

128 John Keats, the ostler's son, was attacked in his lifetime as a "Cockney poet", meaning that he was a Londoner.

129 Herman Melville is famous for *Moby Dick*. His rendering of Victorian Cockney speech is one of the most reliable.

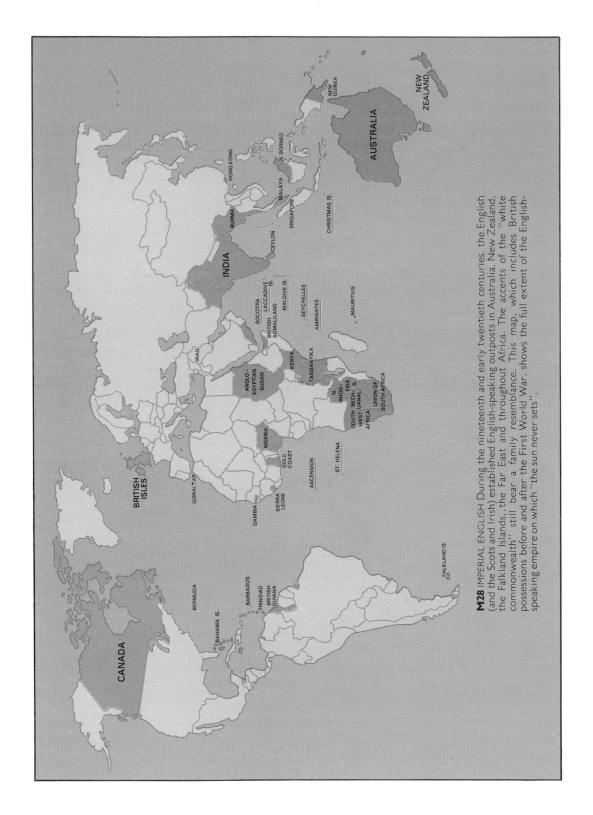

M28 IMPERIAL ENGLISH During the nineteenth and early twentieth centuries, the English (and the Scots and Irish) established English-speaking outposts in Australia, New Zealand, the Falkland Islands...the Far East and throughout Africa. The accents of the "white commonwealth" still bear a family resemblance. This map, which includes British possessions before and after the First World War, shows the full extent of the English-speaking empire on which "the sun never sets".

Map labels: NEW GUINEA; NEW ZEALAND; AUSTRALIA; HONG KONG; N. BORNEO; MALAYA; SINGAPORE; CHRISTMAS IS.; BURMA; CEYLON; INDIA; SOCOTRA; LACCADIVE IS.; MALDIVE IS.; BRITISH SOMALILAND; SEYCHELLES; AMIRANTES; MAURITIUS; IRAQ; KENYA; TANGANYIKA; ANGLO EGYPTIAN SUDAN; N. RHOD-ESIA; S. RHODESIA; BECH-UANAL-AND; SOUTH WEST AFRICA; UNION OF SOUTH AFRICA; NIGERIA; GOLD COAST; ST. HELENA; ASCENSION; GIBRALTAR; BRITISH ISLES; GAMBIA; SIERRA LEONE; BERMUDA; BAHAMA IS.; BARBADOS; TRINIDAD; BRITISH GUIANA; FALKLAND IS.; CANADA distinguishing features of upper- and upper middle-class English speech, the backbone of BBC English, and the inspiration for the famous lyric, "I say tomato and you say tomahto". Another change occurred to words with *oi* like "boiled", "coiled", and "soiled". These previously had been pronounced *biled*, *kiled*, and *siled*, pronunciations which are now, oddly enough, popularly attributed to the British Royal Family. Words like "certain", "learn", and "merchant", for which the "correct" pronunciation had been *sartin*, *larn* and *marchant*, lost their characteristic *ar*, with a few anomalous exceptions like *clerk* and *Derby*. The *r* which is such a mark of American speech, continued to weaken. "More" became *maw*, "harbour" became *hahbah*, and so on. And the *r* at the end of a word like *orator* became what the English critic Raymond Williams has called "a mere glide of the voice" – the distinguishing mark of English in the public schools, the imperial Civil Service, and finally the BBC. At the same time, the received idea of a Cockney became steadily more contemptuous. By the turn of the century, writers like Leigh Hunt and William Hazlitt were scornfully referred to as "Cockney Homers and Virgils". John Keats, the ostler's son, was known, at least to *Blackwood's Magazine*, as the "Cockney poet". Such references were social rather than phonetic. A Cockney was merely a lower-class Londoner who spoke the city's language. The speech of East Enders may have been implicitly despised or laughed at, but it was not labelled "Cockney" in the way that it is today.

It was the Education Acts of the late-Victorian years, with their emphasis on "correct English" and the three Rs, that isolated the speech of the London working class. In the poverty-stricken East End these educational reforms made little impact: the speech of the district remained unreformed. By the turn of the century, it was fast becoming the Cockney of caricature and stereotype. Now we find Shaw, among others, referring to the "Cockney dialect". Only then did Cockney become synonymous with a way of talk as well as with a way of life. The appearance of Eliza Doolittle in *Pygmalion* with her "kerbstone English" of *flars* and *garn* (go on) and *Ay-ee*, *Ba-yee*, *Cy-ee* (A, B, C), consummated the marriage of East End and Cockney.

As the speech of working London began to grow apart from "polite English" it began to attract the attention of many Victorian writers. The first novelist to attempt a rendering of the street-talk with which he had grown up was Charles Dickens – and by all accounts he got it badly wrong. The most famous Dickensian Cockney of them all, Sam Weller, spoke a language which probably has little to do with the streets round Bow Bells. The most famous Wellerism, which has survived in strip-cartoon Cockney to the present day, is the indiscriminate swapping of *w* for *v*, as in: "Bevare of vidders", and "A double glass o' the inwariable", and in sentences like: "I've told her how I'm sitivated; she's ready to wait till I'm ready and I believe she vill."

According to the latest study of Cockney, *The Muvver Tongue*, written by two Cockneys, Robert Barltrop (ex-boxer, schoolteacher, sign-painter and now freelance writer) and Jim Wolveridge (the son of a costermonger who today runs a bookstall in Whitechapel Market), there is not much evidence that Cockneys ever spoke like Sam Weller. If the *v/w* phenomenon has any historical basis, it would be in the "vulgar speech" of London generally. In this there were distinct rules. The exchange of *w* for *v*, as in the *wery* of music-hall songs, is authentic, and apparently persisted in East Anglian speech until very – *wery* – recently. The swapping of *v* for *w* is not. When Sam Weller says, "Vell, if this don't beat cock-fightin', nothin' ever vill, as the Lord Mayor said, ven the chief secretary o' state proposed his missis' health arter dinner", Dickens is truly taking us into the realms of fiction.

If there is a literary representation of Cockney to be trusted it comes from outsiders like Jack London in *The People of the Abyss* or, even earlier, Herman Melville in his second novel, *Omoo*. In this, a landlubber named Rope Yarn is teased for his Cockney speech and ways: if he were back in London, what would he have for breakfast?

> "Well, then", said he, in a smugged tone, his eyes lighting up like two lanterns, "well, then, I'd go to Mother Mill's that makes the great muffins: I'd go there, you know, and cock my foot on the 'ob and call for a noggin o' somethink to begin with."
> "And what then, Ropey?"
> "What then, Flashy", continued the poor victim, unconsciously warming up to his theme; "why then, I'd draw my chair up and call for Betty, the gal wot tends to the customers. Betty, my dear, says I, you looks charmin' this mornin'; give me a nice rasher of bacon and h'eggs, Betty, my love; and I wants a pint of h'ale, and three nice hot muffins and butter – and a slice of Cheshire; and Betty, I wants – "

Melville, writing in mid-century, is an important witness to the emergence of modern Cockney. By the 1880s and 1890s late-Victorian philanthropists and social reformers, following in the footsteps of Henry Mayhew, had discovered what they called the "East End" with a vengeance, a place they found to be "as unexplored as Timbuctoo".

"BORN WITHIN THE SOUND OF BOW BELLS"

The old saying "born within the sound of Bow Bells", does not refer to the Bow of the East End, but to St Mary Le Bow, in Cheapside, in the heart of the City of London, some distance from what is now known as the East End. Traditionally, the East End starts at Aldgate, and runs along Commercial Road and Whitechapel Road as far as the River Lea. It takes in Stepney, Limehouse, Bow, Old Ford, Whitechapel and Bethnal Green. The heart of Cockneyland, though not its geographical centre, is Poplar. In the words of Barltrop and Wolveridge, "as well as being a locality, it is an attitude of mind". Stripped of all the legends, Cockney means East End working class. You can be "born within the sound of Bow Bells" and have no claims to be Cockney.

The life of the street was crucial to the making of late-Victorian Cockney. The close-knit rural communities of East Anglia, Kent and Middlesex from which the majority of East Enders came kept their oral traditions alive on the streets, and in the ale houses and wash houses of Limehouse and Stratford East. When the rural poor were crammed together in the slums of the East End many of the conditions in which the oral tradition of the countryside had flourished were intensified. There was no privacy; everything happened on the street; they were isolated in a particular part of London, not least by the twists and turns of the River Thames. The tradition of spoken English lives on to this day, as Bob Barltrop puts it:

> If there's anything that distinguishes the Cockney, it's his sheer enjoyment of words. He loves to stand them on end and make them jump through hoops and turn circles . . . There's nothing better to a Cockney than to talk – to talk enjoyably, to talk colourfully, to use wonderful phrases. That's Cockney.

This love of nuance, rhythm, word-play and innovation is part of the explanation for the persistent rule-breaking in some elements of Cockney grammar. Some phrases simply *sound* better when the grammar (strictly speaking) is wrong. "That ain't got nothing to do with it" is much more emphatic than the Standard English "That has nothing to do with it".

What does Cockney sound like? Undoubtedly, it has changed since its Victorian days. Then it was, apparently, thinner and reedier in sound. Older Cockneys still say *gardin* for "garden", *year'oles* for "earholes" and *chimbley* for "chimney". There is a continuity in the pronunciation of *th*, which is often replaced by *f*, as in *barf* for "bath", or by *v*, as in *bruvver* for "brother" or *bovver* for "bother". The related loss to this is the "glottal stop", the neglect of the *t* in words like "butter", "bottle", "rotten" which in Cockney can best be represented as *bu!er, bo!le, ro!en*. Similarly, "didn't" becomes *didn* and "haven't" turns into *'avn*. The only alternative to the redundant *t* is *d*, as in *geddoud of i'*, or *you bedder no'*. The characteristic for which Cockney is famous, of course, is the silent *h*. Barltrop points out the dropped *h* has nothing to do with ignorance. He tells the story of the child reading a picture-book with its father. They turn the page and the father says: "That's an 'edgeog. It's really two words. Edge and og. They both start with an aitch."

Then there is a whole class of speech characteristics which betray the rural roots of Cockney. For instance, it is very common to find the *g* missing from *ing* endings like: *eatin'*, and *drinkin'*. This is precisely the speech of Fielding's Squire Western and his heirs in English literature. Even now it is fashionable, in certain parts of the English shires, to talk about *shootin'* or *fishin'*. Similarly, the Cockney pronunciation of "gone", "off" and "cough" (*gorn, orf,* and *corf*) is still used by upper-class country speakers without a trace of class-shame. The characteristic long *o, oo,* for *ew,* almost certainly originated in East Anglia: so it is no surprise that Cockneys and Americans have a number of pronunciations in common, including the *oo* for *ew*. Cockneys say *stoo* for "stew", *nood* for "nude", *noos* for "news", just like many Americans. In some respects, Cockney preserves in a vital form uses of English eradicated by education and the drive towards standardization.

Cockneys will drop letters and slur words in many different ways. "Old" becomes *ol'*. "An" becomes *ern*, as in *ern afternoon*. "You", as everyone who has attempted to render Cockney in print knows, is *yer*. The *o* in words like "tomato" and "potato" becomes *er*, as in *barrer* for "barrow". The main shopping street in Hackney, the Narrow Way, is known as the

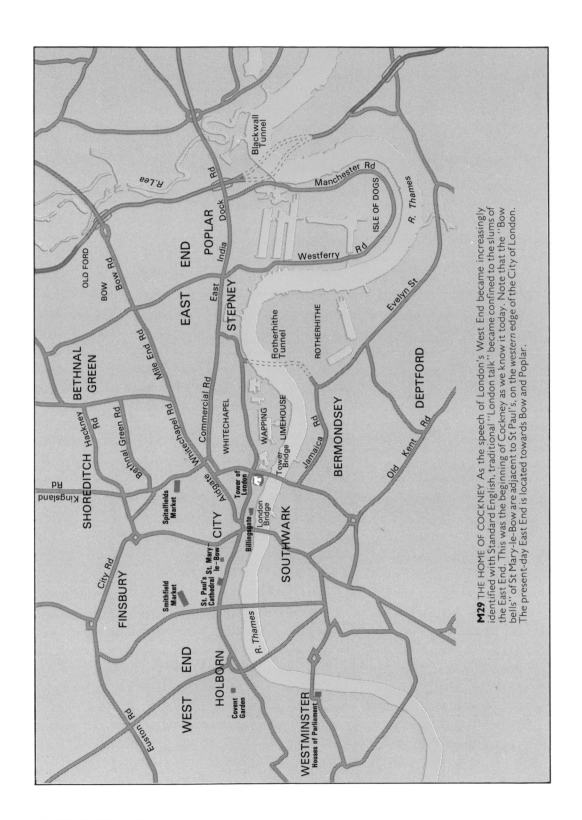

M29 THE HOME OF COCKNEY As the speech of London's West End became increasingly identified with Standard English, traditional "London talk" became confined to the slums of the East End. This was the beginning of Cockney as we know it today. Note that the "Bow bells" of St Mary-le-Bow are adjacent to St Paul's, on the western edge of the City of London. The present-day East End is located towards Bow and Poplar.

Narraway. Words get run together in Cockney. "God help us" becomes *gawdelpus*, and "God blind me" becomes *gorblimey*. Lesser examples like *lotta* for "lot of" pop up in unlikely places. A recent British Milk Marketing Board campaign played on Cockney slang and pronunciation – and an implicit toughness – with the copy-line *Gotta lotta bottle*.

One element of Cockney that has permeated the mainstream of the language is rhyming slang: *a bull and a cow* for "a row", and *Cain and Abel* for "a table". The popular view which holds that Cockney is, essentially, composed of this comes from the music-hall image of the Cockney – the cheeky chappy, with a heart of gold and a joke on his lips, who shows true grit in hard times and knows how to have a party when the day is over. In fact, until the 1930s, the currency of rhyming slang was quite small – Shaw, for instance, never used it. For many Cockneys, it was merely cheerful word play, in which a "suit" became a *whistle and flute*, a "hat" was a *titfer* or *tit-for-tat*, "gloves" were *turtles*, or *turtle-doves* and "boots" were *daisies* or *daisyroots*. Rhyming slang was also used as a form of euphemism: *in the rude* for "nude", and *Bristols* for "breasts" (Bristol City = titty). Some famous examples of rhyming slang also have an undertone of comment – *trouble and strife* (wife), *holy friar* (liar), and *bees and honey* (money). *Rabbit*, which is short for *rabbit and pork* (talk), has now passed into the mainstream of English in the common phrase *rabbiting on*. When the entertainment industry took hold of rhyming slang, however, and put it in the mouths of Cockney characters like Alf Garnett and Arthur "Arfur" Daley, it became elevated into a kind of Cockney code. Bob Barltrop is clear about the myth:

> Everybody knows about rhyming slang. It's very much overdone. A lot of the slang you hear is just the invention of scriptwriters. By the way, it wasn't confined to Cockneys. In the past all kinds of people used it. One of the characteristics of Cockney is to pick up what other people have thrown away and preserve it.

Despite the overstatement, rhyming slang *does* exist, and is springing up all the time. When Edward Heath was prime minister *heath* became rhyming slang for "teeth", prominent features in the premier's smile. More recently, a *John Selwyn* became rhyming slang for a *bummer*, "a bad situation", after the then Chairman of the Conservative Party, John Selwyn Gummer. Another kind of slang that has largely escaped the pens of the scriptwriters is back slang:

> In the middle of the nineteenth century back slang was used as a secret language by street traders and costermongers. The people who use it now are mostly butchers and Thames lightermen. Instead of saying numbers like "one" and "two", you say "eno" and "rouf" and "evif" and "xis". Instead of saying "an old woman", you say "a delo namow". Instead of saying someone's fat, you say they're "taf" ... "Yob" is the best known back slang word. It simply means "boy". "Yobbo" is a different thing. "Yobbo" is the Irishman's "boyo" backwards, and a "boyo" is a fellow who hangs about street corners, one of the lads, a larrikin.

HENRY MAYHEW.

[*From a Daguerreotype by* BEARD.]

130 Henry Mayhew, who wrote about "Irish Cock-neys", did not attribute a specific accent to East Enders.

131 George Borrow's *Romany Rye* has gypsy dialogue, phrases like "Oi, mush".

Cockney survives, but the East End is not what it was. The Blitz flattened much of the area and dealt a body-blow to the London docks, a vital source of local livelihood. The urban planning of the 1960s and 1970s, in particular the creation of high-rise flats, accelerated the erosion of the old community and its traditions. But some aspects of the Cockney way of life die hard: the market at Spitalfields, which has a history running back to the days of Charles II, still does brisk business each morning. Market gardeners and greengrocers trade in fruit and vegetables in the early hours of the morning, as they have for generations. Artie Welsh is a salesman for Mays, the wholesalers.

> When you're serving two or three people at the same time you'll be allowing maybe two or three different prices out as well. I'll talk slang to the bloke who understands it. I'll be talking to someone. I'll say, "Right, George, you can be a rouf there." And he knows I've sold to him at four pounds, and the other person who's buying at five doesn't know.

The numbers have their equivalent in slang. *Nicker* is "one", *bottle* is "two", *carpet* is "three", *rouf* is "four", *jacks* is "five", *Tom Nicks* is "six", *neves* is "seven", *garden gate* is "eight", "ten" is *cock-and-hen*, or *cockle*.

Artie Welsh is surrounded by true Cockneys, all making things up as they go along:

There's no rules. The other day this bloke said, "Do they come to an Alan Whicker then?" Meaning "nicker", which is a pound. That's not a registered slang term, but I knew what he meant ... I get a greengrocer come along. Refers to tomatoes as "Herbert" – Herbert Lom/Tom – Tomatoes.

One of Artie's best customers is George Bonner, who runs a successful fruit and vegetable stall with his brothers in Walthamstow Market. George goes to Spitalfields every morning in the small hours to buy his goods for the day. It is a way of life. He has a laugh with his mates, does the round of the wholesalers, bargaining for a good price, and around three in the morning buys a bowl of jellied eels from Teddy's stall. George has his own Cockney lingo like everyone else:

They'll say, "Morning, George, how's the tomato job this morning? What's trumpy?" Trumpy means short, that's to say, is anything dear (expensive) this morning. Another word that's used a lot in the market is "a cow's". A "cow's calf" is a half. "Do you want a cow's for that?"

Back at his stall in Walthamstow Market, George relies on a very effective patter routine to sell his goods. This is known as "getting an edge".

To get an edge, means you're getting people to line up. You can do it a lotta ways. You lark about, or you come out wiv big words, or I usually say, "You're getting me in a right mucking fuddle." That's to pull an edge. You also pull an edge by cutting an orange, showing people what they're like and giving 'em tasters ... People are like sheep. If they see somebody line up they get on the end of the queue. They think to themself: Well, that's got to be good. Once you got people there, you'll have a trade wiv 'em. They stop. And when you get an edge you say "Oi, 'ere's acky, facky, lacky". They think its's swearing, but it means nothing. This is the way we are. We get an edge by that ... By Saturday night I'm absolutely knackered!

Cockney is as magpie-minded as Standard English. It has borrowed widely: from the Empire, from the gypsies, from the English Jews, from the two World Wars, and, indeed, from any outsider who came up with a word that caught the popular fancy. For instance, *skive*, widely attributed to the Cockneys, a now well-established word for "shirk" or "play truant", is a local Lincolnshire word.

From the armies of the British Empire, stationed in India and the Far East, Cockney picked up words like *buckshee*, the Cockney word for "free", strictly speaking "surplus", or "going a-begging". *Doolally*, from Deolali (a town near Bombay and site of a mental hospital for British troops), is "demented", "barmy". "Let's have a *shufti*", a Hindustani word, means "let's have a look around". One piece of rhyming slang, *khyber* for "backside", came from the British soldiers stationed on the Khyber Pass.

Romany became part of Cockney in the nineteenth century as the population of East

London grew. Gypsy traders – known as *pikeys* – brought their stalls and set up street markets, creating what one writer called a perpetual fair in Whitechapel Road. From the gypsies, Cockney derives words like *mush* (mouth or face), as in *Oi, mush*, meaning, "Here, mate". This Romany derivation is found in the mouths of the gypsies in the novels of George Borrow (*Romany Rye*, for instance). *Pucker*, meaning "to talk", is also Romany, so is *chavvy*, "a child". Romany lingo survives in Cockney talk to this day. As Bob Barltrop says:

> A word that everybody knows is "pal" for friend. This is actually the Romany word for brother. "Dukes" is for hands, and this is the Cockney's favourite word for them, as in "Give us your dukes, mate." Romany palm-reading is called "dukering".

Many Cockney expressions have Yiddish roots. The Jewish community in the East End flourished throughout the last century and reached its cultural peak in the the years before the First World War. Cockney trader and Jewish manufacturer have worked alongside for generations. *Shemozzle*, a favourite Cockney word for "confusion", is obviously Jewish. So is *stumer* for "a dead loss", *schmutter* for "clothing" and *schlemiel* for "an idiot". *Clobber* (clothes) has Yiddish roots; so does *gelt* for "money", and *nosh* for "food". *Gezumph* meaning to swindle has now passed into the lexicon as *gazump*, familiar in estate agencies throughout the land. *Spiel* originates, in Britain, in the East End; so does *donah* for woman. Both have obvious Yiddish roots. All Cockneys know – and still use – *mazel tov* for "good luck".

Finally, the World Wars added their store of words (mainly French) to the Cockney vocabulary. A *parlyvoo* (from *parlez-vous*) still means "a talking session". *San fairy ann* for "it doesn't matter" (from *ça ne fait rien*) is still common. So is *ally toot sweet* (from *allez tout de suite* i.e. "hurry up"). *Bullshit*, a Services word, originally meaning "humbug", has now been intensified to mean "rubbish", "lies", "nonsense". It entered the mainstream of the language through army use in the Second World War.

Part of the Cockney fascination with all kinds of languages comes from what Bob Barltrop calls their love of "grand sounding words to which they can attach a special meaning, words which you can say really majestically". Barltrop has three favourite examples:

> "Diabolical" – and not just "a diabolical liberty". If you can say with presence, "that's absolutely dia-bol-ical, innit", that sounds great. Another word of which Cockneys are immensely fond is "impunity", as in "He walks in and out of 'ere with impunity." Yet another is "chronic". "Chronic" is associated with a long illness, something that goes on for a long time and is terribly painful. So if you ask your friend what the film was like and he didn't enjoy it, he will say, "Gorblimey, it was chronic."

Two elements of Cockney English which were exported directly to Australia were swearing and greetings. (We are not, of course, suggesting that swearing is unique to Cockneys and Australians, but that their *style* and *expression* have common features.) With

132 Australia was settled by the British as a penal colony. These origins prejudiced observers against Australian English from the first.

swearing, it is important to draw a distinction between obscenity and vulgarity. For the Cockney, as for everyone else, there are distinct rules about what is "acceptable" and what is not. For instance, *arse* (widely used) is acceptable, so, in the right context, is *sod* ("He's a cheeky young sod"). But *fuck*, to cite the most obvious, is not. The universal use of *bleeding* and *bugger* make them almost universally acceptable. *Bugger* is freely used to denote a bad person. *You bugger!* – unless there is a note of admiration – will always mean *you shit!* or *you swine! Bugger me!* is for astonishment. *Bugger off* need only mean "go away". *Bugger-all*, as in "won bugger-all at the Derby" means "little" or "nothing"

The distinctive greetings of Cockney include *'Ow're yer goin'* meaning "How are you doing?" "How's things?" "What's new?" Of all the identifying words attached to such questions – from *mate* to *guvnor*, to *chum*, *cock*, *dear*, *love* and *duck*, the most important is probably *mate*, associated with Cockney and Australian English throughout the world. *Mate* covers all relationships that are important, after the family ones (but including wives). A "mate" is more than a friend: it suggests a mutuality and closeness beyond mere friendship. After mate, there are *the mates*, the people you mix with socially.

For all the Londoners and other city folk, Irish immigrants, landless labourers, debtors, hustlers and swindlers who headed for the colonies throughout the nineteenth century, the idea of friendship in adversity, of mates, of pals, even of chums, was fundamental to the experience of exile. New South Wales, New Zealand, and the Cape colony: these were all harsh, unfamiliar environments. And not since the Anglo-Saxons landed in Britain, or the Elizabethans in North America, was there such a need or such an opportunity for word and phrase-making.

THE LANDSCAPE OF DISCOVERY

The story of Australian English starts, appropriately enough, with *kangaroo*. In 1770, when Captain James Cook sailed his ship, *Endeavour*, into the Endeavour River in what is now the state of Queensland his experience was similar to John White's at the Roanoke settlement in North Carolina, in 1584. The first language created by both those historic landings was pidgin. Cook wrote down a number of the Aboriginal words he found useful in his negotiations with the Endeavour River tribes, including the famous *kangaroo*. But like so many European explorers of "primitive" societies, Cook underestimated the sophistication of Aboriginal culture and he did not recognize that there were hundreds of Aboriginal languages. He made his glossary available to later explorers on the assumption that he had been dealing with a monolingual society. When the First Fleet arrived in Port Jackson in 1788 to establish the first penal colony, Governor Philip armed himself with Cook's vocabulary in the hope that he could make friends with the natives. But he soon discovered that the Port Jackson tribes spoke something that was "totally different" from the Endeavour River language. Far from recognizing *kangaroo*, the Port Jackson Aborigines treated the word as a white man's term and applied it indiscriminately to the sheep and cattle that earlier English arrivals had brought with them. The story of *kangaroo* becomes still more confusing. A few years later, another expedition returned to the Endeavour River area, again with Captain Cook's glossary of local words. This time they discovered that although the natives responded to some of the terms in Cook's vocabulary, they did not recognize *kangaroo* as the word for the celebrated marsupial. Like many of the most interesting words in the English language, its origins remain disputed.

Visitors to the new colony soon noticed the pidgin English that was quickly springing up between settler and Aborigine. Less than ten years after the disembarkation of the First Fleet, one new arrival observed that "Nothing but a barbarous mixture of English with the Port Jackson dialect is spoken by either party." The Aboriginal vocabulary of this "barbarous mixture" has now become one of the trademarks of Australian English. The most familiar lines of "Waltzing Matilda" depend on Aboriginal words like *billabong* (a waterhole), and *jumbuck* (a sheep). Other well-known borrowings include *corroboree* (originally an Aboriginal assembly, now any large or noisy gathering), *boomerang* (Australia's curved throwing stick), and perhaps *budgerigar* (from *budgeree*, "good" and *gar*, "parrot").

The Aborigines' contact with the white man was intermittent. The "black boy" and the "black stockman" are part of Australian legend, but they were actually a minority: most Aborigines steered clear of the White settlers. The number of Aboriginal words in Australian English is quite small (though perhaps larger than thought) and is confined to the naming of plants (like *bindieye* and *calombo*), trees (like *boree* and *mallee*), birds (like *currawong* and *kookaburra*), animals (like *wallaby* and *wombat*) and fish (like *barramundi*). As in North America, when it came to place-names the Aboriginal influence was much greater: with a vast new continent to name, about a third of all Australian place-names are Aboriginal. In 1824, the poet J. D. Lang composed this jingle:

> *I like the native names, as Parramatta,*
>   *And Illawarra, and Wolloomooloo,*
> *Nandowra, Woogarora, Bulkomatta,*
>   *Tomah, Toonggabbie, Mittagong, Meroo;*
> *Buckobble, Cumleroy, and Coolangatta,*
>   *The Warragumby, Bargo, Burradoo;*
> *Cookbundoon, Carrabaiga, Wingecarribee,*
>   *The Wollondilly, Yurumbon, Bugarribbee.*

The Aborigines themselves contributed pidgin words that we think of as distinctively Australian. The *Sydney Gazette* of 1828, describing the execution of an Aborigine, gives the first recorded use of the typically Australian word *walkabout*:

> When the executioner had adjusted the rope, and was about to pull the cap over his eyes, he exclaimed, with a most pitiful expression of countenance, "Murry me jerran", I am exceedingly afraid, and immediately afterwards, casting his eyes wistfully around him, and giving a melancholy glance at the apparatus of death, he said, in a tone of deep feeling, which it was impossible to hear without strong emotion, "Bail (no) more walkabout," meaning that his wanderings were over now.

The Aborigines also adopted words from maritime pidgin English, words like *piccaninny* and *bilong* (belong). They used familiar pidgin English variants like *talkum* and *catchum*. Some English words even gained an extra lease of life among the Aborigines. The most famous example is *gammon*, an eighteenth-century Cockney word meaning " a lie". *Gammon* was rapidly adopted by the Aborigines who developed it into a verb. The word then gradually dropped out of everyday White Australian talk but continued to flourish among the Black community. Now, according to anthropologists working in the Northern Territory, *gammon* is coming back into the English of the region, re-borrowed from the Aborigines.

The belief that the Aborigines in Australia are mostly confined to the remote semi-desert regions of the North is misleading. In fact, nearly half live in the south-east corner of the continent, while one in ten live in Sydney – mainly in two communities, Redfern and La Perouse. Here, especially among the schoolchildren, the use of old Aboriginal words like *gowan/gwangy* (stupid), *wadjema* (white girl), *wullung/walland* (money), and *gungie* (police-man), has almost died out. This does not mean that the Aboriginal children are speaking standard Australian English. Far from it. In the context of everyday Aboriginal society, an accurate reproduction of Australian speech is profoundly unacceptable. In places like Redfern such talk is known as *flash language*. An Aboriginal teacher's assistant explains that "If you talk . . . you know, *flash* as they call it at home, that's what they think you are trying to be: stuck up or something, you know, and you've got to talk on their level." A colleague adds, "You've got to have two lots of English in other words: one for home and one for school." There is an irony in this use of *flash* language: unwittingly, it is the Aboriginal community, not the Whites, which has preserved one of the first descriptions of convict English in Australia.

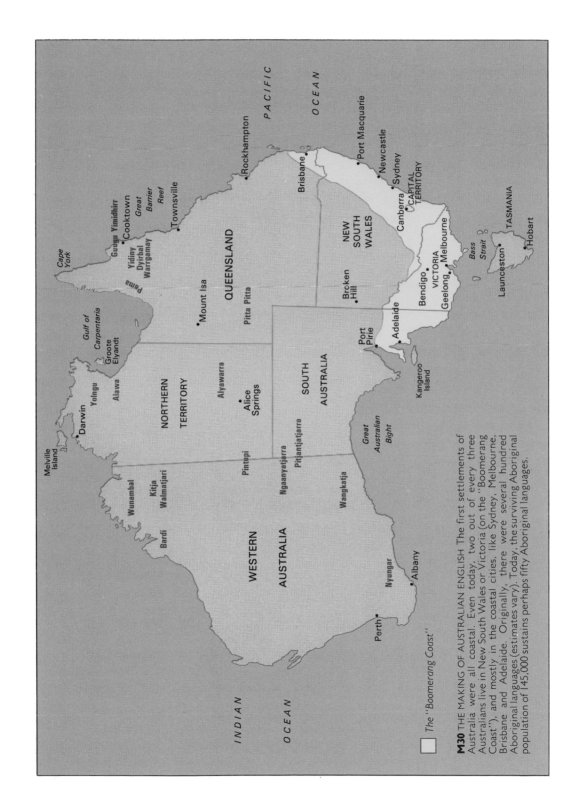

The "Boomerang Coast"

M30 THE MAKING OF AUSTRALIAN ENGLISH The first settlements of Australia were all coastal. Even today, two out of every three Australians live in New South Wales or Victoria (on the "Boomerang Coast"), and mostly in the coastal cities, like Sydney, Melbourne, Brisbane and Adelaide. Originally, there were several hundred Aboriginal languages (estimates vary). Today, the surviving Aboriginal population of 145,000 sustains perhaps fifty Aboriginal languages.

133/134 Aborigines in New South Wales and a mining camp in "the bush".

"THE FLASH LANGUAGE"

Apart from the Aborigines, an estimated 300,000 in 1788, Australia was an empty continent, remote, vast, inhospitable and different in practically every way from its colonial motherland, "a scene too rich for the pencil to portray" wrote one new arrival. The words of E. E. Morris, a nineteenth-century pioneer in the study of Australian English, are hardly an exaggeration:

> It is probably not too much to say that there never was an instance in history when so many new words were needed, and that there never will be such an occasion again, for never did settlers come, nor can they ever come again, upon Flora and Fauna so completely different from anything seen by them before.

Like the first settlers in the United States, the first Australians put some under-employed English words to good use. *Creek*, which at that time meant "an estuary, or arm of the sea", was now applied very widely to streams and watercourses. *Paddock*, which had a similarly restricted meaning in England, was now extended to describe a wide variety of enclosed land. Some typical Australianisms, like *bludger* (originally "a low thief", now "one who evades his responsibilities and imposes on others") evolved from a highly restricted slang use, often criminal. In the early days, it was a makeshift language. The convicts, mostly from an urban, industrial society, were dumped into an empty landscape and thrown back on to their own resources. Words, like things, had to serve many functions. *Back*, for example, has dozens of uses in Australian English, from *back-block* to *outback*. So do *station* and *stock*. It was a frontier society, and its spirit was expressed in its language.

The "settlers" that Morris referred to have, in the past, been the subject of some Australian neurosis. It is now widely – almost proudly – accepted, as Russell Ward, author of *The Australian Legend*, puts it, that "for nearly the first half of its existence White Australia was, primarily, an extensive gaol". Nearly two generations after the First Fleet arrived in

Botany Bay, a staggering 87 per cent of the Australian population were either convicts, ex-convicts or of convict descent.

In the late eighteenth and early nineteenth centuries, the overcrowding and poverty in Liverpool, Manchester, Leeds and London were appalling. In desperate circumstances, people turned to crime. Transportation to Botany Bay was the solution to the overcrowded prisons. The early chapters of Dickens' *Great Expectations* vividly depict the effects of this system: convicts like Magwitch hounded by the law, the prison hulks lying at anchor in the Thames, and an atmosphere of forlorn desperation pervading those who were about to be transported. The early Australians were largely town- and city-bred petty criminals, often first-generation exiles from the Irish or English countryside.

The first consequence of this process for the language of the new colony was that the convicts who were sent to the transports, like the Irish from Lancashire, had probably begun to lose the most distinct aspects of their speech. As outsiders in a new community, they would already have come under pressure to modify their speech to their changed surroundings. Even more important, all the men on the hulks had criminal slang in common. This convict argot was called "flash" language, and James Hardy Vaux published a collection of it in 1812, the *New and Comprehensive Vocabulary of the Flash Language*.

Vaux, who had the distinction of being transported three times (it was customary for convicts to be released after seven years), claimed "an extensive knowledge" of a subject he described as "obviously disgraceful". Most of the words and phrases he listed remained confined to convict circles and have not passed into the mainstream of Australian English. There are a few exceptions, of which the best known is *swag*, defined by Vaux as stolen "wearing-apparel, linen, or piece-goods". In due course this became standard Australian, "a bundle of personal belongings", and was of course the property of "Banjo" Paterson's "Jolly Swagman" in Australia's unofficial national anthem.

> Once a jolly swagman camped by a billabong,
>   Under the shade of a coolibah tree,
> And he sang as he watched and waited till his billy boiled,
>   "Who'll come a-waltzing Matilda with me?
>   Waltzing Matilda,
>   Waltzing Matilda
>   Who'll come a-waltzing Matilda with me?"
>
> Down came a jumbuck to drink at the billabong:
>   Up jumped the swagman and grabbed him with glee.
> And he sang as he shoved that jumbuck in his tucker-bag,
>   "You'll come a-waltzing Matilda with me.
>   Waltzing Matilda,
>   Waltzing Matilda,
>   You'll come a-waltzing Matilda with me."

Swagman, billabong, billy, jumbuck, tucker-bag and *coolibah tree* are all early Australianisms.

Today, Australian English, famous for its air of novelty, is something of a living museum preserving several eighteenth- and nineteenth-century regional words from Cornwall, Wessex, the Midlands, East Anglia, Northumbria, Scotland and Ireland. To take just a few examples, words like *corker*, *dust-up*, *purler* and *tootsy* all came to Australia from Ireland via the cotton mills of Lancashire. *Billy* comes from the Scottish *bally*, meaning "a milk pail". Australians get *larrikin* from Worcestershire and Warwickshire, where the word originally meant "a mischievous or frolicsome youth". A typical Australianism like *fossick*, meaning "to search unsystematically", is a Cornish word, showing the influence of the Cornish miners who settled in Southern Australia. *Fair dinkum* was known in England before it was exported to the Southern hemisphere. *Stonker*, as in "I'm stonkered", a phrase used by some Australians after a large meal, first had the broader meaning of "to destroy, thwart or put out of action", and came from the Midlands word, *stonk*, "the stake in a game of marbles". *Cobber* almost certainly came from the Suffolk verb *to cob*, "to take a liking to someone". *Tucker*, widely used for "food" had various English origins: Robin Hood's fat colleague, Friar Tuck, is well known, and some English schoolboys still go to "the tuck shop". *Clobber* has Romany roots and is originally recorded in Kent as *clubbered up*, meaning "dressed up".

In the middle of the century, the hectic years of the gold rush in Australia drew prospectors from California to the hills of New South Wales, bringing with them a slew of Americanisms to add to the Australian lexicon. G. C. Mundy's account shows how language responds to such upheavals:

> Sydney assumed an entirely new aspect. The shop fronts put on quite new faces ... The newspapers teemed with advertisements ... "Waterproof tents for the El Dorado" – "Quicksilver for amalgamating gold-soil" – "Superfine biscuits packed in tins" – "Cradles, prospecting pans, galvanized iron buckets, etc." – "Digger's Handbook, or Gold Digger's Guide."

This was the first association of "Australian" with *Digger*, a slang shorthand now known to newspaper headline writers throughout the English-speaking world, as well as being the British nickname for the Australian newspaper proprietor Rupert Murdoch.

The invasion of American vogue words marked the beginning of a tension in Australia between the use of British English and American English. Should an Australian say *biscuit* or *cookie*, *nappy* or *diaper*, *lorry* or *truck*? The answer seems to be that Australian English, like its British ancestor (and like Canadian English), borrows freely according to preference. So Australians get water from a *tap* not a *faucet*, but tend to ride in *elevators* as well as *lifts*. Their cars run on *petrol* not *gas*, but they drive on *freeways* not *motorways*. And the oddest of all borrowings from America is *kangaroo court*.

After all these well-attested derivations, we come to the most controversial Australianism of them all – *pommy*, "an Englishman". In the past, this noun, which probably came into the language just before the First World War, has been given several fanciful etymologies. Perhaps it was a shortening of *pomegranate*, a reference to ruddy-cheeked Englishmen;

perhaps it was based on an improbable acronym, POME, Prisoner of Mother England; or on a corruption of *Tommy*, the British slang for "trooper", or on *Pompey*, the sailors' name for Portsmouth, the British naval base; or perhaps it comes from the Breton *pommé*, a colloquialism meaning "complete, downright, out and out" imported by Cornish miners. For the *Macquarie Dictionary*, the origins of the word were "anyone's guess". Now, at last, it appears that the investigations of Dr W. S. Ramson and his colleagues on the *Australian National Dictionary* have arrived at a definitive explanation. Our evidence (Ramson writes)

> is that *pom* and *pomegranate* were first used of an assisted immigrant from the British Isles in 1912, *pommy* (in the form *pome*) in 1913. The significant thing is that all three first appear in the pages of the Sydney *Truth*. *Jimmygrant*, as rhyming slang for "immigrant" had existed from 1845 in Australian, New Zealand and South African use, but seems to have had a fresh flush of use in *Truth* in 1912. The editor of *Truth* at the time, John Norton, favoured witty and eye-catching headlines and indulged in a lot of word-play. Without any reference to a recent arrival's blushing cheeks being intended, *pomegranate* was adopted as rough rhyming slang for *Jimmygrant* and then shortened to *pom* and *pommy*.

With the importation of British (and American) regional slang words, came a spirit of improvisation typical of an oral, largely working-class culture. This inventiveness has now become a vital part of the Australian legend, and it is expressed most memorably by the same editor of *Truth*, John Norton, who claimed credit for the invention of yet another Australianism, *wowser*, "a prudish teetotaller".

> I invented the word myself. I was the first man publicly to use the word. I first gave it public utterance in the City Council, when I applied it to Alderman Waterhouse, whom I referred to . . . . as the white, woolly, weary, watery, word-wasting wowser from Waverley.

The "truth" is that though Norton may have given currency to the word, he certainly did not invent it. Yet he, and many Australians before and since, remain powerfully wedded to a belief in their virtuoso powers of English. For many, this is typified by the witty backchat of Dame Edna Everage, the hilarious stage persona of comedian Barry Humphries who has been partly responsible for the widespread adoption of Australianisms like *chunder* ("to vomit"). The myth is reinforced by outsiders, British and American especially, who look enviously at technicolor phrases like *come the raw prawn, strain the potatoes*, and *exercise the armadillo*. It is, of course, impossible to measure such "inventiveness". Once the excitement of novelty is forgotten, many aspects of British and American English (Cockney and Yiddish usages, for instance), looked at with the same Martian enthusiasm, can seem to have a not dissimilar "inventiveness". But then there are the facts of Australian heritage: the majority of the first arrivals, Cockneys and Irish, were either traditionally in love with talk or traditionally masters of Blarney.

"THE WILD COLONIAL BOY"

"The Cockneys", in the words of one eye-witness, "are, of course, beyond all dispute the worst, and a leaven of a dozen of these is enough to infect a thousand of the country yokels, with whom peace is generally the order of the day." The writer described the Cockneys' "overwhelming oratorical abilities" and the power this gave them over their duller country cousins. The experience of the Cockneys on the transports was expressed in their own street literature, the ballad. The same commentator described the embarkation of some Australia-bound criminals: "It is curious to observe with what nonchalance some of these fellows will turn the jingling of their chains into music whereto they dance and sing."

To many English officials, this behaviour was merely degenerate. One naval surgeon on the transports reported that it was his maxim "never to permit the slightest slang expression to be used, nor flash songs to be sung, nor swearing", but it seems unlikely that he was very successful. He added wistfully that "it was nearly impossible to restrain their almost unconquerable propensity (for song and swearing) while below". Of all the songs brought to Australia by the convicts, one of the most typical was "Adieu to Old England" or "The Transport's Farewell":

> Come all you wild young native lads
>   Wherever you may be,
> One moment pay attention
>   And listen unto me.
> I am a poor unhappy soul,
>   Within those walls I lay
> My awful sentence is pronounced,
>   I am bound for Botany Bay.

135 Released convicts travelled into what they called "the outback", as drovers, graziers or swagmen.

The luckless convict, having been "brought up in tenderness" by devoted parents, becomes apprenticed to a linen draper, but falls into "a harlot's company". To keep his mistress, the apprentice turns to crime, but is "taken" by the authorities, brought before the judge, a "cruel jade", and sentenced with transportation "to Botany Bay".

The experience of the Cockneys on the transports in many ways reproduced the crowded, oppressed society from which they had been expelled. All the old Cockney codes and customs survived (and were passed on to their non-Cockney fellows). None was more typical of this than the notion of mates, of egalitarian class solidarity. A contemporary novel, *For the Term of His Natural Life* by Marcus Clarke, expresses the idea of "mateship".

> "How many mates had he?" asked Maurice, watching the champing jaws as one looks at a strange animal, and asking the question as though a "mate" was something one was born with – like a mole, for instance.

Another Cockney tradition transported to the settlements of New South Wales was swearing. One writer, comparing Australian youth to their paler London cousins, noted that: "your thoroughbred gumsucker never speaks without apostrophizing his 'oath' and interlarding his diction with the crimsonest of adjectives ... One is struck aghast with the occasional blasphemy of his language". A few years earlier, another had commented:

> The two most glaring vices, intoxication and profane swearing, prevail throughout the interior of New South Wales to an extent hardly conceivable but by those who have actually witnessed it contagious in this particular, the native-born youths often inherit this way of talking and grow gradually callous to its enormity, thus handing down to succeeding generations one of the most pernicious legacies of the old Botany Bay convicts.

The Irish experience has already been described in chapter five. Their contribution to Australian culture is not in question, but (as in the Eastern states of the USA) it is exceptionally hard to define phonetically or linguistically. As we have seen so often in this story, it was the first (and largest) group of exiles whose speech proved dominant in the long run. Indeed, almost within a generation of the first landings, visitors to the New South Wales colony were beginning to notice a distinctive Australian accent. What was happening?

The roots of Australian English lie in the South and East of England (the counties of Norfolk, Suffolk, Essex, Middlesex, Hertfordshire, parts of Bedfordshire, Cambridgeshire, Northamptonshire, and, of course, London), but that cannot be the whole story. There is, for instance, virtually no "glottal stop" in Australian English, nor is the "dropped aitch" a feature of Australian speech. Peter Trudgill, who has studied the way varieties of English collide with each other, has his own theory for this. He points out that in the crucial early years of the settlement there were not only "h-less Londoners and south-easterners, but also entirely h-ful Irish and Scottish speakers (as well as East Anglians, RP speakers, and speakers from a few other small h-ful areas of England)". As with the settlers in the United States, these many voices blended to make the distinctive tones of a new variety of English.

It was the children of the immigrants who lost their parents' Irish, or Midland or Scottish accents within one generation of their arrival in Australia. As early as 1820, one writer observed a distinctive – and, for him, euphonious – type of Australian speech: "The children born in these colonies, and now grown up, speak a better language, purer, and more harmonious, than is generally the case in most parts of England. The amalgamation of such various dialects assembled together, seems to improve the mode of articulating the words."

Another writer, struggling to characterize nascent Australian English, spoke of "a voice of that mixed accent which distinguishes the offspring of Dublin parents of the lowest class born in one of our great English cities". A third, a working man called Harris, arrived in Sydney in 1826. On his first night in the new colony, he went to the taproom of a Market Street tavern. This is his description of the scene:

> Most had been convicts: there were a good many Englishmen and Irishmen, an odd Scotchman, and several foreigners, besides some youngish men, natives of the colony ... The chief conversation consisted of vaunts of the goodness of their bullocks, the productiveness of their farms, or the quantity of work they could perform.

There could hardly be a better description of the Australian language melting-pot at work. The unified nature of Australian speech was emphasized from the beginning by the peculiar social conditions of the colony. Beneath the governor and the overseers, everyone was equal. It was, perforce, a one-class society, united in a mixture of hostility and nostalgia towards Mother England, united especially in the isolation and rigour of Australian life.

Charles Darwin, visiting Sydney in the winter of 1835 on the homeward voyage of the *Beagle*, noticed that even the children of Standard English-speaking colonial officials were affected by the convict talk:

> There are many serious drawbacks to the comforts of a family (in Australia), the chief of which, perhaps, is being surrounded by convict servants ... The female servants are, of course, much worse; hence children learn the vilest expressions ...

Apparently, the Cockney element predominated. Another early visitor to New South Wales noted that "The London mode of pronunciation has been duly ingrafted" on "the colloquial dialect" of young Australians. For some observers it was "more harmonious", but for others it was noticeably different, even inferior: "Pure English is not, and is not likely to become, the language of the Colony."

Once again we discover this new Australian English being forged among the children of the second generation: words like *nick* or *cobber* or *dinkum* would pass rapidly into currency if they found favour among the first Australian children who would have cast off whatever regional accents their parents retained, and abandoned most of their parents' usages in conversation with their peers. One scandalized bush-dweller wrote home that she had "never heard a place with as much 'Slang' in it, as this District – every other word nearly is some 'Colonialism' ". The accents would be levelled. Later generations would imitate what went before.

There was also a profound suspicion of good speech. According to one theory, the convict experience established a false equation in the minds of Australians between careful speech and aspirations to social status. *Lah di dah* talk was seen as "uppity". Research has shown that there are still strong pressures on Australian schoolchildren to "de-articulate", that is, talk "badly". For instance, boys who arrive at school with "proper" speech patterns are liable to be regarded as "cissies" or worse, "poofters".

By the middle of the century, the Australian school authorities had become alarmed at the broad speech patterns used by Australian schoolchildren in a way that now strikes us as absurdly deferential to the British Standard. With Victorian rectitude, they thundered against the general lack of education such English suggested. "This dialect", complained one contemporary, "is coarse, vulgar, and representative of all that is least cultivated." Another had his own views about the "Australian twang" as it was becoming known: "The vowel sounds are rolled round in the mouth before utterance and when uttered remind one not infrequently of a cat's miaow or nocturnal caterwauling."

"THE AUSTRALIAN TWANG"
A remarkable feature of Australian English is its comparative uniformity. Australia, a continent roughly the size of Europe, has almost no regional variation of accent. A citizen of Perth can sound much like a citizen of Adelaide or Sydney, or like a stationhand in Alice Springs or Broken Hill. In Britain or the United States, by contrast, even the outsider can probably decide from the local accent whether he or she is in Scotland or Dorset, New England or Louisiana.

Perhaps because the idea of regional English is so deeply rooted in our perception of the language, many Australians consider that the country *does* have local varieties. They report in conversation that you can distinguish a South Australian from a Queenslander. (One property owner assured us that he knew from their speech which families in his district were of Scots ancestry!) But most Australian regionalisms include very few real differences. Queenslanders, for example, tend to use *port* for "suitcase", a *pusher* (baby carriage) in South Australia is usually called a *stroller* in New South Wales, and strawberries, sold in *punnets* in Sydney, appear in *chips* in Melbourne. Some South Australians are said to be identifiable from their pronunciation of *school*, but this hardly compares with the breadth of regional variation we have found elsewhere in the English-speaking world.

There is, undoubtedly, a continuum in the pronunciation of Australian English which cannot be interpreted as regional variation. Linguists estimate that roughly a third of the population speaks what is known as *Broad* Australian, that just over half the country speaks a

136 According to a New South Wales School Commission Report of 1854–5, "Little care is apparently taken to correct vicious pronunciation ... this inattention has a tendency to foster an Australian dialect which bids fair to surpass the American in disagreeableness."

milder English, *General* Australian, and that about a tenth use *Cultivated* Australian – which speaks for itself. The interesting aspect of this widely accepted classification is that it does not follow strict class or occupational contours. Working on the basis of pronunciation alone, there is, in Australia, no reliable means of identifying, say, the prime minister, a Sydney Harbour *wharfie*, a Northern Territory *jackeroo* and a Geelong car salesman. In Britain, by contrast, a trade union leader is expected to sound like a spokesman for the working class, and it would be unthinkable for a Conservative prime minister in Australia to attempt to disguise his lower middle-class accent as Margaret Thatcher is known to have done.

Deeper investigation into the sound of Australian English has shown that women and girls tend towards General or Cultivated Australian (virtually Standard English), and that men and boys, expressing mateship and machismo perhaps, tend towards General or Broad Australian, an observation that is generally true throughout English-speaking communities. Some schoolteachers have suggested that Australian boys tend to be corrected for their speech in school more than girls. The accents of the sports field and the outback tend to be broader than the accents of the office and the city, though this is not as hard and fast a rule as it would be in Britain. In Australia, an institution like Geelong Grammar, one of the top private schools, will contain the full range of Broad, General and Cultivated Australian speakers, which certainly would not be the case, in England, at Harrow or Eton. What is more, there will be virtually no pressure to inculcate any "improvement" in the spoken English there.

The range of Australian English, and its comparative freedom from class or cultural restrictions, is typified by the Hawker family of South Australia. The Hawkers first came to Australia in 1840 and have been in continuous residence at their property, Bungaree, ever since. Their land has now become subdivided among the family, but if you stand on a hill at Anama and look for forty miles in any direction – across some 130,000 acres of burnt grassland and scattered gum trees – what you are surveying is Hawker territory. Today, it is only two hours' drive through the vineyards of the Clare Valley to the city of Adelaide. In the old days it would have seemed remote from civilization, and Bungaree is organized like a small village with homestead, church, post office, stables and shearing shed clustered together in a fold of the hills.

The senior member of the Hawker family, Mrs Joan Hawker, mother of Ryves and James, speaks the kind of Cultivated Australian that would certainly pass for British English anywhere outside England itself, and probably there, too. Her two sons and their cousin, George, speak General Australian. In a convivial context, they might veer towards Broad. Ryves Hawker's three children, educated in Adelaide, speak General Australian, presumably like the majority of their schoolfriends. No Australian, listening to the way that they talk, would have any idea that they came from one of the country's oldest and most distinguished families. Alice, James Hawker's daughter, goes to the local school and likes to shock her family with her accent – she speaks Broad, like some (but not all) of the Bungaree station hands. (For a society that contrasts its classlessness with Britain's, Australians have a sharp ear for speech distinctions.)

The accent strata of Australian English have been identified for some years. A more recent phenomenon is the so-called "rising inflection" that has crept into the Australian speech pattern, (and, to a lesser extent, into the talk of American teenagers, especially on the West Coast). The "rising inflection" is the habit, especially prevalent among women and teenagers, of using a questioning (rising) tone in answer to a question. "Where do you go surfing?" gets the response, "At Palm Beach?" (meaning "Do you know it?" and "Do you approve of my choice?"). The sardonic chronicler of such teenage talk ("vowel cancer") among Australian surfers and their girls is Kathy Lette, author of *Puberty Blues*, a razor-eyed, sharp-tongued account of Australian beach life during the 1970s. Her view, controversial but still widely shared, is that the "rising inflection" is mainly to do with "Australian insecurity".

From the beginning, the insecurities that have pervaded Australian culture and society can be traced in attitudes to Australian English. Once the melting-pot years were over, Australian English suffered the kind of attacks ranged against American English in its infancy. Ironically, it was a self-confident member of the American Philological Society, one Walter Churchill, who delivered the greatest broadside against America's Antipodean sibling. "The common speech of the commonwealth of Australia", he remarked, "represents the most brutal maltreatment which has ever been inflicted upon the mother tongue of the English-speaking nations."

"COME ON, AUSSIE, COME ON!"

Many Australians themselves shared this view. Dame Nellie Melba, one of the first Australians to win international renown, addressing herself to the question of pronunciation, spoke in scathing terms of the way Australians used *oi* for *I*, and *ahee* for *ay* (in "may" or "say"), and spoke caustically of "our twisted vowels, our distortions and flatness of speech which, as I notice with regret, seriously prejudice other people against us".

All these insecurities redoubled with the arrival of broadcasting and films. What should the voice of Australia be? For the *Sydney Morning Herald* in 1932 there were no doubts: "If Australians were to develop an accent of their own, there was no legislative power to prevent them, but the American production, as heard over the wireless, should act as a salutary warning." Until the Second World War, in fact, Australian actors and broadcasters were trained to play down, if not actually to eliminate, all traces of their accent. In one of the film classics of the 1930s, *Dad and Dave Come To Town*, both "Dad" and "Dave" speak with a kind of heavily modified Australian accent that we should call Cultivated, though from all the evidence of their farming lifestyle – and the words they use, like *cobber* and *paddock* – we should expect them to speak General, if not Broad.

The first prominent Australian to urge the use of natural Australian speech on the air was the distinguished phonetician and broadcaster Dr A. G. Mitchell. His proposals, first made during the 1940s, caused an uproar, and a furious public debate ensued. One correspondent in the *ABC Weekly* expressed the traditional view:

> The attempt to create a distinct Australian accent is mischievous. For I make bold to say at present one does not exist. There is not, and should not be, any difference in Standard English as spoken here, in the Motherland, or elsewhere in the Empire, but just that pleasant variation of one person's voice and manner of delivery from another's.

Ranged against such Empire loyalism were an assortment of patriots and progressives. A certain Mr Justice Lowe sided with Mitchell, remarking that "the general thesis is incontestable ... Australian speech has as legitimate a place as a branch of the English language as Scottish, Irish, American, Canadian and South African speech." Another *ABC Weekly* correspondent added a perceptive note of irony:

> First thing in the morning, as I awake from sleep, I now clasp my hands together over my breast, and say to myself fifty times: "Every day in every way I find there is *nothing* wrong with the Australian voice or speech." I repeat this exercise as I drop to sleep at night, and firmly believe it will succeed with me as it has with Dr Mitchell.

The upshot, of course, was the international recognition of Australian English, a slow but inexorable process that began during the Second World War. We have seen how the maturity of American English was marked, at the end of the First World War, by the publication of

Mencken's *The American Language*. Similarly, in 1945, the appearance of Sidney J. Baker's *The Australian Language* can be seen as a milestone in the emergence of a separate Australian Standard. And just as, in the United States, there are still those who believe that British English is "better" (whatever that means) than American English, so there are still Australians who are irrationally ashamed of their mother tongue. As recently as 1974 a letter appeared in the *Sydney Sun-Herald* stating: "The Australian accent at its worst brands every one of us, whether we speak it or not, as uncouth, ignorant and a race of second-class people."

National pride and self-confidence is reflected in language. Since 1945 Australian English, spoken and written, has developed with fewer and fewer glances over its shoulder at the older British and American models. It has even enjoyed (and survived) the ultimate compliment: parody, in the shape of Afferbeck Lauder's *Let Stalk Strine*. For all its popularity, "Strine" was, and is, essentially a comic-strip version of Australian English, matching "Emma chisit?" with "How much is it?", "Aorta" with "They ought to " and "Numb Butter" with "Nothing but a . . . "

The real thing, the Australian vernacular and its traditional love of arresting similes and metaphors, continues to flourish in turns of speech like *as scarce as rocking horse manure, as bald as a bandicoot, as lonely as a country dunny, as mad as a gumtree full of galahs*, and phrases like *a feed, a frostie and a feature*, a rough summary of teenage bliss (food, beer and sex). Sometimes it is hard to distinguish between "real" and "invented" Australianisms. In 1972 the Australian Department of Foreign Affairs noted that "The image of Australians in the minds of many Englishmen may well be more influenced by . . . Barry McKenzie than the activities of Australia House." The Australian passion for abbreviations has now become very widespread. A stevedore (or wharfman) becomes a *wharfie*, a diminutive that made a starring appearance in the memorable simile, *as inconspicuous as Liberace at a wharfies' picnic*. In the same vein, the *garbo* is the "garbage collector", the *cozzie* and the *prezzie* is the "swimming costume" and the "present", and a *smoko* is the equivalent of a "tea-break". A *Westy* is a suburban Sydneysider, and if the afternoon at the beach was enjoyable an Australian might talk about *a beaut arvo*. Barry Humphries claims to have overheard an Australian woman describing her hysterectomy – "She said she'd had a *hizzie* in the *hozzie*."

It has sometimes been observed that advertisements are a better guide to a society than its editorials. Much of Australia's almost jingoistic self-confidence can be detected in Australian television commercials. A generation ago, Australian advertising was a sickly imitation of British and American styles. Now it celebrates national pride, with the heroes of the new Australia – like cricketer Dennis Lillee and Ben Lexcen, the hero of the America's Cup victory – selling anything from Toyota cars to Toohey's beer. The "jingle kings of Australia" are two self-confessed "fair dinkum Aussies", Alan Morris and Alan Johnston, co-partners in a million-dollar agency, Mojo, whose recent campaign theme song, "Come on, Aussie, come on", a counter-blast to the *bludgers* and *knockers* that Mojo felt were doing the country down, also became a topselling record. Ten years ago, say Mojo, "the Australian public was probably ashamed of our pretty grating nasal sort of accent".

In the 1980s Australian English has hit the international headlines. In Britain there has always been an awareness of the vitality of Australian English, but now it was taken up in the United States as well. Films like *Gallipoli* and *My Brilliant Career* have won critical acclaim and found large audiences. "Down Under", advertised by Australian comedian Paul Hogan, has become a fashionable tourist resort, especially among the Californians across the Pacific. And after Australia's victory in the America's Cup (re-christened the Perth Plate by some patriots) some Americans began to wonder if "the Aussies" – as they were now widely known – did not possess the kind of get-up-and-go frontier spirit that had become forgotten at home. The comparisons between the two countries were strengthened by the discovery that far from being the Anglo-Saxon dominion of legend, there were also many "New Australians" (Turks, Yugoslavs, Sri Lankans and Italians), and that Melbourne was now one of the largest Greek cities in the world.

As in the United States, much of the influence of the New Australians on the country's language has been confined to food, like *pizza* and *kebab*. A walk down Lygon Street in the Melbourne suburb of Carlton shows that though Italian Australians behave like Italians (promenading the street and ogling the girls), they talk as "fair dinkum Aussies". Like the European emigrants to the United States, they have changed the landscape but not the language. Appropriately for the decade of Australia's Bicentennial (1988), it is probably not an exaggeration to say that throughout the English-speaking world, there is a greater

137/138 Dennis Lillee, the cricketer, and Ben Lexcen, designer of *Australia II*'s "winged keel", have become integral to the contemporary world's awareness of Australian speech.

awareness of, and respect for, the voice and spirit of Australia than ever before. This "stereotyped Australianness" has been controversially expressed by the New Zealander Dr Robert Burchfield, Chief Editor of the *Oxford English Dictionary*:

> They include a ragged-trousered informality, a laconically expressed desire for independence, an irremovable parochialism, a prolific power to create both euphemisms and also expressions that go beyond normal profanity, and a deeply embedded suspicion of Poms (more recently always called "Whingeing Poms").

Needless to say, this memorable definition can enrage an Australian, but it does perhaps suggest the mild New Zealand resentment that in the playground of the world's English, Australia's voice, now ringing with a new confidence, has drowned the subtler contribution of its Antipodean neighbour.

A "CAREFULLY MODULATED MURMUR"

The similarity of New Zealand English to its Australian cousin is probably as irritating to New Zealanders as the similarity of Canadian and American English is to some Canadians. Actually, it is probably more so, for many New Zealanders believe they speak "better English" than most Australians who, ironically, tend to attribute the half-familiar accent to a remote or unfamiliar part of their own country. A New Zealander in Sydney might well be asked if he or she came from Tasmania. Like Canada, New Zealand has been overshadowed by her larger, richer and more populous neighbour, a truth reflected in the title of the first serious study of English in the Antipodes, *Austral English*. Ironically, according to Burchfield, New Zealand English has more in common with the English of the Falkland Islands than of Australia.

The authenticity of New Zealand English is, however, not in doubt. As the New Zealand writer C. K. Stead has put it:

> There is sometimes argument about whether Katherine Mansfield, who spent almost half of her short life in Europe, can really be called a New Zealand writer.
>
> There is another, apparently unrelated, question: When did a distinct New Zealand speech establish itself?
>
> In his book *The Georgian Literary Scene* Frank Swinnerton describes meeting Katherine Mansfield in 1912. He describes her as "one of the most enchanting young women I had ever met"; but he mentions that she "hummed or intoned her words" "hardly parting her lips". By this I conclude that New Zealand English was established by 1912 and that Katherine Mansfield spoke it.
>
> Any variant of English can be spoken well or badly. Swinnerton was charmed by Mansfield's "carefully modulated murmur". However, if you don't move your lips or your jaw much, some of the sound tends to go up into the nasal cavities, and what happens to it there is seldom pleasant.

> If, as I do, you speak New Zealand English, certain kinds of orotund
> utterance are not possible without faking. It's best to aim for clarity and
> confidence, and hope for a little of Mansfield's music as well.

New Zealand is a younger country than Australia. There were whaling stations established there in the eighteenth century, but it was not formally settled as a colony until 1840, when the British government signed the Treaty of Waitangi with the Maori chiefs. Unlike Australia it was a free colony. Many of its first settlers, if they were not Scots, came from the same urban working-class English background, which is why the accents of the two countries have so much in common. Both, of course, are part of the same English family as RP and Cockney, and it is for this reason that Americans often find it hard to distinguish between an Australian, a New Zealand and a British accent.

From the first, the life of both the North and the South Islands of New Zealand was agrarian. Samuel Butler, the author of the famous Victorian satire on New Zealand, *Erewhon*, spent some time in the place he called "Nowhere". Describing the local conversation in a letter home, he wrote: "The all-engrossing topics seem to be sheep, horses, dogs, cattle, English grasses, paddocks, bush and so forth." Wedded to tradition, socially and politically conservative, English in New Zealand has reflected these traits.

The accents of New Zealand English are generally supposed to be slightly closer to British English than Australian, but are said to share the three levels of Australian speech, Cultivated, General and Broad. According to Burchfield, if a New Zealander and an Australian from the same social background shared a railway carriage only an expert phonetician could tell them apart on the basis of pronunciation. But New Zealand still has an attachment to British English that is unheard of in Australia. New Zealanders still tune into BBC broadcasts, and some still have what the English would call "Home Counties" accents. Within the islands, the sound of New Zealand English is the source of a considerable folklore. The citizens of Canterbury, originally an Anglican settlement, are said to speak "better English" than in other parts of the country. But one other influence is certain: the Scots. Place-names like Dunedin and Invercargill and family names like Murray and McIntosh emphasize the significance of the Highland immigration. The Scots contributed speech habits like the stressed *wh* in words like *when* and *wheat*. Though the New Zealand *r* is generally silent, as in Standard English, in the originally Scottish settlements in the South Island the *r* is rolled, and known as the "Southland burr".

The making of the distinctive New Zealand contribution to English followed the same course as in Australia. There was, first of all, the influence of the native Maori culture, borrowed from an oppressed people (though the Maori vocabulary is, of course, totally different from the Aboriginal). Today, the Maoris number one-tenth of the population and have a significant place in the society. Many schools, for instance, adopted Maori mottoes, and there was a widespread appreciation of the euphony of Maori speech, which is related to the Polynesian languages of Tahiti, Samoa and Hawaii. The New Zealanders borrowed Maori words for local trees, flowers and animals. The kiwi became a national symbol, like the

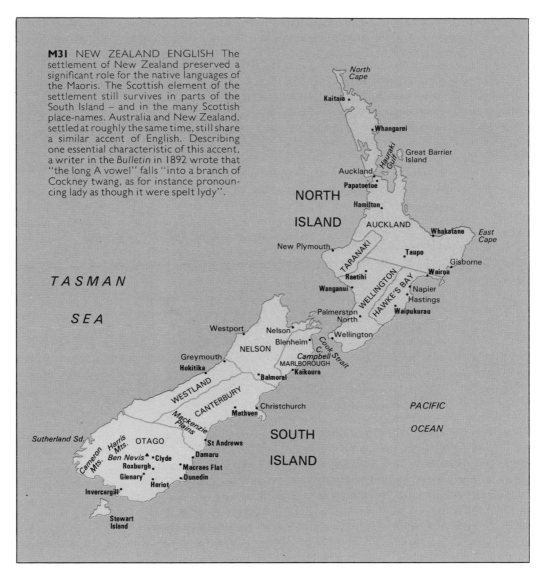

M31 NEW ZEALAND ENGLISH The settlement of New Zealand preserved a significant role for the native languages of the Maoris. The Scottish element of the settlement still survives in parts of the South Island – and in the many Scottish place-names. Australia and New Zealand, settled at roughly the same time, still share a similar accent of English. Describing one essential characteristic of this accent, a writer in the *Bulletin* in 1892 wrote that "the long A vowel" falls "into a branch of Cockney twang, as for instance pronouncing lady as though it were spelt lydy".

kangaroo in Australia. Maori influence is strongest in the North Island, where they have always been more populous. As in Australia, the translations tended to be imprecise. The Maori *kete* became the New Zealand *kit*, for "basket". The language traffic flowed in both directions. *Ranana*, on the Wanganui River, is the Maori pronunciation of "London".

There is rather less slang in New Zealand than in Australia, or perhaps it is simply less well recorded, and certainly no trace of rhyming slang (the Cockney element in Australian English is missing here). On the other hand, New Zealand uses all the familiar Australian abbreviations and diminutives, *beaut*, *arvo* and *smoko*. A slang phrase, common in New Zealand, is *dragging the chain*, a shearing term meaning "to work slowly". *Stop dragging the chain* becomes extended to mean "drink up". *Hoot* is a Maori word for "money". *Razoo*

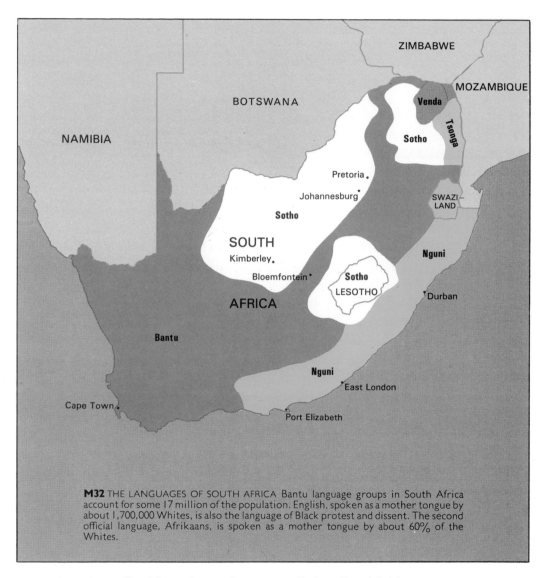

M32 THE LANGUAGES OF SOUTH AFRICA Bantu language groups in South Africa account for some 17 million of the population. English, spoken as a mother tongue by about 1,700,000 Whites, is also the language of Black protest and dissent. The second official language, Afrikaans, is spoken as a mother tongue by about 60% of the Whites.

appears in a phrase like *I haven't got a brass razoo*. Robert Burchfield quotes a contemporary example of New Zealand slang: "A young niece of mine recently said to her English host, 'Well, I suppose I had better rattle my dags and be off.'"

The workaday vocabulary of New Zealand English inevitably reflects the influence of Australia. The *bush*, the most famous example, meaning "uncleared land", "forest" or "scrub", is shared. *Bush* gives rise to many compounds that convey a flavour of the early days: *bushfire*, *bush lawyer* and *bush telegraph*. Equally, there are parts of the New Zealand lexicon which are unique to the islands; the strangeness of the New Zealand experience for the first Whites created plenty of distinct New Zealand vocabulary. An Australian *weekender* is likely to be a *bach* (pronounced "batch") in New Zealand. In some country districts, roads will be called *lines*, as in McDonald's Line. If there is a choice between British and American English usage, the New Zealander will tend towards the British where the Australian may prefer the American. Turning to South Africa, our third example of ex-colonial English, we find that such comparatively fine distinctions are overshadowed by harsher politics.

ENGLISH IN SOUTH AFRICA

In June 1976, English – or rather, the denial of it – was the spark that ignited the explosion on the streets of Soweto, the Black township on the edge of Johannesburg. The Afrikaner authorities had introduced a regulation that forced schoolchildren to learn some of their subjects through the medium of Afrikaans instead of English. The Blacks saw this as both a further limitation of their capacity for self-advancement, and an imposition of a hated symbol, the Afrikaans language. On 16 June, the schools of Soweto erupted on to the streets with slogans like "Away with Afrikaans" and "We are not Boers". The Soweto riots revealed the unusual place of English in South African life: the language of a minority within a minority – there are 25 million Blacks, and 4½ million Whites, of whom about 60 per cent are Afrikaners. This political reality, challenged by the riots, is expressed in one of the most emotive words in the English language: *apartheid*.

English-speaking South Africans have co-existed with the Afrikaner Dutch since the middle of the seventeenth century, and have added a number of Afrikaner words like *spoor*, *trek*, and *veldt* to the language. The main English settlement, drawn largely from the industrial Midlands, occurred at about the same time as the emigrations to Australasia, which accounts for the similarity of accent. Unlike the other White colonial settlers, the English-speaking South Africans were, as they are today, in a minority. The English of the South African Broadcasting Corporation betrays the uneasy non-official status of the language. To British and American ears, it has the clipped formality of BBC English in the 1950s – in other words, the authorities, unable to deny the presence of English in South Africa, broadcast it as a *foreign* language. White South Africans who take elocution lessons – "Speech and Drama" is the euphemism – to improve their English are, perhaps unwittingly, reinforcing the *foreignness* of English in South Africa. There is a distinctive South African English, of course, but it has lacked the confidence of Australian or New Zealand English. Recently, however, the novelist André Brink believes that "a completely new kind of English [has] emerged, strongly influenced by Afrikaans rhythms and syntactical patterns".

A hundred years ago, the position of English in Southern Africa could not have been more different. The language of imperial rule throughout much of the continent, it had its securest base in the English settlements of Natal. After the Boer War (1899–1901) – during which the Afrikaners were briefly *forced* to learn English – positions of power in the government were nearly all in the hands of Afrikaners. An unprecedented evolution now began to occur: English gradually became the language of opposition; and even more so following the declaration of an apartheid policy in 1948, and the final severing of links with the former empire when South Africa left the Commonwealth in 1961. Now, more than ever, English is disapproved of by the Nationalist Party, especially as for the Black majority it is overwhelmingly the preferred medium – an alternative to Afrikaans, a means of self-determination, and a window on to the free world. More and more Blacks are choosing to write in English as a way of reaching an international audience. Blacks who write in Zulu or Xhosa can find themselves accused of promoting ethnicity and apartheid, and of shunning politics. In 1984, Es'kia Mphahlele, Professor of African Literature at the University of Witwatersrand, made the following comment:

> I make bold to suggest that the Black man here has vested interests in English as a unifying force. Through it Africa can be restored to him, and, together with French, English provides a pan-African forum, widens his constituency. English is therefore tied up with the Black man's efforts to liberate himself.

Afrikaans, by contrast, has become the language of the oppressor, the language of the administration boards which issue the hated passbooks. The more bitter the struggle becomes, the more the diehards of Afrikanerdom will cling to this symbol of their authority. Inevitably, English is mistrusted by the Afrikaner authorities who have now been accused directly of wanting to relegate English to the status of "foreign language". The symbol of Afrikaner anxiety is the monument erected just outside Capetown in the late 1970s, dedicated "To the Afrikaner language". As the political situation in South Africa deteriorates the traditional truce between English and Afrikaans may be threatened.

In the Victorian age, there were few such tensions and anxieties. The spreading power of English merely stimulated calls for its universal adoption.

> What should prevent this language of the ruler in every zone, in every clime, and the merchant of every market from extending ... and from supplying the necessities which are growing in their urgency and import-ance wherever our sails are unfurled and our banner floats in the breeze?

In tune with the scientific spirit of the time, quantification of the spread of English followed. In 1907, E. H. Babbitt guessed that the year 2000 would see 1.1 billion English users spread around the globe, a remarkably accurate forecast. Some went further. Albert William Alderson (1908) believed that warfare could be abolished "in perpetuity" if the world spoke a common language. Naturally, he proposed English for this task in a visionary scheme: "The United States should use every endeavour and strain every effort to cause the whole of the New World (North, South and Central America) to speak English." Britain should do the same in Canada, South Africa and India. The result would be the extinction of all other languages – and universal peace would reign. He was both wrong – and right. English was no pacifier. The unfolding century was to be one of the most violent in the history of the world. But it was also the century in which English at last became the international language of the Third World.

139 Bob Marley, reggae super-star, who gave Jamaican English a special place in contemporary culture, symbolizes the emergence of the ''New Englishes''.

9

THE
NEW ENGLISHES

In the ten years between Queen Victoria's Golden Jubilee in 1887 and the Diamond Jubilee of 1897, all eyes were on London as the capital of Empire and the source of English-speaking culture throughout the world. "All [the Australian] knows or even cares for England", wrote one contemporary, "lies in his resentment and curiosity concerning London, with the tale of whose size and wonders the crowd of travelling 'new chums' for ever troubles him." The emotions felt towards "home" by the new settlers in New Zealand, Canada, South Africa, and especially Australia, were, one imagines, a confusion of bitterness, affection, cynicism and longing, but in the harsh, unfamiliar environment of the veldt or the prairie or the bush, the things that bind are stronger than the things that divide. Cockney settler, Welsh fusilier, Essex convict, Irish share-cropper, Scottish engineer, Wiltshire ne'er-do-well: all spoke some version of the Queen's English.

Even American English, the oldest of the overseas variants, was, as many of its writers complained, still overawed by its British parent. The story of the longshoremen of New York greeting visiting British ships with "How is Little Nell?" is a tribute not only to Dickens' powers as a storyteller, but also to the Victorian supremacy of British culture. For a few decades the talk and writing of the places we still know as the City, Westminster, and Grub Street, influenced the English-speaking world in ways that, in some cases, have still to be thrown off. Carlyle, Darwin, Disraeli, Bagehot, Trollope, Thackeray: the English-speaking world looked to London for its opinions, politics, style, sensibility, even its jokes. As one American writer put it: "We may talk of our Western Empire and our admirable ports, of our growth and our growing wealth; but here is and will remain for generations, the centre of the commercial and political world, the focus of intellectual activity and the mint of thought. Here ferments the largest and most highly developed humanity which as yet the universal mother has given birth to, and here the whole world's intellect comes to pay homage."

London boomed, growing from three million people in the early 1860s to four and a half million by 1901. People flocked to this "modern Babylon" from all over England. London had become, as the guidebook writer Karl Baedeker noted, an international city, in which there were more Scotsmen than in Aberdeen, more Irishmen than in Dublin, and more Roman Catholics than in the Eternal City. Bernard Shaw, who loved to mock Anglo-Saxon self-importance, summarized the state of English world rule in *The Man of Destiny*:

> There is nothing so bad or so good that you will not find an Englishman
> doing it; but you will never find an Englishman in the wrong. He does
> everything on principle. He fights you on patriotic principles; he robs you
> on business principles; he enslaves you on imperial principles.

In the coming twentieth century the legacy of those "imperial principles" would mean that for the first time speakers of the mother tongue would be outnumbered by non-native English speakers: Africans, Indians, Chinese and Malays. As we approach the year 2000, English, the legacy of Empire, is the *de facto* international language of the Third World. In four continents, Asia, Africa and the Americas, and in the vast ocean basin of the Pacific, it is an official language in some thirty-four countries, from islands as far apart as Jamaica and Singapore, to states ranging from Sierra Leone to the vast sub-continent of India. The world-journey we have described has scattered the seeds of English far and wide, and the Third World flowering of the language has now produced some exotic hybrids, among them Caribbean English, Indian English, various forms of African English and Singapore English, sometimes known as "Singlish".

The emergence of these new Englishes has been compared to the spread (and subsequent break-up) of Latin throughout the Roman world. In the late 1970s, the Chief Editor of the *Oxford English Dictionary*, Dr Robert Burchfield, made a series of predictions based on this comparison that made headlines all over the world. His controversial thesis was that just as, with the decline of the Roman Empire, Latin broke up into mutually unintelligible European languages like French, Spanish and Italian, so over a period of several centuries, global English will similarly disintegrate into separate languages.

Dr Burchfield pointed out that, historically speaking, languages have always had a tendency to break up – or to evolve. There were, he argued, some "powerful models of the severance of a language into two or more constituent parts, especially the emergence of the great Germanic languages of Western Europe – English, German, Dutch, Norwegian, Swedish and so on – from the mutually intelligible dialects of the fifth century AD." Countering those who pointed, as we did in chapter one, to the existence of a world English, Burchfield argued that such indications overlooked one vital fact:

> English, as the *second* language of many speakers in countries throughout
> the world, is no more likely to survive the inevitable political changes of the
> future than did Latin, once the second language of the governing classes or
> regions within the Roman Empire.

Only time will prove or disprove the Burchfield thesis, but in our travels through the English-speaking world we have found some good evidence for his theory of separate language evolution in countries like India, Singapore and Sierra Leone and, perhaps most dramatically of all, in the Caribbean. In the islands of the West Indies, English is a first and

140/141/142 The English of Trollope, Carlyle and Thackeray was scattered more widely than any previous language. One legacy of the British Empire is the Third World's continuing dependence on the English language.

national language. The spectacularly different form it takes is the legacy of the slave trade described in chapter six. Historically, the creoles of West Africa, the West Indies, and the Southern United States have always had a vigorous separate tradition. Now, with the rise of Third World nationalism, these traditions are finding a political voice as well.

Jamaica probably offers among the best contemporary evidence for the beginnings of what one might call "Latinization", linguistic nationalism or the disintegration of Standard English, a paradigm for the separate development of English. Jamaica has always had a lively independent culture. In the 1970s, during the Manley government, it became internationally renowned as one of the centres of Third World nationalism, the home of reggae and the Rastafarian movement. Of all the varieties of Caribbean English, Jamaican English (with the most speakers) has attracted the most scholarly attention, a path of investigation first blazed by F. G. Cassidy's celebrated *Jamaica Talk* in 1953. But what sort of English is it? Here Jamaican nationalism prompts different responses. E. K. Brathwaite, Professor of Caribbean Cultural and Social History at the University of the West Indies, and the author of a celebrated trilogy of poems, *The Arrivants*, some of them in Caribbean English, speaks of a "nation-language".

> The word "dialect" has so many pejorative overtones. You laugh at a "dialect". It is broken English. "Nation-language" suggests the kind of authenticity which is now becoming part of our expression.

Mervyn Alleyne, Professor of Linguistics, insists that the language is "Jamaican creole". Popularly, it can be known as "patois" or "the dialect". Others, like the poet Jean Breeze, also reject the pejorative associations of the word "dialect", and talk of "the Jamaican language".

A British or American visitor to Jamaica would probably conclude that there were at least two basic levels of language. First of all, in a newspaper like the *Gleaner*, the editorials and news reporting are basically in Standard English. Engaged in conversation, the journalists on

143 "Painting the map red." A Canadian stamp of 1898.

the *Gleaner* will use a spoken version of Standard English, mildly influenced by Jamaican English. This will be fully comprehensible to the visitor, but it might have a number of words – *nyam* (eat) or *tacko* (ugly) – not found in Standard English, and perhaps a few local constructions. Certainly, it would not *sound* like Standard English.

Extending in a speech continuum, the second level – Jamaican English – is virtually unintelligible to the outsider. Here Standard English words take on meanings and pronunciations that are a long way from the English of London or New York. In Jamaican English a word like *form* can mean "to pretend to be", "to feign", as in a sentence like:

> Di kuk di tel mi mi faamin, bot it nat so.
> (The cook told me I was shamming sick, but it's not so.)

This is the language of the streets, of the home, of Jamaica for Jamaicans. Until recently, it remained an essentially *oral* standard, but lately, fuelled by the heat of cultural nationalism, partly inspired by the disc-jockey tradition of performers like Yellowman, and partly by reggae, a new poetry, called "dub poetry", began to emerge that expressed this Jamaican speech in a written as well as an oral form.

"THE BABY OF REGGAE"

Reggae is the heartbeat of Jamaica, and "dub poetry" has been called "the baby of reggae". It is at the crossroads of the oral and the written traditions of poetry. It emerged in the early 1970s when two poets, Linton Kwesi Johnson and Oku Onora (who was then in prison for robbery), began to experiment with a new kind of material. In due course they were joined by two other "dub poets", Mutabaruka (a Rastafarian) and Michael Smith, whose work had

144/145 The dub poets Mutabaruka and Linton Kwesi Johnson are part of a new generation who express Jamaican English in a written form far removed from Standard English.

developed out of his actor's training at the Kingston School of Drama. Linton Kwesi Johnson has described dub poetry as "a new departure in Jamaican protest poetry. Here the spoken/chanted word is the dominant mode. People's speech and popular music are combined, and the Jamaican folk culture and the reggae tradition provide both sources of inspiration and frames of reference."

You can trace the evolution of dub poetry, which uses a highly localized Jamaican form of English, in the work of Louise Bennett. "Miss Lou" – as she is known – is the grandmother of all the dub poets who emerged in the 1970s. In her own words, she has written poems for the last twenty-five years "in the free expression of the people ... a manner of speaking unhampered by the rules of (Standard English) grammar". She writes out of the oral tradition of Jamaica – and Black English – and is inspired by the spoken rhythms of the Bible, the evangelical Sankey and Moody hymnal, and the folksongs of Jamaica.

> *Him sey Englan is foreign, an*
> *Afta dis election,*
> *We mus move King pickcha an put*
> *We own Jamaica man.*

Although many of these poems first appeared in the *Gleaner*, Louise Bennett's work is not meant only for the page. Her poetry is at its best when she performs it, manipulating the full range of the language, playing on nuances of meaning like a music-hall comedian. Her subjects are the life of Kingston – street scenes, public events, local sports and Jamaican politics. In 1962, when Jamaica joined the United Nations, she composed "Jamaica Elevate".

> *We tun Independent Nation*
> *In de Commonwealth of Nations,*
> *An we get congratulation*

From de folks of high careers;
We got Consuls an Ambassadors,
An Ministers an Senators
Dah-rub shoulder an dip mout
Eena heavy world affairs.

Louise Bennett's commitment to writing in the English of her people is expressed in "Bans O'Killing" – meaning "a lot of killing" – which is her declaration of solidarity with ordinary Caribbean speech:

So yuh a de man, me hear bout!
Ah yuh dem sey dah-teck
Whole heap o' English oat sey dat
Yuh gwine kill dialect!

Meck me get it straight Mass Charlie
For me noh quite undastan,
Yuh gwine kill all English dialect
Or jus Jamaica one?

Ef yuh kean sing "Linstead Market"
An "Wata come a me y'eye",
Yuh wi haffi tap sing "Auld lang syne"
An "Comin thru de rye".

Dah language we yuh proud o',
Weh yuh honour and respeck,
Po' Mass Charlie! Yuh noh know sey
Dat it spring from dialect!

When Louise Bennett's poems were first published in a collection in 1966, *Jamaica Labrish,* a glossary of some four pages was provided to translate some of her vocabulary – *bockle* for "bottle", *duppy* for "ghost", *ninyam* for "food". At the time, "Miss Lou" was an almost lone voice in her use of "nation language". Now she is at the centre of a vital tradition. A more conventional Caribbean poet, Edward Brathwaite, describes the condition of Caribbean English today:

With the new generation, the people who are really using nation language, the idea is not really to write it at all, but to have it recorded, and best of all, filmed. There you have a complete correlation between what the culture dictates, and what the media would like, and how you communicate it.

Brathwaite makes the point that English in the Caribbean is refracted through many lenses, historical and local. The traditions of English in the Caribbean are a far cry from Shakespeare and Wordsworth but this society provides an important model for the future development of the new Englishes round the world.

146 Louise Bennett is the grandmother of dub poetry. Her first poems were scorned: now she is anthologized.

> All Caribbean people partake in multiple cultures. They partake in the American culture. Some of us partake in the Latin American culture. Then there's the European culture and the Caribbean culture.

Switching from a localized Caribbean English (i.e. Barbadian, Jamaican, Trinidadian, etc.) to Standard English is the upshot of this fusion, and is natural to any Caribbean child. Standard English, the English of the British and American establishment, the English of the international newspapers, dictionaries and broadcasting authorities, evolves slowly, as we have seen. Caribbean English – "nation language" – is much more mobile, an essentially oral tradition that bubbles up from underneath, searching for new forms of expression. But Brathwaite does not believe that it will remain an unhoused oral form for ever. There are, he believes, the beginnings of a written Caribbean English:

> We are at the stage Chaucer was in his time. That's my assessment of it. Chaucer had just started to gel English, French, and Latin. We are doing the same thing with our creole concepts, our Standard English, our American, and our modernism.

One Caribbean writer whose work typifies the process Brathwaite describes is Michael "Mikey" Smith, one of the dub poets who has established an international reputation. Smith was a young Jamaican, a drama student whose dub poems captured the imagination of his generation in the late 1970s. His most famous poem, "Mi cyaan believe it" (I can't believe it), is a work that is rich with the rhythms and idiom of the street.

> *Mi seh mi cyaan believe it*
> *Mi seh mi cyann believe it*
> *room dem a rent*
> *mi apply widin*
> *but as me go in*
> *cockroach rat an scorpion also come in*
> *waan good*
> *nose haffi run*
> *but me naw go sideung pan igh wall*
> *like Humpty Dumpty*
> *mi a face me reality*

His career was short and tragic. At the age of twenty-nine, Mikey Smith was stoned to death, a victim of Jamaica's political violence. His fellow poet, friend, mentor and patron, Mervyn Morris, is now editing a collection of Smith's work for publication. Morris describes the language of the dub poets like Smith as "Jamaican creole", which relates closely to the language of pop stars like Bob Marley or Peter Tosh. "It's usually very urban. It sometimes has Rastafarian elements." Its subjects are the same as Bob Marley's:

> The concerns are very much the concerns you find in Jamaican pop music.
> They're usually talking about oppression. The need to return to some kind
> of sense of identity which often connects with Africa.

Michael Smith composed orally, and made tape recordings. Only later did he transcribe his work into Jamaican English. The group known as "Poets in Unity", who include the talented dub poet Jean Breeze, compose their work collaboratively, meeting at the Kingston School of Drama, where they transcribe their work on to the blackboard, again representing their words in Jamaican creole.

"NATION LANGUAGE"

Many of the dub poets have had a university education. They are turning their backs on Standard English out of choice. They have chosen to write in the language of their own culture, and to disseminate it throughout the English-speaking world in performance, records, tapes and books. They are extremely alert to the idea that the language of their poetry might become the future standard language of the Caribbean and give their society a distinct Caribbean identity that is not overshadowed by English or American English. Edward Brathwaite likes to make the point, in talking about English in the Caribbean, that the Third World as a whole is "acutely concerned with language". As he says, "We regard words, word play, word power, as an essential part of our personality." The question of the meaning and significance of those words, and the kind of words they should be, is fundamental to all the New Englishes.

147 E. K. Brathwaite: English in the Caribbean is "nation language".

148 The "Poets in Unity" compose collectively. Their poetry is at the crossroads of "nation language" and Standard English.

The debate has changed as the political landscape has changed. In the 1950s before the Caribbean had achieved independence from Britain the emphasis on Standard English was oppressive. Brathwaite recalls the experience of the law courts. "The judge would expect the defendant to speak as best as he could in the Queen's English. This would come out as broken English and the man would be hesitant and embarrassed. Now, with the acceptance of the nation language, the defendant comes in dressed as he is, and he speaks to the judge as himself, and is much more eloquent, and much more successful in his dealings with the court."

Brathwaite believes that Bob Marley achieved a great deal for "nation language". In his lifetime Marley was without doubt the most famous West Indian in the world, invited as guest of honour to Independence Day celebrations and peace rallies. His music swept Britain and the United States, influencing a generation of songwriters. His lyrics gave poignant expression to the Caribbean predicament: an imposed identity that is neither African nor European nor American. His worldwide success gave Jamaican creole international credibility. "I notice now", Brathwaite says, "that announcers on the radio are quite happy to move into nation language." In school, the trend towards a Caribbean English is emphasized by the emergence of examinations devised and adjudicated not in London (as previously), but in the Caribbean.

In the university, the movement towards nation language or Jamaican creole has taken a radical direction. One of the leading spokesmen for the recognition of Jamaican creole is Dr Hubert Devonish, a Guyanese. For him, "the major struggle right now is to fight for the government to recognize that Jamaican creole is as worthy of attention and respect as English." He sees Jamaican creole as "a very old language that the slaves brought from Africa to the Caribbean". He points out that historically it has *always* been on a path of development that is quite different from English. Devonish argues that though the African slaves picked up the vocabulary of English, they retained the grammatical structure of their African languages. No one, he says, can overlook the fact that the structure of all the Caribbean creoles – English, Dutch, French and Spanish – is very similar. "My argument", he says, "is that from a historical and linguistic point of view you're dealing with a separate language."

Devonish argues that English is the language of an elite, cut off from the mass of the Caribbean population. If the people of Jamaica are to participate fully in their society the government should recognize Jamaican creole as an official – and separate – language. "There is", says Devonish, "no reason why any elite group within Jamaican society should determine that only one language, that of the dominant European power, should be the official language." Devonish illustrates the scope of that power with a display of simple Jamaican road signs – NO RIGHT TURN, SCHOOL ZONE BEGINS, NO ENTRY, KEEP LEFT, NO PARKING BETWEEN THESE SIGNS, NO OVERTAKING OR PASSING – all in Standard English. The first step in the recognition of a separate Jamaican standard, he believes, has to come at such a basic level. He has an exhibition of these road signs in Jamaican creole: NO TON RAIT, SKUUL ZUON BIGIN, NO ENTA, KIP LEF, NO PAAK BITWIIN DEM SAIN YA, and NO UOVATEK NAAR PAAS.

The most effective way of getting Jamaican creole accepted by the people who hold power within the society, he believes, is for it to be recognized by the education system. In Jamaica, he says "many people are denied access to education because the education system operates only in English". He has devised an unusual way of breaking down the barriers between the creole and the English, an exhibition of Anglo-American games – Monopoly, Cluedo, Scrabble – written in Jamaican creole. "The idea is that if you are going to establish that Jamaican creole is a language like any other, you have to make the point that it can perform any function within the society. One of the ways you can get people accustomed to using the writing system, Jamaican creole, is by introducing it through games, through fun." On the Monopoly board "Community Chest" is translated into the creole *patcha*. Especially in Scrabble, Devonish experimented with ways of turning an oral language into a written one:

> By bringing Scrabble to creole, what you are doing is turning the language into a written medium and trying to ensure that people, as part of the process of spreading the writing system, will then become used to manipulating their language in a written form . . . and become acquainted with the way that you would spell it as distinct from spelling English . . . A word game like Scrabble is intended to drive home the point that creole is a separate language with a separate writing system.

Not every Jamaican makes such a clear-cut distinction between Standard and creole English. Mervyn Morris, for instance, takes a middle path. "We are a bilingual society," he says. He talks of a continuum in language – from creole at one end ("almost incomprehensible to those who are not living in the society") to Standard English at the other ("something which an awful lot of people are never really fully in touch with"). Morris believes that "most of us operate somewhere in the middle". For Morris, Jamaicans have two co-existing needs, one for creole and one for Standard English. "One values greatly the creole because it expresses things about the Jamaican experience which are not available for expression in the same force in Standard English." Equally, and pragmatically, Morris recognizes the need for Standard English, "not only because it's officially imposed in Jamaica, but because we do not want in the end to cut ourselves off from international communication".

The international power of English is the force that arrests the full, separate development of Caribbean English. Internationalism expresses itself in two pressures, internal and external. Within Caribbean culture, there is still a considerable resistance to the recognition of Caribbean English: a continuing debate about what is "correct", and the absence of a standardized spelling convention makes such debates almost irresolvable. Although much work has been done on compiling a dictionary of Caribbean English, at the time of writing this is still awaiting completion. Schoolteachers prefer to teach a Caribbean version of Standard English rather than a more self-conscious, nationalistic Caribbean English. Most parents who send their children to school for an education still want this to achieve a weakening of "the dialect" and they complain when their children "talk local".

The appeal of Standard English lies in its association with money and success. The outside world, the world of the dollar and of international trade, speaks Standard English and the Caribbean, dependent on the goodwill of the United States and, to a lesser extent, Britain, needs to get on in that world. Lawyers, doctors, businessmen, scholars and economists have little incentive to promote the strongest forms of Jamaican (or other Caribbean) English. There is only a lukewarm enthusiasm among the professional and educated elements in Jamaican society for a separate "Jamaican" language, and the reality of Third World poverty means that for the mass of the population the idea of a nation language is a rarefied concept confined to the seminar rooms of the University of the West Indies. For the majority of the people, the realities are the price of food and fuel.

Ask a Jamaican what he or she speaks and you will have the best expression of the paradox that underlies Caribbean attitudes towards English – and a clue to the future. Jamaicans will say anything from "the dialect" to "patois" to "Caribbean creole" to "Jamaican English" to "the Jamaican language". Caribbean nationalism will prompt them to put as much distance as possible between what they speak and the Standard English of the ex-colonial visitor. On the other hand, if you suggest to the Jamaican that he or she does *not* speak English, they will be insulted or outraged.

"THE FINAL PASSAGE"

The influence of Jamaican English is not confined to the Caribbean. Since the 1950s, there have been large, well-established West Indian communities in Toronto, New York and London. Within the British West Indian community, the "patois" – as it is known – has a special place as a token of identity. One Jamaican schoolgirl now living in London explains the complicated social pressures that frowned on Jamaican English in Jamaica, but that made it almost obligatory in London:

> It's rather weird 'cos when I was in Jamaica I wasn't really allowed to speak it (Jamaican creole) in front of my parents. I found it difficult in Britain at first. When I went to school I wanted to be like the others in order not to stand out. So I tried speaking the patois as well . . . You get sort of a mixed reception. Some people say, "You sound really nice, quite different." Other people say, "You're a foreigner, speak English. Don't try to be like us, 'cos you're not like us."

Despite this mixed reception from her British West Indian friends, she persevered with the patois, and, as she puts it, "after a year, I lost my British accent, and was accepted".

But is this, strictly speaking, Jamaican English? For many Caribbean visitors to Britain, the patois of Brixton and Notting Hill is a stylized form that is not, as they see it, truly Jamaican, not least because British West Indians have come from all parts of the Caribbean. Another British West Indian schoolgirl, who was born in Britain, was teased for her patois when she visited the Caribbean for the first time:

> I haven't lived in Jamaica, right? But what I found when I went out there was that when I tried to speak Jamaican they laughed at me. They said I'm trying to copy them and I don't sound right and that. They want me to speak as I speak now.

The experience convinced her that "in London the Jamaicans have developed their own language in patois, sort of. 'Cos they make up their own words in London, in, like, Brixton. And then it just develops into patois as well."

Within the Black community in Britain, "the patois" is likely to remain a local standard. We found that there were White children in predominantly Black schools who used the British West Indian patois in order to be acceptable to the majority of their friends:

> I was born in Brixton and I've been living here for seventeen years, and so I just picked it up from hanging around with my friends who are mainly Black people. And so I can relate to them by using it, because otherwise I'd feel an outcast.

On the other hand, the same schoolboy knows that this is something for a special set of circumstances. "But when I'm with someone else who I don't know I try to speak as fluent English as possible. It's like I feel embarrassed about it (the patois), I feel like I'm degrading myself by using it." The unconscious racism of such White comments points to the predicament of the British Blacks. Not fully accepted – for all the rhetoric – by the established White community, they feel neither fully Caribbean nor fully British. This is the poignant outcome of what the British Black writer Caryl Phillips has called "The Final Passage".

Phillips, who came to Britain as a baby in the late 1950s, is one of the first of his generation to grapple with the problem of finding a means of literary self-expression that is true to his experience: "The paradox of my situation is that where most immigrants have to learn a new language, Caribbean immigrants have to learn a new form of the same language. It induces linguistic schizophrenia – you have an identity crisis that mirrors the larger cultural confusion." His novel, *The Final Passage*, is narrated in Standard English. But the speech of the characters is obviously a rendering of nation language.

> I don't care what anyone tell you, going to England be good for it going raise your mind. For a West Indian boy like you just being there is an education, for you going see what England do for sheself . . . It's a college for the West Indian.

The lesson of this "college for the West Indian" is, as Phillips puts it, that "symptomatic of the colonial situation, the language has been divided as well".

In the British Black community, and in English-speaking islands of the Caribbean, English – creole or standard – is the only available language. In Africa, the ancestral homeland of the Caribbean Blacks, English plays a quite different role in a society which contains literally hundreds of competing languages.

In the East African states of Kenya, Uganda, and Tanzania, the lingua franca tends to be Ki-Swahili, but English is the main language of all secondary and tertiary education. (The difficulty of rejecting the force of English is illustrated by the career of one of Kenya's best living writers, Ngugi wa Thiong'o. As James Ngugi he found a huge audience throughout the world. In the 1970s, he turned his back on this, and refused to write in the language of his former colonial master, returning to his native Kikuyu. Today, he is known as the author of *Weep Not Child* – not for his more recent writing published in Nairobi in a language that will, until it is translated, confine his audience to Africa.)

149 In the street markets of Sierra Leone, the language of negotiation is pidgin English and Krio.

KRIO: THE HEART OF THE MATTER

In West Africa, English has official status in Sierra Leone, Gambia, Ghana and Nigeria, and we have already seen the way in which pidgin English is widely used as a *lingua franca*. In the words of a primary schoolteacher from Cameroon: "For the first six years I have to use pidgin. If I didn't, the children would not understand *one word*. Only after I have trained them in pidgin can I begin to use proper English." As a result of the slave experience of the sixteenth and seventeenth centuries, the major language of inter-state communication is also pidgin English. In Sierra Leone, this pidgin has evolved into Krio, a language that is developing on a separate path of its own in accordance with the Burchfield model. The attention focused on Krio is due to the fact that it has been studied and now codified in *A Krio-English Dictionary*, a milestone in the English of West Africa. Its co-author, Eldred Jones, comments:

> Krio has been written in casual letters and newspaper articles for a long time. Now it's being used as a vehicle of news broadcasts. It's become very popular as a medium of plays. I thought it was time it was recorded in a standardized form of spelling.

The word Krio itself is derived from *creole*. At the beginning of the nineteenth century, when the British finally abolished the slave trade, they returned some of the creole speakers of the West Indies to Freetown, Sierra Leone. This exposed the speakers of West Indian creole to the influence of their former African languages, especially Yoruba. Anti-slave traders intensified the African element in Krio by recapturing and returning many enslaved Africans to Freetown before they reached the plantations of America and the West Indies. The language that was adopted by these liberated slaves was Krio, a mixture of English and Yoruba, together with some other elements, mainly Portuguese.

Sierra Leone, the setting for *The Heart of the Matter* by Graham Greene, remained under British administration until the 1950s. At the level of the Civil Service we can be sure that Standard English was the language of government administration as it was also the language of the church, commerce and education. Now Krio too has a recognized status: today it is spoken by perhaps two million people in Sierra Leone, about 350,000 of whom speak it as a first language. Since the British departure, Krio has flourished elsewhere: it is the language of the descendants of Sierra Leonean settlers in the Gambia, and it was brought by traders and missionaries to Nigeria and Cameroon, where it has influenced the local pidgin English. Champions of Krio like to emphasize its differences from other West African pidgins but in reality it is very similar. Eldred Jones remarks:

> There are a number of English-related pidgins and creolized languages all the way down the west coast of Africa, in the Caribbean, in parts of North America, which are, with a certain amount of adjustment, mutually intelligible, because they were developed by speakers who originally spoke African languages.

His own experience bears this out. "I have visited Jamaica and I have found a little bit of difficulty in the first forty-eight hours or so understanding Jamaican creole, but after that I found I could understand it very well, although I could not speak it with the right accent."

The strength of Krio is that it is not ashamed of its origins. Most African states still try to pretend that pidgin English does not exist. There is, for example, no complete pidgin English Bible for West Africa. The "wrong way" of speaking has been officially frowned on. African governments, anxious in every other respect to throw off the shackles of imperialism, still show a genuine enthusiasm for speaking "proper". The government of Sierra Leone, by contrast, has expressed a pride in its language and in recent years has promoted a powerful campaign to establish Krio as the national language of Sierra Leone (even though English is still the "official" language). As a result, Krio literature has flourished, and now that it has its own dictionary it may well become the basis for literary pidgin English throughout West Africa.

Official support for this non-standard English reaches high. The former president, Seaka Stevens, told us, in an interview given before he was (peacefully) deposed:

> Once the people chart their own course and know what they are about, they realize that the purpose of education is not to rid yourself of your culture, but to get as much as you can from outside, mix it with your own and get something solid.

For Stevens, Krio perfectly illustrates this philosophy. "Krio is very rich – a bit of Portuguese, a bit of French, a bit of Yoruba, a bit of English, all put together." At the end of the interview, conducted in Standard English of course, it was time to go shopping. President Stevens liked to buy fresh fish the traditional way – from the fishwomen down by the sea. Driven to the beach in the presidential limousine, he haggled with the fish-sellers in Krio, and then, setting off for the presidential palace, remarked (in Standard English again) "They try to charge me a little extra because they see that I am president."

As well as its first-language use in Sierra Leone, especially in Freetown, Krio is used as a *lingua franca* throughout the country and also in the Gambia. It is now used extensively in education, the mass media and in social interactions of all sorts. Despite the new *Dictionary*, its traditions remain largely oral. Krio is the language of informality, of domestic life and of intimacy between family and friends.

For a professional medical man, like Dr Patrick Coker, the two levels of English – Standard and Krio – are a fact of everyday life. Dr Coker will often interview the patients in his surgery in Krio using characteristic Krio sentences like "Open mouth wide-wide", but he uses the greater official authority of Standard English to diagnose and prescribe. His children learn Standard English at school. He prefers them "to leave Krio for when we are at home".

Although at least 80 per cent of Krio is derived from English – as phrases like *a kam fala yu*? (I come follow you? = May I go with you?) suggest – Krio is not a primitive, quaint, or inefficient version of the mother tongue. It is a language in its own right. Its grammatical structure is partly non-English, and, like Chinese and many African languages, it has a system of tones which will affect the meaning of a word. Any page taken at random from the Krio *Dictionary* conveys its flavour. Most Krio words have obvious English roots. A word like *man* transfers unchanged. But then, under the processes of creolization, it begins to work overtime: *man klos* (man's dress) *man pawa* (man power = strength), *manpus* (man puss = tomcat). Equally, there are the words that have African roots. *Manafiki* (deceitful, untrustworthy [Yoruba: *mana fiki*]), *manyamanya* (to pulp something [Twi: *manyamanta*]), *mao* (to be initiated into rituals [Yoruba: *mavo*]), *mara* (to behave foolishly [Mende: *malama*]), *manti-manti* (very large [Temne]). The "spirit" of Krio, for all its English borrowing, is African. The majority of Sierra Leone is speaking a kind of English that is, to the average British or American eye and ear, virtually a foreign language.

Are these the beginnings of a new language? Depending on where one places the emphasis, the experience of English in the Caribbean and in West Africa certainly provides two models for the possible break-up of English. Travelling East, to India and beyond, we find that the story is repeated, with local variations, throughout South-East Asia and the Pacific basin.

ENGLISH IN INDIA

By some estimates, there are now more speakers of English in India than in Britain, about seventy million, and their sounds range from the most *pukka* "Oxbridge" enunciations to the obscure pidgins of the street. A country with many languages has re-made English with many voices. Part of the fascination of English in India to the Standard English-speaking visitor is the richness and completeness of its appropriation by the Indian people.

A few facts: English is the *de facto* language of official life in virtually every sphere. The speakers of English – overwhelmingly from the educated, ruling elites – number more than the speakers of some "official" languages like Assamese or Punjabi. The continuing power and influence of the language is remarkable. It is the state language of two states – Meghalaya and Nagaland – and it is taught as a second language at *every stage* of education in *all* the states of the country. Four of the seven daily papers are in English (*Times of India*, Bombay; the *Pioneer*, Lucknow; the *Mail*, Madras; the *Telegraph*, Calcutta). Out of nearly 16,000 newspapers registered in India in 1978, about 3000 were in English, a figure surpassed only by Hindi newspapers. More important is the fact that English newspapers are published in virtually every state, more than Hindi-Urdu and more than Bengali. The marriage of English and the languages of India has made what Anthony Burgess has called a "whole language, complete with the colloquialisms of Calcutta and London, Shakespearian archaisms, bazaar whinings, references to the Hindu pantheon, the jargon of Indian litigation, and shrill Babu irritability all together. It's not pure English, but it's like the English of Shakespeare, Joyce and Kipling – gloriously impure."

Soutik Biswas is a reporter on the *Telegraph*, Calcutta's English-language newspaper. He was taught British English but he has adopted something of an American style: he refers to rupees as "bucks", reads *Mad* magazine and listens to jazz. On every assignment he will use

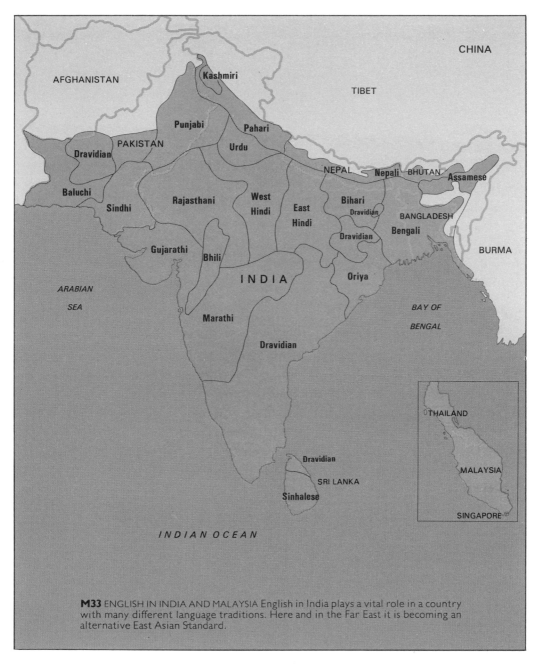

M33 ENGLISH IN INDIA AND MALAYSIA English in India plays a vital role in a country with many different language traditions. Here and in the Far East it is becoming an alternative East Asian Standard.

an extraordinary variety of English (mixed in with two or three Indian languages) and his work, at both the spoken and written levels, typifies the situation of English in India today. If we follow him on one particular story, we find that the international wire service in the *Telegraph* office operates in Standard English, while the editor's briefing – about outbreaks of violence on some neighbouring fish-farms, or *bheris* – is naturally in English with an Indian accent. On the way to the assignment, Mr Biswas collects one of the *Telegraph*'s photographers, Dilip Banerjee. Their conversation is in a mixture of English and Bengali. When they arrive at the fish-farm Mr Biswas discovers that the story is quite a serious one. Bandits – *dacoits* as they are called – have murdered two of the manager's men and are terrorizing the property. It is time to talk to the manager. His command of English is extremely limited. The conversation, in Indian English, goes something like this:

BISWAS:	So what exactly are the problems you are facing now?
MANAGER:	The exactly problem of the fishing . . . and dacoit robbery . . .
BISWAS:	(*writing in his notebook*) Hooligans problems.
MANAGER:	On twenty-ninth June. About nine p.m. We take dinner at the time. They attacked in this hut. They come and they attacked and they fired and they murdered my uncle.
BISWAS:	(*asking about a second attack*): And the second time . . .
MANAGER:	Broad daylight. Three p.m. They attacked and murdered – open daylight – my second manager.

All this is repeated in an umistakable Indian mode, with much nodding of the head, prompting, repetition and suggestion. Sometimes, Biswas will conduct interviews in Bengali or Hindi. But he always takes notes in English: working for an English-language newspaper it is the only sure way of getting accurate quotes.

When Soutik Biswas finally reports this story in the *Telegraph*, he writes in Standard English, with occasional Indianisms, under the headline FISHING OWNERS FEEL INSECURE.

> Frequent dacoits and looting of fish from bheris in the Sonarpur area has created a serious law and order problem. Tension prevails in the entire area which has 60 bheris. Dacoits armed with pipe-guns, swords and sticks strike before the villagers can retaliate. They surround the bheris and loot the fish. For the villagers, the attacks are "straight out of Hindi movies".

This fragment of Indian journalism is an unspectacular but typical example of the everyday uses of English in a society that is continuously indigenizing a foreign language. It is the re-interpretation of the English language by the Indian people – a process echoed in Ireland – that has fascinated visitors from the very beginnings of the British involvement in India.

THE JEWEL IN THE CROWN

The English have had a toehold on the Indian subcontinent since 1600, when the newly formed East India Company established settlements in Madras, Calcutta and later Bombay. By the end of the eighteenth century, the Company controlled virtually all aspects of Indian administration, reinforced, culturally, by the work of English missionaries. In 1813, the East India Company was dissolved and India became the keystone of an English-speaking empire stretching throughout South-East Asia. A flood of English-speaking administrators, army officers, educators and missionaries scattered English throughout the sub-continent, and the English of the subject Indians ("Babu" or "Cheechee" English) became a widespread means of communication between master and servant. Almost from the first many prominent Indian leaders began to pester the East India Company with requests that its officials give instruction in English (not Sanskrit or Arabic) so that young Indians could have access to the science and technology of the West.

The real beginnings of bilingualism in India occurred in 1835, when the historian Thomas Macaulay, as president of the Indian Committee of Public Instruction, proposed the creation of "a class who may be interpreters between us and the millions whom we govern – a class of persons, Indians in blood and colour, but English in taste, in opinion, in morals and in intellect". Macaulay, whose *History of England* had achieved a spectacular popularity, was an out-and-out champion of the superiority of European culture (evaluating the rival claims of Arabic and Sanskrit he once remarked that "a single shelf of a good European Library was worth the whole native literature of India and Arabia"). Macaulay's plan was adopted. At a stroke, English became the language of government, education and advancement, at once a symbol of imperial rule and of self-improvement.

The results of this policy were dramatic. English-speaking universities were set up in Bombay, Calcutta and Madras in 1857, the year of the Mutiny. By the end of the century, with many more colleges and universities established, English had become the prestige language of India, completely supplanting Persian and Indian rivals. When the nationalist movement began to gather momentum during and after the First World War the medium of nationalist opposition was not Hindi, or one of the many other Indian languages, but English.

The imperialists' fascination with India – its people, its culture and its landscape – was expressed in a substantial adoption of Indian words and phrases. Words of Indian origin have insinuated themselves into English since the days of Elizabeth I, words like *brahmin*, *calico*, *curry* and *rajah*. By the end of the seventeenth century, they had been joined by *coolie*, *juggernaut*, *bungalow*, *cheroot*, *pundit* and *chintz*; and at the end of the eighteenth century, by *bandana*, *jungle*, *jute*, *toddy*, and *verandah*. As early as 1624, a letter written by two English traders already shows the local language creeping into their style:

> Their last was of the 15th present, with a copy of the king's "furmand" [*furman*: command]. Since then they have procured the dispatch of two haddies [*ahadi*: a royal messenger], who are ordered to carry to them the royal farman, in command of John Willoughby, 'Cojah [Kwaja Abul Hasan] haveinge given them his parwanna [*parwana*: a written order] to see all things restored unto you and re-established againe in youre formar trad and priviolidges. The messengers should therefore be acquainted with all moneys unjustly taken from them, either by Safi Khan, "Chukedares" [*chaukidar*: here, a custom-guard] or "radarries" [*rahdar*: a road-guard].

Throughout the nineteenth century, the English administrators added more and more local words to their basic vocabularies, words like *chutney*, *guru*, *cummerbund* and *purdah*. A flourishing genre of handbooks for the English visitor to India sprang up, with titles like *The Oriental Interpreter*:

> The new arrival in India, ignorant of the language of the country, is puzzled for some time, to comprehend his countrymen, whose conversation "wears strange suits", and even he, who has been for years a sojourner in India is, to the last, unacquainted with the meaning of numerous words, which occur in his daily newspaper, the Courts of Law, and the communications of his Mofussil or upcountry correspondents.

The scale of English borrowing from Indian speech has had various estimates. The *Oxford English Dictionary* lists about 900 words; a mid-nineteenth-century glossary runs to 26,000. One volume above all, *Hobson-Jobson: A Glossary of Anglo-Indian Words*, compiled and published in 1886 by Colonel Henry Yule and A. C. Burnell, is the classic summary of the mingling of the two cultures before the age of independence, at once stylish and informative. The glossary, whose title showed its authors' understanding of the relationship between English and the languages of India, was published two years after the first fascicle of the *OED*. It was an ambitious volume and, in the words of Yule and Burnell, "was intended to deal with all that class of words which . . . recur constantly in the daily intercourse of the English in India, either as expressing ideas really not provided for by our mother tongue, or supposed by the speakers (often quite erroneously) to express something not capable of just denotation by any English term." *Hobson-Jobson* records thousands of such usages: *amah/ayah* (nurse), *burra-beebee* (lady of high rank), *chota-hazry* (breakfast) and so on. As we shall see, the inventions of Indian English have been sustained to this day.

For a completely unforced, unselfconscious portrait of the state of English in India at the turn of the century, there are the delightful *Letters From India* by Anne Campbell Macleod, who married Sir James Wilson in 1888, and then went to India for a stay of twenty years. Lady Wilson described the experience in a series of letters to her family in England. She writes about the life of Anglo-India with obvious enjoyment, describing her travels to Simla, the Khyber Pass, and Benares with infectious enthusiasm. At the centre of official life, she witnessed the 1903 Durbar, criticized the early independence movement and mourned the passing of Queen Victoria, noting that, "She was worshipped by Her people in India, who identified Her with their gods, and to whom She was an incarnation of Motherhood."

But she was not blindly imperialist. She took a keen interest in Indian culture, art and music. From the beginning her comments on the language of the Raj are highly illuminating. Immediately after her arrival in India she started to learn Hindi; without a basic grasp of the local language she would be unable to communicate with her servants.

> Thanks to my Hindustani grammar, I can make myself understood now by the cook and bearer. I take Akbar's accounts about twice a week, for he keeps the purse and is major-domo, local caterer, middleman between us

150 The empire strikes back: English, once the language of imperial rule, is now being remade by Indian culture.

and the villagers. The rest of our shopping has to be done by correspondence, and is associated in my mind with interminable receipts, which have to be signed by the sender and receiver, as well as by railway and post-office clerks.

She was self-aware enough to contrast her own inadequate struggles with the native language with the achievements of the educated Indians she met in her capacity as Sir James Wilson's wife.

> From all this you may gather that I don't find Hindustani by any means easy. But when one remembers how marvellously educated Indians have mastered our complicated language, with its arbitrary differences in the pronunciation of words spelt in the same way, and its many idioms, so entirely unlike their own, one is ashamed of one's own stupidity, and renews the attempt to learn their language for the pleasure of being able to talk to them in their own tongue.

Quite quickly, Anne Wilson got to know all the local people, and her command of the superior language meant that leading Indian fathers tried out their children's education on the English *memsahib*. "They bring their boys to read English to me, or show me their little English essays." She made a note of the Indian English she encountered:

> I am advancing at least in one branch of my new education, as I am learning by rapid strides the full inner meaning of "chits" – these being scraps of paper with messages from neighbours, to which you are expected to add your answers at once.

Observing the highest echelons of Indian society, she notes the way in which some Indians become completely – almost absurdly – anglicized or deracinated.

> K.S.'s father was cupbearer to Maharajah Duleep Singh's mother, and he was taken by the Maharajah as a boy to England to be educated, with some vague idea of his representing his interests in Parliament. That idea was given up, and K. S. returned to India highly educated and quite denationalized, not even knowing a word of Hindustani.

In 1901, by now thoroughly at home with the Anglo-Indian way of life, her wide-eyed comments about local customs and languages are fewer. It is clear from her letters that in some circles, English was used even by the servants: "Our first essay to enter alien ground (a conversation with an Indian civil servant) was not wholly a success, partly perhaps because of the presence of attendants who understood English, which destroyed some of the intimacy of a three-handed talk."

Three years later, in 1904, Lady Wilson recorded a conversation in Calcutta with "a Bengali writer of plays" that opens a window on to a political landscape with implications she (with her generation) probably could not grasp. " 'We are a conquered race,' said the playwright, speaking very intensely. 'Sometimes I like to write a satire.' He threw back his head and his eyes blazed. 'I like to show up those creatures of my race, who go to England and forget their own traditions, and come back dressed like foreigners, monkeys, beef-eating rascals. I like to hold them up to ridicule, their clothes, their habits, and all their tomfoolery.' "

THE INDIANIZATION OF ENGLISH

The Raj created an essentially bilingual society, Indian English and one (or more) native languages. There were infinite gradations of Indian English ranging from the less-educated varieties (variously referred to by *Hobson-Jobson* as Babu English, Butler English, Bearer English and Kitchen English), to educated or standard Indian English, often very scholarly and bookish. Yule and Burnell, identifying speech patterns we have already noticed in chapter six, described the most pidginized Indian English as follows:

> The broken English spoken by native servants in the Madras Presidency; which is not very much better than the Pidgeon-English [*sic*] of China. It is a singular dialect ... thus *I telling* = "I will tell"; *I done tell* = "I have told"; *done come* = "actually arrived" ... The oddest characteristic about this jargon is (or was) that masters used it in speaking to their servants as well as servants to their masters.

At the other end of the scale, college graduates might occasionally embellish the language of the Raj with an exotic native flourish. The author of *Onoocool Chunder Mookerjee*, a memoir published in 1873, writes that, "The house became a second Babel, or a pretty kettle of fish. His elevation created a catholic ravishment throughout the domain under the benign and fostering sceptre of great Albion." As in the English of some Irish writers, one can almost hear the writer translating into English from his mother tongue. Much more common was the bureaucratic use of Indian English. Below the level of the most highly educated, whose English was invariably modelled on old-fashioned teaching, were the English-using clerks of the Imperial administration. These tended to introduce some characteristic Indian uses into their speech. They would say *I am doing* instead of "I (constantly) do"; *I am doing it* for "I have been doing it"; *when I will come* for "when I come". A question like "Will you please do this?" in Indian English becomes *You will do this?* A scribe in a letter will often give "sympathetic consideration". (See illustrations 153/154.)

In India today, Dr M. P. Jain, of the Indian Institute of Technology, is studying the unique character of Indian English on a computer. He is concerned about the Indianization of English, whose contemporary developments he is charting by storing millions of words in a database. A great collector of "mistakes", Professor Jain distinguishes four important characteristics of Indian English. First, "There is one type of flavour that comes from archaic words." He quotes a sentence like, "What's the time by your *time-piece?*" or "You must have been *out of station* (away)." Second, there is the special flavour gained from words that have been borrowed from Indian languages. We have already seen Soutik Biswas use words like *bheri* and *dacoit*. An Indian might say, "He went to the temple to have a *darshan* of the deity." The word *darshan* means "to offer worship". An Indian might not even say "temple" but use the Indian *gudwarra* instead. Thirdly, another quality of Indian English comes from "a curious combination of two words in English doing a new kind of function". For example, *mixy-grinder* which is Indian English for a food blender. An *Eve-teaser* is someone who harasses women. A *stepney* is a spare tyre. In the same category, we find, *anti-people* is "not in the interests of the people". An *ace-defector* is "a past master at defecting". In Indian films, a *playback singer* is "a singer who provides the voice for an actor who is mouthing the words not singing". Finally, there are the famous Indian English hybrids, *godown space* for "warehouse", *newspaper wallah* (a man who sells newspapers), and *box-wallah* (a businessman).

Another characteristic of Indian English is the literal translation of idiom, echoing the earlier medieval tradition of translation from French into English of phrases like "a marriage of convenience" and "it goes without saying". Today there are several such Indian English translations that may become part of a shared vocabulary: *may the fire ovens consume you, a crocodile in a loin-cloth*, and comparisons like *as good as kitchen ashes, as helpless as a calf* and *as lean as an areca-nut tree*. Abuse in Indian English is a particularly rich source of idiomatic translation. From masters to servants: *you donkey's husband*. From parents to children: *why did I rear a serpent with the milk of my breast?* To women only: *go and lie with a licking male dog*. To oneself: *I am a leper if there is a lie in anything I say*.

In addition to these kinds of translations, Indian English possesses a number of distinctive stylistic features, some of which are inspired by local languages and some by the influence of English educational traditions. For example, there is a drift away from Anglo-Saxon words towards a Latinized vocabulary. An Indian speaker would prefer to say *demise* than *death*. There is a great range of polite forms in Indian English: *I bow at his feet, long live the gods, God is merciful,* and *we only pray for your kindness.* Speakers of Indian English, influenced by their own languages, like to create phrases like *nation building, change of heart* and *dumb millions.* They also abbreviate and rearrange English phrases. "An address of welcome" can become *a welcome address,* and "a bunch of keys" will be *a key bunch.* Some commentators on Indian English have noticed an excessive use of cliché: *better imagined than described, do the needful, each and every,* and *leave severely alone.*

Dr Jain accepts that Indian English must have an "Indian " colouring: "If we are using English in India, we have to integrate it with our social system. It must reflect our social reality. Now to that extent words like *bheri* and *darshan* are appropriate." But he is at odds with those who believe that Indian English should take pride in and develop its native idiosyncrasies. Dr Jain expresses his worries for the future:

> But there is another aspect where we are using English as a window on the world of knowledge. Then it has to be in line with Standard English. Now it is that aspect which is a bit disturbing. There are occasions when Indians are not understood. This is what Mrs Gandhi complained about when she was unable to understand the contribution of an Indian delegate to an international meeting – and the delegate spoke in English.

To emphasize his concerns, Dr Jain cites the example of Indian students, in the social sciences especially, who can no longer understand the Standard English of their textbooks:

> We now have a very interesting industry in India where standard books written by American or British authors are rehashed into a kind of Indian English. A famous textbook by an American economist, *Microeconomic Theory: A Mathematical Approach,* becomes *A Theory of Firm: Economic and Managerial Aspects.*

A sign of "deterioration" for Dr Jain, this for some is the logical and necessary fulfilment of a process that stretches back into the days of the Raj. As in the Caribbean, as in West Africa, the search for an authentically Indian voice in an alien language involves the remaking of the language in a local context.

BY INDIANS FOR INDIANS

Bookish or idiomatic, the making of Indian English was a marriage between the sympathetic elements of English society, typified by writers like Rudyard Kipling (who described Indian English as "a clipped, uncertain sing-song") and E. M. Forster, and the innovative, responsive elements of Indian culture. Nearly half a century ago, before the great watershed of independence in 1947, the Indian writer Raja Rao made a famous summary of the problems of a bilingual community:

The telling has not been easy. One has to convey in a language that is not one's own the spirit that is one's own. One has to convey various shades and omissions of a certain thought-movement that looks maltreated in an alien language. I use the word "alien", yet English is not really an alien language to us. It is the language of our intellectual make-up – like Sanskrit or Persian was before – but not of our emotional make-up. We are instinctively bilingual, many of us writing in our own language and in English. *We cannot write like the English. We should not.* We cannot write only as Indians. We have grown to look at the large world as part of us. *Our method of expression therefore has to be a dialect which will some day prove to be as distinctive and colourful as the Irish or the American.* Time alone will justify it.

Raja Rao also addressed the question of style in Indian English. He wrote: "The tempo of Indian life must be infused into our English expression, even as the tempo of American or Irish life has gone into the making of theirs. We, in India, think quickly, we talk quickly, and when we move we move quickly. There must be something in the Sun of India that makes us rush and tumble and run on."

After independence, the question of language and style became crucial. The Constitution of 1950 recognized fourteen Indian languages of which Hindi was to be the first national language. Prime Minister Nehru declared that it was government policy to shake India free of

151 Indian English is found at all levels of Indian society, including the captions of this comic strip.

English "within a generation". English was to be a transitional language until 1965. In reality, it is still the language that examines students in the universities, conducts foreign affairs and opens the way to a business career. In the words of one scientist, "English is of course not necessary for learning science, but science is an international activity and it's convenient to have a link language which is understood by most people ... If you meet an active, working scientist abroad, then more often than not you can get by speaking English with him."

Indian English has begun, also, to develop its own literary credibility. Before independence, there were English writers, like E. M. Forster, who wrote about India as outsiders; and there were their Indian imitators. These were despised by their colleagues who, remembering Yeats' warning in 1937 that "no man can think or write with music and vigour except in his mother tongue", rejected the "alien" language as a literary form. After independence, this view continued to find vigorous expression. It was said that Indians who wrote in English "do not have a real public in India, where literature is defined in terms of the different native languages, and their claim can be justified only by appreciation in England or the United States". In spite of the controversy, Indian English writing – fiction, poetry, essays and journalism – has gained such a flourishing international reputation as *Indian* writing that it is now being recognized as one of the *Indian* literatures; not as "a blind alley, lined with curio shops, leading nowhere", but as "one of the voices in which India speaks. It is a new voice no doubt, but it is as much Indian as others."

Professor P. Lal, who likes to quote such comments, runs a writers' workshop designed to promote the writing of Indian English. His circle has included the novelist Anita Desai. It is a sign of the times that his efforts on behalf of Indian English, considered laughable in the 1960s, are now widely respected. When his present group gathers to read its work to him, he listens, and reads out a poem – to make a point:

> *Why not let the English language to relax,*
> *And have a truly tropical weekend?*
> *After a course of the choicest Indian rudery,*
> *English may return, chastened, to its prudery.*
> *No? You won't agree?*
> *Forgive me, you look sickened.*
> *In Shakespeare's day,*
> *English was such a dandy ...*

As well as holding seminars for writers who are exploring with him the byways of Indian English ("the Indian languages love elaboration") Professor Lal publishes for India. He has about six hundred books in Indian English on his list, and he makes this prediction:

> You'll always have Indians who speak very good and correct English. But
> in fifteen or twenty years we might have evolved a language which is so truly
> and richly and uniquely and indigenously our own, that you will have to

152 Pandit Jawaharlal Nehru chatting with Mahatma Gandhi. In 1947, Nehru announced that English would be eliminated from India "within a generation". Like many predictions about English, this was not fulfilled.

carry a tourist guide, with footnotes, as to what these words mean. This will be a language written for Indians by Indians. And with no other outside audience in mind ... We will create another indigenous language, like Urdu, like Sanskrit and Hindi ... English is not my mother's tongue, but it is my mother tongue. And that's the way it is with many Indians – we have no choice of it.

Indian recognition of the bilingual traditions and distinctiveness of its culture is being backed up in academic circles by a sharper interest in a serious Indian English dictionary. In 1976 the *Little Oxford Dictionary* included a thirty-two-page "Supplement of Indian Words", drawing on *Hobson-Jobson* and some others. But these, the lexicographer pointed out, "appeared nearly a century ago, before the time of *satyagrapis*, *razakars*, *naxalites*, *gheraos*, *dosas*, *idlis*, *bosons* and *jhuggies*." Not only are there many new developments in Indian English that need to be recorded, some of the definitions in, say, *Hobson-Jobson*, are ludicrously out of date:

> *Butler*. In the Madras and Bombay Presidencies this is the title usually applied to the head-servant of any English or quasi-English household. He generally makes the daily market, has charge of domestic stores, and superintends the table. As his profession is one which affords a large scope for feathering a nest at the expense of a foreign master, it is often followed at Madras by men of comparatively good caste.

House No.3020,
Bhagwanganj, Bahadurgarh Road,
Sadar Bazar, Delhi_6(India).

Dear Miss Vivian Ducat,
I receive with grace your
letter of wishes of 13th instant and I too convey
my best wishes to you for a very cheerful and
prosperous new year.

I remember very well my two
last meetings with you here.But receiving your
kind letter is an exciting experience for me. I
shall feel it to be my endeavour to be amongst
your filming schedule on Friday,March 8 ,1985.
Please do write to me atleast a fortnight in
advance before filming schedule goes on floors,
so as to enable me to be available for the same.

I always feel jolly & strong
as you observed me. This is why I am doing my
business successfully.

I am anxiously waiting for
your arrival in Delhi in mid February.

Yours Sincerely,
(Brij Lal Kochhar).

153/154 A letter from Brij Lal Kochhar to the BBC – in the Indian English of a Delhi scribe.

We have already seen the emergence of dictionaries of Australian English, Canadian English, Jamaican English, and South African English. Indian English has now been sufficiently recognized – internally and externally – as institutionalized on its own terms; and a dictionary of Indian English is now apparently under preliminary discussion at the offices of the Oxford University Press in Delhi.

The traditions of English, as we have seen, are peculiarly deep-rooted in India. Since 1947, there have been three schools of thought about the role of English in an independent India, and they provide a pattern for the likely future debate about English in the Third World generally. A small minority looked for ever-closer ties between International English and Indian English. Then there were those – mainly Hindi – who worked towards the day in 1965 when Hindi would become the official language. In fact, as 1965 drew closer, the hostility of the South to the Hindi supremacy in the North proved decisive in favour of English. In May 1963 there were language riots in Tamil Nadu. The Indian Parliament capitulated. English could "continue to be used, in addition to Hindi, for all the official purposes of the Union . . . and for the transaction of business in Parliament". The third prevailing school argued for the status quo. In due course, this position has become stabilized as the so-called Three Language Formula: English, Hindi and one other Indian language.

Now – in the 1980s – the language debate is focused on questions such as the place of English in education, the proper roles for the three languages, and the model of English to be offered to Indian learners of English. The answers to these questions will be partly shaped by government policy, partly by pressure groups within India (pro-and anti-English), but overwhelmingly by the reality of the society and the culture, the total permeation of Indian life by Indian English, a constant reinterpretation of English in new and changing Indian situations. It is a living language in a living environment, and the result is a new language, yet another of the many new Englishes emerging round the world.

The unique place of Indian English in the spectrum of English today makes it an attractive alternative to many Third World students for whom training in Britain or the United States is either too expensive or politically unacceptable. H. C. Narang, of the Centre for Linguistics and English at Nehru University, New Delhi, has taught students from Iran, Saudi Arabia, Laos, Kampuchea, and Vietnam and believes that "some of these countries feel culturally closer to us, and politically closer, too". There is also the feeling that "at the academic level, there will not be much harm if they come and learn their English in India . . . English has been with us for almost two hundred years". The English taught in this school is not the more idiosyncratic Indian English we have seen in this chapter. Teachers make a point of "exposing our students to the native pronunciation of British English, through the BBC tapes and some of the BBC films". In this school, the teachers believe that they have developed what they like to call "a non-aligned variety of English". For Dr Narang, the learning of English now transcends national boundaries:

> Those countries which have strong groundings in English – like India, or Pakistan, or Bangladesh, or the countries in East Africa and West Africa – share in the task of teaching English to other countries who do not have any English but who do need English. In that sense we are helping the cause of English in a big way. This is no more the cause of England or America, it's the cause of the world.

The immediate and possible future power of Indian English can be seen in the sphere of Indian influence, that is to say, Bangladesh, Pakistan, Sri Lanka and, further afield, the English-speaking parts of South-East Asia, notably Singapore.

THE PACIFIC AGE

The Pacific in the 1980s from Singapore and Malaya in the west, to Japan, Hong Kong and Korea to the north, Hawaii and California towards the east, and Australasia to the south, has become the fastest growing community on the planet, representing one-third of the world's population. The Far Eastern economic miracle is based on the American English of the high-tech industries, the English of shipping and ship-repairing, the English of the auto industry, and the English of scientific research. This English foundation is backed up by the varieties of English spoken in Papua New Guinea, in Hawaii and the South Seas, and above all, in Singapore and Hong Kong.

Singapore, according to the advertisements, is "the most surprising tropical island on earth". To the tourist, the island presents itself as the gateway to the Far East, offering, in a space the size of the Isle of Wight, the quintessence of Chinese, Malay and Tamil culture – exotic temples, fragrant gardens, crowded bazaars and all the spicy riches of the oriental kitchen. But the real business of Singapore is the future. After Japan, it is the most aggressively self-modernizing nation state in the Pacific, a model for Malaya, Korea, Taiwan and the Philippines. The huge international airport has turned a slum-ridden relic of British imperialism into a stop-over city with a high-rise business district, a pan-island expressway, and huge estates of regimented housing blocks. A population of about two and a half million people – Chinese, Malay, Indian – is officially encouraged to speak and write English, from the cradle to the grave.

The English favoured by the government is, of course, the Standard English of international finance, trade and technology. But the English emerging in the multi-racial, multi-cultural society of Singapore is rather different. In the first place, of course, English is not native to the island. The mother tongue of Singaporeans may be any one of several varieties of Chinese, or Malay, or Tamil. For them, English is a learned language, profoundly influenced by the grammatical structure of Mandarin, or Cantonese or Malay. Outside the home, the peer-pressure of the schools reinforces the non-standard nature of Singaporean English, as in:

> I like hot hot curry – very *shink* (terrific, beyond description);
> big *bluff*, man, he! (he's just a show-off);
> you can *drop* here (you can get out here);

155 Singapore in the 1980s. "There is this naive belief that because the language is English, therefore, it is not part of me, so I cannot learn to use it as well as an Englishman. This is utterly wrong." Lee Kuan Yew

my name, you write it with three *alphabets* (letters) not four;
stop *shaking legs* and do some work (*shake legs*, a direct translation
from Malay, means to be idle).

After more than a generation of English-language planning Singaporeans have developed their own kind of English. They have also developed a distinctive accent which the outsider might at first mistake for Japlish. The most celebrated Singlish characteristic is the use of *lah* at the end of sentences: *He is big-sized, lah*. Singaporeans naturally have no difficulty in recognizing their fellow countrymen abroad. T. T. B. Koh, Singapore's representative to the United Nations, has made this into a statement of Singaporean nationalism:

> When one is abroad, in a bus or a train or aeroplane and when one overhears someone speaking, one can immediately say this is someone from Malaysia or Singapore. And I should hope that when I'm speaking abroad my countrymen will have no problem recognizing that I am a Singaporean.

The emergence of a recognizable Singaporean English – both in accent and vocabulary and idiom – has provoked some interesting and contradictory reactions within Singapore society. At one level, there is a distinct pride, mixed with the snob reaction that "Singlish" is the language of hawkers and taxi drivers. There is also a fear that this "new English" will deprive Singapore of the very thing it most wants – membership of the international community of

156 Lee Kuan Yew, prime minister of Singapore, a champion of Standard English. "We were fortunate in that quite fortuitously American technological and economic dominance coincided with our English heritage."

English-speaking nations. In 1978, the prime minister, Lee Kuan Yew, made a rare appearance on television to debate this issue with his people. He remarked:

> The English we are beginning to see or hear our people speak is a very strange Singapore pidgin, a Singapore dialect English which is not ideal but which is the best for the time being, and which we can improve upon if we concentrate our effort and considerable resources.

By 1981, the prime minister's campaign against Singlish had escalated. It was now branded "slovenly" and he lent his authority to the promotion of "clear, clean English". First-language English speakers were hired from abroad to improve the standard of English education. In government, Singapore's bureaucrats were sent on special courses to improve their writing skills. Singapore Broadcasting, modelled on the BBC, began to clamp down on Singlish broadcasts. Singapore's daily newspaper, *The Straits Times*, hired an English language consultant, Lee Sow Ling, to write a regular column entitled "Let's watch our words". Lee Sow Ling is eloquent about Singapore's ambivalence towards English. Singaporeans delight in the access it gives them to the world, but as a language it is "not ours" and "never can be ours". Indigenization of English is the nearest Singapore can get to an internationally viable language of its own.

A sample of Lee Sow Ling's journalism includes advice about the correct use of prepositions ("To get someone *on* your side" not "*to* your side"), the use of singular and plural nouns ("old *guard*" not "old *guards*"), the perils of malapropism ("incredulous" for "incredible"), and the correct placing of commas. The level of Lee Sow Ling's concern does not suggest the emergence of a divergent standard of *written* English in Singapore. At the spoken, idiomatic level, the situation is much more complex, and while Singapore, (despite recent economic troubles) one of the showcase economies of the "New Pacific", enters a period of transition as Lee Kuan Yew approaches retirement, much more attention will be focused on Singlish as a medium of dissent, a rejection of the formal standards of the past and the voice of a new and distinctive nationalism.

Here the champions of Singlish argue that it is a new, unique and vital branch of the great tree of English. They point to an active slang as a sure sign that the language is alive. Defenders of Singlish point out that Standard English has a wide range of spoken varieties, from Irish Blarney, to Cockney, to Strine, and that Singlish is just the latest member of a many-accented club. The Singapore playwright Max Leblond remarks (of the campaigns to improve English in Singapore), "Americans don't feel apologetic about the way they speak English. Why should we?"

An authentic Singaporean English is now beginning to extend to the written word: a recent production of Mike Nichols' *General Hospital* found that the most effective way to represent speech contrasts in one scene was to use Singlish, a decision which alarmed the Ministry of Culture. Like Jamaican creole, Singlish is also finding its voice among writers, valued for a vividness of expression that cannot be equalled by Standard English. The poet

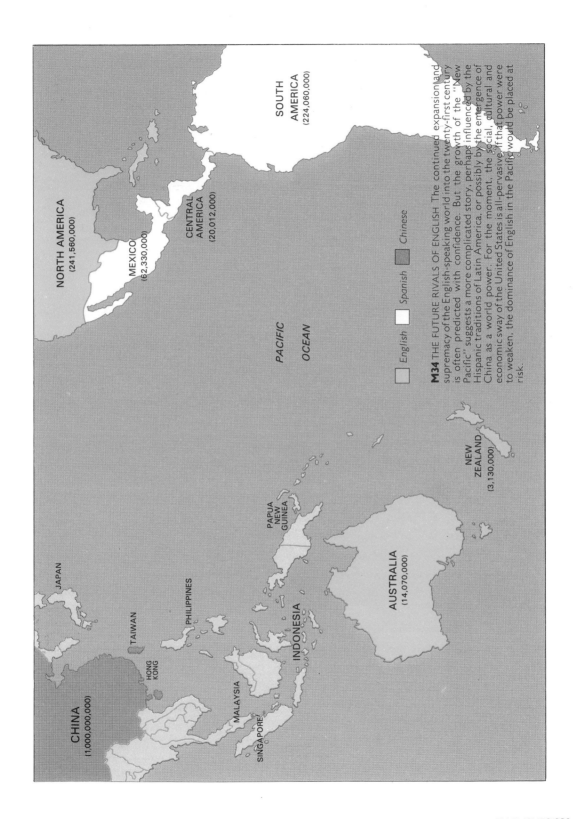

M34 THE FUTURE RIVALS OF ENGLISH The continued expansion and supremacy of the English-speaking world into the twenty-first century is often predicted with confidence. But the growth of the "New Pacific" suggests a more complicated story, perhaps influenced by the Hispanic traditions of Latin America, or possibly by the emergence of China as a world power. For the moment, the social, cultural and economic sway of the United States is all-pervasive. If that power were to weaken, the dominance of English in the Pacific would be placed at risk.

English   Spanish   Chinese

NORTH AMERICA (241,560,000)

MEXICO (62,330,000)

CENTRAL AMERICA (20,012,000)

SOUTH AMERICA (224,060,000)

PACIFIC OCEAN

CHINA (1,000,000,000)

JAPAN

TAIWAN

HONG KONG

PHILIPPINES

MALAYSIA

SINGAPORE

INDONESIA

PAPUA NEW GUINEA

AUSTRALIA (14,070,000)

NEW ZEALAND (3,130,000)

Arthur Yap is one of the island's leading writers in the local idiom:

> *Ah Beng is so smart*
> *already he can watch tv and know the whole story*
> *your Kim Cheong is also quite smart*
> *what boy is he in the exam?*
> *this playground is not too bad, but i'm always*
> *so worried, car here, car there.*

Later the poet uses Singapore English *jamban* for "toilet bowl", *toa-soh*, Hokkien Chinese for "sister-in-law", *ah pah*, Hokkien for "father" and Singlish phrases like "I scold like mad but what for?" None of this is hard to understand, nor is this extract from another Singlish writer, Catherine Lim:

> Yes, Madam, quite big family – eight children, six sons, two daughters. Big family! Ha! Ha! No good, Madam. In those days, where got Family Planning in Singapore.

Is this the beginning of a new language, as Burchfield would insist, or is it an example of the kind of local variety we have seen from the first landing of the Angles and Saxons in Britain? It is certainly true that this kind of local "corruption" can be found throughout the English-speaking countries of Asia, and in the Philippines and Malaysia especially. Here, in traditionally important outposts of American English and British English respectively, the rise of nationalism has strengthened the claims of Filipino and Bahasa Malaysia. But English is still everyone's second language, the passport to economic and intellectual liberation, the means of Third World development – in other words, the language of an elite, the educated few. This, Dr Burchfield would say, is precisely what happened to Latin in the Middle Ages.

Our own view, based on observation throughout the English-speaking world, is that, given a world of satellites, televisions and telephones, English will probably continue to flourish at two quite distinct levels: International Standard (internationally functional) and Local Alternative (locally functional). The former will evolve more or less uniformly throughout the Standard English-using world. At this educated level, the differences between British English, American English and a Third World variety like Indian English are *probably* not so severe as to require, in the way some have suggested, a simplified, international "Nuclear English". The latter, the Local Alternative, will become more and more distinctive and will indeed throw up local literatures, though these are always likely to be overshadowed by the International Standard. Take away the technology of mass communications and the picture changes dramatically. In that (unthinkable) situation, Dr Burchfield is almost certainly right in his predictions. (Our own experience in recording the material for this book around the world bears out this thesis. Time and again, in pursuit of a particular local English oddity, Gullah, for instance, or Barbadian creole, we found – to our intense frustration – that our informants would drop their "local" speech and approximate to the International Standard, partly to be understood and partly to show off their command of "prestige" international form. It was often difficult to create the right conditions in which to record the "local" English – as shy, in its way, as the world's rarer wildlife.)

In the end perhaps the most serious potential challenge to World English will come from outside. In the age of the New Pacific should we not consider those two historical rivals to English: Spanish and Chinese? The economic power of Latin America, many experts believe, has yet to be fully deployed. The Hispanic question is now on the minds of many Americans. Might Spanish not mount a serious challenge to the hegemony of American English? It seems unlikely today, but no one, presumably, paid much attention to the English-speaking merchants of the fifteenth century. The influence and potential of Chinese is of quite a different order, however. It is widely spoken throughout the Far East. A decline in American power might encourage a country like Singapore, whose children are bilingual in Mandarin and English, to switch its support to Mandarin as the medium of Far East Asian business. And then there is the "x factor" of technological change. Will computerized translation machines finally overthrow the myth of Babel? When we look into the dark crystal of predictions about language we find the words of T. S. Eliot:

For last year's words belong to last year's language
And next year's words await another voice.

Epilogue

NEXT YEAR'S WORDS

What, finally, is the future of the English language in its two homelands, Britain and the United States? As we have seen, every new stage in the evolution of English has provoked the same questions: does change mean revitalization, or does it mean corruption and deterioration? English is in a constant state of renewal. The quicker the tempo of change, the quicker the rate of renewal. In a century of uniquely rapid social and cultural transformation, thanks mainly to the technology of mass communication, fears for the future of English have become one of the staples of newspaper columns, television chat shows, and even, in Britain in 1978, the subject of a special debate in the House of Lords.

The record of the debate – *The English Language: Deterioration in Usage* – makes very interesting reading. All but one of the speakers accepted without question that the language *was* deteriorating, and unloaded a truckload of familiar complaints. English usage was going to the dogs, witness the misapplication of words like *parameter* and *hopefully*. The language was being cluttered with monstrosities like *ongoing*, *relevant* and *viable*. Good old words were acquiring bad new meanings. "It seems to me", remarked one peer, "virtually impossible for a modern poet to write, *the choir of gay companions*. What has happened is that a word has been used for propaganda purposes which have destroyed its useful meaning in English."

Pronunciation, another familiar bugbear, was also considered to be slipping in words like *controversy* and *formidable*. In this context, as in many, the BBC came in for a substantial amount of criticism for failing in its "clear duty to uphold the standards of English". There was praise for the Plain English Campaign (which has waged a vigorous and successful war against Civil Service gobbledygook) and complaints about the prevalence of jargon and obfuscation in official documents. There were laments over the latest revised translations of the Bible and the revisions in the Book of Common Prayer. And there were familiar sallies against American usage such as *elevator* for "lift" and *location* for "place". "A great deal of the long-windedness and ambiguity which is creeping into our usage", observed one peer, "originates in America." Another noble speaker, Lord Somers, observed that "if there is a more hideous language on the face of the earth than the American form of English, I should like to know what it is!" (The bitter tone of some English pronouncements about American English often recalls nothing so much as the tone of French complaints about Franglais.)

The noble lords blamed this parlous state on the schools, the universities, and the mass media. Children and students were no longer educated in grammar or the classics. Newspapers, radio and television were familiarizing the public with "a language that depends on generalizations which are usually imprecise and often deliberately ambiguous ... a language that makes unblushing use of jargon whenever that can assist evasion". Britain's peers also exhibited more than a touch of xenophobia. "A major cause of deterioration", noted one, "in the use of the English language is very simply the enormous increase in the number of people who are using it." Perhaps the most revealing of many comments came from Lord Davies of Leek who remarked:

> Am I right in assuming that in an age tortured by uncertainty with respect to religion, God, family, self, money and property, there is a worldwide collapse of not only the values of the past but of our language which, more and more, tends to be vague, indecisive, careless and often callous?

In one sense, Lord Davies is right. The relativism of the century probably does encourage a more permissive approach to language. In a deeper sense though, it was the decline of respect for God, the family and property, "a worldwide collapse of the values of the past", that really concerned Lord Davies and his colleagues, and he used *language-change* (what he called "deterioration") as a way of complaining about *society*.

The House of Lords debate highlighted many important fears about English in the future. They are matched across the Atlantic in the now-familiar cry from a number of American commentators and organizations that the language is in danger. American English has two fundamental characteristics which are slightly at odds with each other. On the one hand, a highly mobile population with a strong sense of national identity has always stimulated a trend towards a national variety of spoken English. At the written level, this centralizing tendency has been reinforced by generations of vigorous textbook learning. But on the other hand, American society is astonishingly plural, and its language is correspondingly eclectic. There is a very hazy line of demarcation between what is or is not acceptable, especially in written English. This is the no-man's-land in which the horrors of contemporary English are often first discovered.

There has been, first, the fear of *jargon* – a word to set alarm bells ringing in the minds of many English speakers, connoting a language that is restricted to a particular group, usually professional, and that has enough technical terms to make it virtually incomprehensible to an outsider. The contemporary use of jargon was parodied in Alan Simpson's "translation" of the first verses of the Twenty-third Psalm:

1. The Lord is my external-internal integrative mechanism.
2. I shall not be deprived of gratifications for my viscogeneric hungers or my need dispositions.
3. He motivates me to orient myself towards a non-social object with affective significance.

4. He positions me in a non-decisional situation.
5. He maximizes my adjustment.

It is perhaps no accident that a society dominated and controlled by science and technology should express itself in a science-inspired jargon, larded with Greek and Latin prefixes and suffixes (*sanitize*, *prioritize*), and loaded with hyphenated compounds like *total-incarceration facility* for "city gaol". The association of jargon with science has contributed to an additional meaning: the use of self-important words to obscure and evade meaning, a use that is popularly attributed to civil-service and administrative flak-catchers. For instance, during the Watergate scandal, Ron Ziegler, explaining the lies of the White House, stated that "All previous statements are inoperative."

In a permissive age we have also generated euphemistic jargon: words and phrases that (in an effort to please) obfuscate, circumnavigate and ameliorate. The White House, describing the invasion (or, as it preferred, "incursion") of Grenada, referred to a parachute drop as a "pre-dawn vertical insertion". The nuclear industry has a phrase for things that go wrong all the time: "normally occurring abnormal occurrences". The world of euphemistic jargon is the world in which "second-hand" cars become "experienced", a hospital death is "a therapeutic misadventure", and an airline reports a fatal aircrash to its stockholders as "the involuntary conversion of a 727". California appears to be the natural habitat for such usages. In San José, the Department of Physical Education became the Department of Human Performance. When, in the late 1970s, spurred into action by various kinds of Plain English campaigns, President Carter issued an instruction that Federal regulations should be written in Plain English, it was California that took the most dramatic action. The Planning Division of San Mateo County hired a specialist in plain writing whose blue pencil was to change *utilize* into "use", *inaugurate* into "start", and *at this point in time* to "now". (The arguments about "obfuscation" and "exactness" are abetted by the sheer size of the English lexicon: there are always three or four ways to express the same thought.)

Next to the attack on jargon and officialese, has been the renewed concern with "correct" English, a championing of "standards" that is probably linked to the mood of conservatism running throughout British and American society. The high priests of correct English usage are Edwin Newman, John Simon and William Safire, who remarks, "I don't like stiff English. I don't like euphemism. If you raise your taxes, don't call it 'revenue enhancement'." Variously described as "pop grammarians", "self-appointed guardians of linguistic purity", "language vigilantes" and "gurus of grammar", these commentators have one thing in common: their newspaper columns and television appearances play to a wide public anxiety about the changing language. Their book titles alone express their attitude to English. Newman is the author of *Strictly Speaking – or Will American be the Death of English?* John Simon's *Paradigms Lost* has a typical attack on the permissive approach to language:

> Why does language keep changing? Because it is a living thing, people will
> tell you. Something that you cannot press for ever, like a dead flower,

between the pages of a dictionary. Rather it is a living organism that, like a live plant, sprouts new leaves and flowers. Alas, this lovely albeit trite image is – as I have said before and wish now to say with even greater emphasis – largely nonsense. Language, for the most part, changes out of ignorance.

The concern in all these pronouncements is not so much with the intellectual or moral content of what is written or spoken, but with the expression of it. This, the argument usually runs, is owed to declining educational standards. Schools are producing "functional illiterates". Unless educators get back to the three Rs, the next generation will not be able to spell its name: as the title of a best-selling book had it, *Johnny Can't Read*. Confronted by the unprecedented rate of change (and an unprecedented public awareness of it), commentators like Newman believe (with Jonathan Swift) that the language is being corrupted.

The "gurus of grammar" complain about *he don't* for "he doesn't" and *different than* for "different from". They attack the triteness of *ongoing situation*, the misuse of a word like *hopefully* and the confusion of *owing to* and *due to*. Many of their complaints about usage pre-suppose an unchanging standard of written and spoken English. These commentators rarely address the ethical side of language misuse.

The gurus of grammar, who are journalists not academics, have been reacting partly to the fashion within the universities to explain that there is no single all-purpose standard for language any more than there is for dress. The advent of tape-recorders, radio and television has encouraged linguists to become preoccupied with spoken rather than written English, a territory in which it is the varied richness, not the standardization, that seems most noticeable. Some linguists have stated that *any* variety of a language is as "good" or "correct" as any other variety. In this context, it is easy to see why the Newmans and the Simons have felt impelled to mount a defence. The anxious tone of their writing is a powerful indication of the speed and depth of change in English today.

There is another kind of fear expressed by the watchdogs of English in America, the fear of what is called "bilingualism", especially directed, as we have mentioned, against the rise of Spanish as a rival language. In the 1980s, the Hispanic population of the United States (officially 14.6 million, but estimated by the census authorities, who cannot count the illegal immigrants crossing the Mexican border, at closer to twenty million) has become increasingly significant. Half of the recorded Hispanics are bilingual, but Spanish is a growing force in the media: there are now 247 Spanish-language newspapers in the United States, as many radio stations and a television network (SIN) which claims twelve million viewers in one hundred cities. The difficulty of dealing fairly with large numbers of Spanish-speaking children led, in the 1970s, to the concession known as Bilingualism. New waves of immigrant children (mainly Hispanics) would not have to be dropped into the deep end of the English language (like the "huddled masses" of the past) but would have "bilingual education" until they had acquired English skills. This policy was extended to other new immigrant groups, Vietnamese, for example, but it was the Hispanics who drew the conservatives' fire.

In places like San Diego or San Antonio some educators feared that children taught English in school but speaking Spanish at home would fail to learn either Spanish or English properly and grow up poorly educated in both. More seriously though, wherever there is a sudden concentration of newly arrived Spanish speakers – Miami, California, or New York, now 20 per cent Hispanic – some Americans fear that Bilingualism means these immigrants will *never* learn to speak American English. In part, this is a re-run of the 1970s debate about Black English (and the even earlier debate about the place of German) and the danger of recognizing alternative standards. But Black English is still a variety of the mother tongue and the Blacks have a secure if partly begrudged place in American society. The Hispanics are not merely new arrivals, they speak a language that has nothing to do with English. Opponents of Bilingualism speak darkly of Balkanization and Quebec's secessionist struggle. A substantial Hispanic population not speaking American English, they say, is simply a dangerous legacy for the future.

Black Power, Hispanic Rights, Feminism, Gay Liberation, anti-Americanism: these are some of the issues of our time, and the English language will always be used by conservatives as a stick with which to beat the opposition. As long as there are Democrats and Republicans, Tories and Socialists (or whatever), linguistic conservatives and radicals will go on firing at each other across the water. The argument about where English is heading is, as we have seen, one of the oldest in the book. Conservatives will take a prescriptive, authoritarian line. Liberals will prefer a tolerant, descriptive approach. There will be battles on a shifting battlefield – now vocabulary, now grammar – about "unacceptable" or "incorrect" English, about the speed at which *de facto* English becomes *de jure*. The direction of change can, perhaps, be influenced more than is sometimes acknowledged. Swift, for instance, opposed *phizz* and *hipps* as well as *mob*. But in the end, the Darwinian process by which *perclitation* ("jeopardie, hazard") expires and *animadversion* ("the turning of the attention") survives, is beyond the power of individuals to explain or control. The only issue, finally, is the speed of change, and that, as the row about *Webster's Third New International Dictionary* suggests, will be disputed to the crack of doom.

THE CITY OF LANGUAGE

At the end of our journey through the English-speaking world, what can we add by way of general observations to this debate about the state of the language, and its evolutionary processes? From the point of view of word-making, the twentieth century is similar to the sixteenth. New words and new uses are being coined at a furious rate to describe new inventions and new experiences. As always, language is being created at the frontiers of science, industry, culture and society. The new usages of English are often generated by in-groups as a code. This can be used to *include* the members of the circle and to *exclude* outsiders. The language code is one of the simplest and most effective ways of defining a social group or class, from peers to policemen. And when the group becomes favoured socially or politically, then parts of the code become adopted by outsiders.

A good example of this process is the widespread adoption of – *pace* the House of Lords – "gay" usage. It is quite common, for instance, to describe the clothes we wear to the office as *business drag*. Newspapers might say of a politician who finally revealed his true ideological colours that he had *come out of the closet*. The use of *cruising* has been widely adopted by heterosexual as well as homosexual society. The way in which the specialized language – essentially a code – of a sub-culture becomes more widely adopted and in turn affects social attitudes can be seen in the latest edition of the *Random House Dictionary*. Many words from the gay community have now been added for the first time: *closet queen* (for the homosexual who denies his homosexuality), *drag queen* (a male transvestite), *fag hag* (for the heterosexual female who enjoys the company of male homosexuals), *faggy* (resembling male homosexuals – "disparaging" or "offensive", a further reflection of the increased awareness of homosexuals of homosexuals – jokingly defined by the gay comic Tom Ammiano as "the irrational fear that three gays will break into your house and redecorate it against your will").

The *Random House Dictionary* now labels terms such as *fruitcake*, *fruit* and *pansy* as "disparaging" or "offensive", a further reflection of the increased awareness of homosexuals in modern society. Stuart Flexner, Editor-in-Chief of the dictionary, adds: "At certain other non-gay entries I find that I am rewriting definitions of various physical and emotional relationships so that they can include gays when necessary. For example at *ménage à trois*, *necking*, *foreplay*, etc., our definitions have often been worded, sometimes unconsciously, to imply that only heterosexuals were involved, whereas in updating such definitions we now tend to rewrite them so that gay couples are included."

A related theme that emerges strongly from our journeys is that language follows its own path. It can bridge gulfs of class and geography in the most remarkable ways. This is not least because innovation in language is as old as human nature. It is simply the way one generation announces its superiority to, and perhaps even disdain for, the previous one. New words and phrases mark out a new experience, a new lifestyle, and a new society. We found a vivid example of this in the Far Out West. The beaches of California have been fashionable ever since the Beach Boys caught the ear of the English-speaking world with songs like "Let's Go Surfing". But even before the pop revolution, there had been a community of tall, blonde, salt-caked surfers in search of the ultimate wave. The climate of Southern California means they can surf all year round and the sport – for aficionados a way of life – has created a slang (or argot) all its own. Surfers tend to be laconic. They will say that a wave (or an experience) is *awesome* or *outstanding*. If they agree with you, they will say *for sure*. They use abbreviations. A can of Heineken becomes a *Heinie*, a Lowenbräu becomes a *Lowie*. The surf-language changes so frequently that surf-talk glossaries published in the past have recently been discontinued. *Getting air*, a new surfing manoeuvre, was coined in 1984. By the time this book is printed, the term may already be obsolete.

Surf talk was – and is – the hip slang of California's youth. What is interesting is the way in which the talk, and its style, have gradually drifted off the beaches and inland. Originally, the surf culture flourished on the beach but, because it was slightly *outré*, did not extend beyond the beach area. As surfing became more popular with middle-class Los Angeles, and as the teenagers from the middle-class suburbs of the city began to come to the beach at weekends and during vacations, there was a mild culture-clash between the beach-dwelling surfers and the suburbanites from places like Ventura Boulevard, Sherman Oaks and Burbank. In order to get along with the surfers, the outsiders adopted the language of the beach. By an almost Darwinian language-process teenager slang in Los Angeles became a processed, educated version of surf talk.

The evidence for this is a kind of teenage slang that burst into national and even international prominence in 1982, so-called *Valspeak*. The occasion for the media's sudden discovery of this extraordinary lingo was the appearance of a hit record, "Valley Girl", by the outrageous Frank Zappa and his daughter, Moon Unit, a five-minute soliloquy on the Valley Girl lifestyle, from school to shopping mall and back again. "The Valley" of the song is hardly a valley at all, more a huge, sprawling continuous suburb of about a million affluent middle-class Californians stretching into the San Fernando Valley north of Los Angeles. The "Valley Girl", who is probably called Andrea, Roni, Jayne, Cori, Kelli, Kim, Kristi, Michelle, Stacy, Tracy or Tricia, is a well-heeled, suburban, middle-class child with time on her hands and money to spend, a kind of ultimate consumer. Valspeak turns out to be middle-class American girl-talk, depending on an infinite variety of gurgles, squeaks, exclamations, sarcasm, eye-rolling and lip-curling. When she speaks English, the Valley Girl speaks her version of surf talk, including some words, like *barf*, that go back to the 1940s and earlier. *Awesome* means "good"; *bag your face* is an expression of disagreement; *max* means "maximum", or "to score high"; *mondo* is the Valspeak for "very"; *billies* are "dollars bills", or "money"; *for sure* is an expression of either support or scorn; *grody* is "unspeakably awful"; *totally* is "very good": *tubular*, which originated in surfing to describe a well-curved wave, also means "very good"; *vicious*, which seems to owe something to Black street talk, is "extremely desirable".

Valspeak, as a special language confined to the San Fernando Valley, is a media myth, but its dissemination is typical of our language. A year or two later, it was matched by the craze for so-called *Preppy talk*, a teenage slang inspired by the popular *Preppy Handbook*: the terms used by students in Eastern "prep" (private boarding) schools. Here *awesome* would be matched by old usages like *neat* or *tremendous*. Other preppy words included *rude* (in bad taste), *a dork* (an outsider who does not understand Preppies), *bones* (a marijuana cigarette), *poo* (champagne, from "shampoo") and *booted* (expelled).

The Valley Girls and the Preppies introduce another important theme in the evolution of language: the power of schools. In almost every episode in the story of English, there have been evolutions of accent and vocabulary that are attributable not to parents (speakers of English whose habits have been formed) but to children growing up in a new environment in which it is more important to be acceptable to their playmates than to their teachers. This is as true of Anglo-Norman children playing alongside English country children, as of Anglo-Irish children with Gaelic schoolfellows, as of Southern White boys and girls living among the children of Black slaves, as of the children of the first Australian settlers. It is the power of the playground that probably explains how, within one generation, and particularly if it is transplanted, language can undergo significant shifts.

It is often said that radio and television are steamrolling the fascinating bumps and crannies of English, the strange local accents, the odd usages and bizarre throwbacks, from Gullah to Cockney. We believe, on the contrary, that such variety has proved remarkably resilient to the standardizing pressures of the mass media. In the isolated communities where most of these language fossils are found, improved roads and larger schools are much more damaging to the local speech than television and radio. The roads increase mobility and enlarge horizons; larger schools tend to promote accent levelling within a particular region. Radio and television enable you to understand another variety of English, but they do not force you to speak it. But if you go to school where another kind of English is the norm, then you *have* to adopt it.

And then there is tourism. In the seventeenth century, language was sea- and river-borne, moving at the speed of the fastest ship. The cousinly relationship of pidgin English round the world demonstrates the significance of sailors and sea-routes. In our time, air travel and tourism have helped to spread a similarly simplified international English, and perhaps to break down the isolation of places like the Tangier Island fishing community.

But there are some perils in the avalanche of world English for those countries for whom English is the mother tongue. In the United States, the "tongue-tied American" is giving cause for concern. The English-speaking tourist armed with the motto "Speak slowly and loudly in English" is becoming a prisoner of his or her monolingualism – and something of a oddity in a world that is essentially polyglot. In Africa, as we have seen, most Africans, who are gifted linguists, will know at least three languages. In India, there is a *de facto* bilingualism. In Europe, English is widely understood – and taught – in all countries, even in France. It appears that the British and Americans, lacking many levels of language competence, are exceptional – and exceptionally handicapped, perhaps.

Speakers of Standard British English have, as this narrative has unfolded, sometimes taken second place to various kinds of outsider – among them the Scots, the Irish, the Founding Fathers, the Blacks, the Jews, and the Cockneys. It is worth re-emphasizing that, as the twenty-first century approaches, some significant future developments of spoken English will also occur in the British Isles among the speakers of Standard English. If, for instance, the use of the "glottal stop" becomes part of the fashionable speech of the London professional classes (and there is evidence that this is already happening among middle-class children and teenagers), this will be as significant in its own time as the shift from *greet* to *grate* discussed by Dr Johnson (chapter five). It is important to note that, historically, such influential changes have always occurred at the centre not the periphery, in Britain, not the United States – or anywhere else for that matter. From this perspective, the much-abused Standard British English is the radical force, while the "colonial" variants remain conservative. However, within the British Isles, it is often a mistake to look to the "high ground" of the language for evidence of change. Just as, in the ninth century, the significant fusion of Old English and Old Norse was happening far from the centres of trade and administration in the South, so in our own century, it is the neglected Cockneys who are providing the influential "glottal stop" and the "*l* vocalization". Changes in language tend to come from below.

Finally, and perhaps most fundamentally, our journey through the English-speaking world confirms the view that the English language cannot be controlled by legislation or re-made by committees. Towards the end of his life, Walt Whitman, reflecting on language, defined it as "something arising out of the work, needs, ties, joys, affections, tastes, of long generations of humanity" and having "its basis broad and low, close to the ground". English has its own momentum and its own laws. Tourism, satellite television and word processors spread English faster and farther than ever before, and if a particular usage or a particular pronunciation finds favour or answers a need there will be no controlling it. In 1972, the editor of the *Supplement to the Oxford English Dictionary* estimated, in the preface to the first volume, *A–G*, that his work would be complete with the definition of some 50,000 words in three volumes. In fact, the spate of new English and new uses means that there will be four volumes and more than 60,000 words, some of which derive from sources that Dr Johnson could scarcely have dreamt of: Eskimo English (*qiviut*, the underwool of the arctic musk-ox), Finnish English (*rya*, a knotted pile rug), and Hawaiian English (*oo*, a black and yellow bird).

Language has always been – as the phrase goes – the mirror to society. English today is no exception. In its world state, it reflects very accurately the crises and contradictions of which it is a part. In Britain, its first home, it has become standardized and centralized in the South, apparently cautious of change. The English of the United States (heard on television, films and radio through the world) has become the voice of the First World in finance, trade and technology. Within the United States, the huge socio-economic significance of the South and West – oil, beef, and the high-tech aerospace and computer industries – has given the voice and accents of the South-West a new and preponderant influence. In the British Commonwealth, the independent traditions of Australia, Canada and New Zealand have breathed new life into the English that was exported from Britain two hundred years ago. In the Caribbean, it is the focus of an emergent nationalism. In Africa, it is a continent-wide form of communication. In South Africa, it is the medium of Black consciousness. In India and South-East Asia, it is associated with Third World aspirations, and, reflecting the confidence of these Asian countries, it is taking on its own distinctive Asian forms. In the words of Emerson, with whom we began, "Language is a city, to the building of which every human being brought a stone."

NOTES AND SOURCES

The books, articles and informants are referenced to the relevant pages of the text and are intended to allow the reader to follow up particular aspects of the narrative in further detail.

INTRODUCTION: SPEAKING OF ENGLISH

p.12 Logan Pearsall Smith: *The English Language* (Oxford, 1966; Darby, 1930).

p.13 George Orwell is often credited with a special understanding of English. But see W. F. Bolton: *The Language of 1984* (Tennessee, 1984). Bolton points out, for instance, that when Orwell recommends pure "Anglo-Saxon" usages he is, in fact, recommending words that were themselves originally borrowed from abroad.

The subject of linguistics has produced one of the greatest literatures (measured in shelf-space) of any subject in our time. Most readers will find all they need in Peter Trudgill: *Sociolinguistics* (London, 1974; New York, 1983) and David Crystal: *Linguistics*, (London, 1971; Baltimore, 1982), both of which have sensible bibliographies for those who wish to venture further into the Chomskian interior. The source itself, *Syntactic Structures* by Noam Chomsky (The Hague, 1957; Hawthorne, 1978), one of the most influential of all linguistic theories, is probably best approached by way of John Lyons: *Chomsky* (London, 1970). One of the shortest and most entertaining books on language (with some characteristically incisive chapters about English) is *Language Made Plain* (London, 1975) by Anthony Burgess. C. L. Barber: *The Story of Language* (London, 1964), is more thorough, but less vivid. Ludwig Wittgenstein: *Philosophical Investigations* (Oxford, 1973; Chicago, 1980) is a must for anyone who wishes to explore the philosophy of language. *Speech Acts* by John R. Searle (Cambridge, 1969; New York, 1970) and *Forms of Talk* by Erving Goffman (Philadelphia, 1981) are both extraordinarily perceptive about the oral aspects of the language.

The phrase "the world is his oyster" is actually – like so many in the language – from Shakespeare. "Why, then the world's mine oyster, which I with sword will open." *Merry Wives of Windsor* Act II, scene ii.

p.14 The full text of Denis Forman's lecture was published in *Index on Censorship*, October 1984. For those who doubt these statistics, compare the known sales of successful English as a Foreign Language (EFL) textbooks: as many as three to four million per title per annum.

William Safire is the author of *What's the Good Word* (London, 1982; New York, 1983), and *On Language* (London, 1980; New York, 1981). Both are breezily readable and full of good sense. For someone who is rather conservative about English usage, Safire has a hip, racy style that makes a refreshing change from the club-footed pronouncements of some commentators.

p.15 Charles Berlitz: *Native Tongues* (New York, 1982), is a very readable, though unreliable, compendium of "facts" about language.

For the idea of "dialect" see "Dialects, Accents and Standards" in W. R. O'Donnell and Loreto Todd: *Variety in Contemporary English* (London, 1980; Pikesville, 1980).

I AN ENGLISH-SPEAKING WORLD

p.19 We are indebted to Dr Christopher Craft, formerly "the voice of NASA" for the benefit of his experience with NASA. There were two Voyager space-shots. The logic of NASA meant that Voyager One was preceded by Voyager Two (on 20 August 1977). The full text runs as follows: "As the Secretary-General of the United Nations, an organization of a hundred and forty-seven member states who represent almost all of the human inhabitants of the planet Earth, I send greetings on behalf of the people of our planet. We step out of our solar system into the universe seeking only peace and friendship, to teach if we are called upon, to be taught if we are fortunate. We know full well that our planet and its inhabitants are but a small part of this immense universe that surrounds us and it is with humility and hope that we take this step."

p.20 The "facts" of English are widely available and often reproduced. Each version invariably disagrees on points of detail, but the broad picture is consistent. For the argument that there are "more than one billion English speakers" see Richard W. Bailey's article in *English Today*, Vol. 1, No. 1. Some of the contemporary quotations in this chapter are taken from "English, English Everywhere", *Newsweek*, 15 November 1982.

"The Queen's English"
p.21 For varieties of English in the British Isles, see Philip Howard, *The State of the Language* (London, 1984), an entertaining Cook's Tour.

The first English citation of "received pronunciation" is in A. J. Ellis' classic, *On English Pronunciation* (1869).

p.24 For the relationship of Received Pronunciation and BBC English see Randolph Quirk's essay, "Speaking into the Air", in *Style and Communication in the English Language* (London and Baltimore, 1982).

For RP and the Public Schools see John Honey: *Tom Brown's Universe* (Blandford, Dorset, 1977) from which these details are taken. See also John Honey: "Acrolect and Hyperlect: The Redefinition of English RP", *English Studies*, Volume 66, No. 3, 1985.

The development of "Standard English" is treated very elegantly and concisely in Raymond Williams: *The Long Revolution* (London and Westport, 1971).

p.25 The development of Cockney (see chapter eight) means that we should draw a distinction between Cockney (the English of the East End of London) and the "Cockney" sometimes referred to in earlier generations which is essentially "London English", perhaps with a slight overtone of scorn. For a full and fascinating etymology – including hints of "the Land of Cokaygne" – see the *Oxford English Dictionary*.

Afferbeck Lauder, the author of *Fraffly Well Spoken*, also published *Let Stalk Strine* (see chapter eight).

There are many accounts of Kipling's life and work. A recent one is by Angus Wilson: *The Strange Ride of Rudyard Kipling*, (London, 1977; New York, 1979). It should be read alongside T. S. Eliot (Ed.): *A Choice of Kipling's Verse* (London, 1979; Winchester, Mass., 1963).

"Nation shall speak peace unto nation"
p.26 We are grateful to the BBC for permission to use the ACSE archive. See also Howard Davis and Paul Walton (Eds.): *Language, Image, Media* (Oxford, 1983; New York, 1984).

Alistair Cooke himself is doubtful about the notion of "BBC English": "There really never was any such thing as the BBC accent. What the Advisory Committee was doing was just seeing that the announcers used a Standard Pronunciation for everything, and 95 per cent of them would pronounce things in the same way. But remember, the BBC was going out all over the country. And a great many of the regions, the Midlands, and the North country, were hearing Southern upper middle-class pronunciation for the first time. So they said, it's the BBC accent. They didn't see it as the accent of the army, the church and the clubs because most of them had never heard one."

Lord Reith's remarks were made in an interview with Malcolm Muggeridge on Granada Television in 1957.

p.27 For the idea of "Standard English", see "What *Is* 'Standard English'?" by Professor Peter Strevens (RELC Journal, Singapore, 1982).

p.28 For the famous U and Non-U debate, see *Noblesse Oblige*, edited by Nancy Mitford (London, 1980; Westport, Conn. 1974).

For an evaluation of accents, see John Honey's "Accents At Work" in *Personnel Management*, January, 1984.

"The Best Kind of English"
p.29 John Honey: *The Language Trap* (Kay–Shuttleworth Papers, No. 3, Middlesex, 1983) explores the desirability of the spread of Standard English, and echoes Henry Higgins:

Why can't the English teach their children how to speak?
These verbal class distinctions by now should be antique.

In the recent BBC-2 documentary, "Talking Proper", the BBC broadcaster, Susan Rae, a Scot, said: "People write to me and say, 'Please don't take this personally'. They then proceed to say how much they hate me, and how much they hate my accent, and then tell me to get back to the hills and the heather."

p.30 The best and fullest account of English accents is by J. C. Wells: *Accents of English*, three volumes (Cambridge, 1982).

The Voice of America
p.31 For the richness of American English, the two indispensable volumes are by the Editor-in-Chief of the Random House Dictionary, Stuart Berg Flexner: *I*

Hear America Talking (New York, 1976), and *Listening to America* (New York, 1982).

SNAFU (situation normal, all fucked up) is a member of a lively family, including JANFU (joint army and navy fuck-up).

For more army slang, see Park Kendall (Ed.): *Dictionary of Service Slang* (London, 1945).

p.33 See Barton J. Bernstein and Allen J. Matusow: *The Truman Administration* (New York, 1966) for "Iron Curtain" speech in full.

The "Network Standard"
p.35 It should be made clear that we are not suggesting that the networks themselves actively sponsored the "Network Standard". Some American broadcasters are ignorant of the term, which was developed by linguists. The current ABC "anchorman" is the Canadian Peter Jennings. He recalls that for a long time he had a "mental block about the word 'lieutenant'". In fact, a short film about his experiences in America was titled "Spell it Lootenant for Jennings", because that was how it had to be spelled on the teleprompter.

p.36 The details of Abraham Lincoln's speech come from Carl Sandburg: *Abraham Lincoln* (San Diego, 1975).

English Where It's At
p.37 The hacker talk of Silicon Valley has produced a plethora of handbooks to the jargon: one of the best is by Patty Bell and Doug Myrland: *The Official Silicon Valley Guy Handbook* (New York, 1983). Essential for all recent jargon is Jonathan Green's *Newspeak: A Dictionary of Jargon* (London, 1984). For some of the wilder shores of jargon see Dwight Bolinger's essay, "The jargonauts and the not-so-golden fleece" in *Language: The Loaded Weapon* (London and New York, 1980).

A Universal Language
p.38 There are various estimates of the spread of Esperanto: some go higher. The figures quoted are the estimate of Professor Mario Pei. The Esperanto Society produces a great deal of interesting literature. Their offices in 140 Holland Park Avenue, London W11, are worth a visit.

p.39 Professor Lal's claim is high. Professor Braj Kachru reckons the figure is nearer 25 million. It is, of course, a question of definition. For the Third World aspects of English, see Braj Kachru: *The Other Tongue: English across Cultures* (Illinois, 1982), especially Kachru's own contribution, "The Other Side of English." According to Peter Strevens of Wolfson College, Cambridge, "Within India alone, the practised ear can distinguish ten or twenty varieties of English – differentiated by geography (the speech of a man from Bombay does not closely resemble that of a man from Madras), and by social and educational level – all identifiably 'Indian' and not Maltese or West African, and all identifiably 'English' rather than German or French."

p.41 For essays on many aspects of English in the contemporary world, from Plain English Campaigns to Israeli Attitudes to English, see Sidney Greenbaum (Ed.): *The English Language Today* (Oxford, 1984).

From Japlish to Franglais
p.43 An antidote to the idea that English is infiltrating all the world's languages is Alan Bliss's fascinating *A Dictionary of Foreign Words and Phrases in Current English*, (London and Boston, 1966), which reveals the extent to which English has also borrowed from abroad, from *avant-garde* (15th century) to *voyeur* (20th century).

p.46 The full population of Bangladesh is, of course, much larger – some 89 million.

"Wealth, Wisdom and Strict Economy"
The classic account of the English language is A. C. Baugh and Thomas Cable: *A History of the English Language* (London, 1978; Des Moines, 1983). We are indebted to their work, which must be the starting place for anyone who wants to make a serious study of the subject. A good follow-up is G. L. Brook: *A History of the English Language* (London, 1977).

We should make it clear – it is a fundamental proposition in linguistic studies – that we are *not* saying that "sounds have spellings". In fact, the whole system works the other way round. Thus, the question "Why don't we pronounce the *t* in *castle*?" is meaningless. We *can* ask, however, "Why do we spell [kasl] with a letter *t*?" Historically, writing is a (rather complicated) representation of speech. And speech is absolutely not a speaking of writing.

p.47 There have been many attempts at a simplified English, from BASIC to Anglic. See C. K. Ogden: *Basic English: A General Introduction with Rules and Grammar* (London, 1930).

2 THE MOTHER TONGUE

p.51 The making of English from AD 450 to 1500 has been described by innumerable scholars. If we have added anything new, this is owed to many conversations with Early and Middle English scholars whose research we have benefited from. This chapter relies on A. C. Baugh and Thomas Cable: *A History of the English Language*, on another influential classic, Otto Jespersen: *The Growth and Structure of the English Language* (Oxford, 1982) and on Logan Pearsall Smith: *The English Language* (Oxford, 1966; Philadelphia, 1982). For a slightly different perspective see Dick Leith: *A Social History of English* (London and Boston, 1983).

p.52 There is an excellent and more detailed summary of the latest research into the origins of the Indo-European languages in Robert Claiborne: *Our Marvellous Native Tongue* (London, 1984). For the prehistory of Europe see J. Bronowski: *The Ascent of Man* (London, 1973; Boston, 1974).

The "clever detective work" referred to here is the matching of specific vocabularies with what archaeologists and anthropologists know about the climate, flora and fauna of prehistoric Europe.

The Celts
p.53 For the relationship of Celtic to the other European languages, see also Anthony Burgess: *Language Made Plain* (London, 1975). For more on the other languages of Britain, there is a popular account by Victor Stevenson (Ed.): *Words* (London, 1983; New York, 1984) and a scholarly one by Glanville Price: *The Languages of Britain* (London and Baltimore, 1984).

p.57 Tacitus' account is taken here from *The Agricola and the Germania* (Translated with an Introduction by H. Mattingly (London, 1970; New York, 1971).

p.58 For the full story of the *Moorleichen*, see P. V. Glob: *The Bog People* (London and Ithaca, 1969).

For the information about Friesland and its language, we are indebted to Marten Sytema, Robert Fox and Marianne Fox. Other English-Frisian word-pairs include: *bread-brea*; *wheat-weet*; *corn-koarn*; *sheep-skiep*; *butter-butter*; *dream-dream*; *green-grien*; *sweet-swiet*; *thread-tried*; *well-wel*; *house-hus*; *cooper-kuper*; *fork-foarke*; *bull-bolle*; *key-kaai*; *ox-okse* and *sunshine-sinneskine*. The list is all the more remarkable in that many Frisian words are closer to English than to neighbouring Dutch.

The Making of English
p.60 *The Anglo-Saxon Chronicle* was, of course, written after the event. For the beginnings of English, see "From Runes to Printing" in Robert Burchfield, *The English Language* (Oxford, 1985).

p.61 For the historical background to the Anglo-Saxons, see Dorothy Whitelock: *The Beginnings of English Society* (London, 1977; New York, 1959) and David Wilson: *The Anglo-Saxons* (London, 1966; New York, 1984).

p.62 Some very common words – *they, get, till, both* – are Old Norse. The point is that the English language has very deep roots. The emotive power of Anglo-Saxon words – simple, direct, traditional – in British political oratory has been confirmed by subsequent linguistic psychology. (*Street* has Latin roots but arrived in OE via Germany.)

p.64 The poems referred to are found in Michael Alexander (Trans.): *The Earliest English Poems* (London and New York, 1966), and the riddle comes from Kevin Crossley-Holland (Trans.): *The Exeter Book of Riddles* (London, 1978; New York, 1980).

The Words of God
p.65 For the full account of the early English church, see Bede: *The History of the English Church and People* (Translated with an Introduction by Leo Sherley-Price, London, 1968; New York, 1935). See also H. Mayr-Harting: *The Coming of Christianity to Anglo-Saxon England* (London, 1972).

p.68 The Lindisfarne Gospels and the other Anglo-Saxon illuminated manuscripts are widely reproduced, and are indispensable to a re-evaluation of the Anglo-Saxon achievement.

The Viking Invasions
pp.68–9 For the Viking invasions see Gwyn Jones: *A History of the Vikings* (Oxford and Totoura, 1968). For the impact of the Vikings on the English landscape see W. G. Hoskins: *The Making of the English Landscape* (London, 1979).

The story goes that Alfred hides from the Danes in the house of an English peasant whose wife, not knowing that their guest is the king, asks him to mind some cakes she is baking. Alfred, weighed down with worry about his country, and absorbed in planning for victory, forgets to mind the fire and the cakes are burnt. When the peasant's wife starts to scold him, she is interrupted by her horrified husband who points out that she must not speak to the king in such words . . .

p.69 Alfred's Preface to St Gregory's Pastoral Care should be read in full. See Michael Swanton (Ed.): *Anglo-Saxon Prose* (London and Totoura, 1975).

p.71 *Borough*, a fortified place, is both English and Viking. There are shelves of books about English place-names. We used *Names* by Leslie Dunkling (London, 1983) which also has an excellent bibliography. For surnames, see Basil Cottle: *The Penguin Book of Surnames* (London, 1980; New York, 1984).

p.72 The lines quoted from *Beowulf* are 2260–2266. We acknowledge that many scholars believe that *Beowulf* was composed before the Viking age.

The Norman Invasion
p.73 For the Norman Conquest, see the excellent summary by H. R. Loyn: *The Norman Conquest* (London, 1982; Dover, New Jersey, 1984). It is estimated that the Normans introduced 10,000–12,000 new words into the vocabulary of English.

p.74 For the continuities in English speech, see M. F. Wakelin: *English Dialects* (London, 1978). See also G. L. Brook: *English Dialects* (London, 1963; New York, 1978). We also acknowledge Richard W. Bailey and Manfred Görlach (Eds.): *English as a World Language* (Cambridge, 1984; Ann Arbor, 1982), a thorough and scholarly survey of many varieties of English including an essay on the varieties of English in the United Kingdom.

p.75 There is a myth, expressed most powerfully by Sir Walter Scott in *Ivanhoe*, that the English *swin, cyna* (cow) and *calfru* tended by the English peasantry, became the Anglo-Norman *porc, mouton* and *veel*: that the English did the *werc* (Old English) and the Normans enjoyed the *leisir*. This is at best only half true. See Robert Burchfield: *The English Language* (Oxford, 1985), pp.17–19.

An excellent account of the survival of English under the Normans is Michael Clanchy: *From Memory to Written Record* (London and Cambridge, Mass., 1979).

"Common Men Know No French"
p.76 The first essay that examined the evidence for the survival of English under the Normans is by R. W. Chambers, "On The Continuity of English Prose", Introduction to *The Life of Sir Thomas More*, Early English Text Society (London, 1932; New Haven, 1962).

Middle English
pp.77–8 The Middle English texts quoted here are given in literal translation. The ME spellings are given in A. C. Baugh and Thomas Cable: *A History of the English Language* (London, 1978; Des Moines, 1983).

"First Foundeur and Embellissher of Our English"
p.80 The phrase is William Caxton's, whose own "Prologue" to his edition of Chaucer's work is probably the most famous publisher's blurb in the history of the English language. In it he extols "that noble & grete philosopher Gefferey Chaucer, the whiche for

his ornate wrytyng in our tongue may wel have the name of a laureate poete."

The essential details of the Middle English period are summarized in Boris Ford (Ed.): *The Pelican Guide to English Literature, The Age of Chaucer* (London, 1980; New York, 1984), which also has a full, annotated bibliography – perhaps the best part of the book.

p.81 The fullest account of Chaucer's life and career is by Derek Brewer: *Geoffrey Chaucer* (London, 1953), and, updated, *Chaucer in His Time* (London, 1963; Westport, Conn., 1973).

p.84 The name-ending *-ing*, as in Stebbing, is the OE equivalent of *-son*, which is Scandinavian.

For Henry V's role in the emergence of English see Malcolm Richardson, "Henry V, the English Chancery, and Chancery English", *Speculum*, 55, 4 (1980).

p.85 The best serious account of Caxton's life, about which only the salient facts are known, is by George D. Painter: *William Caxton* (London, 1976).

p.87 For the texts of Medieval English Drama, see P. Happe (Ed.): *English Mystery Plays* (London, 1975; New York, 1980), and A. Crawley (Ed.): *Everyman and Medieval Miracle Plays* (London and Totoura, 1974). For criticism, see Richard Axton: *European Drama of the Early Middle Ages* (London, 1974; Pittsburgh, 1975).

3 A MUSE OF FIRE

p.91 The two sources for many of the quotations in this chapter are an excellent anthology by W. F. Bolton: *The English Language* (two volumes, Cambridge, 1966 and 1969), and Arthur Quiller-Couch (Ed.): *The Oxford Book of English Prose* (Oxford, 1925). We have also drawn on A. C. Baugh and Thomas Cable: *The History of the English Language* (London, 1978; Des Moines, 1983) and on C. L. Barber: *The Story of Language* (London, 1964).

"The New World of English Words"
pp.93–4 For the transition from manuscript to printing, see Robert Burchfield: *The English Language* (Oxford, 1985).

For truly compendious lists of continental borrowings, see Robert Claiborne: *Our Marvellous Native Tongue* (London, 1983).

For the lives and letters of the numerous Elizabethans, see the indispensable Paul Harvey: *The Oxford Companion to English Literature* (Oxford and New York, 1967).

For the authentic spellings (and pronunciations) of early Renaissance English, see "The Paston Letters".

"Englishe Matter in the Englische Tongue"
p.95 The phrase is Roger Ascham's, in his *Toxophilus*.

Next to Shakespeare, Ben Jonson is himself rather like the poet Marston, windy and verbose. A fellow writer, comparing their wits, observed that it was like the difference between a Spanish galleon, overloaded with sail, and an English man o' war, with deadly firepower.

The Brave New World
p.96 For the "lives" of Ralegh, Shakespeare (and other improbable biographies), see John Aubrey: *Brief Lives* (London, 1972; Chicago, 1983).

p.97 For a short route to Hakluyt's *Voyages*, see Roger Sharrock (Ed.): *The Pelican Book of English Prose* Vol. I (London and Magnolia, 1970).

pp.97–8 The account of the John White expeditions is told fully in Charles Porter: *Adventurers to the New World*. Perhaps the most prophetic vision of the future of English was expressed by the poet, Samuel Daniel, in 1599 when he wrote:

*And who in time knows whither we may vent
    The treasure of our tongue? To what strange shores
This gain of our best glory shall be sent,
    T'enrich unknowing nations with our stores?
What words in th'yet unformed Occident
    May come refined with th'accents that are ours?*

The Bard of Avon
p.98 From a mountain of possible biographies, there is the entertaining one by Anthony Burgess: *Shakespeare* (London, 1972), and the sensible one by Peter Quennell: *Shakespeare* (London, 1963). Both have good bibliographies. See also L. P. Smith: *The English Language* (Oxford, 1966) for many insights into Shakespeare's language.

p.99 See Bernard Levin: *Enthusiasms* (London and New York, 1983).

The First Folio citations for Shakespeare's vocabulary are not always reliable evidence of his inventiveness, but no one challenges his extraordinary *range*.

p.101 For the Warwickshire terms in Shakespeare see C. T. Onions: *A Shakespeare Glossary* (Oxford, 1911; New York, 1919).

For Shakespeare and the Folios see S. Schoenbaum: *Shakespeare, The Globe and the Word* (Oxford, 1970; New York, 1979).

p.104 In *Love's Labour's Lost* the character Don Armado is thought to portray Walter Ralegh. In one exchange, Armado says "Chirrah!" and the schoolmaster Holofernes replies, "Quare (why) chirrah, not sirrah?" This is possibly a reference to Ralegh's West Country accent.

p.105 George Puttenham: *The Arte of English Poesie*, edited by Gladys Doidge Willcock and Alice Walker, (Cambridge, 1970; Kent, Ohio, 1971).

For the development of "Standard English" (written and spoken), see Raymond Williams: *The Long Revolution* (London, 1971). For the "Irishness" of Elizabethan English, see J. Braidwood: "Ulster & Elizabethan English" in G. B. Adams (Ed.): *Ulster Dialect Symposium* (Ulster Folk Museum, 1964).

The First Americans
p.106 For a masterly survey of the spread of the English abroad, see Angus Calder: *Revolutionary Empire. The Rise of the English-Speaking Empires from the Fifteenth Century to the 1780s* (London, 1981). For a readable account of the beginning of the English settlement in the United States, see Alistair Cooke: *America* (London, 1973; New York, 1977).

p.108 For the life of Chesapeake Bay, see William W. Warner: *Beautiful Swimmers: Watermen, Crabs and the Chesapeake Bay* (London and Boston, 1976).

We are indebted to David Shores for his paper on the speech of Tangier Island. For the "hoi toiders" and their history, see David Stick: *The Outer Banks of North Carolina* (Chapel Hill, NC, 1958).

p.109 For the best treatment of English in the Bahamas see John A. Holm: *Dictionary of Bahamian English* (New York, 1982). We are extremely grateful to Dr Holm for his assistance.

The Authorized Version
p.109 The basic facts of James I's reign are well summarized in *English History: A Survey* by George Clark (Oxford and New York, 1971).

p.112 The little-known John Bois story is told in Ward Allen (Ed.): *Translating for King James* (London, 1970; New York, 1969).

p.113 The aesthetic and spiritual companion to the Authorized Version is the Book of Common Prayer, largely the work of Thomas Cranmer (who was also martyred) but also revised by the Hampton Court Conference. The Prayer Book marks the days of a man's life with unforgettable majesty, from baptism, "renounce the devil and all his works", to marriage "With this ring, I thee wed", to eternity "Earth to earth, ashes to ashes, dust to dust".

East Anglia and the Puritans
p.115 For the Puritans and East Anglia, see G. M. Trevelyan: *English Social History* (London, 1946; New York, 1978).

p.116 The excerpt from William Bradford's *History of Plimouth Plantation* is in many anthologies. There is a typical extract, with a good commentary, in Albert H. Marckwardt and J. L. Dillard: *American English* (Oxford and New York, 1980).

"Broken English"
p.120 The definitive work on pidgin English in America is by one of the few who bring a stylish grace as well as information to their writing on the English language – J. L. Dillard: *American Talk* (New York, 1976). We are indebted to Professor Dillard in chapters three and six especially.

"New Words, New Phrases"
p.122 See A. C. Baugh and Thomas Cable, London, 1978; Des Moines, 1983.

The Sound of American English
p.123 The best summary is in Stuart Berg Flexner: *I Hear America Talking* (New York, 1976).

Dagoes, Cajuns and Yankees
p.123 We use "Dagoes" in its historical sense: no anti-Hispanic sentiment is implied.

p.125 The most recent work by J. L. Dillard has the fullest account of the integration of English in the United States: *Towards a Social History of American English* (Hawthorne, 1985)

4 THE GUID SCOTS TONGUE

p.127 Technically, Scots is a variety of English, but politics and nationalism, together with the sheer difficulty of drawing a line of demarcation between "language" and "dialect", have often given Scots the status of a language – usually with reference to the Scots of pre-Union Scotland. Addressing this question, a scholar has recently written, "I have changed my mind four times, and, in the end, I devote a separate chapter to Scots not because I necessarily accept that it is a 'language' rather than a 'dialect' but because it has proved to be more convenient to handle it thus . . ."

On the question of Scots and nationalism, see "Language and Nationhood" by Randolph Quirk in *Style and Communication in the English Language* (London and Baltimore, 1982).

For a fine range of Scots vocabulary, see William Graham: *The Scots Word Book* (Ramsey Head Press, 1977).

We are indebted to Professor A. J. Aitken for his advice on this chapter. See also his forthcoming article in the Proceedings of the Northern Ireland Speech and Language Forum, "What's So Special about Scots?"

"Mac" is actually of Irish origin.

pp.127–8 The broadcast in Scots was written by Billy Kaye, whom we thank.

"The Corruptions in Our Language"
p.128 For the latest version of this debate see "Epilogue: Next Year's Words". See John Dryden: *Discourse Concerning Satire*. For the literary background, see Boris Ford (Ed.): *Pelican Guide to English Literature* (London, 1966; New York, 1984).

p.129 For the background to the developments in the language, see A. C. Baugh and Thomas Cable: *History of the English Language* (London, 1978; Des Moines, 1983).

pp.131–2 For the best selection of Swift on the English language, see W. F. Bolton (Ed.): *The English Language* (two vols, Cambridge, 1966 and 1969; Boston, 1965). Swift defined "Enthusiastick Jargon" as "the exalted language of bigoted sectarians claiming private inspiration".

For another use of abbreviations see George and Ira Gershwin's "'S'Wonderful":

Don't mind telling you
In my humble fash
That you thrill me through
With a tender pash.

p.133 For the gap between written and spoken English see Raymond Williams: *The Long Revolution* (London, 1971; New York, 1984).

Dr Johnson's Dictionary
p.133 For lexicographical matters generally, see Robert Burchfield: *The English Language* (Oxford, 1985). An even fuller treatment is by Sidney I. Landau: *Dictionaries* (New York, 1984).

p.133–5 For the story of the *Dictionary*, see "Storming the Main Gate" in Walter Jackson Bate: *Samuel Johnson* (London, 1978; San Diego, 1977). The significant Scottish contribution to Johnson's *Dictionary* was echoed in the making of the *Oxford English Dictionary* which was two-thirds edited by Scotsmen, Sir James Murray and Sir William Craigie. The

Scottish tradition of dictionary-making goes back to 1808 when Dr John Jamieson produced his *Etymological Dictionary of the Scottish Language*, but despite this richness of lexicographical record the Scots language itself languishes and in 1986 *The Dictionary of the Older Scottish Tongue* is still awaiting completion.

p.136 The Preface to the *Dictionary* is reproduced in W. F. Bolton, op cit.

A Tour of the Highlands and Islands
p.137 The handiest edition of both Johnson's *Journal to the Western Isles of Scotland* and Boswell's *Journal of a Tour to the Hebrides* is a combined edition edited by Peter Levi (London and New York, 1984). All quotations are from this edition.

For a moving account of the '45 Uprising see John Prebble: *Culloden* (London, 1961).

p.138 For the history of Scots Gaelic see Glanville Price: *The Languages of Britain* (London, 1984).

p.140 According to Norman MacDonald, president of the Gaelic College on Cape Breton Island, over 6000 people in Nova Scotia still speak Gaelic. The figure comes from informal studies and an estimate based on the 1973 Canadian Census Report. Many people believe that the figure should be higher – others lower!

The Older Scottish Tongue
p.141 For the most reliable account of Scots English see A. J. Aitken (Ed.): *Lowland Scots* (Association for Scottish Literary Studies, 1973). See also A. J. Aitken in Peter Trudgill (Ed.): *Language in the British Isles* (Cambridge, 1984), and A. J. Aitken and T. McArthur: *Languages of Scotland* (Edinburgh, 1979), B. Glauser: *The Scottish-English Linguistic Border* (Berne, 1974), and W. B. Lockwood: *The Language of the British Isles* (London and New York, 1975).

p.143 It is difficult to date the composition of the Sir Patrick Spens Ballad, but it dates from this period.

The great names of the "Golden Age", Dunbar, Douglas and Lyndsay were all dead or old by 1550: in other words, by the mid-sixteenth century, Scots was already in flight to English. The English writers, Chaucer, Gower, and Lydgate had started the anglicization. Shakespeare et al. were setting the seal on a process that goes back to the fourteenth century.

For the wider cultural background to the Older Scottish Tongue, see T. C. Smout: *A History of the Scottish People* (London, 1969).

"A Bible in the Vulgare Tongue"
p.144 For the New Testament in Scots see W. L. Lorimer (Trans.): *New Testament in Scots* (Southside, 1983). Lorimer was not the first to translate the Scriptures into Scots (see W. W. Smith's *New Testament* (1901), but his was the first to be widely available and to catch the popular imagination. There is still no complete Bible in Scots.

From Burns to Lallans
p.146 For Robert Burns, the life and works, see David Daiches: *Robert Burns and His World* (London and New York, 1971), H. W. Meikle and W. Beattie (Eds): *Robert Burns. Poems* (London, 1972), S. G. Smith (Ed.): *A Choice of Burns's Poems and Songs* (London, 1966).

p.147 A. J. Aitken points out that "most working-class city Scots speak a dialect heavily laced with Scottish features."

p.148 For Walter Scott, see David Daiches: *Sir Walter Scott and His World* (London, 1971). A longer list of his best works would include *Rob Roy, Guy Mannering* and *Old Mortality*.

p.149 For Lallans, see J. K. Annand (Ed.): *Lallans, the magazine for writing in Lowland Scots*.

p.151 The words of Stanley Robertson are taken from Barbara McDermitt "Stanley Robertson" (unpublished article, 1984), which we gratefully acknowledge.

The Scots in Ireland
p.152 We are most grateful to Professor John Braidwood for his advice in this section. See Eric Montgomery *The Scotch-Irish and Ulster* (Ulster-Scot Historical Society, 1965). See also Linde Connolly: "Spoken English in Ulster in the Eighteenth and Nineteenth Centuries", *Ulster Folklife*, Vol. 28, 1982. See also Robert J. Gregg: "The Scotch-Irish Dialect Boundaries in Ulster", in Martyn Wakelin (Ed.): *Patterns in the Folk Speech of the British Isles*, (London, 1972). We are also grateful to Dr Alan Gailey of the Ulster Folk and Transport Museum, Cultra Manor, Holywood, Co. Down, Northern Ireland, for his paper, "The Scots Element in North Irish Popular Culture." See also James Milroy: *Regional Accents of English, Belfast* (Dundonald, 1980).

p.152 The name given to the Lowland Scots in Ulster varies. In the United States, they are "Scotch-Irish". In Ireland, they are known as "Ulster Scots". We have adopted a neutral term "Scots-Irish".

For an excellent essay "The Dialects of Ulster" by G. B. Adams, from which we quote, see Diarmaid Ó'Muirithe (Ed.): *The English Language in Ireland* (Cork, 1977).

p.153 See John Braidwood on Ulster English generally in "Ulster and Elizabethan English", in G. B. Adams (Ed.): *Ulster Dialect Symposium* (Ulster Folk Museum, 1964).

"Fornent" can also be spelt and pronounced "fornenst". The phrase "a wee colour" means "a small drop of " (milk, whisky, etc.).

For the history of Ballymena and district see *Mid-Antrim*, passim. We are grateful to Ivan Herbison for bringing it to our attention.

"The American Plantations"
p.157 For the Scots-Irish generally, see Stuart B. Flexner, op. cit.

For the German influence, see Leo Rockwell: "Older German Loan-words in American English" (*American Speech*).

pp.159–61 For the English of Appalachia, see Linda Blanton: "Southern Appalachia. Social Considerations of Speech" in J. L. Dillard (Ed.): *Towards a Social History of American English* (Hawthorne, 1985). See also, for Daniel Boone, John Bakeless: *Master of the Wilderness. Daniel Boone* (1939), and Walter Blair: "Half Horse, Half Alligator" in *Native American Humor*. See also Alan Crozier: "The Scotch-Irish Influence on American English", *American Speech*,
59.4, 1984. The landscape of Appalachia (and the American view of its people) is luridly depicted in John Boorman's film *Deliverance*.

p.160 *Whae-aw* (who all) is also Northumbrian and Scots.

For the stories of the Appalachians and the Ozarks generally see Vance Randolph: *Pissing In The Snow* (New York, 1976).

For the Scots-Irish influence generally see Jack W. Weaver (Ed.): *Selected Proceedings of the Scotch-Irish Heritage Festival at Winthrop College* (1980)

p.161 See T. W. Moody: "The Ulster Scots in Colonial and Revolutionary America" (*American Studies*, 1945).

For his advice on the "sunbelt English" of the New South, we are grateful to Professor John Fought, at the University of Pennsylvania.

5 THE IRISH QUESTION

p.163 We would like to thank Professor Alan Bliss for his generous assistance with this chapter. The best account of Irish English is provided by a series of half-hour broadcasts, the Thomas Davis lecture series, edited by Diarmaid Ó'Muirithe under the title *The English Language in Ireland* (Cork, 1977), to which Professor Bliss contributes the opening lecture. For other summaries of English in Ireland see Michael V. Barry "The English Language in Ireland" in Richard W. Bailey and Manfred Görlach (Eds.): *English as a World Language* (Cambridge, 1984; Michigan, 1982), and also Glanville Price: *The Languages of Britain* (London, 1984) and Victor Stevenson: *Words* (London, 1983).

The "Irish joke" is taken from "On Conceptions of Good Grammar" in Randolph Quirk: *The English Language and Images of Matter* (Oxford, 1972).

p.164 For the Blarney story see Sean Jennett: *Cork and Kerry* (London, 1977). We are grateful to Sir Richard Colthurst for his advice about the origins of the Blarney.

The *oral* culture of Ireland is all-important: sung and spoken ritual were fundamental to the rural society of medieval Ireland.

The Irish critic and writer Seamus Deane has called the early nineteenth century the golden age of "shamrockery". It is interesting to note that this was the period when the Highlands were also being romanticized. See Eric Hobsbawm and Terence Ranger (Eds.): *The Invention of Tradition* (Cambridge and New York, 1983).

"The Pagan Speech"
p.164 Yeats could read Irish, but he couldn't speak it. See P. L. Henry "Anglo Irish and its Irish background" in Diarmaid Ó'Muirithe (Ed.): *The English Language in Ireland* (Cork, 1977).

p.165 The Irish golden age is real enough. After Greece and Rome, Ireland had the oldest written vernacular literature and grammar in Europe.

The Gaelic Factor
pp.167–8 The "long line" is found in a Yeats poem like "Down by the Sally Gardens . . ."

p.168 See J. H. Delargy: "The Gaelic Story-teller" (From the *Proceedings of the British Academy*, vol. xxxi, 1945).

Other examples of Irish idiom include: "He has a long face to wash in the morning" (He's bald) and "He has hands on him for anything" (He is an excellent workman). See Loreto Todd: "Tyrone English", (*Transactions of the Yorkshire Dialect Society*, 1971). We are grateful to Professor Todd for her exceptionally generous assistance with this chapter. It has been pointed out that, strictly speaking, the Irish *Sí* does not mean "fairy", but "magic, enchantment, abode of fairies".

p.169 The varieties of present tense are also attributable to regional variation.

In Irish Gaelic "yes" and "no" are achieved by repeating the verb positively or negatively.

p.172 For the condition of English in Ireland today, see a characteristically eloquent essay, Tom Paulin: "A New Look at the Language Question" (Belfast, 1983).

"The Irish Brogue"
p.172 See Alan Bliss: "Spoken English in Ireland: The Background to Literature" (Private paper, 1985). Also Alan Bliss: *Spoken English in Ireland: 1600–1740* (Portlaoise, 1979).

p.174 Thomas Sheridan, the actor, also lectured the citizens of Edinburgh about "marks of rusticity." His *General Dictionary* is an important source-book for eighteenth-century pronunciations.

p.175 See also for the self-conscious use of the Anglo-Irish idiom Somerville and Ross: *Experiences of an Irish R.M.* (London, 1969). In the less well-known *Children of the Captivity*, they write:

"The very wind that blows softly over brown acres of bog carries perfumes and sounds that England does not know; the women digging the potato land are talking of things that England does not understand. The question that remains is whether England will ever understand."

p.176 The impression of variety in Irish English is enhanced by different translations of Irish idioms in different areas.

Irish Galore
p.176 Loreto Todd tells us that in Nigeria the common mispronunciation of words like *mischievous* and *grievous* as "mischievious" and "grievious" are generally attributed to the teaching of Irish missionaries in the nineteenth century.

Galore may owe its present currency to Sir Walter Scott. If so, it is Scottish Gaelic, and has little or nothing to do with Ireland.

p.177 It is said that the Irish in Newfoundland kept up a traditional hostility to the English even in World War II, selling salt fish to German U-Boat captains sheltering in the Straits of Belle Isle.

For details of English in Newfoundland, see the excellent introduction in G. M. Story, W. J. Kirwin, and J. D. A. Widdowson (Eds.): *Dictionary of Newfoundland English* (Toronto, 1982).

We are indebted to Professor Harold Paddock for his help in Newfoundland.

p.179 We should like to thank Thomas Nemec for his assistance in our research in St Shott's.

p.180 For the Irish in the Caribbean and a full account of the origin of "redleg" see Jill Shepperd: *The "Redlegs" of Barbados* (KTO Press, 1977).

p.181 For the best reading on the Irish in Australia, see the notes to chapter eight "The Echoes of an English Voice".

For the influence of Irish English on Australian English, we acknowledge, with gratitude, Peter Trudgill's forthcoming book, *Dialects in Contact*, an exceptionally stimulating and provocative study.

p.182 For the sportswriting tradition in Australia (with special reference to Australian Rules Football) see Jack Hibberd and Garrie Hutchinson: *The Barracker's Bible* (McPhee Gribble, 1983), see also Garrie Hutchinson: *From the Outer* (London, 1984).

The Naturalization of Irish English
p.182 There are no reliable figures for Ireland at the time of Union. Those quoted are the generally accepted estimates.

The claims for and against a future for Irish Gaelic reflect the political and cultural preferences of the speaker. Our feeling, echoing Seamus Heaney, who observes that Irish is "on hold", is that it neither lives nor dies and that this is likely to be the case well into the future.

p.183 The Irish for "Irish Free State" is *Saorstat Éireann*. The name *Éire* first appears in the 1937 Constitution. According to Article 4 (in the English translation), "The name of the State is Éire, or in the English language, *Ireland*." This means that it is only proper to use the form *Éire* if you are writing in Irish. The constitutional statement that Irish is the "first official language" is a statement more of hope than fact, and it is seen by some as a fairly hypocritical statement. The fact is, as Randolph Quirk has put it, that "the chief national language of the Irish Republic is cultivated Irish English" (in "Language and Nationhood" in *Style and Communication*, op. cit.).

The Irish Revival
pp.184–5 For Yeats and the Irish revival, see W. B. Yeats: *Essays and Introductions* (London, 1961).

p.185 For Synge's visit to Aran and the story of the "Playboy" see J. M. Synge: *The Playboy of the Western World* (various editions), and J. M. Synge: *Aran Islands* (Oxford, 1979).

p.187 See Thomas E. Connolly: *Scribbledehobble: the Ur-Workbook to Finnegans Wake* (Evanston, 1961).

The Land of Youth
p.188 See Hugh Brody: *Inishkillane: Change and Decline in the West of Ireland* (London, 1973).

p.189 See "Dialect and Literature" by Benedict Kiely in Diarmid Ó'Muirithe, op. cit.

The Ulster pronunciation of *d* and *t* ("budder" for *butter*, and "wadder" for *water*) is also prevalent in American English, and may have been transplanted there by the Scots-Irish.

pp.189–90 For the Irish in America see Stuart Berg Flexner: *I Hear America Talking* (New York, 1976). The Irish were always literate. It has been estimated that during the eighteenth century 55 per cent of the population could read and write in Irish.

p.190 For some of the arguments about the derivation of words like *shenanigan, shanty, shebang* and *smithereens* see Stuart B. Flexner (op. cit.) vs. Alan Bliss in *Notes and Queries*, ccxiii, (1968) pp. 283–6.

On the *buddy* controversy, Loreto Todd adds that in West African Krio *padi* (Paddy) means a close friend.

Among several speeches, Kennedy made the following comment: "My country welcomed so many sons and daughters of so many countries, Irish and Scandinavians, Germans, Italian, and all the rest, and gave them a fair chance and a fair opportunity. The speaker of the House of Representatives is of Irish descent. The leader of the Senate is of Irish descent. And what is true of the Irish has been true of dozens of other peoples. In Ireland I think you see something of what is so great about the United States; and I must say that in the United States, through millions of your sons and daughters – 25 million, in fact – you see something of what is great about Ireland."
(Remarks at Redmond Place, Wexford, 27 June 1963)

The Mersey Sound
p.191 For the Irish in Victorian England see Asa Briggs: *Victorian Cities* (London, 1968)

For the Liverpool accent see Peter Trudgill: *Accent, Dialect and the School* (London, 1975; Baltimore, 1979), and also Arthur Hughes and Peter Trudgill: *English Accents and Dialects* (London and Baltimore, 1979) and J. C. Wells: *Accents of English: The British Isles* (Cambridge, 1982).

The English public probably identify two kinds of Irish English – Northern and Southern.

p.192 The remarks by Terry Wogan and Anthony Clare appeared in "Blarney at the BBC" by Hunter Davies, *The Sunday Times*, 19 December 1982.

p.193 We are grateful to the directors of Field Day: Seamus Deane, Brian Friel, David Hammond, Seamus Heaney, Tom Paulin and Stephen Kea. See also Seamus Heaney: *An Open Letter* (A Field Day Pamphlet, 1983).

The growing recognition of Irish English (Hiberno-English) was marked by the first conference of Hiberno-English in Dublin in September 1985.

The idea of "language death" and also the fate of Manx is explored in Dick Leith: *A Social History of English* (London and Boston, 1983).

For the fate of the Cornish language see the tombstone in Mousehole: *Here lieth interred Dorothy Pentreath who died in 1777, said to have been the last person who conversed in the ancient Cornish, the regular language of this county from the earliest records till it expired in the eighteenth century in the parish of Saint Paul.*

6 BLACK ON WHITE

p.195 For the preparation of this chapter we are especially grateful to Professor J. L. Dillard and Dr John Holm. The inspiration for much of our argument has been J. L. Dillard: *Black English* (New York, 1973), and J. L. Dillard: *American Talk* (New York, 1976).

The origin of *tote* ("carry") is unclear, possibly a convergence of Kongo *tota* "to pick up", Mbunda *tuta* "to carry", with the Old English *totian* "to lift".

The first British fort in what is now Ghana was built in 1631.

The Atlantic Triangle
p.196 For blacks in Britain see Peter Fryer: *Staying Power. The History of Black People in Britain* (London, 1984).

The Making of Pidgin English
p.197 For another account of pidgin see Randolph Quirk: *The English Language and Images of Matter* (Oxford, 1972).

For maritime pidgins see Loreto Todd: *Pidgins and Creoles* (London and Boston, 1974).

"The Tower of Babel"
p.200 Strictly speaking, they did not become slaves until they were sold in America or the Caribbean.

For the making of Black English see also Dwight Bolinger: *Language: The Loaded Weapon* (London and New York, 1980).

For Maritime Pidgin English see "Creole Languages" by Derek Bickerton in *Scientific American*, July 1983.

p.201 For Krio see Clifford N. Fyle and Eldred D. Jones: *A Krio-English Dictionary* (Oxford and New York, 1980).

The trading language on the Congo is "Lingullah": presumably related.

p.203 For West African pidgin see W. R. O'Donnell and Loreto Todd: *Variety in Contemporary English* (London, 1980).

Caribbean Creole
pp.203–07 For this section on the English of the Caribbean we gratefully acknowledge the help of Professor Richard Allsopp. See also his *Caribbean English as a Challenge to Lexicography* (Lexeter, 1983).

p.204 For English in Central America, see John Holm (Ed.): *Central American English* (Heidelberg, 1983).

For English in the Caribbean see David L. Lawton's essay in Richard W. Bailey and Manfred Görlach (Eds.): *English as a World Language* (Cambridge, 1984), see also John Holm's forthcoming "The Spread of English in the Caribbean" in M. Gorlach and John Holm (Eds.): *Focus on the Caribbean* (Amsterdam, 1986).

pp.204–5 See George Lamming: *In The Castle of My Skin* (London, 1979; New York, 1983).

"Bajan" tends to be the word used by the Caribbean Whites and it is now considered to have racist overtones.

"An Echo of Plantation Talk"
p.208 See Lorenzo Turner: *Africanisms in the Gullah Dialect* (Ann Arbor, 1974).

p.209 For our research in Charleston and on Johns Island we would like to thank Al and Bill Saunders, and Deborah and Robert Rosen.

For the link between Gullah and Caribbean Creole see John Holm's fascinating article "On the Relationship of Gullah and Bahamian" in *American Speech* 58.4 (1983).

p.209 The inclusion of Krio here should acknowledge the special contribution of Gullah-speaking returnees in the nineteenth century (see chapter nine.) See also Allen Walker Read, "The Speech of Negroes in Colonial America", *The Journal of Negro History*, Vol. xxiv, July 1939.

p.210 The literary evidence for Gullah is found in Fanny Kemble: *A Journal of Residence on a Georgia Plantation in 1838–39*. She reported: "That 'spect, meaning *expect*, has sometimes a possible meaning of *suspect*, which could give the sentence in which it occurs a very humorous turn, and I always take the benefit of that interpretation." Gullah tends – like Black English – to have an elided or omitted initial syllable. The single best literary attempt to reproduce it was made by Colonel Thomas Wentworth Higginson, a white Massachussetts aristocrat who commanded a Black regiment in the Civil War in *Army Life in a Black Regiment*.

Most of the quotations here are taken from J. L. Dillard: *Black English* (New York, 1972).

For the latest research on the Black English of the American see J. L. Dillard: *Towards a Social History of American English* (Hawthorne, 1984).

"The Negro Dialect"
p.211 For the tradition of Black writing in the nineteenth century see Paul Brennan (Ed.) *You Better Believe It, Blank Verse in English* (London, 1973) and Joan R. Sherman: *Invisible Poets, Afro-Americans of the Nineteenth Century* (Champaign, 1974). For the Brer Rabbit stories and a very revealing introduction by the author, see Joel Chandler Harris: *Uncle Remus* (London, 1959). See also Joel Chandler Harris: *Uncle Remus. His Songs and Sayings*, edited with an Introduction by Robert Hemenway (London, 1982; Cherokee, 1981).

p.213 For many Blacks, Joel Chandler Harris is an unacceptable reminder of the racist past and his work is rejected. We feel obliged to report, however, that many linguists, Black and White, endorse the opinion that Harris's stories are remarkably accurate transcriptions of Plantation Creole.

p.213 The J. C. Harris story is told by Mark Twain: *Life on the Mississippi* (New York, 1981)

For the Negro dialect in a landmark of black American fiction, see Harriet E. Wilson: *Our Nig: Sketches from the Life of a Free Black* (London, 1984; New York, 1983).

"The Thick Negro Speech of the Southerners"
p.214 The "implosive consonant" Dillard mentions is the prenasalized stop, sometimes written [mb].

p.215 For the speech of Southern Whites see also Albert H. Marckwardt: *American English* (Oxford and New York, 1980).

The Blacks Move North
p.217 For the Blacks and jazz see J. L. Dillard: *American Talk* (New York, 1976). The Minstrel show is, of course, of both Black *and* White origin (cf. Amos and Andy p.225), but this does not detract from its place in our story.

For the origin of jazz, we have been told by *Jazz Journal* that "jassing around" is Black slang for "fucking around." See also Clarence Major: *Black Slang* (London, 1971).

p.220 See also the Black use of "signifying", "sounding", "doing the dozens" etc. In the words of Ann Cook and Herb Mack (Eds.): *Tell It Like It Is: A Dictionary of Black Slang*, this means, "kidding one's friends about their intellectual ability or family." Examples: "*Your hair is so short it's like blowin' dust off a jug,*" and "*Your teeth are so yellow you put the sun out of business.*"

"Mr Hepster's Jive Talk Dictionary"
p.221 See also Miles Davis: *The Birthplace of the Cool*. See Albert Murray: *South to a Very Old Place* (New York, 1972).

pp.223–5 For the Blues, see Robert Palmer: *Deep Blues* (New York, 1981).

p.226 The intensifier "stone" is familiar in "stone cold" and "stoney broke".

"I Have A Dream"
p.228 For Cassius Clay see the *New York Times*, 21 February 1964: "When he and his cohorts throw back their heads and bellow, 'Float like a butterfly, sting like a bee; rumble, young man, rumble,' they always crack themselves up. It's all a colossal gas for Cassius." The wording was probably made up by one of Clay's entourage, Drew (Bundini) Brown, probably before the Doug Jones fight in 1963. Clay was definitely using it before the Sonny Liston fight in 1964.

p.229 For the Black English of the ghettos and twentieth-century United States see Charles A. Ferguson & Shirley Brice Heath (Eds.): *Language in the USA* (Cambridge, Mass., 1981).

p.230 The inversion *aks* for *ask* is a traditional one in Black English and is found throughout the American South and the Caribbean.

pp.230–31 The words of Judge Joiner are found in "Objectivity and commitment in linguistic science: The case of the Black English trial in Ann Arbor" by William Labov, in Dell Hymes (Ed.): *Language and Society* (Cambridge, 1982). For the Black English debate, see also Geneva Smitherman and Monroe K. Spears in Leonard Michaels and Christopher Ricks (Eds.): *The State of the Language* (Berkeley, 1980).

p.231 The report in the *Philadelphia Inquirer* (21 October 1983) was by Russell Cooke.

p.232 For the street talk of the Blacks see Thomas Kochman (Ed.): *Rappin and stylin' out* (Champaign,

1977). In 1985 Black English again hit the headlines in the United Kingdom and the United States with a report by William Labov which suggested that the street talk of Blacks and Whites is diverging – contrary to the assumptions of many linguists.

7 PIONEERS! O PIONEERS!

p.235 The indispensable guide to American English is H. L. Mencken: *The American Language* (4th edition, New York, 1979). Next to that for an entertaining A–Z see Stuart Berg Flexner: *I Hear America Talking* (New York, 1976), and also Stuart Berg Flexner: *Listening to America* (New York, 1982). We are indebted to Mr Flexner for his advice on this chapter.

The argument about the course of American and British English – divergence or convergence? – (see chapter nine) naturally affects one's view of the evidence of *American* English in 1776. Even allowing for mutual antipathy, it is clear that there were *some* differences in 1776, but that the tempo of change increased – as we describe – significantly during the nineteenth century. For the two opposing views see Robert Burchfield: *The English Language* (Oxford, 1985) and "Philology, Politics and American English" in Randolph Quirk: *The English Language and Images of Matter* (Oxford, 1972).

The irrationality surrounding the Amer-English debate is summed up by S. T. Coleridge's attack on *talented*, a word that was actually coined in England.

p.236 See Allen Walker Read: *British Recognition of American Speech in the Eighteenth Century* (Dialect Notes, 1933).

"The American Language"
pp.236–9 There is a good account of American English in A. C. Baugh and Thomas Cable, op. cit.

p.237 For the polemical side of American English in the early years see Dennis E. Barron: *Grammar and Good Taste* (New Haven, 1982). See also Shirley Brice Heath: "A National Language Academy? Debate in the New Nation" (*International Journal of Sociology of Language*, 1976).

p.239 For the idea of "American" see Allen Walker Read: "The Adjective 'American' in England" (*American Speech*, 1950).

Canadian English
p.244 There is, and always has been, an important ethnic mix in Canada – linguistically distinctive in Scots and Irish settlements in inland (as well as Atlantic) Canada, and linguistically absorbed in socially mobile offspring of Italians, Portuguese, Ukrainians, etc.

p.245 We are grateful to Professor J. K. Chambers for his advice about Canadian English. In addition to his help we acknowledge Walter S. Avis (Ed.): *A Dictionary of Canadianisms on Historical Principles* (Toronto, 1967): J. Bartlett Brebner: *Canada: A Modern History* (Ann Arbor, 1960); Bruce Fergusson and William Pope: *Glimpses into Nova Scotia History* (Windsor, Nova Scotia, 1978); Neil MacNeil: *The Highland Heart in Nova Scotia* (Toronto, 1958); Andrew H. Malcolm: *The Canadians* (New York, 1985); R. Montgomery Martin: *History of Nova Scotia* (London, 1837); David Millet, "The Social Context of Bilin-

gualism in Eastern Ontario", *American Review of Canadian Studies*, Spring, 1983, pp. 1–12; Mark Orkin: *Canajan, Eh?* (Don Mills, Ontario, 1973).

p.247 See Richard G. Bailey "English in Canada" in *English as a World Language* (op. cit.).

The Loyalists were not the first by any means, but along the Atlantic coast, in the territory now occupied by Newfoundland and the maritime provinces of Nova Scotia, New Brunswick and Prince Edward Island, there was a patchwork of English-speaking settlements dating as far back as 1583. To this day, there is more variety of speech in the Maritimes than anywhere else in Canada, and, we are tempted to say, North America. In the south-west corner of Newfoundland, for instance, the small communities of Highlands and St David are inhabited by Highland Scots. Nearby Heather Town belongs to West Country Englishmen with "Mummerzet" accents. St Theresa and Flatbay are inhabited by English-speaking Micmac Indians (with Gaelic accents), and French "Jacatars". Close by is Stevenville, occupied by the Acadian French, and there are other communities of French speakers on the Port au Port peninsula.

These French speakers are an important reminder that much of Canada was French before it was British. To this day, the province of Quebec remains committed to a French not an English tradition. In this century, Canada has had three francophone prime ministers, Sir Wilfred Laurier, Louis St Laurent and Pierre Trudeau. The French Canadian accent (scarcely evident in Trudeau, very noticeable in his would-be successor, Jean Chrétien) is another important ingredient in the mixture of Canadian sounds. Canadian place-names reflect their French ancestry, from the Gaspé peninsula on the Atlantic to Belleville (Ontario), Portage la Prairie (Manitoba), Fort Qu'Appelle (Saskatchewan), Lac la Biche (Alberta), and Jumeau (British Columbia). *Concession, portage* and *cache* are direct borrowings from the French. There is also a long list of words that came into Canadian English from Indian languages via French: *caribou, papoose* and *pemmican*. The very word Canada itself probably comes from the Iroquois *kanata*, meaning "village", adapted by the French.

p.248 For the condition of Canadian English today see J. K. Chambers and Margaret F. Hardwick: *Dialect Homogeneity and Incipient Variation: Changes in Progress in Toronto and Vancouver* (Sheffield Working Papers in Language and Linguistics 2, 1985, ed. J. Harris and R. Hawkins, School of Modern Languages and Linguistics, University of Sheffield).

For Canada generally see June Callwood: *Portrait of Canada* (New York, 1981).

For a full bibliography see Walter S. Avis and A. M. Kinloch: *Writings on Canadian English, 1792–1975: An Annotated Bibliography* (Markham, Ontario, 1976).

"Go West, Young Man, Go West!"
p.249 See Charles Dickens: *American Notes* (London, 1895).

pp.249–51 For a full treatment of American English in the Wild West see J. L. Dillard: *Towards a Social History of American English* (Hawthorne, 1985). We owe to Professor Dillard many of the examples we quote here.

p.250 The introduction of "American ice" into drinks occurred during the nineteenth century, see Allen Walker Read, op cit. For *angeliferous, explunctify* and other bizarre coinings see Allen Walker Read: *The Criteria for a Class of Jocular Words in English* (Maledicta, 1982).

"To See the Elephant"
p.251 By far the best book on the California gold-rush is J. S. Holliday: *The World Rushed In* (New York, 1981).

"The Real McCoy"
p.254 The origin of the "real McCoy" is, naturally, disputed. Flexner (op. cit.) gives no less than five versions, but we are sticking to our story!

"Mark Twain"
p.259 T. S. Eliot's verdict is found in "American Literature and the American Language" on p. 45 of *To Criticize the Critic and Other Writings* (London, 1978; New York, 1965).

pp.260–1 For the Twain quotations given here see Mark Twain and Charles Dudley Warner: *The Gilded Age* (London, 1883); and Mark Twain: *Life on the Mississippi* (London, 1985; New York, 1984); and Mark Twain: *Roughing It* (London and New York, 1981).

For some entertaining Twain correspondence see Bernard De Voto: *The Portable Mark Twain* (London, 1982; New York, 1983).

p.262 The best biography of Whitman is by Justin Kaplan: *Walt Whitman* (London and New York, 1980). See also Mark Doren (Ed.): *The Portable Walt Whitman* (London and New York, 1977).

Walt Whitman expressed his love of *American* English in *An American Primer* (1855): "The Americans are going to be the most fluent and melodious-voiced people in the world – and the most perfect users of words.... Words follow character – nativity, independence, individuality.... These States are rapidly supplying themselves with new words, called for by new occasions, new facts, new politics, new combinations. ... Far plentier additions will be needed, and, of course, will be supplied ...

"American writers are to show far more freedom in the use of words.... Ten thousand native idiomatic words are growing, or are today already grown, out of which vast numbers could be used by American writers, with meaning and effect – words that would be welcomed by the nation, being of the national blood – words that give that taste of identity and locality which is so dear in literature."

"The Huddled Masses"
p.263 For immigrants and American English see Albert H. Marckwardt: *American English* (Oxford and New York, 1980).

p.264 For the emigrant experience in the days of the railroad, see a minor classic, Robert Louis Stevenson: *The Amateur Emigrant* (London and New Hampshire, 1984).

p.264 The list of German Yiddish words is from S. Flexner: *I Hear America Talking*. Some of these derivations are disputed.

p.265 There is, of course, a fanciful sense in which the Italian invasion of America can claim to be the oldest of all: it was Christopher Columbus and Amerigo Vespucci who were the first Europeans to explore the New World. To this day, Columbus is remembered in many ways: the District of Columbia, Washington; Columbia University; Columbus, Ohio (and at least 21 other towns and cities) and Columbus Day, 12 October, the anniversary of the first landing at San Salvador Island, 1492. Amerigo Vespucci, who came five years later, was the first explorer to realize that North America was not part of Asia but a new continent. He himself called the place *Mundus Novus*, New World. It was Vespucci's German publisher who is supposed to have suggested that the new territory should be named after him, America. After that, there was very little Italian immigration until the nineteenth century.

p.267 For the influence of Yiddish on English see Leo Rosten: *The Joys of Yiddish* (London, 1971) and *Hooray for Yiddish!* (London, 1983). For fuller definitions of the "Yinglish" quoted here see Rosten *passim*.

"Over there"
p.269 For H. L. Mencken see Huntington Cairns (Ed.): *The American Scene* (New York, 1982). For the Master's choice see *A Mencken Chrestomathy* (New York, 1982).

For an excellent memoir of H. L. Mencken, see Alistair Cooke: *Six Men* (London and New York, 1977).

In a way that is typical of English, the origin of *doughboy* is obscure and controversial. One theory goes that "doughboy" was a small biscuit served to American sailors, which was then borrowed to describe the brass buttons on some Civil War infantry uniforms and finally adopted to describe the troops themselves. Alistair Cooke says that the nickname came from the biscuity complexions of the American soldiers in Britain, a fact attributed to the lack of sun in cities full of skyscrapers. Another theory has it that the US infantry used to wear white belts which had to be cleaned with pipe clay dough, hence *doughboys*. Finally, there is the suggestion that the word has a Spanish-American origin, and comes from *adobe*, slang for "soldiers" among Spanish-speakers of the American South-West, and derived from the fact that most soldiers were housed in *adobe* quarters.

Mencken's estimate of the vigour of American English received an unexpected endorsement from Virginia Woolf, who wrote that Americans are only "doing what the Elizabethans did – they are coining new words ... one may search English fiction in vain for a single new word ... All the expressive, ugly, vigorous slang which creeps in among us ... comes from across the Atlantic."

We have here used the phrase "the English languages", but it should be noted that for many scholars this is an unacceptable usage and, strictly speaking, we should write about American English, Australian English, Canadian English, etc.

8 THE ECHOES OF AN ENGLISH VOICE

p.271 We are very grateful to Professor John Bernard and Dr W. S. Ramson for their advice on this chapter.

For the history of the White Commonwealth in the nineteenth century see Asa Briggs: *The Age of Improvement* (London, 1979) and Asa Briggs: *Victorian Cities* (London, 1968).

"The London Language"
p.272 For Henry Machyn see H. C. Wyld: *A History of Modern Colloquial English* (Oxford, 1953). See George Bernard Shaw: *Three Plays For Puritans* (London, 1983), and also J. C. Wells: *Accents of English* (Cambridge, 1982).

For the condition of the poor in the East End, see G. S. Jones: *Outcast London* (London, 1984).

p.273 For the changes in the sound of Standard English see Raymond Williams: *The Long Revolution* (London and Westport, 1971).

p.276 See Henry Mayhew: *London Labour and the London Poor* (1861).

For Sam Weller see Charles Dickens: *Pickwick Papers*.

"Born within the Sound of Bow Bells"
p.277 We are indebted to Robert Barltrop and Jim Wolveridge for their help with the section on Cockney. See also Robert Barltrop and Jim Wolveridge: *The Muvver Tongue* (London, 1980). Robert Barltrop is completing a Cockney dictionary for the Athlone Press, see his Introduction. See also the earlier standard work, William Matthews: *Cockney Past and Present* (London, 1972).

Ford Madox Ford claimed that "pikey" was derived from "turnpike", i.e., one who travelled on the turnpike.

"Put up your dukes" means "put up your fists".

No chapter on the Cockney would be complete without acknowledging a debt to Eric Partridge whose *Usage and Abusage* (London, 1973) and *Dictionary of Slang* are among the indispensable books on the language.

p.279 W. S. Ramson notes an increased incidence of "rhyming slang" at the turn of the century.

The Landscape of Discovery
p.284 For the Aboriginal element in Australian English see Bob Dixon: *Searching for Aborigine Languages* (Queensland, 1984). See also Robert Eagleson et al.: *English and the Aboriginal Child*, Canberra, 1982). See also A. W. Reed: *Aboriginal Words of Australia* (French's Forest, NSW, 1983).

Professor John Bernard offers a definite Aboriginal source-word "gangurru" which, in the language Gungu Yimidhirr means "a large black kangaroo". But if this is so why did the natives not recognize the Anglicized version?

The *kangaroo* story is told in *The Macquarie Dictionary* (Sydney, 1981), currently the only Australian English Dictionary, and full of interesting Australianisms.

p.285 For the first days of English in Australia see W. S. Ramson (Ed.): *English Transported* (Canberra, 1970).

See the compendious Sidney J. Baker: *The Australian Language* (Melbourne, 1970) from which J. D. Lang's poem is taken.

"The Flash Language"
p.287 We should make it clear that "flash language" referred to "convict slang". Australian English is, of course, drawn from many sources.

p.288 For the connections between Cockney and Australian see A. J. Ellis: *Early English Pronunciation* (1889).

pp.288-9 For the early history of Australia see Geoffrey Blainey: *The Tyranny of Distance* (Melbourne, 1982) and Peter Taylor: *Australia. The First Twelve Years* (London, 1982).

p.289 *Corker*, *dust up*, *purler*, and *tootsy* mean "something very good of its kind", "a fight", "a heavy fall", and a "foot".

For the first account of English in Australia, see E. E. Morris: *Austral English* (London, 1898).

See also W. S. Ramson: *Australian English* (Canberra, 1966)

p.290 W. S. Ramson's account of *Pommy* is a private communication to the authors. The definition will be in the forthcoming *Australian National Dictionary*.

Chunder has two derivations: 1) as an abbreviation for "watch under", an ominous courtesy on board ship shouted from the upper decks for the protection of those below, and 2) rhyming slang *chunder loo = spew* (from a long-running cartoon series).

"The Wild Colonial Boy"
p.291 For the place of the Cockneys and the Irish in the making of Australia see a brilliant survey, Russel Ward: *The Australian Legend* (Oxford, 1978). Some scholars resist the close association of Australian and Cockney, but it is an identification favoured by the majority.

p.294 For the spread of the English language throughout the White Commonwealth see Dick Leith: *A Social History of English* (London and Baltimore, 1983); for the prevalence of "Slang", see Lucy Frost: *No Place for a Nervous Lady: Voices from the Australian Bush* (Victoria, 1984).

For the poetry of Australia see Russel Ward (Ed.): *The Penguin Book of Australian Ballads* (London, 1981).

The account of English in Australian schools comes from Richard Yallop: "Why Strine ain't English" (*Guardian*, 2 September 1982).

For a fine collection of Australian slang and its origins see the authoritative G. A. Wilkes: *A Dictionary of Australian Colloquialisms* (London, 1978).

"The Australian Twang"
p.296 For the properties of Australia, including Bunagaree and Anama see Peter Taylor: *Pastoral Properties of Australia* (London, 1984). The "class" aspect of English in Australia is controversial: those who believe that Australia is a "classless" society tend to support most strongly the idea that there is no social variation. The differentiations in Australian speech seem to come partly from the social image different people wish to project, a preference not confined to

Australia. *Broad* tends to be most common among the less privileged sectors of society. *Cultivated* is most often used by the educated elite. *General* is used by the majority, the people in between.

Cathy Lette: *Puberty Blues* (London, 1980). For a brilliant essay on Dame Edna Everage (alias Barry Humphries), see John Lahr: *Automatic Vaudeville* (London and New York, 1984).

"Come on, Aussie, Come on!"
p.297 For "Strine" see Afferbeck Lauder (pseud.): *Let Stalk Strine* (Sydney, 1966). For the image of Australia, see Mimmo Cozzolino: *Symbols of Australia* (London, 1980).

p.299 There is a myth, perpetrated by the editor of a Greek language newspaper in Melbourne, that his city is the *third-largest* Greek city in the world. This is not true, Chicago and New York easily outstrip it. This is not to say that its Greek population is not significant!

A "Carefully Modulated Murmur"
p.300 We are most grateful to C. K. Stead for this personal communication.

p.301 We are indebted to Dr Robert Burchfield for his advice on New Zealand English. See also Robert Burchfield: *Opening Words* (The *Age* Monthly Review, March 1982). In the view of Dr W. S. Ramson, "the New Zealand accent is shifting rapidly and is in some cases so different that an Australian would have difficulty communicating."

p.302 For New Zealand English and its relationship to Australian English see G. W. Turner: *The English Language in Australia and New Zealand* (London, 1966).

p.303 The New Zealand writer Gordon Slatter conveys some of the flavour of New Zealand slang in his novel *A Gun In My Hand*, in what he calls "the jargoning of the working man at rest": "I was shikkered to beat the band. He's a randy old coot always hanging about the cat's bar. I been carryin ya all mornin. He was full on nines and I was full on jacks. He got on to me about smoking in the shed. No sense bustin ya guts out. Blow that for a joke. Time for a coupla draws before the bell goes. An it ran like a hairy goat an I did me chips."

English in South Africa
p.304 The Soweto story is told in Nancy Harrison: *Winnie Mandela: Mother of a Nation* (London, 1985). For English in South Africa see the essay by L. W. Lanham in Richard W. Bailey and Manfred Görlach (Eds.): *English as a World Language* (Cambridge, 1984).

For South African English see Jean Branford (Ed.): *A Dictionary of South African English* (Cape Town, 1978)

p.305 For the place of English in the Black community see Gilbert Marcus: "Blacks treated more severely", *Index on Censorship*, Vol. 13, No. 6, 1984

For English in South Africa see also Randolph Quirk: "Coda: Considering Your English", in *Style and Communication in the English Language* (London, 1982).

For a fascinating insight into the language situation in South Africa, here is the novelist André Brink's view:

First of all, there is no doubt that South Africans identify with British, not American, English – although in the Black townships, mainly through music, American has a strong influence. Certainly, Blacks identify largely with English as their *lingua franca*, as they regard Afrikaans as the language of the oppressor.

English is very firmly ensconced in the economic world, even among Afrikaans speakers; but ever since the Nationalist Party came to power in 1948 the importance of English in politics has been steadily eroded. It is, for instance, interesting that the main White opposition party, the Progressive Federal Party, could make no important headway while its leadership was English-speaking: only with the advent of Van Zyl Slabbert, an Afrikaner, did it become viable as a political factor. (Even so, the top hierarchy of the party is English-orientated, which still hampers it severely in practical politics.)

As I see it, there used to be three completely different "streams" of literature in South Africa until about a decade ago: Afrikaans (then largely the language of the White proletariat), English written by Whites (dominated by a colonialist/imperialist outlook), English written by Blacks (usually in a very self-conscious attempt to escape the linguistic bonds of political oppression). But it seems to me these three streams have been converging steadily. In the work of Athol Fugard and John Coetzee, for instance (as in the earlier stories of Herman Charles Bosman), a completely new kind of English emerged, strongly influenced by Afrikaans rhythms and syntactical patterns: I find in it a more complete identification with the here-and-now, the physicality of the land and the landscape. Even in Olive Schreiner the English language was something of a stumbling-block: something extraneous brought to indigenous experience, which is why she had to resort to strained Dutch words for a sense of local colour. And local colour for a very long time remained just that: a picturesque addition, nothing vital and intrinsic to the experience grasped in the act of writing. Whereas this, it seems to me, is precisely what is happening now. And I think one sees it even in Nadine Gordimer's style – *July's People* and *Something Out There* have a linguistic element new to her writing: a perception of Africa, an acuity of observation, a sense of the tangible and the immediate, which may have rubbed off from Afrikaans. (Just as Afrikaans, in the process, opened itself to the expression of more "abstract", "philosophical", "metaphysical" experience . . .) It is not so much a matter of vocabulary as of syntax, of rhythmic patterns, cadences – which Afrikaans initially acquired when the Dutch brought from Europe became distorted in the mouths of non-Dutch speakers: slaves, "Hottentots", etc.

I find this vitality within the South African language scene one of the most vital and exhilarating aspects of living in this country: living right *inside* it, through the language one uses, (private communication).

p.305 The works of an anonymous Victorian pamphleteer in 1846.

9 THE NEW ENGLISHES

p.307 The two indispensable guides to English today are Loreto Todd: *Modern Englishes* (London and New

York, 1984) and J. Platt, H. Weber and M. L. Ho: *The New Englishes* (London and Boston, 1984) whose title we gratefully acknowledge.

For London in the days of Empire, see Asa Briggs: *Victorian Cities* (London, 1968).

The overshadowing of American literature was expressed by James Russell Lowell in "A Fable for Critics":

*You steal Englishmen's books and think Englishmen's
    thought;*
With their salt on her tail your wild eagle is caught;
Your literature suits its each whisper and motion
To what will be thought of it over the ocean.

Henry James wrote of London's "horrible numerosity" and Thomas Babington Macaulay described the expansion which, in 1881, was christened Greater London: "Long avenues of villas, embowered in lilacs and laburnums, extended from the great centre of wealth and civilization almost to the boundaries of Middlesex and far into the heart of Kent and Surrey."

p.308 For Dr Robert Burchfield's original remarks see *Encounter*, October 1978, and for his latest position *The English Language* (Oxford, 1985).

p.309 See F. G. Cassidy and Robert Le Page: *Dictionary of Jamaican English* (Cambridge, 1980), and F. G. Cassidy: *Jamaica Talk* (London, 1961).

"The Baby of Reggae"
p.310 For her advice on Jamaica and the "dub poets" we are grateful to Anne Walmsley. For a summary of the "dub poetry" movement see Linton Kwesi Johnson in *Race Today*, May/June 1985, page 27, and Mervyn Morris' article "People Speech" in *Race Today Review*.

p.311 For the poems of Louise Bennett see *Jamaica Labrish* (Sangster's Bookstores, 1966).

p.312 For Edward K. Brathwaite's poetry see *The Arrivants* (Oxford, 1973).

p.314 For Michael Smith's work see "Fallen Comet" by John La Rose in *Race Today Review 1984*, p. 4.

"Nation Language"
p.315 For E. K. Brathwaite on the linguistic heritage of the Caribbean see "English in the Caribbean", Leslie A. Fiedler and Houston A. Baker Jnr. (Eds.): *English Literature* (Baltimore, 1981).

p.316 For Hubert Devonish on Caribbean creole see his paper "Creole Language Standardization in Guyana". See also Mervyn Alleyne, "Theoretical Issues in Caribbean Linguistics" (The Language Laboratory, the University of the West Indies).

p.317 For the missing Dictionary of Caribbean English see the writings of Professor Richard Allsopp, University of the West Indies, Cave Hill, Barbados.

"The Final Passage"
p.318 Caryl Phillips: *The Final Passage* (London, 1985). Phillips is the heir to George Lamming (quoted in chapter six) who wrote (in the 1950s):

I am not much interested in what the West Indian writer has brought to the English language; for English is no longer the exclusive language of the men who live in England. That stopped a long time ago; and it is today, among other things, a West Indian language. What the West Indians do with it is their own business. A more important consideration is what the West Indian novelist has brought to the West Indies. That is the real question; and its answer can be the beginning of an attempt to grapple with that colonial structure of awareness which has determined West Indian values. (*The Pleasures of Exile*, London, 1984.)

p.319 As James Ngugi, he was the first writer in East Africa to publish a novel in the English language. Ngugi wa Thiong'o's most recent publication was *Ngaahika Ndeenda* which was subsequently translated as *I Will Marry When I Want*.

Krio: The Heart of the Matter
p.320 For Krio, see Clifford N. Fyle and Eldred D. Jones, *A Krio-English Dictionary* (Oxford, 1980).

The returned slaves formed a society which had its own English creole.

English in India
p.322 The essential text, from which some of the quotations in this section have been derived, is Braj Kachru: *The Indianization of English: The English Language in India* (Oxford, 1983). Kachru is the leading spokesman of English for the Third World, see the collection edited by him *The Other Tongue* (Champaign, 1982). Professor Kachru is also the author of the forthcoming *The Alchemy of English* (Oxford). See also Professor Kachru's paper in the collection "Progress in English Studies" given at the 50th anniversary conference of the British Council.

Estimates vary, but between three (17 million) and ten (70 million) per cent of the population of India speak English.

The Jewel in the Crown
p.324 For the full riches of Indian English during the Raj see Col. Henry Yule and A. C. Burnell: *Hobson-Jobson: A Glossary of Colloquial Anglo-Indian Words and Phrases, and of Kindred Terms, Etymological, Historical, Geographical and Discursive* (Munshiram Manharlal Publishers Ltd, 1979). The phrase itself, "Hobson-Jobson", is defined as "A native festal excitement ... an Anglo-Saxon version of the wailings of the Mahommedans (sic) as they beat their breasts in the procession of *Moharram* – 'Ya Hasan! Ya Hosain!'"

p.326 Lady Wilson: *Letters from India* (London, 1984).

The Indianization of English
p.328 Some of the examples quoted here are from Braj Kachru: *The Indianization of English* (Oxford, 1983) whose title and assistance we gratefully acknowledge.

p.329 See also Paroo Nihalani, R. K. Tongue, Priva Hosali: *Indian and British Usage* (Oxford, 1979).

By Indians for Indians
p.331 See Raja Rao: *Kanthapura* (London, 1974).

The Pacific Age
p.335 For English in Singapore see R. K. Tongue: *The English of Singapore and Malaya* (Singapore, 1984), also Evangelos A. Afendras and Eddie C. Y. Kuo (Eds.): *Language and Society in Singapore* (Singapore, 1980).

p.336 We are grateful to Professor Edwin Thumboo for his advice; see his *The Second Tongue: An Anthology of Poetry from Malaysia and Singapore* (London, 1976).

p.338 We are indebted to Lee Sow Ling for her assistance and for copies of her columns on the use of English.

At the same meeting with his civil service, Lee Kuan Yew also remarked, "If I ask you at your age to try to speak the Queen's English that will be a waste of your time because your oral speech patterns are set."

p.340 For Singapore English writing see Robert Yeo (Ed.): *Singapore Short Stories* (London, 1982).

p.341 For the idea of Nuclear English see Randolph Quirk's essay in *Style and Communication*, (op. cit.).

T. S. Eliot: *Four Quartets* (London, 1944).

EPILOGUE: NEXT YEAR'S WORDS

p.343 The House of Lords Debate is found in *Hansard*, 21 November 1979.

p.345 The condition of English today is explored in Leonard Michaels and Christopher Ricks (Eds.): *The State of the Language* (Berkeley, 1980).

p.346 For the "pop grammarians" see John Simon: *Paradigms Lost* (Clarkson Potter, 1980), and (much more entertaining) William Safire: *What's the Good Word?* (London and New York, 1982). For a splendid and witty counterblast to the "gurus of grammar" see Jim Quinn: *American Tongue and Cheek: A Populist Guide to Our Language* (London, 1980). The English newspapers have devoted less space to issues of language and English; but see Philip Howard: *The State of the Language* (London, 1984).

See Dwight Bolinger: *Language: The Loaded Weapon* (London and New York, 1980).

For "functional illiterates" see the calculation in A. and C. Tibbetts: *What's Happening to American English* (1978) that roughly fifteen per cent of American children are "functional illiterates".

p.347 For the *US English* position see Jacques Barzun, "Language and Life", published by the US English committee.

The resistance to Bilingualism took a big step forward in November 1983, again in San Francisco. "Proposition O", a non-binding referendum opposing the practice of printing city ballots in Spanish and Chinese as well as English, passed to 2 to 1, and came close to winning even in Chinatown and in the Hispanic district around Mission Street. Elsewhere – in the heavily Hispanic areas of South Florida – the issue has become so inflamed that it has spilled over into educational politics. A local requirement that all high-school students take two years of a foreign language course to be admitted to state universities was blocked by the state legislature in a gesture of loyalty to the mother tongue.

As with Black English, Hispanic bilingualism has its own powerful Hispanic critics. Richard Rodriguez is the author of *Hunger of Memory*, a touching memoir about growing up a Mexican American. He argues that a bilingual policy in schools is crippling to the Hispanic minority because it reduces learning, delays assimilation, reinforces separateness and keeps the minority in the ghetto:

"What I needed to learn in school was that I had the right – and the obligation – to speak the public language of *los gringos*. Only when I was able to think of myself as an American, no longer an alien in *gringo* society, could I seek the rights and opportunities necessary for full public individuality."

For the hostility to feminism see the lively press reaction to the new edition of *Roget's Thesaurus* which included "chairperson". Not all the fears about language are conservative. Some feminists, and their supporters, have, for example, mounted an attack on the English gender, neutering words like "Chairman", turning God from He to He/She, and in some cases (duly reported in the press) names like Terman into Terwoman (and perhaps, in due course, Terperson).

For the more exotic blooms of Californian English see Cyra McFadden: *The Serial* (London, 1979).

The row about *Webster's Third* centred on the editor's permissive approach to language, a willingness to include the full range of contemporary "words in use" and to accept their contemporary definitions even if, in the case of *disinterested* and *infer*, for example, these definitions were not "correct". As one critic put it, "Webster III, behind its front of passionless objectivity, is in truth a fighting document. And the enemy it is out to destroy is every obstinate vestige of linguistic punctilio, every surviving influence that makes for the upholding of standards, every criterion for distinguishing between better usages and worse . . ."

The City of Language

p.348 We are grateful to Stuart Flexner for his notes on Gay English.

Surfer Magazine, July 1984.

We are grateful to Dennis Dragon and "Mark the Shark", both of "the Surf Punks" for their encouragement and advice in this section.

p.349 *New Generation Dictionary* (London, 1981).

Lisa Birnbach (Ed.): *The Official Preppy Handbook* (New York, 1980).

In Preppy talk, the spirit of the private school is found in the use of mystifying acronyms B.M.O.C. (Big Man On Campus), N.O.C.D. (Not Our Class, Dear) and P.D.A. (Public Display of Affection). Typical of all private school slang (and, surprisingly, Australian slang) are the boastful euphemisms for sex: *hopped on a babe, played hide the salam/salaami, had a horizontal rumble*, or *done some parallel parking*. In Britain, the Preppy movement was matched by first the "Sloane Rangers" and subsequently, the "Young Fogeys" – both defined in fashionable handbooks.

p.350 Readers who would like to contribute their experience of the English language in the world today should write to the authors c/o Faber and Faber in the United Kingdom or The Viking Press in the United States.

TABLE OF MAPS

The maps were drawn by Maureen Dewick and Anne Leleu, who gratefully acknowledge the assistance of various publications:

Maps 1, 2, 6, 8, 11, 14, 15, 16, 23, 25, 26, 27, 28, 29, 30, 31, 34: Geoffrey Barraclough (ed.), *The Times Concise Atlas of World History* (London and New York, 1982); Malcolm Falkus and John Gillingham (eds.), *Historical Atlas of Britain* (London and New York, 1981).

Maps 3, 7: Victor Stevenson (ed.), *Words* (London, 1983).

Maps 4, 5: A. C. Baugh and Thomas Cable, *A History of the English Language* (London, 1978, and Des Moines, 1983).

Maps 9, 33: *Language Variation and Diversity* (Milton Keynes, 1981).

Maps 10, 24: Charles A. Ferguson and Shirley Brice Heath (eds.), *Language in the USA* (Cambridge, Mass., 1981).

Map 12: Glanville Price, *The Language of Britain* (London, 1984).

Maps 13, 17: Diarmid Ó'Muirithe (ed.), *The English Language in Ireland* (Cork, 1977).

Map 19: Garret FitzGerald, *Proceedings of the Royal Irish Academy*, Volume 84, C, Number 3 (Dublin, 1984).

Maps 20, 21: J. L. Dillard, *Black English* (New York, 1973).

Map 22: John Holm (ed.), *Central American English* (Heidelberg, 1983).

PICTURE CREDITS

132 Photo: The Australian Information Service, London
133 © National Library of Australia
134 Photo: The Australian Information Service, London
135 © Rex Van Kivell Collection, National Library of Australia
136 By T. Baines, Sketchbook X86 number 018845. Royal Geographic Society
137 Photo: © AllSport/Adrian Murrell
138 Photo: © AllSport/Duomo
139 Photo: Camera Press
140 Photo: Mansell Collection
141 Photo: Mansell Collection
142 Photo © BBC Hulton Picture Library
143 By courtesy of Stanley Gibbons

144 Photo: Anthony Brennan
145 Photo: Julian Stapleton, 1982
146 Photo: © London Weekend Television Ltd
147 Photo: © David South
148 Photo: © David South
149 Photo: © David South
150 Photo: © British Library
151 From *Folk Tales of Bengal*
152 Photo: Associated Press
153 By kind permission of Vivian Ducat
154 Photo: © David South
155 Photo: Singapore Tourist Board
156 Photo: Camera Press

ACKNOWLEDGEMENTS

For permission to reprint verse and prose extracts from copyright material the publishers gratefully acknowledge the following: William Collins Sons and Co Ltd for "Jamaica Elevate", "Bans O'Killing" and "Jamaica Ant'em" from *Jamaica Labrish* by Louise Bennett; Faber and Faber Ltd and Harcourt Brace Jovanovitch, Inc, for *Four Quartets* by T. S. Eliot; for "Summertime" composed by George Gershwin and written by Dubose Heyward, copyright 1935 Gershwin Publishing Corp, used by permission of Chappell Music Ltd, London; Macmillan London Ltd for "Danny Deever" by Rudyard Kipling; Jonathan Cape Ltd and Crown Publishers Inc for *Enthusiasms* by Bernard Levin; W. L. Lorimer Memorial Trust Fund for *The New Testament in Scots* translated by William Lorimer; Longman Group Ltd and Schocken Books Inc for *In the Castle of My Skin* by George Lamming; W. G. Gage for "I'll Stay in Canada" by Stephen Leacock in *Canadian Anthology* (eds.) C. F. Klink and R. E. Watey; The Estate of the late Sonia·Brownell Orwell, Secker and Warburg Ltd and Harcourt Brace Jovanovitch, Inc for *Burmese Days* by George Orwell; Oxford University Press for *The English Language* by Logan Pearsall Smith; Greenwood Press and New Directions for *Kanthapura* by Raja Rao; *Race Today* for "Mi cyaan believe it" by Michael Smith; Charles Scribner's Sons for *Look Homeward, Angel* by Thomas Wolfe; Macmillan London Ltd for *Essays and Introductions* by W. B. Yeats.

For permission to reproduce the illustrations on the jacket, the publishers gratefully acknowledge the following: Mansell Collection, Scottish National Portrait Gallery, Peter Newark's Western Americana, the Estate of the late Sonia Brownell Orwell, Colorific Kobal Collection, Camera Press, National Portrait Gallery, IBM, Popperfoto, Coca-Cola Great Britain Ltd ('Coca-Cola' and 'Coke' are registered trademarks which identify the same product of the Coca-Cola Company), Associated Press.

INDEX

as "national" language, 14, 39, 309

as official language, 39, 41, 319, 321, 322

place-names taken to America, 122

plays, 87, 88, 95, 98, 100, 102

poetry, 25, 61, 62, 64, 77, 81, 82, 85, 86, 91, 95, 96, 98, 129, 143

politicians and actors (accent), 29, 30

pronunciation, 11, 21, 27, 29, 46, 123, 137, 148, 174, 175, 177, 189, 192, 193, 195, 197, 241, 242, 243, 245, 247, 277, 279, 294, 295, 343

as second language, 20, 38, 39, 308, 322, 340

speech patterns, 35, 62, 79, 99, 108, 116, 122, 208, 242, 294, 296

spelling, 38, 46–7, 85, 86, 105, 132, 133, 148, 240, 241, 242, 245, 317

spoken, 12, 21, 76, 110, 133, 346, 350

usages, 12, 14, 27, 29, 79, 93, 101, 122, 132, 174, 290, 343, 345, 347

varieties, 13, 21, 79, 122, 128, 141, 163, 167, 179, 195, 269, 292, 293, 335

vocabulary, 13, 19–20, 26, 38, 39, 47, 67, 79, 102, 128–9, 142, 172, 188, 193, 204, 205, 236, 244, 245, 257, 279–83, 347, 349

written, 12, 21, 76, 110, 133, 172, 346

English (language):

African English, 308

AmerEnglish, 15

American English, 31–8, 40, 44, 45, 116, 117, 120, 122–5, 163, 188, 189, 208–17, 220, 223, 230, 235–69, 289, 290, 296, 297, 298, 300, 304, 307, 313, 335, 340, 341, 343, 344, 347

Anglo-Irish, 164, 167, 168, 169, 189

Anglo-Saxon English see Old English

Appalachian English, 159, 160

Australian English, 14, 181, 182, 271, 283, 284–300, 301, 302, 304, 334

Barbadian English ("Bajan"), 180, 204–5, 207, 313, 340

BBC English, 14, 27, 28, 30, 35, 275, 304

Black American English, 125, 194, 195, 207, 208, 209, 211, 221–6, 231

Black English, 11, 169, 195–233, 311, 347

British English, 14, 31, 38, 40, 45, 123, 237, 239, 240, 243, 245, 268, 269, 289, 290, 298, 301, 304, 313, 335, 340, 350

"broken English", 45, 120–1, 314–5, 328

Canadian English, 44, 45, 244–8, 289, 297, 300, 334

Caribbean English, 204, 207, 308, 309, 312, 313, 315

Cockney, 14, 25, 29, 31, 35, 272–83, 290, 293, 295, 301, 302, 338, 350

"common" English, 272

Deutschlish, 20

Elizabethan English, 96, 101, 106, 110, 159, 172, 173, 185

Englisc, 19

"English languages", 11, 269

Franglais, 14, 15, 43, 343

Hiberno-English, 167, 168, 172, 176, 179, 187

Indian English, 39–40, 175, 308, 324, 326, 327, 328–35, 340

International Standard English, 340

Irish English, 167, 169, 172, 173, 175, 176, 177, 182–8, 192, 193, 297

Jamaican English, 306, 309, 310, 311, 313, 314, 316, 317, 318, 334

Japlish, 20, 43

jargon, 344–5

King's English, 25

Local Alternative English, 340

London English, 80, 87, 144

Middle English, 78–80, 86

Miskito English, 204

Modern English, 78

New Zealand English, 271, 300–4

Nigerian English, 40

Nigger English, 211

non-standard English, 24, 29–30, 174

"Nuclear English", 340

Old English, 58, 60, 61, 62, 64, 65, 67, 68, 70, 71, 72, 75, 78, 79, 81, 86, 95, 102, 160, 172, 176, 329, 351

pidgin English, 45, 117, 120, 121, 123, 125, 196, 197–200, 201, 203, 207, 208, 211, 230, 254, 284, 285, 319–21, 322, 328, 350

"posh English", 28, 30, 31, 272

"Queen's English", 21, 24, 144, 307, 314

Scots English, 13, 29, 72, 80, 127–61, 247, 273, 297

Shakespeare's English, 101

Singaporean English ("Singlish"), 43, 48, 308, 336, 337, 338

slang, 28, 37, 95, 226, 265, 279, 288, 289, 290, 294, 302, 303, 338, 348–9

"Slanguage", 48

South African English, 271, 297, 304–5, 334

Southern White English, 214–7

"Spanglish", 48

Standard English, 13, 21, 24, 27, 28, 38, 45, 56, 79, 80, 101, 105, 121, 127, 128, 135, 144, 145, 146, 149, 151, 168, 169, 172, 174, 176, 192, 195, 199, 204, 205, 245, 269, 273, 277, 281, 293, 294, 295, 301, 309, 310, 311, 313, 314, 315, 316, 317, 319, 320, 321, 322, 323, 324, 330, 336, 337, 338, 340, 350

"Swinglish", 44

Welsh-English, 56

World English, 308, 341, 350

Yinglish, 267

English-language

education, schools and training programmes, 38, 41, 42, 45, 46, 137

policy (China), 14, 42

English-speaking

international aid bodies and diplomatic exchanges, 42, 43

institutions and corporations, 31

multinational companies, 41

(to the Press) contemporary world figures, 41

world, 26, 28, 31, 33, 37, 41, 45, 57, 58, 62, 69, 73, 77, 97, 100, 112, 140, 141, 142, 151, 163, 172, 177, 183, 197, 245, 267, 289, 294, 299, 304, 307, 308, 314, 319, 340, 347, 348, 351

English, the, 57, 61, 67, 69, 73, 74, 75, 97, 120, 156, 157, 161, 164, 165, 172, 176, 177, 180, 196, 201, 245, 248, 262, 271, 272, 273, 288, 289, 293, 304

English Jews, 281, 282

Northern English of Scotland, 141–2

Epistle of the Excellency of the English Tongue, An, 91

Erewhon, 301

Esperanto, 38

Ethandune, the battle of, 69

Europe, 28, 31, 33, 47, 52, 53, 56, 57, 68, 70, 77, 93, 95, 96, 120, 135, 188, 203, 220, 239, 243, 248, 260, 268, 294, 300, 308, 350

European Economic Community, 183